Modern Sufis and the State

RELIGION, CULTURE, AND PUBLIC LIFE

RELIGION, CULTURE, AND PUBLIC LIFE

Series Editor: Matthew Engelke

The Religion, Culture, and Public Life series is devoted to the study of religion in relation to social, cultural, and political dynamics, both contemporary and historical. It features work by scholars from a variety of disciplinary and methodological perspectives, including religious studies, anthropology, history, philosophy, political science, and sociology. The series is committed to deepening our critical understandings of the empirical and conceptual dimensions of religious thought and practice, as well as such related topics as secularism, pluralism, and political theology. The Religion, Culture, and Public Life series is sponsored by Columbia University's Institute for Religion, Culture, and Public Life.

For a complete list of titles, see page 345.

Modern Sufis and the State

The Politics of Islam in South Asia and Beyond

EDITED BY
KATHERINE PRATT EWING
AND ROSEMARY R. CORBETT

Columbia University Press
New York

PUBLISHER'S CIRCLE

COLUMBIA
UNIVERSITY
PRESS

Columbia University Press gratefully acknowledges the generous support for this book provided by a Publisher's Circle member.

Publication of this book was made possible in part by funding from the Institute for Religion, Culture, and Public Life at Columbia University.

Columbia University Press
Publishers Since 1893
New York   Chichester, West Sussex
cup.columbia.edu

Library of Congress Cataloging-in-Publication Data
Names: Ewing, Katherine Pratt, editor. | Corbett, Rosemary R., editor.
Title: Modern Sufis and the state : the politics of Islam in South Asia and beyond / edited by Katherine Pratt Ewing and Rosemary R. Corbett.
Description: New York City : Columbia University Press, 2020. | Series: Religion, culture, and public life | Includes bibliographical references and index.
Identifiers: LCCN 2019051465 (print) | LCCN 2019051466 (ebook) |
ISBN 9780231195744 (cloth) | ISBN 9780231195751 (paperback) |
ISBN 9780231551465 (ebook)
Subjects: LCSH: Sufis—Political activity—South Asia. | Sufism—Political aspect—South Asia. | Islam and politics—South Asia. | South Asia—Politics and government.
Classification: LCC BP188.8.S64 M63 2020 (print) | LCC BP188.8.S64 (ebook) |
DDC 322/.10954—dc23
LC record available at https://lccn.loc.gov/2019051465
LC ebook record available at https://lccn.loc.gov/2019051466

Columbia University Press books are printed on permanent and durable acid-free paper.
Printed in the United States of America

Cover design: Noah Arlow
Cover image: Sam Panthaky/Getty Images

Contents

PART IV

Sufism in Indian National Spaces

Acknowledgments

This book would not exist without the people who animate the Institute for Religion, Culture, and Public Life (IRCPL) at Columbia University. Not long after editor Katherine Ewing's arrival at Columbia University, Karen Barkey, who was then director of IRCPL, was organizing a series of conferences and workshops on Sufism as part of a larger project on "Religious Toleration and Plural Democracies." She encouraged Katherine to organize the 2015 conference "Rethinking Islam, Democracy and Identity in Pakistan and India: The Role of Sufism," out of which this volume has emerged. Editor Rosemary Corbett was originally brought onboard as a postdoctoral fellow to help coordinate the overall project, which was generously funded by the Henry Luce Foundation, with the enthusiastic guidance of Toby Volkman. We would like to thank Jessica Lillien and Zachary Hendrickson for helping out at various stages of the project, and especially Walid Hammam for being there at every step of the way. He was an invaluable partner as Katherine took over the directorship of IRCPL. Bill Carrick of the South Asia Institute has also contributed in countless ways.

In addition to the contributors included in the present volume, the conference was enriched by the presence and contributions of Pnina Werbner, Thomas Gugler, Jamal Malik, Akbar Zaidi, Anand Taneja, Zahid Hussain, Rob Rozehnal, Souleymane Bachir Diagne, and Mamadou Diouf. Bruce Lawrence gave a keynote address. We would like to thank them all. Contributors to an early planning workshop entitled "Pluralism: Sufi Thought and Practices" included Cheikh Babou, Souleymane Bachir Diagne, Carl Ernst, Katharina Ivanyi, Karen Barkey, Mamadou Diouf, and Leonardo Villalon. Thanks also to

Columbia Religion Department PhD students Quinn Clark, Ilona Gerbakher, Zehra Mehdi, and Ebadur Rahman, who have been great conversation partners as their own research projects on related themes have developed along the way. Colleagues Gil Anidjar, Rachel McDermott, Jack Hawley, Courtney Bender, Brinkley Messick, and Gauri Visvanathan are among those who have made Columbia University a rich intellectual environment for the pursuit of this project.

We thank Taha Poonawala and Fidahussain Yamani for their hard work on making transliterations across several languages as consistent as possible. We also thank Wendy Lochner of Columbia University Press for overseeing publication of the book, and we thank the anonymous reviewers whose detailed and thoughtful comments have made this a better book.

Katherine appreciates the steadfast support of her husband and intellectual companion, Thomas DiPrete, three loving daughters, the wonderful young men they have brought into the family, and Charlotte, who is the promise of the future. In the time between the convening of the conference from which this volume evolved and the book's publication, Rosemary added another child to her family and also navigated the illness of her partner. There are simply too many people to thank for the tremendous support received during those years, but eternal gratitude will always be due David Kaiser for his unflagging faith, endless encouragement, and abiding love.

Note on Transliteration

Words found in *Merriam-Webster's Collegiate Dictionary* are considered part of English lexicon and do not contain any markers/diacritics.

When transliterating names of living people, we use the preferred or popular spelling. For names of the deceased, we either transliterate or use spelling as used by them self-referentially as found in their works.

ا/ء ʾ	ر r	ف f
ب b	ز z	ق q
پ p	ڑ ṙ	ك k
ت t		گ g
ث th	س s	كھ kh
ٹ ṫ	ش sh	ل l
ج j	ص ṣ	م m
چ ch	ض ḍ/ż	ن n
ح ḥ	ط ṭ	ں ñ
خ kh		ه/ة h
د d	ظ ẓ	و w
ذ dh	ع ʿ	ي y
ڈ ḏ	غ gh	ے e

Long

آ/ا	ā
و	ū
ي	ī

Doubled

ـِيّ	iyy (final form ī)
ـُوّ	uww (final form ū)

Diphthongs

وَ	aw
يَ	ay

Short

ـَ	a
ـُ	u
ـِ	i

Modern Sufis and the State

Introduction

Sufis and the State: The Politics of Islam in South Asia and Beyond

KATHERINE PRATT EWING

When we, as a public living at this particular historical moment, ask, "What is Sufism? Is Sufism part of Islam? What is the relationship between Sufism and the modern state?" our concerns have been largely shaped by a pervasive, globalized media- and policy-driven discourse about how Sufis might save the world from intolerant forms of Islam. Sufism, usually understood today to mean the mystical side of Islam, has been swept up into globalized debates that are increasingly framed as an opposition between "Sufis" and "Salafis."[1] Policy makers within the American government and in many countries with large Muslim populations have promoted Sufism and popular traditions associated with local shrines in an effort to discourage the spread of Islamists who may be prone to violence. A rhetorical chasm has developed between something that has come to be called Salafi, or "fundamentalist," Islam and Sufism, and this chasm has come to shape the understandings and practices of Muslims themselves. Sufism has undergone a reification in recent years that has transformed local practices into a new kind of cultural, religious, and political object, understood as a vestige of local culture and tradition that can be preserved and revived, much as the colonialism and Orientalist scholarship of the nineteenth century turned Sufism into something quite different from what it had been during the time of the great Muslim empires.

Within the world of South Asian Sufism today, perhaps the most dramatic phenomenon we have seen in recent years is a series of violent attacks against the shrines of Sufi saints, especially in Pakistan, but also in India. While the destruction of shrines certainly has precedent in other parts of the Muslim world, especially in connection with the Wahhabi movement in Saudi Arabia beginning in the eighteenth century, this is something new in South Asia. There is a sense among many Muslims that Sufism, however imagined, is beyond the pale of true Islam—a kind of "Sufiphobia" among Muslims themselves. In some circles this discursive process has gone so far as to split Sufism from Islam, a split that has led various reformist thinkers to recast earlier Islamic reformers as anti-Sufi, reshaping the past to create historically deep intellectual lineages for their own reformist projects. As Itzchak Weismann has noted, "the fundamentalists' critique of Sufism as backward, superstitious, and apolitical involved the collective forgetting of the leading role that Sufi reformist brotherhoods had filled in premodern Islam."[2] We explore in this volume how and why this polarization has happened, how this dynamic is playing out in South Asia, and what the consequences of current public representations and their politics are for both Sufis and the shape and direction of Islam today.

The contributors to this volume were brought together for the workshop "Rethinking Islam, Democracy, and Identity in South Asia: The Role of Sufism," held under the auspices of the Institute for Religion, Culture, and Public Life (IRCPL) at Columbia University in September 2015 and funded by a grant from the Henry Luce Foundation. The workshop was part of a research project, "Sufi Islam in 21st Century Politics," itself part of a larger project, "Religious Toleration and Plural Democracies."[3] The broader Luce project aimed to better understand the political theologies of secular and religious leaders, asking what forces promote a discourse of democracy, inclusion, and toleration and foregrounding localized practices of accommodation and coexistence that could be found at shared sacred sites. The overall plan for the Sufi component of the project was to ask what has made Sufism successful and effective at managing religious pluralism and ethnic diversity in various parts of the world, a question that is consistent with the goals of a number of foundations and granting agencies over the years to promote democracy and modernize Islamic societies.

Though springing from this rather problematically conceptualized agenda, the present volume and the workshop out of which it emerged have had a different aim. Instead of contributing to an ongoing effort to spread the good news about what practices seem to work to promote democracy and toleration, workshop participants were asked to consider what might be the effects and unintended consequences of policy-driven efforts to link Sufism with the propagation of peace, democracy, and toleration and to consider what role scholars and governments have played in shaping what Sufism has become in the twenty-first century. The chapters challenge three common assumptions that are made about Sufism in public discourse today: (1) that Sufism is peaceful and apolitical; (2) that Islamic reform and Sufism are antithetical; and (3) that shrines are sites of harmony and toleration. They consider the effects of these assumptions on what "Sufism" is becoming in India and Pakistan and offer specific analyses of the diversity, multivalence, and local embeddedness of Sufi political engagements. The volume also foregrounds differences in the political environments of Pakistan and India and the effects of these environments on Sufi political action and self-representations, connecting Islamic rituals, sacred spaces, and theological debates to national and global issues of power, profit, and violence.

The Emergence of "Sufism" in the Colonial Period

"Sufism" is an aspect of Islam that has been particularly subject to the effects of a European gaze and government policies involving the close intertwining of scholarship and public discourse since the beginning of the colonial era. This history has played an important role in shaping how Sufism is imagined and practiced today. As a category, "Sufism" was first coined by British Orientalist scholars working primarily in colonial India in the late eighteenth and early nineteenth centuries. It was one of an array of "isms" taxonomically subsumed under the category of "religions."[4] The term "Sufi" emerged as early as the eighth century to designate a fringe group of ascetics, and much of what is now designated as Sufism, or *taṣawwuf,* had become an important aspect of Islamic practice and education by the tenth century.[5] Nevertheless, these Arabic terms were part of a conceptual map very different from the Orientalist classification scheme associated with "Sufism," and there was no single label that was consistently used to refer to ascetics, mystics, "friends" of God, and those who belonged to the *ṭarīqah*s, or Sufi orders. In his commentary on part 1 of the present volume, Carl Ernst traces the Orientalist process of category formation and its implications for current scholarship.

In the South Asian colonial landscape, the concept of "Sufism" in Orientalist sources was founded on at least two conceptual splits that helped shape Sufism's boundaries and its relationship to Islam. Though most Muslims, including the ulama, were also Sufis or followers of Sufis, Sufism was imagined by colonial observers as having origins separate from Islam, as having roots elsewhere—such as Aryan Persia—apart from the Semitic environment that produced the Prophet Muḥammad, the Quran, and the institutional beginnings of Islam. Reflecting Protestant Christian understandings of religion, the concept of Sufism as a form of mysticism stemming from the individual's relationship with God was split off from legalistic Islam in the writings of late eighteenth-century and early nineteenth-century scholars associated with the East India Company,[6] a distinction that continued to appear in the work of twentieth-century scholars of South Asia and Islam who played an influential role in shaping scholarship on Sufism in the American academy.[7]

A second split was the bifurcation in nineteenth-century writings between, on the one hand, the Sufi as mystic and producer of poetry and other literature to be deciphered and translated by the Orientalist scholar and, on the other hand, the *pīr* as the living holy man who was studied by colonial anthropologists/administrators and monitored as either a dangerous wanderer, a corrupt hereditary descendant of a Sufi ensconced at a shrine, or a charlatan purveyor of talismans and superstition, described in publications like colonial government-produced gazetteers and the late nineteenth-century periodical *Panjab Notes and Queries*, which focused on popular religion and folklore.[8] Within colonial settings, "the Oriental was either common in spirit but distant in time or of a common era but distant in space and culture, in either case denied the status of "modern."[9]

Regardless of the vicissitudes of how differences between Sufism and Islam or between Sufism and popular practice were characterized by various nineteenth-century writers—whether Sufism was "good" in its sophisticated mystical inspiration and Islam was "bad" because of its legalism, or the inverse, in which Sufism was "bad" because of its ties to superstitious rituals and Islam was "good" because of its rationality and strict monotheism—it was the split itself and its political and rhetorical force in the colonial environment that was to be crucially significant for the subsequent evolution of Sufism/*taṣawwuf*. Echoes of this split can be heard in postcolonial Islamic reformist writings that distance themselves from Sufism. Muhammad Iqbal, for example, drew inspiration from Sufi poets such as Jalāl al-Dīn Rūmī (1207–73), yet he also denounced "Persian mysticism" based on a spiritual aristocracy of saints that was manifest in the institution of *pīrī-murīdī*, which he felt contributed to the thralldom of the people.[10]

Echoes of the split of Sufism as mystical philosophy from local practices associated with shrine networks are still readily visible in the disciplinary boundaries of scholarship even today. Thus, Rex O'Fahey and Bernd Radtke have pointed out that though "Sufism" is "a term used indiscriminately to describe both the complex thought of Ibn ʿArabī and the variegations of popular Islam," there is still a disciplinary divide between scholars of medieval Islam who study Sufism as mystical philosophy and anthropologists and historians of modern Islam, who assume that postclassical Sufism "can be dealt with simply as a set of symbols, litanies, prayers, miracles, tomb visitations and the like, the paraphernalia of maraboutic credulity."[11]

In everyday conversations about Sufis/*pīrs* that I participated in during the 1970s and 1980s in Pakistan, many people did not recognize *pīrs* or shrines as having any connection to Sufism, which they associated with well-known local Sufi poets such as Shāh ʿAbd al-Laṭīf Bhittāʾī and Bulle Shāh. The conceptual splits between Sufism and Islam that were pervasive in colonial discourse have facilitated the imagining of Sufism, even in its philosophical and literary forms, as something apart from and even antithetical to Islam, a position that has been taken up by some Islamic reformers in subsequent eras. It is not a great leap from this location of Sufism outside of the discursive tradition of Islam by Orientalists in the colonial era to the sense among many modern Muslims that Sufism, however imagined, is beyond the pale of true Islam and to the sense of urgency among certain radical Muslims that Sufism is *bidʿah* (innovation) and must be wiped out.

Though the *silsilahs* (genealogical linkages) based on chains of *pīr*-disciple relationships that organize the Sufi orders continue to be important for South Asian Sufis, new forms of organization and religious identity emerged in the nineteenth century in the colonial environment and have continued to evolve in the twentieth and twenty-first centuries. During the colonial period, Sufi practices and organizations were affected not only by Orientalist understandings of Sufism but also by organizational forms introduced by the British as they imposed a new administrative structure on the subcontinent and by Christian missionizing efforts, which partially inspired the Hindu and Islamic reform movements that were transforming the religious landscape of India. Thus, within Hinduism, the colonial period saw the emergence of the Brahmo Samaj, Arya Samaj, new *sampradāyas* (devotional systems), and even the new idea of Bhakti as a broad movement that was said to have swept across India over the course of a thousand years.[12] Among Muslims, multiple reform movements also emerged at this time, including the reformist Ahl-e Hadith (often called "Wahhabi" by critics);[13] the controversial Ahmadiyyah, whose founder claimed to be the promised messiah at the end of time; the Deobandis; and the Tablīghī Jamāʿat, an offshoot of the Deobandis, in the early twentieth century. The Deobandis established a new madrasa system modeled partly on British bureaucratic and educational forms such as classrooms and a fixed curriculum, creating an institution that replaced an earlier madrasa model based on the metaphor of kinship ties. This organizational shift enabled the creation a transnational network of educational institutions, the Dār al-ʿUlūm , that now goes well beyond South Asia.[14]

Though the Deobandis did not reject Sufism, they did reject popular practices associated with local shrine culture. In reaction to this perceived threat to local shrine culture, many South Asian Sufis and their followers organized under the new identity of "Ahl-e Sunnat wa-l-Jamāʿat" (the people of the Sunna and the community), often called "Barelwi" (especially by opponents), in order to resist the modernizing and purifying efforts of Deobandis and other Islamic groups such as the Ahl-e Hadith while simultaneously organizing madrasas with a structure and curriculum similar to the Deobandi madrasas.[15] "Deobandi" and "Barelwi" came to be seen as competing identities. These new forms of organization have continued to develop and evolve in the twenty-first century. Although both Barelwis and Deobandis each emerged under the leadership of Sufis, Barelwi and Deobandi networks have evolved in different directions, with Barelwis particularly concerned with preserving Sufi practices associated with shrine culture and rituals focused on respect and love for the Prophet Muḥammad. In the present volume, chapters by Hermansen, Ingram, Sanyal, and Philippon address various aspects of this Barelwi-Deobandi split.

Sufism and Its Modern Engagements with a Global Order

A key subject in the "Rethinking Islam" workshop was how Sufism has been understood by scholars and outside observers and what implications such understandings continue to have for government policy and the politics of Sufi practice. In an earlier essay,[16] Rosemary Corbett traced perceptions of Sufism as a liberal Islamic mysticism to roots in American Transcendentalist and Protestant interest in Eastern mysticisms in the late nineteenth and early twentieth centuries. She described how this idea of Sufism became established in both popular culture and American scholarship through the efforts of Wilfred Cantwell Smith and his colleagues. These colleagues included Sayyid Hossein Nasr, H. A. R. Gibb, Annemarie Schimmel, and Pakistani scholar Fazlur Rahman. These scholars debated the nature of mysticism at the new Islamic studies programs at McGill and Harvard, which had been established with extensive funding from the Ford and Rockefeller Foundations in the post–World War II period. The funding for the current Luce project can in many respects be viewed as a descendant of the efforts of the Ford and Rockefeller Foundations in the 1950s to reshape Islamic societies into liberal democracies through the work of scholars.

For this volume, Rosemary Corbett extends her argument further in chapter 1 to examine the Rockefeller Foundation's role in shaping U.S. policy makers' impressions of Sufism as the peaceful Islam that could counter dangerous extremism. She explores how, despite some efforts to engage French Orientalists, who were more aware of the Sufi-led, highly politicized anticolonial efforts in North Africa than were the Rockefeller-funded scholars who shaped early Islamic studies departments and influenced U.S. policy makers, these latter scholars relied heavily on ideas about Sufism that had been drawn from South Asian contexts and were shaped by Orientalist racializing stereotypes about passive South Asians and aggressive Arabs. Such assumptions about the peacefulness of Sufism continue to be widespread today. Essays in the present volume question such preconceptions in order to examine the effects of such representations on the complex political dynamics of Sufism today.

An important figure in the close interconnection between scholars and policy makers in the modern development of Sufism is Fazlur Rahman, who was hired by W. C. Smith at McGill, as a sort of diversity hire during Smith's efforts to develop an Islamic Studies Department at McGill.[17] After teaching in Canada, he was invited by Pakistani president Ayub Khan in 1963 to head the Central Institute of Islamic Research in Karachi. Under Ayub, he promoted a form of Islamic modernism that was based on *ijtihād* (independent reason) and was sympathetic to certain forms of Sufism. Inspired by the thought of Muhammad Iqbal, Rahman rejected popular Sufism as ignorant superstition but felt that a form of dynamic Sufism combined with modern education could form the basis for reforming sharia in Pakistan. He tried to weave Islam into the workings of government but was forced to leave Pakistan in 1968 when conservative ulama denounced him as an apostate. He moved to the United States and resumed his teaching career, ultimately taking a position in the Islamic Studies Department at the University of Chicago, where he played a role in shaping a generation of scholars, including some of the workshop participants.

In chapter 2, Verena Meyer focuses on Fazlur Rahman's Indonesian PhD student Nurcholish Madjid, who studied with Rahman at the University of Chicago between 1978 and 1984 and went on to become a major figure in Indonesian religious and political life. Meyer's goal is to complicate the assumption that Madjid simply transmitted Rahman's program of *ijtihād* from Pakistan to Indonesia via Islamic studies in the Western academy. Rather, she argues, Madjid was reframing Sufism in ways that addressed specific conditions in Indonesia, countering the authoritarian regime with ideas of secular democracy by strategically drawing on and altering Rahman's concept of "Neo-Sufism" while dissociating it from colonial images of paganism. He was nonetheless a part of what became a transnational project to recast Sufism in the service of modernization and the secular state, thereby reinforcing the idea of Sufism as the "good" Islam.

Rahman introduced the concept of "Neo-Sufism" to refer to various Sufi-related movements of the late eighteenth and early nineteenth centuries that were concerned with renewal and reform.[18] He used the term in his general introduction to Islam to refer to "Sufism reformed on orthodox lines and interpreted in an activist sense."[19] He was foregrounding reformist efforts to bring Sufi practices in line with Islamic "orthodoxy" by rejecting many of the popular practices associated with the old Sufi orders. Rahman identified orders in both South Asia and Northwest Africa that could be characterized in these reformist terms as Neo-Sufi.

The term has provoked controversy among scholars of Sufism about whether the specific features that one scholar or another has identified with Neo-Sufism are really new practices and doctrines. While O'Fahey and Radtke argued that these features were not actually new,[20] Islamic historian John Voll stressed that, in terms of organizational structure, Sufi orders that developed in the late eighteenth and early nineteenth centuries were, in fact, new.[21] According to Nehemia Levtzion, there was a change in the eighteenth century, when brotherhoods became larger-scale, self-supporting, and more centralized organizations: "In the eighteenth century, brotherhoods transformed from old patterns of decentralized diffusive affiliation into larger-scale organizations, more coherent and centralized."[22] Even the formation of the supposedly traditionalist Ahl-e Sunnat wa-l-Jamāʿat (Barelwis) in South Asia was a move toward a new form of organization in response to the political forces of the late nineteenth century. This trend has developed even further in the twentieth and twenty-first centuries, as some Sufi organizations have begun to operate on a global scale.

Marcia Hermansen explores new modes of recruitment and mobilization in chapter 3. She asks how the idea of the "Barelwi" itself is changing by examining the organizational structure that has emerged with the rise to prominence of religious leader and politician Tahir-ul-Qadri, founder of the transnational Minhaj-ul-Quran movement. As she notes, Qadri also founded a political party, won a seat in the Pakistani national assembly, and rose to political prominence for a short time in 2014 by drawing on Sufi tropes and the idea of Sufism as the peaceful Islam to mobilize a large following to pressure government reform. Qadri also operates on a global scale, using the media in new ways to capitalize on the image of the Sufi as a peaceful alternative to violent Islam. Hermansen argues that Qadri is an example of how there has been a shift from *ṭarīqah*-based Sufism to Sufism as a globally based "traditional Islam" that challenges several features of Barelwism, such as the *pīr*-disciple relationship: Qadri rejects the title of *pīr* and preaches that one can become a member of the Qādirī Sufi order by filling out a Minhaj-ul-Quran membership form.[23] Qadri's political activities as a Sufi leader on a very public Twitter- and YouTube-fueled stage exposes tensions between Sufi sources of authority and the expectations of a disenchanted, secular public sphere and raises questions about the effects of his form of populism on democratic order.[24]

An assumption commonly made in public discourse is that in contrast to the political threat posed by orthodox Islam, Sufism's adherents are apolitical and should be supported as a way of fending off extremism. This is a form of the "good Muslim, bad Muslim" split that, according to Mahmood Mamdani, has driven U.S. foreign policy since 9/11. Mamdani critiques the distinction between the secular, Westernized Muslim and the fanatical, premodern/antimodern Muslim made by scholars such as Bernard Lewis, who provided an intellectual justification for his conceptualization by arguing that the idea of freedom and a nonreligious society are totally alien to traditional Islam.[25] Though Mamdani emphasizes how the good Muslim is thought to be secular and modern, this public discourse that he is critiquing also constitutes the Sufi as a good Muslim, with the help of scholarship such as that funded by the Luce Foundation, which aims to draw close connections between various aspects of Sufism and the values of secular democracy. Part of this perceived compatibility stems from the Protestant Christian lens through which Sufism continues to be seen. Thus, even Ernst, in his *Shambhala Guide to Sufism*, which aims to disrupt Orientalist assumptions that have shaped the study of Sufism and is focused on Sufism as a fundamentally social and historical phenomenon, offers a definition of "Sufi" in terms of an individual's orientation toward ethical and spiritual goals.[26] This definition focuses on the individual, just as talk of democracy rests on the individual as a bearer of rights and freedoms founded on the idea of the individual's autonomous will. This definition of the Sufi also separates the individual from the social and political, making this form of religion apolitical: Sufi experience is fundamentally private and thus compatible with the place of religion in a secular society when framed in terms of individual spirituality.

The chapters in this volume disrupt the assumption that Sufism is apolitical by focusing on the political engagement of Sufis in South Asia. In some respects this inquiry is more in line with a definition of Sufism offered by Nile Green in his 2012 global history of Sufism, which, like Ernst's guide to Sufism, attempts to recast our understanding of Sufism away from the grand narrative of decline associated with the development of the Sufi orders and their institutional forms. Green prioritizes Sufism's social dimensions in his definition of Sufism as "a tradition of powerful knowledge, practices and persons."[27] Sufism, like all religions, is a social and political practice, despite modern efforts to relegate religion to the private sphere.

Sufis, Sharia, and Reform

Another assumption that dominates public discourse about Sufism is that Islamic reformism stands in opposition to Sufism, which is associated with traditionalism and shrine visitation and continues to bear the shadow of the colonial label that linked popular Sufism with superstition. The chapters in part 2 focus on the issue of Sufis and Islamic reform. Muhammad Qasim Zaman's commentary calls attention to how the very term "reform" and its deployment are politically fraught. Each chapter questions the idea that Islamic reform is necessarily anti-Sufi or that Sufis themselves are unconcerned with reform. They also disrupt any neat categorization of Deobandis as pro-reform and Barelwis as anti-reform.

One of the ways that the past is rewritten is through the misrecognition of earlier distinctions, judgments, and practices that are taken to be the same as what is happening today. Thus, for example, an earlier criticism of shrine visitation is taken to be a rejection of Sufi practices. Before the modern era, most Muslim scholars and teachers were also Sufis, and the Sufi *ṭarīqah*s (orders) were a central element of Muslim social worlds. Thus, the medieval theologian Ibn Taymiyyah of Damascus, who in the modern era has been claimed as a predecessor by anti-Sufi reformists such as the eighteenth-century Arabian reformist Muḥammad ibn ʿAbd al-Wahhāb and the Indian/Pakistani reformer Abū al-Aʿlā Mawdūdī, was himself a Sufi *shaykh* of the Qādirī order.[28] Ibn Taymiyyah had been critical of the of the growing use of elaborate tombs erected in the twelfth and thirteenth centuries to enhance the legitimacy of local rulers such as the Mamluks and was also concerned about reforming the popular practice of worshipping the dead and petitioning them as intermediaries with God. But this to him was not the same as Sufi practice, and he had considerable praise for contemporary *shaykh*s. Similarly, though Deobandis today are assumed by many to be anti-Sufi, especially by their critics, they have always retained a tie to the Sufi orders, even as they have sought reform and condemned popular practices associated with the shrines.

Focusing on Deobandi discourse as manifest in the writings of major Deobandi scholars whose madrasas in Northwest Pakistan have trained members of the Taliban, Brannon Ingram in chapter 4 shows us how ambivalent these Deobandis have been toward Sufism: Like Deobandis in the nineteenth century, they feel that Sufism is essential to the cultivation of piety yet place strict limits on what is permissible at shrines, which they feel are sites that cultivate illicit beliefs and practices. Ingram cautions us against assuming that the Taliban attacks on shrines, including those of Dātā Ganj Bakhsh and Bābā Farīd, two of Pakistan's most important, arise from a general critique of Sufism. He argues that they have more to do with local Barelwi-Deobandi contestations and Taliban conflicts with the Pakistani government.

Usha Sanyal, in chapter 5, foregrounds the extent to which Barelwis defy easy classification as rural, traditional, or "unreformed" in their Sufi orientations. Sanyal describes a Barelwi girls' madrasa in India that teaches a disciplined regimen for how to be a "good" Muslim through daily prayer and study so that these girls become role models for their families. This commitment to sharia is interwoven with Sufi orientations that include love of the Prophet and honor of saints of the Qādirī *silsilah*. At the same time, she argues, the teachings and routines of this madrasa do not prioritize other Sufi institutions such as shrine visitation, despite the Deobandi assumption that shrine visitation is a key and unlawful element of Barelwi practice.

In chapter 6, Brian Bond addresses the question of Sufi orientations toward Islamic reform in India by focusing on the issue of music and its performance at Sufi shrines in Kachchh, Gujarat, very close to the border between India and Pakistan. He traces reactions among Muslim musicians to a legal opinion (fatwa) issued by a prominent local Barelwi preacher who stated that music is impermissible in Islam. This is a "reformist" position, part of a more general context of reformist activities undertaken by Sufi-oriented Barelwis in this part of India. Bond argues that musical performance is a critical site around which competing ethical stances among Sufis are articulated and enacted. Such contestations, arising from local splits among Barelwis, are eclipsed when "Sufis" are pitted against "legalists" or "orthodox Muslims" in literature on music and Islam.

These chapters are not the first scholarship to demonstrate that Sufi practice can be contiguous with reformist sentiments and concern for orthodoxy. Indeed, the same Orientalists and Islamic studies scholars who argued for the liberality of South Asian Sufis made such arguments as early as the 1940s. Those thinkers—especially H. A. R. Gibb—did so prescriptively as much as descriptively, however, hoping to write the future of Islam in terms of an idealized past, interpreted through what they believed to be the universal template of European Protestant history. As Corbett has pointed out, Gibb and several of his students positioned Sufism and reformism (they were the first to apply the

Protestant label "fundamentalist" to Muslims) as antithetical in the Hegelian sense: as opposing forces that required synthesis for the sake of progress and religious evolution.[29] Although few contemporary scholars argue for synthesizing Sufism and reformism in such ways now, Gibb's heuristic division between Sufis and so-called fundamentalists remains powerfully influential. By charting movements that blend reformist impulses with Sufi traditions, these chapters challenge the idea that Sufism and reformism are necessarily opposed, but do so without romanticizing the convergence of these traditions or prescribing a formula for using one to combat the perceived excesses of the other.

Sufis and Politics in Pakistan

Despite a shared past, the situations of Muslims in Pakistan and India are very different, and their political possibilities are in many respects incommensurable. During the late colonial period, communal violence in the subcontinent began to escalate,[30] culminating in a massive loss of life during the Partition of India and Pakistan at the moment of Independence in 1947. In India, Muslims were positioned as a minority in the Nehruvian secular order that was established with Partition. Anti-Muslim sentiment intensified as Hindu nationalism became the dominant political force. Muslims were rhetorically labeled the historical enemy who invaded and illegitimately controlled India. The post-Independence era continues to be punctuated by periodic attacks against Muslims. The tension between Sufism and Islamic reform thus takes on a very different valence in this political environment from that of Pakistan, where debates about Islamic reform and the legitimacy of Sufi Islam have been intertwined with struggles to negotiate the type of Islamic state and society that Pakistan aspires to be.[31] In both India and Pakistan, the shrines associated with Sufism are key sites where Sufi practice intersects with government policies and regulation. When it comes to the incursions of government into the operation of shrines and representations of Sufism, we see stark differences between India and Pakistan in the significance of shrines for the state and in state efforts to shape its citizenry. In parts 3 and 4, focused on Pakistan and India, respectively, some of these differences are vividly on display.

The history of *awqāf* law in Pakistan demonstrates the close intertwining of governmentality—the shaping of and caring for a modern population—and policies toward shrines. Sufis continue to be organized as *ṭarīqahs* (Sufi orders, literally, "paths") with a chain of spiritual succession (*silsilah*) passing from master/teacher (*pīr*) to disciples, along the lines of a kinship model, in which fellow disciples of a single *pīr* often called themselves *pīrbhā'ī*, or brothers of the same teacher, and *silsilahs* can be traced back for centuries, to the early founders of the orders and, ultimately, to the Prophet himself. These chains of succession link networks of Sufis across time, space, and national boundaries. Such chains of succession are perpetuated not only through links between a Sufi teacher and his spiritual (*rūḥānī*) successors but also through hereditary families whose descendants retain the spiritual authority of their Sufi ancestors within communities in which the *pīr-murīd* (teacher-follower) relationship itself is passed down through generations. The status of hereditary *pīr* families was reinforced by colonial policy.

In 1959, less than a decade after the establishment of Pakistan, President Ayub Khan initiated a new administrative policy intended to undercut the political and economic power of both the hereditary *pīr* families and the ulama as he sought to create a modern state, a policy that in its general outlines was continued and extended by his successors. The Pakistani government did not choose to undercut the power of Sufi *pīrs* by abolishing shrines and *pīrs* entirely. They did not ban them, as Ataturk had done in Turkey, in order to advance the cause of secularism. Nor did they destroy them, as was done in Saudi Arabia for the almost opposite reason of returning to a more fundamentalist interpretation of Islam that was also a manifestation of modernity.[32] One of the main sources of inspiration for how to deal with the perceived problem of *pīrs* and shrines in Pakistan was the thought of Muhammad Iqbal, who inspired much of the ideology for Pakistan, and his son Javid Iqbal, who advised the creation of a Ministry of Auqaf. He suggested that this ministry should take possession of and administer all religious endowments (*awqāf*) in Pakistan.[33] The first of a series of Auqaf ordinances was passed in 1959. These ordinances gave the government the power to take direct control over and manage shrines, mosques, and other properties dedicated for religious purposes, with each successive act further extending the authority of the Auqaf Department.[34]

As part of the direct assault on the role of the *pīr*, the Auqaf Department has stressed the aspect of Sufism that Iqbal had drawn on and himself embodied: the original Sufi as poet and social reformer. The government published pamphlets describing several of the major Sufi poets of Pakistan. In sharp contrast to traditional hagiographies, they do not give accounts of the miracles performed by the saint. Rather, they stress pious actions of the saint, actions within the capacity of the ordinary person.

Under successive governments, the Auqaf Department also concentrated on shifting the focus of activities at the shrines away from those that directly involved the leadership of the *gaddī nashīn* (hereditary caretaker of a shrine).

The goal was to make the shrines centers of more general social welfare by building hospitals, schools, and other facilities for poor and rural people. The hospitals are, in a sense, in direct competition with the *gaddī nashīns*, who claim as one of their spiritual powers the ability to heal, though many see the two approaches to healing as complementary. This policy of providing modern services at major shrines has continued and been extended, even as Islamization developed in subsequent decades. Policies have evolved and shifted over successive regimes, but the structure of the Auqaf Department has meant that the government has been able to carry out specific policies through on-the-ground administration of the shrines.

Despite post-Independence efforts to diminish the political and economic roles of hereditary *pīr* families in Pakistan, their power and influence persist, as Sarah Ansari discusses in chapter 7. Ansari questions the suggestion often raised in Pakistani public discourse that Sufism might be a panacea for extremism and intolerance by examining how local *pīr* families continue to wield extensive religious and political authority in Sindh. She argues that, though middle-class Sindhi nationalists view Sufism as a defining characteristic of the province, many of these *pīrs* are actually members of large land-owning families who serve as intermediaries and power brokers between the countryside and the Pakistani central government and whose political interests thus do not usually coincide with the urban interests of the Sindhi nationalists who evoke Sufism as an ideal of equality and toleration.

Pakistan's 1973 constitution dictated that all laws must conform with sharia, setting the stage for intensifying debates about what constitutes the limits of true Islam and how Sufi practice associated with shrines should be understood and regulated. When Mohammed Zia-ul-Haq became president in 1978, he pursued a program of Islamization, including a tightening of blasphemy laws in 1986. Though he and subsequent leaders also promoted certain activities at shrines,[35] these have in recent decades increasingly been the target of criticism and even violent attacks, including bombings at several shrines. Though often framed in terms of the proper practice of Islam, Ingram emphasizes in chapter 4 that these attacks arise from specific conflicts with the Pakistani government rather than from the pressure of Islamic reform itself, which can be enacted at shrines, and not just against them. In such cases, "reform" becomes a signifier for more context-specific power struggles.

Political leaders in recent years have supported Sufis to counter Taliban pressure. For example, as president, Pervez Musharraf established the short-lived National Sufi Council, discussed in chapter 8 by Alix Philippon. Current global perceptions of Sufism as a moderate antidote to fundamentalism have been directly translated into local conversations and social activism, as in headline-grabbing protests in Pakistan led by Sufi and scholar Dr. Tahir-ul-Qadri, founder of Tehreek-Minhaj-ul-Quran International, discussed by Hermansen in chapter 3. The political involvement of Barelwis has led to their mobilization on a national level using new methods of recruitment based on charismatic leadership and preaching rather than the traditional oath of allegiance to a *shaykh*, a process that could fall under the category of "Neo-Sufism."

Some scholars and local actors are concerned that the association of Sufism with Western efforts to foster a more moderate Islam is having a negative impact on the politics of Sufism within Pakistan. Some of the religious violence in recent years has involved attacks on Sufi shrines, but there are also Sufi-oriented Barelwis who have become anti-Western and less tolerant of pluralism. Philippon, in chapter 8, explores aspects of Barelwi involvement in contemporary Pakistani politics and considers the effects of public and government-sponsored discourse about the nature of Sufism on Barelwi politics. Philippon argues that Sufism in Pakistan has been politicized through a process of culturalization, in which the shrines and Sufi art forms have been identified as a central element of Pakistani heritage that must be protected against radical Islam, following the model of Turkey, where Sufism, which had been banned during the early days of the new republic in the 1920s, was allowed to return as a form of cultural performance. She points to the ways that General Pervez Musharraf, who was president of Pakistan in the period immediately following 9/11, promoted a vigorous ideological reformulation of Sufism as an Islam "of peace and love"—a component of the War on Terror against the Taliban and a policy that was continued by subsequent governments. Aiming to give Sufism added legitimacy in the wake of anti-Sufi pressure from "Talibanization," the government organized conferences, promoted Sufi cultural performances on TV, and publicized festivals at shrines, activities that were also supported by the U.S. government in various ways. Barelwis, especially those who were shrine custodians, were organized by the government into a National Sufi Council. Local critics saw this use of Sufism as a military dictatorship's efforts to legitimize itself to Western powers through the harmless symbols of Sufism. The ironic result is that some Barelwis themselves became radicalized and have mobilized to defend Islam, sometimes violently. Philippon demonstrates that the state-sponsored ideology of peaceful Sufism was just one position among many and that Barelwi groups have taken an array of political positions, including struggle for their version of an Islamic state, in opposition to Deobandi and Ahl-e Hadith groups that have targeted Barelwis and shrines as un-Islamic.

We see another form of shrine-based conflict examined by Noor Zaidi in chapter 9. Zaidi focuses on sectarian conflict that developed in the 1970s between the Shiʿi community and Sunni-oriented government authorities who administer the shrine of Bībī Pāk Dāman in Lahore, Pakistan. She examines how the rise of Sunni conservative theology associated with the government in the 1970s exacerbated existing tensions at the shrine, despite government efforts to "non-sectarianize" the shrine as a way of promoting public order. This shrine is an important site for South Asian Shia because it is purported to be the burial site of the daughter of the first Shiʿi imam. This chapter provides an example of how sectarianism can be produced and amplified on the ground and how a shrine, even as it draws visitors of different backgrounds, can become a flashpoint for conflict despite government claims that the shrines transcend religious difference.

Such conflicts take particular forms within the context of Pakistani politics. As Thomas Guglar, who participated in the workshop, has pointed out, moments of Barelwi violence have been inspired by Pakistan's blasphemy laws, which were strengthened in the 1980s under President Zia-ul-Haq. The Islamization policy initiated by Zia has become a key vehicle of religious intolerance, supported by factions within the government itself. Gugler has traced how mass sentiments have been generated by a rhetoric of threats to Islam, focused particularly on insulting the Prophet, which Barelwis feel is a particular outrage perpetrated by Deobandis, who criticize rituals intended to honor the Prophet. These affective politics, rooted in Sufi practices, have stirred mass protests and disruptions of the criminal justice system.[36]

Sufism in Indian National Spaces

In recent years Muslims in India face escalating hostility from Hindu nationalists and the Bharatiya Janata Party (BJP), now firmly established under Prime Minister Narendra Modi, who came to power in 2014 and won sweeping reelection in 2019. Under his government, Hindu nationalists have targeted Muslims as the dangerous, alien enemy of the nation, and mob lynchings have become more common.[37] Although this Hindutva rhetoric positions Muslims as outsiders, Sufism continues to play a special and rather different role within this national imaginary. As Arshad Alam has noted, the Hindu Right has for decades engaged in a vitriolic tirade against the madrasas, calling them " 'dens of terror' training *jihadis* to massacre Hindus and turn India into an Islamic nation."[38] The historical memory of Sufis and their place in India plays into this narrative of Muslims by way of contrast: Unlike the Turko-Afghan dynasties who invaded India in the medieval period, Sufis are depicted as the peaceful mystics who syncretized Islam with Hinduism, a perpetuation of the distinction articulated by colonial Orientalists. Sufi shrines play an important role in the Indian national imaginary as sites of toleration and communal harmony,[39] an idea that continues to be promoted by the Indian government. Modi himself spoke at the World Sufi Forum in Delhi in 2016, a conference "encouraged by the government . . . to convey India's message of peace and harmony."[40] In 2019 Modi presented a *chādar* (sheet for covering a body or grave) to be laid on the grave of the thirteenth-century Sufi saint Muʿīn al-Dīn Chishti during the annual *ʿurs*.[41] In contrast, Modi's BJP has sought to erase the importance of the shrine of Ghāzī Miyāñ in Delhi, a shrine that, according to Shahid Amin, disrupts their nationalist narrative because Ghāzī Miyāñ is purported to have been the invader-turned-Sufi nephew of the quintessential invader Maḥmūd of Ghazni. In his study of competing narratives about the shrine, Amin argued that the sense of community around the shrine is constituted because of this memory of conquest, not in spite of it, thereby disrupting the dichotomy between invading, violent Muslims and quietistic Sufi syncretism.[42]

The government-promoted assumption that Sufis are the bearers of peace and harmony and that shrines are thus sites that exemplify secular pluralism has also generated a considerable amount of research in recent years that examines how the peaceful co-presence of Hindus and Muslims is managed at various shrines, in apparent defiance of the growing communal tension and violence between Hindus and Muslims as Hindutva has become politically ascendant.[43] The framing of scholarly inquiry on Sufism in these terms has been quite different from the concerns of scholars working in Pakistan, and it is usually rather detached from questions of Muslim politics in India today, in effect reinforcing the idea that politics can somehow be transcended in environments controlled by Sufis. This narrative is, of course, a political one, promoted in many corners of Indian officialdom and reinforced by diversely situated actors, from NGOs to Sufis themselves. Thus, Torsten Tschacher has discussed with considerable irony his own description of his observations at a local shrine, which he gave in his exit interview to a government official in Pondicherry, South India: "I told of the astonishing harmony between Hindus, Muslims, and Christians visiting the shrine and the shared culture of worship I supposedly encountered." He went on to explain that this was the "politically correct answer" that extolled India's "unity in diversity."[44] Tschacher has described how shrines and Sufi poetry have been taken up in Tamil nationalism as examples of a shared ethos.[45] In this and other cases, Sufism and shrines have become vehicles for promoting various ideological and political messages in India, serving nationalist discourses or "suffer[ing] the fate of propagating syncretic dialogues of Hindu-Muslim secularism."[46]

In chapter 10 of this volume, Carla Bellamy's ethnographic study of a Muslim shrine in a Mumbai neighborhood in India makes the point that the devotional atmosphere at a shrine can reinforce religious difference rather than simply subsuming it. She shows how the experiences at a shrine can be very different for different categories of people. Yet she also nuances this point by depicting how devotees may form "transgressive" relationships across sectarian boundaries that they value because these relationships allow them to overcome the religious differences that increasingly divide people in their everyday lives. She thus documents an example of the possibilities for how difference is actually negotiated. In an essay from the 1990s, Peter van der Veer depicted analogous differences between Hindu and Muslim experiences of a shrine, describing how the shrine was a place of danger for Hindus in a way that it wasn't for Muslims, who understood the spiritual forces at the shrine differently.[47] Anand Taneja's presentation at the workshop offered yet another model of the shrine's potential with respect to difference: He argued that Hindu-Muslim interactions at a Muslim shrine in Delhi offer new ethical potentialities in which nameless, anti-identitarian intimacies become the basis for healing, a point that he explores more fully elsewhere.[48]

The Nehruvian vision of secularism in which minorities are to be tolerated and brought into the mainstream through education can be seen in action in chapter 11, where Helene Basu illustrates an effort to use the shrines as sites for education and modernization. This chapter foregrounds how governmentality—the Indian secular state's efforts to simultaneously care for and modernize its population—penetrates shrine spaces as sites of healing, even though the Indian government does not directly control the shrines, as in Pakistan. Psychiatrists established cooperative programs with shrines in Gujarat, India, and attempted to collaborate with Sufi healers. But their efforts at purifying mental health care from contamination by ritual healing were, in effect, an abjection of the enchanted world of the *pīr* and were experienced by the *pīrs* in charge of the shrine as a process of stripping the shrine of meaning. The outcome was growing resistance from the healers at the shrines, resulting in the failure of the program. This effort to use Sufi shrines as a site for educating or modernizing populations is reminiscent of policies emanating from Pakistan's Auqaf Department, but it seems to lack the kind of infrastructural support and trust from Muslim communities that we see in Pakistan.

In chapter 12, we see a very different example of the ways that modern forms of governmentality, whether through state or nonstate institutions, draw on the idea of the Sufi and the identification of Muslims with Sufi shrines to shape a national imaginary. Rachana Umashankar, like Brian Bond in chapter 6, focuses on *qawwālī* (Sufi music) performed at shrines. Umashankar examines how *qawwālī* has been used in Indian cinema. She demonstrates that since the turn of this century and the rise of violence associated with Hindu nationalism and interreligious strife, Sufi themes and music have been used in films to evoke the desire for a morally higher unity and a renewal of the promise of an egalitarian, secular, and pluralist society that the Indian state has failed to keep as it moves further toward Hindutva as its core political ideology. The image of Sufism as the peaceful Islam is here used to invoke the ideals of the secular state. We see here a setting in which the idea of the Sufi shrine as a place of peace, pluralism, and tolerance has been reinforced in the Indian national imaginary through film.

Bellamy's and Basu's essays, as well as Modi's photo-ops with the caretakers of major shrines, offer glimpses of the enduring institutional structure of Sufism in India, which is supported by the Indian legal system and the structure of *awqāf*: The authority of the Dewan to represent the shrine and to run events at the shrine has been guaranteed by the Indian courts since the colonial era.[49] India's central Wakf Council,[50] which oversees the administration of shrines as well as a range of other charitable bequests, was established in 1954. State wakf boards were established under the 1995 Wakf Act. Since 2006, the administration of *awqāf* is under the general oversight of the Minister of Minority Affairs, who is ex-officio chair of the central Wakf Council. Muslims writing about *awqāf* in India have focused on the poor governance, corruption, and expropriation of *waqf* properties,[51] a problem foregrounded in a 2017 *India Today* exposé: "Waqf Land Grab Exposed: India's Biggest Land Scam," which documented how custodians of *waqf* estates had been caught selling these charitable assets for a profit, sometimes with a shrine included, often with kickbacks to the state Wakf Board.[52] Another concern has been the sectarian affiliations of official caretakers (*mutawalīs*), some of whom are unsympathetic or even opposed to the activities at the shrines that they administer.

In contrast to research questions focused on how religious difference is managed at Sufi shrines in India, there has been little research on the power struggles among Muslim leaders with respect to orientations toward Sufism. Sectarian splits among Muslims, including the Barelwi-Deobandi divide, continue to be salient for Muslims in India as well as in Pakistan, despite the minority status of Muslims in India. These splits generate similar struggles over control of shrines and institutions such as wakf boards. Based on fieldwork at the most important Barelwi madrasa in India, the Jamiat al Ashrafiya Misbahul Ulum in eastern Uttar Pradesh, Alam has shown that "for students of this *madrasa*, the 'other' is not a Hindu, but a Muslim from another *maslak*," even as members of the Hindu right were calling madrasas "dens of terror."[53] Tracing the history of the Deobandi-Barelwi contestation in Mubarakpur, the town where the madrasa is located, Alam notes its roots in a class divide in which wealthy Deobandis sought to reshape popular practice in the area. Van der Veer makes a similar observation based on his fieldwork at the shrine of a Rifāʿī saint in the North Indian city of Surat in Gujarat in the early 1990s: He notes that the reform-oriented "Tablighi Muslims" who oppose rituals at the shrine are not concerned with Hindu participation or with maintaining a communitarian boundary between Hindus and Muslims, but rather with critiquing the Rifāʿī *faqīrs* themselves as un-Islamic.[54]

Greater scholarly attention needs to be paid to Sufi political voices in the public arena and how these voices have been shaped by the growing perception in the late twentieth and early twenty-first centuries that Sufis represent peace and toleration, in contradistinction to Wahhabis or Salafis. In the Indian political environment, where Muslims are viewed with such hostility and suspicion, the stakes of claiming an association with peace-loving Sufis are high. Within the Indian political arena, some Barelwis have played the Sufi card and claimed to be peace loving, contrasting themselves with Deobandi Jihadis, a stance that U.S. diplomats have bought into and used as a basis for policy recommendations, as evidenced by WikiLeaks' revelations of confidential diplomatic cables.[55] Kelly Pemberton has discussed how Chishtī Sufis in India have responded to common stereotypes in India of Muslims as backward and intolerant by increasing efforts to foster intercommunal harmony through interfaith activism, especially since the bombings of shrines in India by right-wing Hindu groups.[56] While her emphasis is on the fact that this movement to promote communal harmony is a "continuation of extant forms of social activism among Chishtis,"[57] she is talking about an ideological shift that has occurred since the 1990s, in which a Sufi message developed that was similar to that of artists, musicians, and NGOs that were also promoting communal harmony. These various actors draw on themes and images from hagiographies of the early Chishtī Sufis, but they are recast and embellished in new ways,[58] much as successive Pakistani governments have recast the hagiographies of saints associated with major shrines to foreground contemporary themes.[59] Ronie Parciack, examining the visual culture that has developed in relationship to Chishtī Sufi shrines and is disseminated through new media, has demonstrated a popularly negotiated visual formula that has borrowed motifs drawn from Hindu nationalist iconography in ways that have the potential to make Hindu nationalism attractive to Muslims who are drawn to Sufis associated with Chishtī shrines.[60] These new images have had an impact on sectarian struggles.

Umashankar has shown how, paradoxically, the Indian secularist incorporation of Muslims by embracing Sufism (which is often associated with local shrines) has exacerbated suspicion of Sufism among conservative Muslim groups. This is in part a consequence of secularist and spiritualist claims that Sufism has little to do with Islam.[61]

Sectarian struggles among Muslims are playing out through new organizations that transcend local politics, with institutional structures that reflect those of many other modern organizations. Several Sufi *pīrs* have sought to be national representatives of Muslim communities through various Sufi-based organizations. The Centre for Islamic Studies at Bareilly Sharif, for instance, was founded in 2000 by Akhtar Rażā Khān, who claimed the title Grand Mufti of India. These organizations are engaged in contests over this ideological divide between Sufis and Islamic reformists.[62] The All-India Ulama and Mashaikh Board was founded by Mohammad Ashraf Kichhouchhwi as "a representative body consisting of the *Sajjada Nasheen* (Patrons-in-Chief) of Dargahs, imams of mosques, Muftis and teachers of madrasas,"[63] and was set up with subcommittees in each state. The board has been holding large gatherings of Sufi *shaykhs* and others to push back against anti-Sufi Wahhabi and Deobandi influence by supporting secular political candidates. In 2011 they staged a "coming out" event at which they denounced Muslim extremists and complained that, despite representing 80 percent of Sunni Muslims in India, "they have not been able to assert themselves because the Deobandis and the Wahabis have captured key Muslim institutions such as the Wakf Board and the madrasas."[64] In 2016 they held the World Sufi Forum, which was launched by Prime Minister Modi and was attended by Sufis and scholars from several other countries, including Tahir-ul-Qadri.[65] Their aim has been to shape government policy concerning Muslims as a minority, including laws that would affect succession and leadership of shrines and mosques, which leaders such as Syed Babar Ashraf claim have been usurped by "people of extremist ideology."[66]

The tension between Sufism and Islamic reform, which is playing out all across the Muslim world, is thus a force shaping the significance of shrines for Muslims in India. This tension intersects with the growing discrimination against Muslims as the Indian state moves away from secular democracy toward the promotion of Hindu nationalism. In this environment, Sufis have been involved in promoting Muslims as Indian citizens, and shrines have been cultivated as sites of interfaith forms of belonging, while the Indian government and creators of popular culture use Sufi shrines and cultural forms such as *qawwālī* to promote an Indian national imaginary of secular tolerance.

Beyond South Asia

Though most of the chapters focus on either Pakistan or India, this volume is also an effort to think critically about the role of public discourse in shaping the place and trajectory of Sufism today in a way that situates what is happening in Pakistan and India within a broader global context that goes beyond South Asia. Though *Modern Sufis and the State* only touches on this "beyond," two chapters, by Rosemary Corbett and Verena Meyer, make clear the far-reaching influence of South Asian Islam on modern ideas of Sufism. Corbett contrasts the experience of French colonizers with Sufis in North Africa, many of whom were involved in anti-colonial militias, with British colonizers, who imagined Sufis as pacifist. Meyer examines the influence of Pakistani scholar Fazlur Rahman, who had played an important role in the development of Islamic Studies in the United States, on Neo-Sufism in Indonesia.

Islamic studies continue to have an Arab-centered bias, an overemphasis on the beginnings of Islam, and an assumption that the core of the Islamic tradition lies in its Arab institutions as revealed in Arabic sources. This is true despite the occasional efforts of some scholars to move away from this Arabic-centric view of Islamic studies, beginning with Hodgson's 1974 epic *The Venture of Islam*,[67] which posited a multicentered world order in which Persianate, Turkic, and Indic societies were key components of the Islamicate world; and including Richard Bulliet's *View from the Edge*,[68] which not only looked at the concerns of recently converted populations who were far from the "center" of the Caliphate but also argued that the religious scholarly elites on the "edge" and the institutions they developed in their unsettled regions eventually had a transformative effect on the "center" itself. Recently, Shahab Ahmed's *What Is Islam?* generated a scholarly sensation because of its focus on the "Balkans-to-Bengal complex," away from a prioritization of Arabic sources as somehow being closer to a true Islam.[69] Ahmed's book is also important for the way that it firmly encompasses Sufism within normative Islam in an era when it is increasingly excluded. Green's 2012 overview of Sufism similarly tried to give an even amount of attention to developments in Sufi institutions across all regions of the Islamic world.[70]

In the modern period thinkers from South Asia, far from being on the periphery of developments in the Islamic world, have been key players in the generating new interpretations of Islam that have had a global impact. Abū al-Aʿlā Mawdūdī's articulation of the need for reform and his anti-Sufi position, forged in the crucible of the late colonial period in India, have had a deep influence on Islamic reformers, and his books—translated into Arabic, Turkish,

Farsi, and other languages—are still widely read across the Middle East.[71] Similarly, Muhammad Iqbal, the South Asian poet who is credited with the idea of Pakistan and often called its "Spiritual Father," was an inspiration for the first president of independent Senegal, Léopold Senghor.[72] Building on this legacy of Iqbal, the Senegalese government today is committed to supporting a form of Islam inspired by Sufism as they seek to contain the influence of foreign-trained Islamic reformists. These examples suggest that it is important to take seriously developments in Sufism in South Asia, not just as relevant for the history of Islam in South Asia, but for the broader Islamic world. Sufis are on the move, forming transnational networks, getting involved in translation projects, setting up shrines in new homes outside of South Asia, transmitting dreams across the world and blowing blessings through phone lines, communicating through Skype and the Internet, and engaging in arguments with anti-Sufis in new forums.

One guiding question at the empirical level has been how do the very different political climates for Sufis shape what's going on in India versus Pakistan? In Pakistan, Muslims run the show, and Sufism has become a controversial issue in shaping the contours of Muslim/Pakistani identity. A spate of bombings at shrines would seem to reinforce the conclusion that Sufis are in dire peril in the face of Islamist efforts to set narrow limits on what is properly Islam. But this is a view that is far too simple and blinds us to the complex dynamics of Sufism in Pakistan today. In India, Muslims are a minority subject to discrimination in many arenas. Communal violence between Hindus and Muslims has been a feature of India's political and social landscape since the colonial period, but this violence and the role of Muslims in it is imagined very differently than "Islamic terrorism." In this setting, Sufism and its shrines are doing quite different things than in Pakistan, not only for local populations but also for Indian national imaginings of Muslim minorities, democracy, tolerance, and diversity. Furthermore, scholars are asking rather different questions about Sufism in these two environments.

What are the effects of policy-based efforts to promote Sufis as the friends and allies of democracy, tolerance, and peace, an effort supported by the very Luce-funded project through which this volume's contributors were gathered? The political project can be simply stated: How can scholars contribute to making Muslims and the nations to which they belong into modern democratic global citizens? One important answer has been to identify peaceful players, and thus to promote (but also possibly to delegitimate) Sufism.

But this volume's goal is to consider how we can understand this act of positioning of the Sufi as the peaceful Muslim, the bearer of tolerance and democracy. Gayatri Chakravorty Spivak has described how in modern Western philosophy and postcolonial reason, the "native informant" functions as a foreclosed other on which the modern subject is founded,[73] meaning that this native is visible only through the traces of erasure—first negated and then affirmed as something other than itself. From this perspective, we could say that the Sufi has become the other of the other, in a kind of double foreclosure. The Sufi has been recovered from the oddly bifurcated realm of superstition and Oriental spirituality to become "the enemy of my enemy" (the intolerant, violent Muslim). The Sufi is my friend, but not in the lateral plane that the term "friendship" implies. In the process, the Sufi of a global discourse that has developed over the past half century has become increasingly removed from the complex politics of Sufi practice in South Asia, though Sufis in India and Pakistan are in turn shaped by this discourse of "the good Sufi."

Perhaps an analogue would be the Muslim woman in Europe, who is more easily assimilable than the Muslim man, but only through a process that both reinforces the stigmatization of Muslim men as dangerous and abusive and positions the Muslim woman as a victim to be saved by the Western liberal. Thanks to this complex and politically powerful discourse, it has become increasingly difficult to claim a Sufi identity in the modern world.

PART I

Sufism and Its Modern Engagements with a Global Order

1

Anti-Colonial Militants or Liberal Peace Activists?

The Role of Private Foundations in Producing Pacifist Sufis During the Cold War

ROSEMARY R. CORBETT

In 2007, the United Nations Educational, Scientific, and Cultural Organization (UNESCO) commemorated the eight-hundredth anniversary of the birth of Jalāl al-Dīn Rūmī, a Persian-language writer whom they hailed as a "spiritual master" and "one of the greatest poets, philosophers, and scholars of the Islamic civilization."[1] UNESCO was far from the only organization to celebrate the Sufi sage that year. The Turkish government, for example, placed giant exhibits on Rūmī and the Mevlevis, the Sufi order that claims him, in the Hagia Sophia in Istanbul for the benefit of domestic and international tourists. These celebrations and demonstrations were hardly inspired just by the anniversary of Rūmī's birth. Rather, they both reflected and arose from the increasingly politicized ideas that Sufi practices are both the most mystical *and* the most moderate of Islamic traditions, and are even able to counter radicalization among Muslims—particularly those in Pakistan. The year after the anniversary, for example, the *New York Times* published nearly three dozen articles mentioning Sufism in its pages, with titles such as, "Turkish Schools Offer Pakistan a Gentler Vision of Islam" and "In Pakistan, Islam Needs Democracy."[2] *Smithsonian* magazine joined in that December with a cover story accompanying the photo of a brightly clad Pakistani dervish. "The Sufi Question: Can the Joyous Muslim Movement Counter the Forces of Extremism?" it asked.[3]

By 2008, American pundits and policy makers had been hoping Sufis would help counter "radical Islam" for years. In 2003 and 2007, for example, the RAND Corporation identified Sufis as partners for the U.S. government in "Building Civil and Democratic Islam" and "Building Moderate Muslim Networks," respectively.[4] Indeed, the idea that Sufis could be considered "moderate" or particularly pacifist took root in policy circles even decades before that: Since 1947 it has been particularly appealing for those concerned with the strategically crucial nation of Pakistan.

As I have demonstrated elsewhere, during the early years of the Cold War several prominent Orientalists and Muslim scholars began to regard Sufis from India-turned-Pakistan as potentially more liberal in their religious interpretations than Arab Muslims. Some, such as Wilfred Cantwell Smith, who established the Institute of Islamic Studies at McGill University with Rockefeller Foundation funding in 1951, even hoped to move the center of Islamic orthodoxy away from Arab lands to South Asia.[5] In what follows, I examine the Rockefeller Foundation's role in funding the research that led to such partial impressions of Sufism and that helped to create for American policy makers an enduring picture of Sufis as Muslim pacifists opposed to the kinds of political violence increasingly ascribed to "fundamentalists."

As we shall see, Rockefeller Foundation (RF) officials involved in sponsoring area studies and Islamic studies after World War II, and working in close cooperation with Ford Foundation officials and U.S. diplomats undertaking the same pursuits, relied heavily on British- and American-trained Orientalists for their impressions of Islam. Foundation officials shared some of the racial and religious biases that animated the work of even the most sympathetic Orientalists, and only occasionally sought to counter what seemed to be problematic oversights, such as the tendency of scholars at the McGill Institute of Islamic Studies to rely too heavily on ideas about Sufis drawn from Indian and Pakistani contexts. Had foundation officials put more energy into diversifying their sources of information, not least by including more French-trained Orientalists in their inquiries, they might have developed a more nuanced understanding of the variety of Sufi traditions and tendencies. In North and West African colonies once held by the French, Sufis had played active roles in conflicts ranging from local rivalries to anti-colonial militia movements and could hardly be considered pacifist or apolitical.[6] As it was, however, foundation officials tended to rely heavily on particular British Orientalists, including Hamilton A. R. Gibb, and on those trained by them. Consequently, they often viewed Islam in the dichotomous terms provided in Gibb's 1947 *Modern Trends in Islam*—a book first delivered as a series of lectures at the University of Chicago and published in the United States with Rockefeller Foundation support. The dynamic Gibb presented was one of perpetual conflict between two Muslim factions: generally pacifist "Sufis" and more aggressive (often racially coded as "Arab") "fundamentalists."[7]

Rockefeller Foundation officials charged with funding Islamic studies did not perpetuate Gibb's overly schematic understandings of Muslims simply because they overlooked bias or ignored Francophone scholars and territories. To the contrary, foundation officials sought to work with scholars whom they believed to be least antagonistic toward Arabs, they involved at least one French scholar in RF-sponsored international study groups in the early 1950s, and they sent a British Orientalist through French-occupied North Africa during the same period to gather information about contemporary Islam. Thanks to their overreliance on a close network of British scholars and their acolytes, however, RF officials were still rarely presented with information that disrupted the idea of Sufis that they otherwise funded and disseminated. But how did the Rockefeller Foundation come to be involved in such work to begin with?

Private Foundations, Government Officials, and the Creation of Area Studies

The role of private foundations in funding area studies before the 1958 National Defense Education Act was passed is now well known.[8] At the forefront of such work were the Rockefeller and Ford Foundations and, to a lesser extent, the Carnegie Corporation. After World War II, with the United States assuming a larger role in international affairs, both government officials and leaders of private foundations (sometimes the same people) believed it necessary to better educate policy makers and the general public about the rest of the world. Even before the war's end, the Carnegie Corporation and Rockefeller Foundation supported the Smithsonian's Ethnogeographic Board, the mission of which was to "furnish to governmental war agencies, military and civilian, needed information of all sorts relating to any areas outside the United States where military, economic, or other action is carried on or planned."[9] After the war, the Ethnogeographic Board redistributed some foundation grants to aid the growth of area studies. But, as I have discussed elsewhere, the RF also participated much earlier and more directly in funding studies of religion in what they then called the "Near East."[10]

The RF officer who would be put in charge of postwar Near East studies, John Marshall—an agnostic Harvard PhD who once taught English and medieval literature[11]—was hardly an expert in the region when he joined RF as assistant director for the humanities in 1933. Promoted to associate director of the Division of Humanities in 1940, Marshall focused primarily on fostering the arts in Europe and North America. During the late 1940s and most of the 1950s, however, Marshall was tasked with overseeing studies of Arab countries and fostering modern developments within them. (Also interested in what he and others considered the comparatively modern Muslim societies of Iran and Turkey, Marshall found his work in Iran cut short by Mohammad Mosaddegh's election, which the RF believed created a hostile climate for American foundations. And secularized Turkey, Marshall thought, belonged mostly to Europe, anyway. Arab countries, however, seemed most in need of his attention.[12])

Although Rockefeller-related foundations had funded studies of the ancient Near East for decades, Marshall's endeavors in the region during the early Cold War years occurred at a time when the newly formed Central Intelligence Agency sought to co-opt the work of foundations to combat the spread of communism.[13] Relationships between intelligence agencies and foundation officers during this era were often quite close. John McCloy, for example, who had served as assistant secretary of war before becoming president of the Ford Foundation, created an administrative unit designed specifically to work with the CIA. While concerned that this open relationship could undermine Ford's credibility, he reasoned that the CIA would otherwise only operate through the foundation covertly.[14] At the Rockefeller Foundation, where two foundation presidents (Dean Rusk and John Foster Dulles) went on to become secretaries of state, the relationships among trustees, officers, and members of the intelligence services were particularly strong. Not only was Nelson Rockefeller (an RF trustee and head of Latin American intelligence during World War II) appointed to Eisenhower's National Security Council in 1954, but David Rockefeller (another RF trustee) routinely received personal briefings from and provided funding to Tom Braden, the assistant to CIA Chief Allen Dulles (brother of John Foster Dulles).[15]

Several RF officers (including Charles B. Fahs, director of the humanities in the 1950s) had also worked in Truman's intelligence bureau, the Office of Strategic Services (a CIA predecessor), before joining RF. And at least one—Chadbourne Gilpatric, who oversaw humanities in South Asia and would join Marshall in funding Islamic studies—came to the RF directly from the CIA. Marshall's and Gilpatric's officer diaries display occasional resentment over government interference in their grant making. (Marshall, for example, befriended an Iraqi parliamentarian whom, he noted, the State Department had erroneously warned him to steer clear of because of alleged Nazi sympathies.[16]) More frequently, the diaries recount collaboration with such officials, domestically and abroad.

Foundation officers routinely checked in with U.S. and British diplomats, consular officials, and intelligence service officers, as well as with local government functionaries, on their trips to South Asia and the region increasingly called the "Middle East." They meticulously researched possible grantees and used the information provided by those officials to ensure that they did not sponsor anyone known to have communist sympathies. During such investigative meetings, foundation officers also informed government officials of their projects. When, for example, Marshall sponsored a multiyear series of conferences involving Arab intellectuals and a few Westerners (the latter to guide discussions) on prospects for modernizing education, law, and religion in the Arab world, he invited the American ambassador in Lebanon to the opening ceremonies.[17] Years later, when one of those Western intellectuals—Wilfred Cantwell Smith—hosted a series of RF-funded workshops on Pakistan at McGill University, the RF consulted Nicholas Thatcher of the State Department's Pakistan Desk on the proceedings and invited the educational and cultural attaché at Pakistan's Washington embassy to attend.[18]

Such consultation with diplomats and intelligence officials was deemed crucial to the success of the RF area studies programs—in part to compensate for the staff's lack of knowledge. Not only was there no Near East/Middle East expert on staff at the RF, the program's focus on contemporary (rather than ancient) culture had only really begun after World War II. But government officials were not the only people Marshall consulted. Despite his own marked racial prejudices against Arabs, Marshall believed that most of the world had a more negative opinion of Arabs than they should. The foundation needed to cultivate Arab spokespersons who could represent the Arab world to Westerners in a way Westerners could understand, he insisted, and who could simultaneously learn to think like Westerners when directing the affairs of their newly independent countries. His ultimate guide on who to enlist in this project was the British Orientalist the foundation had first sponsored in 1945, hoping to bring sympathetic understandings of Arabs and Islam to the United States: Hamilton Gibb.

Under that first 1945 grant, Gibb had traveled to the University of Chicago to deliver the prestigious Haskell Lectures on Comparative Religions.[19] Two years later, his lectures were published as *Modern Trends in Islam.* This was the same work that argued for the perpetual confrontational dialectic between creative Sufis and overly orthodox "fundamentalists"—and it became, in effect, Marshall's field guide to the Near East.[20] Marshall knew Gibb had not traveled to any Arab country in over a decade. "Gibb was one of the first to say [his book] was not up-to-date and that it was relatively superficial," he acknowledged. "Really valid interpretations had to come from Muslims themselves."[21] Still, in his early visits to the region, he would frequently ask locals whether they had read the book and, if so, what they thought. (If they had not read it, he often offered to send a copy.)[22] Eventually, the Muslims recruited to RF-financed projects at McGill would also be those trained by Gibb or trained to think like him.

As the overlap between Marshall's interests in the Near East and in Muslims suggests, he regarded Islam as synonymous with the region. (Marshall was hardly alone in this. RF documents frequently spoke of sending scholars to travel "in Islam.") Indeed, in contrast to proponents of complete secularization, Marshall—following Gibb—saw Islam and Muslims as crucial to modernizing the Near East.[23] And more than trusting Gibb's 1945 assessment of Near Eastern trends, Marshall put a great deal of stock in the scholars Gibb identified as most knowledgeable about Islam, as well as in the Muslims he identified as most promising for sparking some kind of Islamic intellectual reform. This, after all, was an early goal of the RF's Islamic studies program (to which I turn shortly). The academics Gibb thought most highly of included the noted French scholar of Sufism Louis Massignon as well as Smith, who had spent the war years in Lahore and, thus, had more recent experience with Muslims than did Orientalists stranded in their home countries by the conflict.[24] As to Muslims who might spark reform, Gibb mentioned just one person—a man about whom Smith was initially ambivalent but whom Smith would also later regard as a guide for liberalizing and modernizing Islam: the intellectual father of modern Pakistan (as he is often called) and the Sufi who wanted to do away with "medieval" mysticism, Muhammad Iqbal.[25]

Despite his general focus on Arab-language countries and his favoring of scholars trained in or hailing from Pakistan, Gibb did note in the preface to his 1947 book that "some valuable regional studies have been published by French scholars on North and West Africa."[26] Gibb did not name them, however, and Marshall was not tasked with overseeing grants in those regions. Nevertheless, with the French still very active in Lebanon and Syria, Marshall believed it prudent to include a French Orientalist in his Arab study group. The contemporary French Orientalist Gibb most frequently referred to and whom Marshall ultimately involved in their Arab world conferences was Henri Laoust, a scholar trained by Massignon who was then spending part of each year as the director of a research institute in Damascus. Laoust, who specialized in the work of Ibn Taymiyyah, was "only a symbol of some French participation," Marshall assured Mohammed Awad, the former director of cultural affairs in Egypt's Ministry of Education. But in his diaries, Marshall gave evidence of Laoust's possible importance and, more so, his preference for scholars sympathetic toward Sufism. If Laoust "is in the Massignon tradition," Marshall wrote, "he may well be the Frenchman to be included."[27]

Laoust, who did not speak English well, did not turn out to be a memorable participant in the study group. Marshall rarely mentions him in his diaries from the time and does not refer to him at all in his memoirs (where a great deal of fond reflection is devoted to Gibb and laudatory comments are afforded

Smith). Importantly, Marshall did at least once try to gain an impression of Muslim life in French territories. After the RF decided to fund Islamic studies, and not just studies of regions where Muslims lived, Marshall sought out—on Gibb's recommendation—the British Orientalist Arthur John Arberry, commissioning him to make an investigatory trip through North Africa. He presented A. J. Arberry, who had translated the works of Rūmī and Iqbal, to the RF as a "great scholar of mystical Islam."[28]

One of just a few Orientalists whom RF officers deemed both intellectually competent and not condescending toward Muslims, Arberry was only too happy to accept a travel grant. He outlined an ambitious itinerary through Spain, Morocco, Algeria, and Tunisia (the last of which he failed to reach), and the RF helped him gain visas into French territory. Upon his return however, and with apologies, Arberry refused to submit a report to the foundation. Instead, he complained that the French did not understand Arabs and that French officials were completely unhelpful in his travels, directing him only to those who echoed official opinions.[29] (Arberry did not say what those opinions were, but it seems likely—given the history of Sufi anti-colonial activity in the region—that French officials in Algeria presented a different picture of Sufism than the one Arberry promoted). Although they remained cordial, Marshall did not involve Arberry in any subsequent Islamic studies grants. Neither did he make any further efforts to investigate French perspectives on Sufism.

Rockefeller Foundation Funding for Modernizing Islam

The RF's reasons for funding Islamic studies were similar to its reasons for funding Near East studies. In the "General Description" section of their first major Islamic studies grant (dated May 31, 1951), foundation officers wrote:

> In every predominantly Muslem [*sic*] country Islam is . . . a force to be reckoned with—even in Turkey where the political power of Islam seems now to have been eliminated by Ataturk's reforms. This fact is increasingly recognized by educated Muslems, particularly those of western education. For them, the urgent need is for a rethinking of Islam which would, they are convinced, furnish the religious sanction for the modernization their countries must undergo. As a result they are more and more inclined to challenge the conservatism of present popular leadership in Islam in an effort to redefine the role which Islam should play in the lives of present-day Muslems.[30]

Although modernization and liberalization (that could "challenge the conservatism of present popular leadership") were central aims, RF officers did not believe they were exporting a particular agenda or mode of being to the Near East or to Muslim-majority societies. Rather, they envisioned themselves as partners (albeit sometimes admittedly paternal ones) in an enterprise their educated Near Eastern Muslim contacts supported. During a 1954 conference on Arab countries in Egypt, one of the "Western" interlocutors (Ralph Turner, a cultural historian at Yale) proposed that what participants really sought was not a way to deal with the Westernization of Muslim societies but modernization—which, he reasoned, was different from imposed Westernization because all societies would inevitably have to confront issues of modernity in their own ways at their own times. According to Marshall, "the effects of this assertion were instantaneous. This obviously was THE way to tackle the problem. Everyone present had something to say."[31]

Smith, who also participated in the conference, held a similar view. Thanks to Gibb, RF officials considered Smith "the leading Western authority on contemporary Islam," and he was quickly selected for the RF's first round of Islamic studies travel grants in 1951. Primarily designed to reintroduce scholars of Islam who had spent the war stranded stateside (or in Britain) to the people about whom they so frequently wrote, these grants also aimed "to stimulate Muslem [*sic*] thinking" out of its "backwardness." Only by so inspiring indigenous intellectuals could the RF help spark what Westernization had so far failed to effect: "an amalgamation of what is best in the West and the sources of growth in the East."[32]

When later, in 1951, Marshall and Smith began discussing the possibility that RF might fund an Institute of Islamic Studies at McGill, they bonded over their similar impressions of Muslim-majority lands. In his diaries Marshall frequently invoked the Orientalist stereotype of the calculating Semite, and more than once described Arabs as particularly "shrewd." In later years, he would describe Arabs in more base terms, saying that his work in Arab countries—especially when juxtaposed with his time in Turkey—had shown Arabs, except for a small educated elite, to be "stupid" and "a little crazy," and even a "menace" to the rest of the world.[33] The Turks, on the other hand, in Marshall's opinion, had secularized and depoliticized Islam and "made something beautiful of it."[34]

While not overtly racist, Smith also tended to accept the Orientalist dichotomy that divided Muslims into Semites and Aryans, and believed that Semites (Arabs) were overly rigid, while Aryans (Indians and Persians) were more flexible and creative. These impressions influenced his thinking about how future studies of Islam should take shape. When Marshall and Smith met in 1951,

Smith told Marshall he believed Islamic reform was not likely to originate in the Arab world. Rather, he argued, they should look to Turkish or Pakistani Muslims for leaders of the needed reformation.[35]

So committed was Smith to the idea of fostering a Turkish or Pakistani-led Islamic reformation that he initially envisioned this as the McGill Institute's purpose. In fact, it was Marshall who insisted that it focus on other Muslim populations, including Arabs (Africa seemed not to be on anyone's radar), and treat Islamic reform as incidental to the larger study of Islam.[36] Smith agreed to diversify the institute's focus and faculty, though his first proposed hires were still Pakistani and Turkish: Fazlur Rahman, once a student of Gibb's, and Nizai Berkes, who translated Gibb's *Modern Trends in Islam* into Turkish. He also agreed to downplay his reformist aims for the sake of "diplomacy."[37] Three months into the institute's inaugural semester in 1952, however, Smith wrote to Chadbourne Gilpatric (the RF officer in charge of humanities in South Asia, with whom Smith had spoken during a 1951 interview about the possibility of Pakistani-led Islamic reform) to once again impress upon him their mutual interests.[38] It would not be long before Smith's hopes to foster studies of and reform in Pakistan materialized.

In 1953 and 1954, Gilpatric was in frequent communication with Freeland Abbott, a Tufts University professor then working courtesy of a Ford fellowship in West Pakistan. Simultaneously, Gilpatric was in close contact with Ishtiaq Qureshi, Pakistan's first minister of education, who was then working as a visiting researcher at Columbia University. In January of 1955, Qureshi emphasized to Gilpatric that "modern and liberal movements" in Arab countries "have not been paralleled with attempts to rethink and modernize Islam" as they had in Pakistan.[39] The day after speaking with Qureshi, Gilpatric contacted Smith about forming a group of scholars to study Pakistan.[40]

Smith confessed to Gilpatric that his administrative duties at McGill were quite heavy and would likely prevent him from organizing such a group personally. Still, he submitted a formal funding request to the RF that March, arguing that "Pakistan is a very major nation in the modern Orient, of conspicuous importance to present policy of the United States, and through the Colombo Plan to Canada."[41] While Smith agreed to chair the first meeting that year (to involve Abbott, Qureshi, and Keith Callard, a political science professor at McGill), Abbott would organize it.[42] Soon, philosopher Stanley Maron of the Human Resource Area Files also joined as an ongoing participant.

The work of what came to be known as the "Group on Pakistan Studies" is charted elsewhere.[43] What is important here, and what has been otherwise glossed over, is the early members' joint belief that Pakistani Muslims, following and improving on the work of Muhammad Iqbal, might foment Islamic reform. As Maron (who later chaired the group) argued at one point, a "renaissance of Islam, which is indicated by historical evidence, will probably be successful only if it concentrates on the individual and his relations to God and man. . . . The efforts of the liberal philosophers should be oriented towards Being, for it is only there that man can find fulfillment."[44]

Scholars listening to Maron's call for supporting liberal existentialists could likely not have avoided thinking of Muhammad Iqbal's Sufi-centered, quasi-existentialist philosophy. Ultimately, Maron found Iqbal's work to be overly eclectic in some ways. Others, though—particularly Qureshi, who defended Iqbal and other Muslim modernists—disagreed and continually promoted what they saw as Iqbal's insights.[45] For his part, Smith secured the appointment of an aspiring Iqbal scholar, Fazlur Rahman, to his Institute of Islamic Studies at McGill. (Earlier, when Rahman had applied for an RF fellowship to go to Pakistan from Durham, North Carolina, where he had been teaching in March of 1955, Smith informed RF officials that he did not think Rahman's project on Iqbal was sufficiently advanced to merit the trip.[46] However, he then procured Rahman for McGill, where Rahman pursued his studies of Iqbal's reformism in conversation with Smith and the institute's faculty and students.[47]) At the Pakistan group's 1956 meeting, Smith reported that he had signed Rahman to a five-year contract. In the meantime, Callard assumed the role of proposing an institute for Pakistan studies to the university and to the RF. Among its possible tasks, he suggested, would be training diplomats and members of the military about the new nation.[48]

The Group on Pakistan Studies, with Callard at the helm, focused increasingly on questions of political science. In the meantime, Smith and Rahman spent years discussing the possibilities of Iqbal-inspired educational reform in Pakistan. When Rahman's five years at McGill concluded, he moved to Pakistan to join Qureshi there in reforming the nation's education system. In 1961 he was appointed to help direct President Ayub Khan's Central Institute of Islamic Research. Among Rahman and Qureshi's first major endeavors there was publishing a new journal, *Islamic Studies.* They, along with other editors, sent several issues of the new publication to the Rockefeller Foundation, including the inaugural volume, still housed in foundation archives, which included an article on Rūmī by A. J. Arberry.

With Smith's, Rahman's, and others' hopes for the future of Islamic reform (orthodox Islam infused with Sufi liberalism) in Pakistan seeming promising, Smith left McGill for Harvard in 1963 and turned to the task that would consume the rest of his life: how to promote "world community" among members of all religions. Rahman, in the meantime, turned to reworking Gibb's ideas about Sufis and fundamentalists.[49] As I have discussed elsewhere, this included somewhat re-entrenching the notion that liberally minded Sufi philosophers could dialectically balance out the influence of Muslims who were rigidly orthodox (and generally depicted as Arab, or "Wahhabi"—a British colonial term).[50] After falling out of favor in Pakistan, Rahman returned to the United States in 1968. He eventually secured a position at the University of Chicago, enjoyed Ford Foundation support of his work, and occasionally shared his perspectives with U.S. State Department officials.[51]

Fighting the Tide of Liberal Protestant Perspectives on Authentic, Modern Religion

As the history of Rockefeller Foundation funding for Islamic studies demonstrates, it was not inevitable that American pundits and policy makers came to see Sufis as inherently pacifist or anti-fundamentalist. On the contrary, it could almost be seen as accidental—due mostly to the liberal Protestant biases of white American foundation officers (Marshall was not only rather anti-Arab but somewhat fascinated by mystics and fond of quoting William Blake) and, especially, to the biases of the academics RF officers consulted. Despite such biases and the uneven power relations that made the perspectives of affluent white Euro-American men seem synonymous with modern knowledge itself, opportunities to see things differently did arise. They did not, however, arise with enough frequency or force to crest above the growing tidal wave of "common sense" created by the intersecting currents of postwar scholarly consensus and U.S. statecraft.

Long after Arberry's excursion, for example, RF officers again funded work in Africa that could have complicated their understandings of Sufism. In 1959 the RF deemed Islamic studies crucial to educating newly independent Nigerians in their history and traditions. As with Arab nations and Pakistan earlier, their hope was that critical studies of Islam would yield openness to other kinds of liberal criticism. Further, according to RF officers, studies of Arabic and contemporary Islamic traditions in other parts of the Islamic world would educate the "archaic"-minded "desert people" of Nigeria in how Islam is compatible with modernity.[52] Proper Islamic education would lead to modernization. Thus, the RF added Islamic studies to the list of programs they funded at University College in Ibadan, Nigeria.

Principal John Parry believed that adding Islamic studies to the college's existing programs would contribute to pluralism, helping to educate non-Muslim Nigerians from the south and east in the traditions of their new northern compatriots. The many African studies scholars, political scientists, and anthropologists RF officials consulted during the spring and summer of 1959 seemed to concur. So dedicated to Islamic studies was Parry that he managed to turn the original grant for additional professors in religious studies, history, and languages into funding for a new Islamic and Arabic Studies Department from which, he suggested, faculty might undertake research into the relationship between Sufis orders and jihad.[53]

Despite Parry's intentions and the enthusiasm of foundation officers for the project, the program suffered problems from the beginning. Because of difficulty finding faculty, it began a year later than expected, and the department continually struggled to staff its curriculum, with the two RF-sponsored lecturers severely overburdened by teaching and having no time for independent research. By 1968, when RF funding for the program concluded, required courses were finally staffed. These included one on "Islamic Cultures," readings for which involved Arberry's Quran, Margaret Smith's work on Islamic mystics, and Montgomery Watt's translation of al-Ghazālī.[54] The proposed research on Sufi orders and jihad, however, never did take shape.

In 1968, the same year that the RF ceased funding University College in Nigeria and that Rahman returned to the United States, a young American anthropologist, dramatizing the lives of rural Moroccans, wrote about an "axial figure" he christened "the warrior saint." Such saints were active throughout Moroccan history, he noted, including after 1911. When, at that time, "the French and Spanish moved in to take direct control of the country, it was a series of such martial marabouts, scattered along the edges of the crumbling kingdom, who rallied the population, or parts of it, for the last, brave, desperate attempt to revive the old order."[55] He elaborated on the sometimes anti-colonial mores of these Sufis in 1979.[56] By then, however, Sufism was newly *en vogue* in the United States—so much so that even in his earlier piece, Clifford Geertz could speak to readers of the "usual image of Sufi practice": the "famous sort of whirling dervish performances."[57] Geertz's work appears to have done little to dislodge what was then becoming conventional wisdom about the pacifist, spirituality minded Sufi character.

Not only was Sufism popular in the United States at that point, it was soon deemed a positive influence in North African politics. During and after the bloody conflict in Algeria—sparked by government suppression of the Islamist parties that won democratic elections in the early 1990s—Algerian officials promoted Sufism as an indigenous, and pacifist, form of Islam that contrasted favorably with the ostensibly Arab-imported Salafism of the Islamists.[58] A few years later, when a Lebanese Sufi immigrant to the United States (Hussein Kabbani, who established a new Naqshbandi order in America) told a State

Department gathering (where he hoped to make allies against anti-Sufi Muslims) that most non-Sufi Muslims in the United States were influenced by Saudi Arabian Wahhabis, the idea did not seem unfamiliar. And two years after that, in the wake of the 9/11 attacks, this idea was once again turned from conventional wisdom into statecraft.[59]

Since 9/11, policy analysts and diplomats in the United States and officials abroad, often working in tandem, have given even more weight to the idea that Sufis are the natural antidote to "radical" Muslims. Several scholars have explored the ramifications of such ideas, and the ways these ideas have translated into policy in Pakistan, in their contributions to this volume (see Brannon Ingram, chapter 4, and Alix Philippon, chapter 8, in particular). As in India, where government officials endorsed Sufism earlier and more widely than U.S. officials did for similar reasons, promoting Sufism as a way to moderate extremism has failed to achieve the desired results.[60] Not only has it blinded leaders to the historical and contemporary diversity within Muslim communities and the ways communal politics stubbornly refuse to yield to romantic ideals about interreligious cohesion (see Carla Bellamy, chapter 10, this volume), but it has made many peaceful Sufis into the targets of antigovernmental forces while leaving government officials unprepared for the occasions on which contemporary Sufis, like some historical ones, pursue their ends through violence. While scholars have increasingly turned to how twentieth-century American liberal Protestant perspectives on religion have shaped U.S. imperial encounters around the globe, we have yet to really grasp the manifold ways such dynamics will ramify within and across discrete nations and local communities as various actors adopt aspects of these discourses that resonate with their needs and traditions and make them their own. As mentioned, the chapters that follow bring some of these developments into focus. But the necessary work has just begun.

2

From *Taṣawwuf* Modern to Neo-Sufism

Nurcholish Madjid, Fazlur Rahman, and the Development of an Idea

VERENA MEYER

In his *Islam and Modernity*, the Indo-Pakistani scholar Fazlur Rahman (1919–1988) called for "a reworking and restructuring of sociomoral principles that will form the basis for a viable social Islamic fabric in the 20th and twenty-first centuries."[1] Similarly, Nurcholish Madjid (1939–2005), Rahman's Indonesian doctoral student at the University of Chicago, sought in his book *The True Face of Islam* "to put the understanding and implementation of Islam in the framework of the actual and real demands of time and place."[2] Greg Barton calls Rahman and Madjid's version of reformist Islam "Neo-Modernism," a "new phase of Islamic modernism" that "represents a genuine attempt to combine progressive liberal ideals with deep religious faith."[3] Whether or not one accepts Neo-Modernism as a distinct Islamic orientation, Barton points to a significant overlap in Madjid's and Rahman's scholarly activism and reformist agendas, which has led to some debate about the extent to which Madjid adopted Rahman's thought.[4] More recent studies have proposed a move away from a one-directional model of influence and transmission and consider Madjid a participant in global discourses and regimes of knowledge whose career and thought was shaped by the possibilities and challenges of the New Order Regime.[5]

This chapter builds on this scholarship by analyzing Madjid's understanding of Neo-Sufism, a term famously coined by Rahman and adopted by Madjid after his return from Chicago. While tracing the intellectual genealogies of which Madjid was a part, I also use Madjid's deployment of this term as a lens to investigate how Muslim intellectuals in New Order Indonesia participated in global debates on the role of Islam in contemporary politics while navigating the marginalization and instrumentalization of Islam under Soeharto's regime. As Rahman's doctoral student funded by the Ford Foundation, Nurcholish Madjid's formation at the University of Chicago needs to be understood against the background and political agenda of Western academia outlined by Corbett in this volume, but is not reducible to Western interests. Indonesian Muslim intellectuals educated in the West navigated a complex array of agendas and power dynamics, including not only postcolonial regimes of knowledge but also the complicated terrain of Indonesian politics. While appropriating Western academic concepts like Neo-Sufism, Madjid strategically deployed them to intervene in religious and political discourses back home.[6]

Madjid's Indonesia and Indonesia's Madjid: Historical and Biographical Background

Nurcholish Madjid was born in 1939 in the eastern Javanese region of Jombang, known for the strong presence of Nahdlatul Ulama (NU), Indonesia's traditionalist Islamic mass organization, and its many *pesantren* (Islamic educational institution in Indonesia, comparable to the madrasa elsewhere in the Islamic world).[7] Madjid attended a public school while also receiving an Islamic education, first with his father and later at Darul ʿUlum Rejoso, a renowned, progressive *pesantren* with strong NU ties. His childhood was characterized by the emergence of Islam as an ideologically distinct force in the anti-colonial movement. Snouck Hurgronje, the first adviser on Arabian and Native Affairs (1899–1906), had recommended the toleration of apolitical Islam while fighting Islamic political activities.[8] However, his recommendations could not stop the emergence of Islamic nationalist movements that largely evaded Dutch control.[9] After their invasion in March 1942, the Japanese empowered political Islam to counterbalance the power of nationalist groups. It was in this context that members of NU joined constituents of the modernist Islamic mass organization Muhammadiyah in the creation of Masyumi, a political organization founded in 1943. During the last months of the occupation, the Japanese withdrew their support from Muslim nationalists, suspending the artificial balance between secular and Islamic interests and allowing the former to take initiative.[10] As Muslim and secular nationalists fought over the role of Islam in independent Indonesia, Sukarno attempted to resolve the crisis by introducing the nonconfessional Pancasila state ideology with the obligation to believe in one God. But because the Pancasila eventually excluded the proposed Jakarta

Charter, a preamble requiring Muslims to abide by sharia, it failed to placate many Muslim nationalists.[11] In the first years of the Republic, Muslim activists not only promoted their respective agendas for Islam in the Indonesian state but also struggled with the uneasy compromise that constituted the platform of Masyumi, encompassing both modernists and traditionalists. In 1953, frustrated by the dominance of the modernists in Masyumi, NU split off to found their own political party and adopted a more conciliatory attitude toward Sukarno's dismantling of the parliamentary democracy than Masyumi, which, under the leadership of Muhammad Natsir (1949–1958), kept pushing for the replacement of the Pancasila with Islam as foundation of the state until the party was prohibited in 1960.[12] In 1956, Madjid transferred to the *pesantren* Pondok Modern Gontor in Ponogoro, which was renowned for its cosmopolitan outlook and hybrid curriculum, and for being supportive of Masyumi's agenda. His education thus exposed him to a variety of ideological and political visions at a time characterized by controversies about the role of Islam in the new republic and strategies to adopt vis-à-vis the government.

After his graduation, he taught at Gontor until he left for Jakarta in 1961 to study Islamic history and Arab literature at the Islamic State University (IAIN) Syarif Hidayatullah. During this time, he became personally acquainted with Hamka (1908–1981), a Muslim public intellectual who played a significant role in directing theological orientations within the Malay-Indonesian community in the twentieth century. Hamka was a modernist reformer well known for his uncompromising attitude toward what he deemed syncretistic practice in Indonesian Islam as well as his defense of Sufism, rightly understood, as indispensable for modern Indonesian Muslims' cultivation of spirituality. Madjid would later articulate very similar ideas. His student years furthermore coincided with the change of regime from Sukarno's Guided Democracy to Soeharto's New Order, which was accompanied by political unrest, culminating in the mass killings of alleged communists in 1965–66. After the increasing marginalization of political Islam under Sukarno with the prohibition of Masyumi and the neutralization of NU, the old elites of these organizations hoped that Soeharto would rectify the mistakes that were made with the Pancasila. However, Soeharto's determination to centralize power and to prioritize development resulted in a renewed marginalization of the established Islamic organizations. Simultaneously, Soeharto welcomed the cooperation of a group of reform-oriented Muslims, many of whom were educated in the West, thus causing a rift among Muslim modernists: Whereas some, especially the former Masyumi leadership, opposed Soeharto's agenda, others found common cause with his development agenda and cooperated with the regime. Focusing on what they considered a revitalization of Islam through intellectual freedom and progress, this group of modernists shifted their focus away from political Islam to social reform.[13] Madjid was to play a major role in this division.

While at IAIN Syarif Hidayatullah, Madjid also got involved in student activism. In 1963, he joined the Islamic Students Organization (Himpunan Mahasiswa Islam), which had close ties to the former Masyumi leadership, and was appointed president in 1967. In this role, he was expected to dedicate himself to the struggle for political Islam. However, as he noted in retrospect, he was already doubting whether he truly stood behind these objectives.[14] He also served as the head of the Union of Southeast Asian Islamic Students (1967–1969) and deputy secretary general of the International Islamic Federation of Student Organizations (1969–1971), for which he traveled abroad to several countries in the Middle East as well as the United States. His trip to the United States left him "deeply impressed," while he found Arab society "disappointing," and he returned to Indonesia convinced that Islamic thought needed "radical renewal."[15] It was these thoughts of renewal that provided Madjid with a prominent and controversial spot in Indonesia's Muslim community. In January 1970 he presented a paper titled "The Necessity of Renewing Islamic Thought and the Problem of the Integration of the Umma" at a meeting of Muslim youth organizations.[16] In the paper he criticized Indonesian Muslims for their reluctance to embrace change in Islamic thought and, advocating for increased intellectual vitality, bemoaned the loss of the spirit of *ijtihād*. His renewal program included a commitment to secularization encapsulated in the slogan "Islam yes, Islamic parties no!," a proper separation of worldly and sacred affairs that precluded the involvement of Islam in party politics or the state. A politicization of Islam not only led to stagnancy and obstructed reform but was also a mis-sacralization, violating the Islamic tenet of *tawḥīd*, the oneness of God.[17] Simultaneously, Madjid acknowledged that innovation and intellectual invigoration would cause disagreement among Indonesian Muslims. His propositions predictably furthered the polarization between Muslim intellectuals and activists with different views of the role of Islam in postcolonial Indonesia.[18]

In the midst of this controversy and Madjid's sudden appearance in the limelight, he first met Fazlur Rahman and Leonard Binder when they visited Indonesia on a trip in 1974 to conduct research and recruit an Indonesian participant for a workshop, part of a four-year research program titled "Islam and Social Change" funded by the Ford Foundation at the University of Chicago,[19] where Rahman had been a professor since 1969. Madjid was recommended by local Ford Foundation representatives and thus chosen for this role. While at

Chicago in 1976, he accepted the offer to stay and to take up postgraduate studies, which he began in 1978, again funded, among others, by the Ford Foundation.[20] Initially Madjid intended to undertake his doctoral studies in political science with Binder, but Rahman convinced him to focus on Islamic studies instead, saying that "the Muslim world needed modern scholars of Islam more than it needed political scientists,"[21] a possibly apocryphal statement that reflects Rahman's reputation and belief that a reform of Islam would result in political and social reform as well. Madjid wrote his dissertation on the medieval Islamic scholar Ibn Taymiyyah (d. 1328), whose views have been cited in support of a wide range of modernist agendas in the twentieth and twenty-first centuries. While Muḥammad ʿAbduh and Muḥammad Rashīd Riḍā admired Ibn Taymiyyah's uncompromising criticism of *bidʿah,* Rahman made use of Ibn Taymiyyah for furthering the cause of liberal modernism. Rahman saw his own reform program as the latest in a series of renewal efforts that began with Ibn Taymiyyah, something Madjid would also do years later.[22] Influenced by his advisor, Madjid credited the medieval scholar with bringing Sufism closer to orthodox ideals and credited him with the promotion of reform through *ijtihād* (independent reasoning).[23] Madjid then took his interpretation of the medieval scholar as an example and aimed to reform Sufism in a similar manner, using *ijtihād* to respond to contemporary problems.

By the time Madjid returned to Indonesia in 1985 to take up a teaching post at his alma mater, IAIN in Jakarta, Islamic political parties had been effectively neutralized.[24] By the mid-1980s, a new urban and well-educated middle class of Muslims attracted to the cultivation of personal piety and morality rather than political Islam was emerging. Desiring to reach this new middle class, Madjid founded Paramadina, a religious organization for teaching and publishing, to offer a spirituality compatible with these social changes. He sought to devise a "balanced program of renewal" in which Sufism and modernism, respectively framed as the inner and outer dimensions of Islam, balanced and corrected each other.[25] At this point, even the older generation of the former Masyumi elite, including Natsir, had resigned themselves to putting party politics aside, focusing instead on a program of expansion and revitalization of religious life through preaching and education. In a sense, the controversy Madjid had exacerbated in the early 1970s had been resolved in favor of the position he had advanced.

But the detachment from Indonesian politics was never a total one. The years between 1989 and 1994 marked a phase of increased openness in the New Order, likely because of tensions between Soeharto and the military, and increased calls for democratization and reform. In 1990, hoping for support from Western-educated Muslims, Soeharto allowed the creation of the Indonesian Muslim Intellectuals' Association (Ikatan Cendekiawan Muslim Indonesia, ICMI) under the chairmanship of his right-hand man, Habibie. Madjid was active in this group in a central capacity, and while he defended ICMI as being more than just an extension of Soeharto's administration, his leadership role brought him closer to the centers of power and Soeharto himself.[26] During these years of increased openness, Madjid also spoke and published widely, advocating democratic reform and thus, as Kull suggests, challenging the limits of Soeharto's openness.[27] Perhaps as a result of these challenges, in 1994 Soeharto's strategy shifted once again as he took steps to neutralize the pro-democracy movement. With new limits on what could be talked about in public, Madjid and others turned to the idea of what they called *masyarakat madani* (civil society), emphasizing solidarity and nonviolence,[28] and it was at this time that he began to use the term "Neo-Sufism." After Soeharto's fall in 1998, which Madjid helped to precipitate by publicly demanding the president's resignation, he continued to shape public political discussions until his health failed in 2004. When he passed away in 2005, he received a state burial at which he was honored as one of the most influential thinkers in modern Indonesia and as instrumental in interpreting modern global Islam in the Indonesian context.

Madjid and His Teachers: Transmissions and Innovations

In this section I trace some of the intellectual traditions that influenced Madjid, especially his understanding of Sufism and his use of the term "Neo-Sufism." While acknowledging Rahman's influence on Madjid, I argue that Madjid's conceptualization of Neo-Sufism points to his participation in multiple intellectual genealogies, comprising more than Rahman's legacy. Since Madjid was an eclectic fusionist who drew on a wide variety of scholars,[29] establishing the extent of distinct sources of influence is beyond the scope of this chapter. But his story shows how processes of influence are embedded in complex webs and networks of knowledge and transmission: The following three examples, which could be expanded with others, suggest that Madjid's understanding of Sufism and his deployment of the term "Neo-Sufism" built on different, interconnected sources. Sources that Madjid himself elevated as formative in his works are his *pesantren* education, Hamka's ideas, and, finally, Fazlur Rahman.

Darul ʿUlum

As elsewhere in the Islamic world, denunciations of popular or ecstatic forms of Sufism had been ongoing for centuries in the Malay-Indonesian world, but gained momentum in the nineteenth century.[30] With increased mobility between Southeast Asia and the Hijaz, more Southeast Asians went on the hajj and studied in the Middle East, encountering debates about reforming Islam to meet the challenges of modernity. These debates were transmitted to Southeast Asia through print media, in particular the Egyptian reformers ʿAbduh and Rashīd Riḍā's journal *al-Manār*, which was read among the archipelago's elites. Southeast Asians began to participate in these debates in their own print media, adopting and appropriating modernist discourses and frameworks for their own contexts.[31] Criticism and polemics against what were considered degenerate forms of Sufism, especially those associated with the *ṭarīqahs* (Sufi orders), became entangled in the rivalry between religious leaders of different affiliations.[32] With its ties to the Qādirīyyah wa Naqshbandīyyah in East Java and NU, Darul ʿUlum became a site of such rivalry and polemics while Madjid was a student there. His early religious education thus took place in an environment where legitimate forms of Sufism and political participation were regularly negotiated and contested. Years after he had left Darul ʿUlum, Madjid reflected on Sufism, the *pesantren,* and his own *pesantren* education in two articles. Of course we must assume that his retrospective reflections are colored by later experiences and encounters; neither Madjid's own awareness of others' influence nor the nature of that influence was static.

In a 1974 article titled "Tasauf and Pesantren,"[33] Madjid began by delineating the boundaries of Ashʿarī Islam, which emphasized Allah's transcendence and *tawḥīd*, therefore sharply prohibiting monistic tendencies. He further described legitimate forms of Sufism practiced in *pesantren* that follow the teachings of al-Ghazālī, which he called the "*modus vivendi,*" bridging the rationalism of *kalām* and Sufi intuition. Most Sufis in the *pesantren*, he claimed confidently, know that Sufism cannot be separated from the observance of Islamic law. He elevated his former *kyai* (teacher of Islamic sciences in Indonesia and community leader in traditionalist circles) Ramli at Darul ʿUlum as a good teacher, an example who influenced his students and society at large in a positive way.[34] He was also aware of the dangers of a Sufism that tended either toward monism or "primitive animism" and that included practices like magic, veneration of saints or teachers, and "free sex."[35] On the other hand, a total rejection of Sufism would lead to spiritual dryness that was particularly prevalent in the West but increasingly affected the Islamic world as well.

In an article Madjid wrote in 1977 on his education at Darul ʿUlum, he noted that, since the *pesantren* was a local center for the Qādirīyyah wa Naqshbandīyyah at the time, the students were socialized according to the traditions of this *ṭarīqah*.[36] He presented his school as already engaged in discussions around the idea of a piety that both embraced a Sufism that held itself accountable to the law and was politically engaged. Specifically, he described tensions that arose concerning the presence of aspects that were considered to be outside the bounds of orthodoxy: a certain *kyai*, Khalil, displayed forms of religious practice that were considered problematic from the viewpoint of Islamic law, and so some local religious authorities staged an intervention and brought the unruly *kyai* back on the right path. Khalil's successor, the above-mentioned Ramli, was also active in the *ṭarīqah* but emphasized the significance of Islamic law in Sufism. In retrospect, Madjid found that the debates around the significance and scope of legitimate and beneficial Sufism he would later share with Hamka and Rahman were already present in his early education. At the same time, he contributed to shaping perceptions and memories of which figures and institutions were within the scope of this legitimate Sufism.

Hamka

During his studies at IAIN Syarif Hidayatullah, Madjid came into contact with Hamka, the head imam of a newly built mosque and school named Masjid Agung al-Azhar in suburban Jakarta. Hamka's main affiliation was with the modernist organization Muhammadiyah. Never having been involved in party politics, he was one of the first to call for a shift away from politics toward a more comprehensive revival of society. As he put it, "All this time . . . we've neglected the mosque because we've been too busy in parliament." Now, "We'll take up our struggle from the mosque."[37] Even though Madjid would later clash with Hamka over the question of secularism,[38] he nonetheless called Hamka "without doubt one of the paramount [Muslim] leaders of recent times"[39] and specifically acknowledged that he drew on Hamka's ideas on Sufism.[40]

From 1936 until the beginning of Japanese occupation in 1942, Hamka was the editor-in-chief and main contributor of a successful magazine published in Medan titled *Society's Compass*. This appointment constituted the beginning of his career as a public intellectual and writer. Beginning in 1937, the magazine regularly included a column titled *Tasauf Modern* ("Modern *Taṣawwuf*") written by Hamka himself. He collected and published these columns in 1939 as a book with the same title, which is widely available today and significantly contributed to the popularization of Sufism among Indonesian Muslim modernizing elites—one of the first groups to embrace Sufism, thus breaking with the view that Sufism and modernism are mutually exclusive.[41] In these columns, Hamka, who had little in the way of formal education, did not offer a systematic argument or a consistent definition of Sufism, let alone modern Sufism. He explored Sufism via the topic of happiness, which he considered to be connected to Sufism: A healthy Sufism would make people and their communities happier. Hamka thus took a stance on the vexed status of Sufism and argued that there had been good and bad forms in the history of Islam. He agreed with other modernists that much of the Sufism in Indonesia at his time was bad. *Ṭarīqahs*, he reproved, were characterized by arbitrary norms and rules that had nothing to do with Islam, and by religious leaders deliberately withholding knowledge and religious education from their followers to exploit their ignorance for their own purposes. This was un-Islamic in spirit because Islam encouraged learning and independent reasoning.[42] Hamka also admonished his fellow Muslims for misunderstanding the meaning of *zuhd* (asceticism). *Zuhd*, properly understood, he wrote, did not mean withdrawal from the world, but merely not to let worldly concerns impede one's spiritual journey.[43] Withdrawal, Hamka argued, was inimical to the spirit of Islam, which encouraged the spirit to fight and "to sacrifice, to work, not the spirit to be lazy, weak, and inactive."[44] The consequences of bad Sufism were dire: Hamka thought colonialism was an effect of Sufism having weakened Islamic nations.[45]

In contrast to these problems he diagnosed in Indonesian Sufism, Hamka held up the Prophet Muḥammad as the paragon of good and healthy Sufism, but added that at the time of the Prophet, all Muslims were good Sufis. Good Sufism aimed to purify and improve one's character, which would result in being "calm in the face of all agitations of the heart, peaceful on the path toward God's approval," and never ceasing to be industrious. For Hamka's Sufi, "the goals for one's own benefit are overcome by the goals for the benefit of the umma,"[46] not just aiming at the sanctification of the individual, but society as a whole. Hamka's Sufism was thus explicitly this-worldly, an attitude he also found among the first Muslims, the best Sufis: "They sacrificed themselves and they fought on the battlefield . . . with only one intention, to raise the name of Allah above all else."[47] If Muslims strove to be successful and prosperous, the entire *ummah* would benefit and progress. Madjid's co-worker Munawar-Rachman reflected that, for Hamka, Sufism was a "double-edged sword" in that it could be used to criticize both a "dry" kind of *fiqh*-oriented spirituality as well as a practice of Sufism that would cause the adherents to be too absorbed in their practices and to "run" from the world while forgetting the social aspects of piety.[48] While generally critical of *ṭarīqah* Sufism, he considered philosophical Sufism compatible with Islamic modernism as it was a way to cultivate a deeper spirituality and moral integrity in the face of the challenges of the modern world.

Rahman

Fazlur Rahman, the son of a Deobandi scholar from what would become Pakistan, graduated from Oxford University with a doctorate before assuming a position at Durham University. While this exposure to the modern, secular study of Islam initially posed a challenge to his religious beliefs, by the time he took up a permanent position at McGill in 1958, he had come to be convinced of the compatibility and complementary potential of academic methodologies and Islam, thus making him an ideal candidate for Wilfred Cantwell Smith's McGill Institute of Islamic Studies.[49] Rahman's explicit articulation and justification of modernist reform on the basis of the canonical texts of Islam was readily shared by Madjid. There are, in fact, many parallels between Rahman's and Madjid's visions and general perceptions of the potential and role of Islam in the modern world, including perhaps most importantly their perspectives on the political and social role of Quranic exegesis. Rahman articulated his program of Quranic exegesis as a hermeneutic process for determining political action in contemporary Islamic societies in his *Islam and Modernity*, which he wrote in 1977–78, the period during which Madjid began to study with him at Chicago. As Rahman saw the Quran as embedded in a particular historical context, he suggested a hermeneutic practice consisting of a "double movement, from the present to Qur'anic times, then back to the present,"[50] a process he called *ijtihād*. Such an interpretation would yield ideas that, albeit contingent on their social and historical background, are faithful to the teachings of the Quran.[51] In Madjid's later works, we see a very similar understanding of an Islam relevant for the modern world through *ijtihād*, as the reinterpretation of Islamic beliefs in the modern context occurring "within the principle of *maṣlaḥah* (public interest)," which demonstrated the "relevance of Islam to modern life."[52] This principle allowed for differences in opinion or competing ideologies while nonetheless ensuring that these opinions or ideologies were compatible with "the spirit of Islam."[53] Resonances between Rahman's and Madjid's works are thus undeniable, and Madjid's formation at the University of Chicago resulted in his scholarly work and activism becoming firmly rooted in both Islamic tradition and Western academic discourses. However, this fusionism was not only characteristic of Rahman's and Madjid's work, but also of many other Muslim scholars of their generation, especially those connected with Smith's program at McGill.[54]

Moreover, if we consider Madjid's use of the term "Neo-Sufism," we see that he gave the term a role and meaning in his work that was different from Rahman's, indicating that he had agendas of his own. Throughout his career, but especially in his early years, Rahman was at best ambivalent about Sufism in general and its role as a vehicle for Islamic modernization in the contemporary world in particular. In a 1963 article on Iqbal, Rahman still distinguished between negative forms of Sufism that had world-denying and weakening tendencies and Sufism's positive spiritual aspects, which he saw represented by Rūmī, among others.[55] A more pessimistic view about Sufism can then be found in an article from 1970, in which he derided the "system of moral gymnastics" of Sufism, which was "incurably individual" and therefore "a permanent challenge and threat to orthodoxy,"[56] causing the degeneration of Muslim cultures. In these two articles Rahman recognized that Sufism could possibly be brought into the fold of orthodoxy but did not perceive it as making valuable contributions within the framework of his own reform program. Although Rahman recognized that constructive theology often failed to produce doctrines that were both intellectually sound and emotionally satisfying, he never promoted Sufism as a means by which his contemporary Muslims were to reintroduce devotional aspects to political Islam.

When Rahman coined the term "Neo-Sufism" in his *Islam*, it was to describe a historical phenomenon he saw at two moments in the history of Islam. The first and prototypical Neo-Sufis were Ibn Taymiyyah and his student Ibn Qayyim al-Jawziyyah.[57] According to Rahman, these two thirteenth-century thinkers were succeeded by Sufi brotherhoods that were similarly reform-minded in the eighteenth and nineteenth centuries, such as the North African Sanūsī order and the Muḥammadīyya in South Asia.[58] Rahman presented these Neo-Sufi movements as strictly orthodox while inculcating an activist and this-worldly attitude, thus reconciling a populist Sufi tradition with orthodox Islam and a positive and active attitude to the world. Movements were Neo-Sufi movements if they emphasized the controlling force of *fiqh* and recognized that Sufi practices had social and political utility. Unlike other kinds of Sufism characterized by mass spiritual hypnotism and uncontrolled speculation, Neo-Sufism distinguished itself by sound intellectual processes and puritanical thought and action.[59] Furthermore, Rahman identified the activist impulse to political action as representative of Neo-Sufi movements, in which the teachings were geared toward practical goals derived from orthodox understandings of Islam, such as a jihad against British rule in India or the Sanūsī project of combining religious and professional education to improve society comprehensively. Traditional Sufism, on the other hand, "had stressed primarily the individual and not the society."[60]

Unlike Rahman, Madjid did not consider reformed Sufism to be only a historical movement, but, more like Hamka, he thought of it as having potential for forming contemporary Islamic societies. Nonetheless, Madjid did not think that Hamka's "*tasauf* modern" and Rahman's Neo-Sufism were substantially different from one another. In 1993, reflecting on the differences and similarities between Hamka and Rahman, Madjid found that the two terms only differed in nuance, as Rahman's Neo-Sufism sounded more neutral whereas "modern" sounded more optimistic.[61] He furthermore observed that both thinkers considered Neo-Sufism to have originated with Ibn Taymiyyah and Ibn Qayyim al-Jawziyyah since they advocated a Sufism that was closely tied to Islamic law and that took an active part in society, following a reform-minded agenda that made use of *ijtihād* and spiritual techniques while strictly enforcing the boundaries of Islamic orthodoxy. Madjid agreed with Hamka's and Rahman's assessment of the medieval scholars, as well as their differentiation of their reformed Sufism from traditional Sufism by rejecting monist tendencies, seeking instead a close connection with the spirit of the Prophet Muḥammad.[62] But Madjid's thought was more than just a synthesis of his two teachers. His remarks on his *pesantren* education suggest that he recognized many of his ideas in discourses that were widely present in Indonesian Islam; and as suggested by other chapters in this volume, including Marcia Hermansen's contribution on the Pakistani Qadri in chapter 3, they reflect trends in global Sufism. While it is clear that Madjid's ideas emerged in conversation with his mentors, their respective ideas were rooted in concerns and movements that transcended the intellectual ownership of any one person. This makes the tracing of intellectual influences not only difficult but also indicates that Madjid's formation was a process in which he, like his conversation partners, responded to ideas that were important across the Islamic world while simultaneously shaping these ideas to his own situation and concerns. As he addressed ideas that reflected global trends, Madjid's ideas were articulated in the Indonesian milieu, responding to particular circumstances and thus widening the scope of these discussions. This was also true for his use of Neo-Sufism, to which I turn next.

Sufism Across the Decades: Madjid's Articulations of an Idea

Even though Madjid adopted the term "Neo-Sufism" from Rahman, he did not use it in his works until the mid-1990s, more than a decade after he returned from Chicago. However, even without Rahman's terminology, the concept of a socially engaged orthodox Sufism can be found throughout Madjid's earlier writings beginning in the 1970s, and it reappeared frequently. I have described how Madjid discussed the Sufism practiced in the East Javanese *pesantren*, including his own Darul ᶜUlum, in terms of the scope and merit of what he considered legitimate Sufism. Here I specifically focus on Madjid's works about Sufism written after his return from Chicago, addressing both his conceptualization of Sufism and the terminology he used. I argue that Madjid's choice to adopt the term "Neo-Sufism" should not be attributed as much to Rahman's influence as to wider intellectual trends as well as Indonesian politics, which Madjid hoped to influence with his writings.

In 1985, the year he returned from Chicago, Madjid published the essay "Taṣawwuf as the Essence of Religiousness."[63] The conceptualization of Sufism presented in this text, referenced here variably as *taṣawwuf* or *Sufisme* (Sufism), is strikingly similar to the one in his 1974 article on Sufism and the *pesantren* discussed above. Locating his thought squarely within Ashᶜarī Islam, he argues that *taṣawwuf* is a "built-in" aspect of Islam due to its roots in the Quran. *Taṣawwuf* could furthermore complement the observance of Islamic law and therefore enrich Islam, which would become dry without this inner dimension. Again, Madjid warns of the dangers of a *taṣawwuf* outside of the framework of *tawḥīd* and proceeds to delineate the boundaries of commendable and "healthy" Sufism. He argues that healthy Sufism presupposes a high level of education, especially in *fiqh*, which needs to be mastered before concerning oneself with Sufism. Furthermore, healthy Sufism avoids "negative excesses," such as worshipping saints and fetishizing teachers, or withdrawal and passivity.[64] He again references Ibn Taymiyyah as a vanguard for this active and engaged Sufism. While crediting al-Ghazālī with the successful reconciliation of *fiqh*, *kalām*, and *taṣawwuf*, he echoes Ibn Taymiyyah's criticism of al-Ghazālī's withdrawal from the world.[65] In short, Madjid's healthy *taṣawwuf* is engaged in the world and observes Islamic law.

We find another discussion of Sufism in Madjid's *Islam: Doctrine and Culture* from 1992. In two consecutive chapters, Madjid discusses *fiqh* and *taṣawwuf* as the two traditional disciplines,[66] hinting at the related and complementary nature of the two branches of Islamic science and practice. In his chapter on what he references interchangeably as *taṣawwuf* and an Indonesian rendering, *kesufian*, he takes a historical approach, explaining the emergence of *taṣawwuf* as an opposition movement to both the Umayyad caliphate and an Islam that had become dry by overemphasizing *fiqh*. He describes that in its subsequent development *taṣawwuf* did not remain primarily a political opposition movement, although the spirit of opposing or counterbalancing established power structures was preserved. It was thus from this historical contingency that the separation of the disciplines of *fiqh* and *taṣawwuf* emerged.[67] And, Madjid continues, both disciplines are present in the Quran and the traditions of the Prophet.[68] Having thus vouched for the authenticity and significance of Sufism, Madjid proceeds to discuss the limitations of Sufism: because mystical experiences are ineffable, Sufis tend to act in eccentric ways as though they were drunk or withdrawn from the world into passivity and escapism. On the other hand, he argues that *taṣawwuf* had an important contribution to make to worldly affairs, as Sufi teachings emphasize morality like no other discipline.[69] While in this book Madjid reiterates many of his longstanding points, he particularly emphasizes Sufism's potential as a movement of political resistance through the teaching of morality.

The term "Neo-Sufism" then appears for the first time in Madjid's 1993 article "New Sufism and Old Sufism." Although Madjid uses a different terminology here, he simply reiterates the points he had been making for years. He begins by pointing to the supposed dichotomy between *taṣawwuf* and Islamic law just to argue that these two orientations are in reality not opposed but complementary, as demonstrated by al-Ghazālī.[70] But, as spearheaded by Ibn Taymiyyah and emphasized by Hamka and Rahman, Sufism also needs an activist spirit. Then, using "Neo-Sufism," he calls for a Sufism with a "moral motif" and a "positive attitude toward the world,"[71] or a Sufism engaged in political and social activism, and substantiates his claims by referencing both scholars at Western institutions and hadith. Calling Neo-Sufism a kind of *ijtihād*, an idea for which he again credits Ibn Taymiyyah, he links normative Sufism not only to the law but also to the independent reasoning of *ijtihād*. Old Sufism, on the other hand, was characterized by a "passive and anti-worldly . . . asceticism" and an "isolating spiritualism" that rendered people "weak and egotistical."[72] Comparing these texts that demarcate healthy, new, or legitimate Sufism from its unhealthy, old, and illegitimate counterpart, recurrent themes are immediately apparent: Madjid emphasizes that legitimate Sufism is never in conflict with *fiqh*, as the two are just external and internal expressions of the same thing, but he presupposes that followers have a high level of education, especially in the legal sciences, resulting in personal accountability rather than blind submission to a teacher or *ṭarīqah*. Furthermore, normative Sufism is characterized by an active engagement with the world instead of withdrawal.

What caused Madjid to suddenly adopt Rahman's terminology after writing for decades about *taṣawwuf*, *Sufisme*, or *kesufian* as a socially and politically active orientation that was complementary rather than inimical to *fiqh*? His change in terminology was likely caused by trends in Western scholarship, with which he likely became familiar during a short tenure as a research fellow at McGill in 1991–92. After the term "Neo-Sufism" was first used by Rahman, it was adopted by scholars like Nehemia Levtzion and John Voll as a distinct historical movement and had become a well-known, albeit disputed, term by the time Madjid began to employ it in his works.[73] Although in Western scholarship it was still primarily used in Rahman's sense, as a descriptor for certain historical movements rather than as a program for contemporary Islamic societies, the increased currency and name recognition of the term likely led Madjid to adopt it. But what did he hope to affect by doing so? We may find the reason for his choice in the changing landscape of political Islamic thought in Indonesia in the early 1990s, which, as described above, was characterized, on the one hand, by a short period of political openness and public discussions of democratization in which Madjid was an active participant. On the other hand, prominent Muslims had to maneuver in the face of Soeharto's and Habibie's attempts to co-opt Islam for their own purposes, especially through their involvement in ICMI. In one sense, Madjid returned to his long-standing concern, beginning in the 1970s, about Islam influencing politics and public life while he also rejected the subordination of Islam to regimist ploys. The challenges of the late New Order now led him to articulate these concerns in the idiom of Western scholarship while also explicitly rooting its content in the history and tradition of Islam.

Madjid's other speeches and publications from this time give further indication of his navigating and seeking to influence Indonesian public life. In 1992, he presented his views of the state of religion and its main problems in a well-known speech titled "Some Reflections about Religious Life for the Next Generation."[74] The main problems Madjid diagnoses in this speech are people's alienation in modern society and social inequality, giving rise to fundamentalism.[75] He frames these trends not only as a religious but as a social problem that causes a separation of people from society. Referring to examples drawn from Western countries to illustrate his points and remarking that the problems he described are particularly prevalent in the United States, he then uses these examples to indirectly problematize recent developments in Indonesia, specifically Soeharto's instrumentalization of Islam, resulting in increased religious intolerance as well as social inequality and unrest. The solution to this problem, he claims, can be sought in the Quranic principles of spiritual independence and the primacy of truth. These same principles were articulated by Erich Fromm and Ibn Taymiyyah, among others, because "every true thing comes from the same source, that is, God."[76] His references to an eclectic selection of Western and Islamic writers throughout history allowed Madjid to frame his social reform program in the idiom of both Islamic tradition and history and Western academic discourses that, he argues, express the same truth. He articulates a similar view in his article "Islamic Roots of Modern Pluralism: Indonesian Experiences" from 1994. Religious pluralism, he claims, is a basic value of the Pancasila, which he compares to the constitution of Medina, thus framing pluralism as an intrinsically Islamic and Indonesian ideal.[77] Similarly, he states, the norm of religious tolerance also characterized Islam from the onset. This ideal of pluralism, however, despite its rootedness in Islam and the Indonesian nation, was not always realized because Muslims did not adapt well to the modern age. One reason for this, he argues, is that Muslims were not sufficiently socialized according to "ideas of modern tolerance and pluralism as understood and followed in modern western nations."[78] He moreover demands that Muslims revisit the basic tenets of Islam and its history as the basis for religious tolerance and pluralism.[79] In both pieces, Madjid presents Islam as a set of universal norms and virtues and affirms its compatibility, even equivalence, with modern secular democratic values.

These two pieces thus show that Madjid's use of the term "Neo-Sufism" coincided with his increased appeal to Islamic values to advocate for a reform following a political system favored in the West, namely a democratic, pluralistic, and secular society, along with the claim that Islam and Western liberalism had the same goals and virtues. It seems unlikely that this sudden adoption of what was originally Rahman's term, more than a decade after Madjid's return from Chicago, should be attributed to Rahman's influence, but should instead be sought in wider trends in Western scholarship and the fact that Neo-Sufism had become a well-known category in Western academia at that point. Whether or not Madjid himself believed in the validity of Neo-Sufism as a historical category, the appropriation of Rahman's term was likely a tactical choice. His reference to this term allowed him to put the reform efforts of contemporary Indonesia into a wider context, equating it with historical movements that Western scholars considered to have been sober, rational, moral, democratic, and scientific. At the same time, he was able to appeal to an Islamic audience by drawing their attention to the fact that his program of religious and political reform had a concrete tradition in the history of Islam, a tradition that was associated with resistance to unjust political rule and increased religious zeal, which he also equated with the norms of the Pancasila. Madjid thus derived legitimacy from Western academic discourses and accepted funding from the institutions that promoted them while appropriating these debates to frame his own agendas. These agendas arose from his commitments as a Muslim and an Indonesian, as well as longstanding conversations in Indonesia and elsewhere in the Islamic world about how to best embody those commitments in any particular historical and political circumstance. The shift to the terminology of Neo-Sufism in the early 1990s encapsulated Madjid's strategy of rooting his views on the one hand in Islamic history and tradition, and on the other in Western scholarship. As Soeharto variously sought activists' support and withdrew his support of them when they became too critical or influential, these legitimizing discourses, neither of which Soeharto would have been interested in rejecting, allowed Madjid to strategically advocate for his own program while navigating the president's shifting policies toward Islamic activists.

3

Beyond Barelwiism

Tahir-ul-Qadri as an Example of Trends in Global Sufism

MARCIA HERMANSEN

This chapter considers how episodes and shifts in the career of well-known Pakistani religious leader Tahir-ul-Qadri, founder of the Minhaj-ul-Quran movement, illustrate evolving forms of Sufi identity in Pakistani social and political contexts that in turn engage global trends in Sufism that have emerged in recent decades.

Why Tahir-ul-Qadri? He is a particularly suitable figure to consider at the center of Pakistani debates about Islam/Sufism, identity, and democracy since until recently he has played a controversial and very public role. Qadri is the founder and head of a large international Islamic social movement, Minhaj-ul-Quran. He has operated as either a protégé or an opponent of a series of regimes in Pakistan and at one point founded a political party, the Pakistan Awami Tehreek (PAT), which won a single seat (his) in the National Assembly. Multiple and conflicting narratives,[1] assorted videos, and even biographical movies about Qadri are part of public awareness about him, often based on a strong and orchestrated social media presence, including the Minhaj-ul-Quran website,[2] Tumblr and Twitter accounts, memes, and political cartoons.

Who is Tahir-ul-Qadri? Depending on who is asked, the answer might be: a Sufi, a scholar, or a politician. Now in his late sixties, Qadri's career over recent decades has spanned many transitions in Pakistani politics and culture, developments in global Islam, and changes in the role of Sufism in both local and international contexts. Particularly salient in the light of the topic of the workshop from which this volume emerges, "Rethinking Islam, Democracy, and Identity in Pakistan and India: The Role of Sufism," is Tahir-ul-Qadri's prominent role during the Inqilab (Revolution) March on Islamabad in August 2014 in which thousands of his supporters joined throngs of Imran Khan's followers in an attempt to put pressure on the Nawaz Sharif government to resign or at least to enact certain internal reforms. Qadri's 2010 London launch of his well-publicized book-length *Fatwa on Terrorism* also signaled his emergence as a Muslim actor on a global scale, as did his subsequent (2015) positioning as an insider Muslim scholarly expert on deradicalization and counterterrorism strategies.[3] The fact that Qadri relocated to Canada in 2005 and launched his *Fatwa on Terrorism* in London amid media fanfare also indicates his turn toward the West as the locus of global outreach, audience, and support.

Perceptions of Qadri's relations with power and the state in Pakistan, the political and religious themes and causes that he has espoused during his career, the international expansion of Minhaj-ul-Quran, and the manner in which his image and religious discourse are projected, can all serve as taking off points for rethinking Sufism in contemporary Pakistan. This chapter argues that the changing manner in which Tahir-ul-Qadri has projected his role as a Sufi embodies an ongoing shift from an earlier Sufism based on affiliation with a specific order (*ṭarīqah*) to a Sufism discursively identified as "traditional Islam," thereby enabling conceptual and cooperative connections to be forged and maintained across diverse scholars and Islamic institutions worldwide that espouse similar views and increasingly challenge opposition from Islamists and Muslim literalists.

The idea of traditional Islam has been identified as a return to the *ahl al-sunnat wa-l jamāʿat* (Sunni) consensus of the four schools (*madhhabs*) of Islamic law in Islamic jurisprudence,[4] Sunni Ashʿarī theology, and *taṣawwuf* (Sufism) of the sober variety.[5] With a resurgence in global Sufism, often in new, more affective, post-*ṭarīqah* forms, especially among the new generation born to Muslim immigrants to the West from South Asia and the Middle East, "traditional Islamic" piety is often characterized by punctilious observance and mastery of the discourse of *fiqh* (Islamic jurisprudence)—to the extent that elsewhere I have suggested "fiqhsation" and "authenti'fiqh'ation" as neologisms to describe this orientation, which I have alternatively termed "authenticity" Sufism.[6] As we will see, in many ways Qadri is well positioned to claim this type of authority through his mastery of the Arabic language, command of the traditional sources of Quran and hadith, and expertise in the discourses of Islamic law, including issuing legal opinions.

The Trajectory of Tahir-ul-Qadri's Career

Muhammad Tahir-ul-Qadri was born on February 19, 1951, in Jhang, a city in the Punjab. As a child, Qadri attended the Christian "Sacred Heart" school. He studied hadith (reports from the Prophet Muhammad) and the fundamental principles of Islam from a well-known expert in hadith studies, al-Sayyid ʿAlawi ibn ʿAbbas al-Maliki al-Makki (d. 1971), who was known as "Muḥaddith al-Ḥijāz" (Hadith expert of the Hijaz), during a year that he spent in Saudi Arabia in 1963. Upon his return from Saudi Arabia, Qadri completed his *dars-e niẓāmī* (the curriculum taught in Islamic madrasas) from Jamia Qutbia Madrasa, Jhang, and then continued his higher religious education at Madrasa Anwar ul-Uloom in Multan, a renowned Barelwi institution in Southern Punjab.[7] According to a biographical appraisal, Qadri is multilingual and can fluently speak Urdu, Punjabi, English, Arabic, and Persian, skills that makes him popular among religious scholars from multiple countries.[8]

Qadri studied Sufism with Tahir ʿAlauddin al-Qadri al-Jilani (d. 1991) and remained under his guidance for twenty-five years. The fact that Jilani was originally from Iraq and was a member of the family of custodians of the Baghdad shrine of the great Sufi ʿAbd al-Qādir al-Jīlānī (d. 1166), eponymous founder of the Qādirī Sufi order, anticipates the future global positioning of Tahir-ul-Qadri's Sufi outreach. Later in his academic career, Qadri studied law at the University of Punjab, where he graduated with an undergraduate degree in 1974 as the valedictorian of his class. He also taught at Punjab University and pursued his doctorate in Islamic law. Many observers feel that the patronage of Pakistan's powerful Sharif family was crucial to the rise of Qadri to national prominence. The late Pakistani political scientist Mumtaz Ahmad wrote, regarding this aspect of his career:

> For a while after completing his PhD, Qadri served as a lecturer in Islamic Studies at Law College, Lahore. It was during this time that he was introduced to the family of Nawaz Sharif, the twice former prime minister of Pakistan. Nawaz Sharif was so impressed with Qadri's oratorical skills and Islamic scholarship that he persuaded him to leave the Law College and accept the position of *khatib* (the person who delivers the sermon during Friday prayers) at the Jamia Mosque in Model Town, Lahore. At the request of Qadri, Sharif, who was at that time the chief minister of Punjab, allotted him a substantial tract of prized land in Lahore to build an institution of higher Islamic learning that would integrate the teaching of traditional Islamic sciences with modern disciplines. Qadri soon developed some differences with the Sharif family, but by that time he had become a well-known Islamic scholar and preacher in his own right and no longer required the family's patronage.[9]

Qadri founded the organization Minhaj-ul-Quran (The Quranic Paradigm) in October 1981. Minhaj now claims to have expanded to more than ninety countries, mostly through diaspora Pakistani communities.[10] In an article published in 2012, political scientist Alix Philippon cited Minhaj membership statistics of 500,000 in Pakistan and 25,000 internationally.[11] Qadri also founded and is the chairman of the Board of Governors of Minhaj University in Lahore, an institution that provides education in multiple disciplines including social sciences and management as well as religious subjects. Minhaj-ul-Quran materials emphasize Qadri's Islamic credentials as the author of more than one thousand books, especially works on hadith that consist primarily of topical compilations of sayings of the Prophet Muḥammad. In addition to Qadri's scholarly credentials, Minhaj produces materials that celebrate him as a neutral advocate of honesty in politics and a pioneer in antiterrorism and deradicalization activities.

According to Ahmad, Qadri became a media star in the mid-1980s when he was recruited by the Sharif government to replace host Israr Ahmed (d. 2010) on the government channel PTV, after the latter made some unpopular statements that were considered antinationalist.[12] Qadri, who was younger and more personable than Ahmed, attracted a large following on his version of the program, *Fahm-ul-Quran* (Understanding the Quran). According to Ahmad, Qadri was "charming, more lucid and articulate, and spoke in popular idioms, illustrating his points through analogies from everyday life. In addition, having gone through both traditional and modern Islamic education, Qadri was able to attract a wider audience than any other contemporary Islamic scholar."[13]

Qadri's media career then took off from this point. In 2008 Ahmad counted Minhaj-ul-Quran Publications in Lahore as listing 1,034 VCDs and DVDs of Qadri's lectures, sermons, and interviews in Urdu, Punjabi, English, and Arabic recorded in Pakistan, India, Kuwait, the UAE, Oman, Syria, South Korea, Taiwan, Denmark, Norway, Greece, and South Africa. His programs and lectures were broadcast on popular Pakistani Islamic channels such as QTV, ARY, PTV Prime, Roshni, Labbaik, and Indus, which were proliferating during this period. Religious channel QTV has been broadcasting Qadri's talks regularly on an almost daily basis since the channel's inception in 2003.[14] As of 2019 the Minhaj website bookstore page stated that Qadri has published 551 books, and 449 are "in the pipeline."[15] YouTube videos of Qadri garner hundreds of thousands of views, thereby demonstrating his popular appeal, and his Facebook account has attracted 3,365,548 followers.[16]

In May 1989 Qadri founded a political party called the Pakistan Awami Tehreek (PAT). The main objective of the party was stated as "providing law and order for the general public, respect for human rights, the elimination of poverty, and quality education for all."[17] According to Philippon, the platform of the party also included some version of calling for an Islamic state.[18] The importance of an Islamic state is dealt with extensively in Qadri's writings,[19] although it is clear that his understanding of such a state encompasses democracy and pluralism. In 1990 a number of candidates from the PAT unsuccessfully contested the general elections, and in 2002 Qadri alone was elected a member of the National Assembly from Lahore. Qadri remained a vocal one-man opposition voice, but eventually he resigned from his seat on November 29, 2004, "seemingly in protest against the Musharraf regime's corruption, institutional instability, and 'undemocratic democracy.'"[20]

In what I term a trajectory of renewal and reinvention in the new millennium, in 2005 Qadri next embarked on a tour of the Middle East with a circle of some 250 devoted followers, mostly from outside of Pakistan.[21] This initiative could be construed as a move to establish himself on the stage of global "traditional Islam." Furthermore, this rebranding was symbolically represented by Qadri's adopting a new honorary title, "Shaykh al-Islam,"[22] and his sartorial switch to from wearing clothes more common in Pakistan to wearing an Azharī-style turban and long Arab-style *thawb*,[23] thereby signaling his positioning within a new generation of global Sufi leadership that is part of the "traditional Islam" coalition as well as his deriving of authority from both Islamic and Sufi sources beyond local Pakistani traditions. On this tour he visited with his entourage the shrines of notable Sufis of the past, including Ibn ʿArabī in Damascus and Rūmī in Konya, Turkey. He also met during and after the trip with a range of contemporary Sufi leaders, especially those with global constituencies, including Shaykh Nazim in Cyprus,[24] al-Habib Umar Salim ibn al-Hafiz and al-Habib Ali al-Jifri, and Shaykh Hisham Kabbani.[25] It is noteworthy that these global leaders were drawn from multiple Sufi *ṭarīqah* affiliations and command significant international youth followings.

Another watershed moment in Qadri's career occurred with his immigration to Mississauga, a suburb of Toronto, Canada, in 2005. Ostensibly he moved due to security concerns, and, indeed, with the breakdown in law and order and proliferation of targeted killings in his native Pakistan, this seems like a logical rationale. In the turbulent environment in Pakistan at that time targeted killings were eliminating leaders and activists across the religious and political spectrum, and Qadri could have fallen victim to such an attack due to his Sufi associations, his political affiliations, or even due to his program of advancing Christian-Muslim relations in Pakistan. Removing himself to North America marks another stage of Qadri's "going global."

Qadri further garnered extensive international publicity in 2010 with the launch of a six-hundred-page *Fatwa on Terrorism* in London that drew on his expertise and authority in jurisprudence, rather than Sufism. Subsequently, in June 2015, Qadri and his organization launched a deradicalization curriculum in London in response to the recruitment efforts of groups such as ISIS among disaffected Muslim youth in Europe and North America.[26]

We therefore can describe multiple ways in which Qadri transformed his scope of operations: (1) by expanding the Minhaj-ul-Quran organization internationally, especially within the Pakistani diaspora in Europe; (2) by situating himself within global "traditional Islam" Sufism; and (3) by positioning himself as an authentic and moderate Muslim legal expert who could formulate an antiterrorist discourse from within the classical Islamic sources.

Yet Pakistan and its political landscape did not drop off of Qadri's radar. Indeed, his forays into the Pakistani political scene continued. His sudden return to Pakistan in December 2012, to "save the state, not your politics,"[27] after having spent nearly seven years in Canada, became a subject of controversy and debate among the country's political circles.

As part of this initiative, in December 2012, Qadri addressed a large audience at the Minar-e Pakistan, Lahore, saying that the current system adopted by the Sharif government had failed and if the military intervened in the future, he would be the first Pakistani to protest against it. He gave an ultimatum to the government that if the situation failed to improve, he would lead a "Long March" to Islamabad. On January 1, 2013, Qadri, together with his new found ally, Altaf Hussain, chief of the Muttahida Qaumi Movement (MQM),[28] vowed to turn Islamabad into the Tahrir Square of Pakistan. He predicted that on the aforementioned day, "millions" of peaceful demonstrators would pour into the capital to install what was described as a neutral and independent caretaker administration to introduce long overdue electoral reforms.[29] This alliance, however, proved to be short lived because Altaf Hussain backed out before the anticipated rally. Qadri and his supporters did march with some results, since on January 17, 2013, the Sharif government agreed to negotiations and struck an agreement termed the "Islamabad Long March Declaration," thereby ending the protest. At that time Prime Minister Nawaz Sharif called Qadri's views an "imported agenda" aimed to disrupt the electoral process.[30]

This reengagement of Qadri with Pakistani politics was evidenced most notably in August and September 2014 in what was this time billed as an "Inqilab [revolution] March" on Islamabad. Its aims included the revamping of Pakistan's political system, the removal of Prime Minister Nawaz Sharif's government, the introduction of social welfare reforms, and the establishment of merit-based local governing bodies throughout the country.[31] In mid-August 2014 Qadri was able to draw thousands of followers in hundreds of cars, buses, and trucks to proceed toward the federal capital from his primary base in Lahore. The Pakistan satellite TV channels and airwaves were completely saturated with images of Tahir-ul-Qadri along with his ally, ex-cricketer turned politician Imran Khan, and their supporters, as well as broadcasts of their long orations condemning the government and issuing ultimatums. Many Pakistanis expected some kind of meaningful change, but when this failed to materialize both opposition figures, Khan and Qadri, were somewhat discredited, and their alliance fizzled out. Some analysts say that this failure to effect change was due to their lack of support from the Pakistani military. The role of media was very prominent during the Inqilab March, and a number of private Pakistani satellite channels, such as ARY, which favored Qadri and Imran Khan, were temporarily closed down by the Nawaz Sharif government, while journalists seen as favoring one side or the other were attacked by either police or demonstrators.[32] As is well known, the political movement of Imran Khan and his political party, Tehreek-e Insaf (PTI), continued to gather momentum and triumphed in the 2018 elections, installing him as prime minister. Qadri, however, seems to have abandoned any personal political ambitions in Pakistan, and he and his party declined to participate in the 2018 elections.

Tahir-ul-Qadri as a "Post-*Ṭarīqah*" Sufi

The category of "Barelwi," or, as proponents of this position call themselves, "Ahl-e Sunnat wa-l-Jamāʿat,"[33] has generally been considered the default religious orientation of the masses of India and Pakistan. Works discussing South Asian Islam often claim that up to 90 percent of the population are Barelwi, as opposed to being either Deobandi or Ahl-e Hadith.[34] But these claims fail to distinguish the exact nature of Barelwi identity and affiliation. Is a diffuse belief in the power of the Sufi saints the qualifier for being a "Barelwi"? Or is the criterion rather performative, for example, celebration of *mīlāds*,[35] standing (*qiyām*) for salutations (*salām*) to the Prophet after the ritual prayers in mosques, or performing certain devotional practices at Sufi shrines? Are Barelwis losing ground since the 1980s with the Talibanization of Pakistan and the influence of Saudi-style Wahhabism, or are they becoming more unified and politically mobilized?[36]

While Barbara Metcalf notes the greater appeal of Barelwiism among the less-educated, along with their justification of "mediational, custom-laden Islam, closely tied to the intercession of *pīrs* of the shrines,"[37] the formal designation of being a "Barelwi" emerged with the career and efforts of an eponymous founder, Ahmed Raza Khan Barelwi (d. 1921).[38] Usha Sanyal presents Barelwi as a reformist whose devotionalism and appreciation of typical South

Asian pious beliefs and rituals venerating the Sufi saints were combined with his being able to articulate a defense of such practices that drew on the authority of classical Islamic sources such as the Quran, hadith, and *fiqh*.[39]

Three factors underlie recent challenges to Barelwiism—modernity, migration, and globalization. In terms of modernity, the main pressure on Barelwis today would be the disenchantment that induces widespread skepticism of claims to the miraculous and favors scriptural literalism. The proliferation of Saudi-style Wahhabi ideas through patronage, funding of madrasa education, and influences on Pakistani guest workers residing in the Gulf has also worked against Barelwiism since the 1970s, and this combines modernity with the other two factors of migration and globalization in terms of the promotion of Islamist and Saudi-style ideas and practices and the resulting devaluation of local cultural traditions. The rise of militant literalist groups in Pakistan has further led to attacks on Sufis and their shrines. In her analysis of Barelwi mobilizations, Philippon argues that government policies during both the Zia-ul-Haq and subsequent eras have favored the Deobandis and Ahl-e Hadith as part of Islamic and even jihadist mobilization, thus laying the groundwork for eventual push back by some Barelwis.[40]

Ethan Epping draws attention to the fact that traditional Barelwiism focused on the charismatic authority of Sufi leaders, which became routinized in their descendants, who were often powerful feudal landlords able to succeed in elections as powerful *pīrs*. This is one leading aspect of how Sufism has influenced Pakistani politics. Sarah Ansari, in chapter 7 of this volume, provides extensive discussion of this aspect of Sufi influence on Pakistani politics. More recently, however, the way that Sufism functions on the political stage has become more complex, as have internal differentiations among diverse streams of Barelwiism. As Anatol Lieven observes, "Every attempt at creating [Barelwi] parties over the decades has foundered on the deep rivalries and jealousies between (and indeed within) the great pir families."[41] Ethan Epping presents a similar view in that, "There simply has not existed the sufficient ideological common ground to overcome the regional locus of Barelwi practices. One's identity as a Barelwi provides connections on the tribal and regional levels, but little beyond that, which has tended to inhibit political activism beyond such levels."[42]

Now, in contrast to Lieven and Epping's observations, Pan-Barelwi organizing in Pakistan seems to be taking place at the national level. And I would characterize Qadri's mobilizing through the Minhaj and other activities as being more successful internationally and also as being more diffuse in terms of translating into any local political influence. This is perhaps one reason why Qadri and his party did not succeed in politics at the national level, despite efforts in that direction. Philippon elaborates, in chapter 8 of this volume, on recent political and social mobilizations of Pakistani Barelwis. In an earlier publication she notes that "one phenomenon that has hardly attracted much attention from academia has been the emergence since the 1980s of multiple organization hailing from the Barelwi school of thought, such as Minhaj al-Quran, Dawat-e Islami, Sunni Tehreek, or ʿAlami Tanzeem Ahl-e Sunnat. The founders of these organizations all belong to the Qādiriyyah, one of the four main Sufi orders present in Pakistan."[43] These dynamics raise the question: can affiliation with a particular Sufi order lead to more effective collaboration? The answers remain beyond the scope of this chapter, other than to suggest that Qadri and the Minhaj seem to move away from local *ṭarīqah* bonds to global Sufi authority grounded in traditional (hadith and *fiqh*) credentials.

Common characteristics across these diverse Barelwi movements are, according to Philippon, that they recruit along modern lines and involve preaching. The leaders are charismatic, and their devotees believe they are representatives of the Prophet. Most of these groups are also involved in forms of social activity, such as education, and may be politically mobilized.[44]

Regarding modernization and its impact on Barelwi/Sufi identity in Pakistan, Philippon observes how traditional aspects of Sufi *ṭarīqah* affiliation, such as taking an oath of allegiance to the *shaykh*, are not the main focus of these more recent Barelwi mobilizations, suggesting that these are a form of "Neo-Sufi" orders, following the usage of this term by Olivier Roy.[45] In fact, as Verena Meyer, in chapter 2 of this volume, discusses at length, the term "Neo-Sufism" has proven both fruitful and contested in understanding how the methods and roles of Sufi orders have evolved before, during, and after colonialism. In addition, Carl Ernst's reflection on part 1 of this volume picks up on the significance of using the concept of Neo-Sufism to describe the struggle with change and continuity in forms of Sufi identity and practice, both locally and globally. Since the term "Neo-Sufism" in academic literature was previously defined by Fazlur Rahman,[46] and subsequently applied to developments such as emphasizing the need for Sufi authority to be grounded in classical Islamic hadith study and legal injunctions while exhorting social and moral reform, the expression "post-*ṭarīqah* Sufi movements" may be more suitable for describing mobilizations that include features such as deemphasizing allegiance to a specific Sufi order.[47]

Sociologist Amer Morgahi explains in similar terms new elements that indicate nontraditional approaches within Qadri's Sufism. Qadri does not give *bayʿah* (formal initiation as a Sufi) and states explicitly, "I am not a Pir." He rejects terms such as "*shaykh*" and prefers modern forms of address such as "Dr." or "Professor," according to Morgahi.[48] His adoption of the title "Shaykh al-Islam" after 2005, then, is not in the Sufi sense of "spiritual master" but rather grounds his authority on the foundation of Islamic law and hadith. At the same time, by joining Minhaj-ul-Quran, affiliates may consider themselves disciples of the Qādirī order, since "filling a form of the MQ membership puts one within the lineage of the Qadariyya."[49] Some Minhaj adherents have been further promised that they will be raised in the company of the founding Sufi saint ʿAbd al-Qādir al-Jīlanī on Judgment Day, and, additionally, Qadri has recounted a dream promising that all of his followers will be guided by Jīlanī.[50]

One impact of migration on Barelwiism is that in the diaspora, that is, Western Europe or the United States, traditional South Asian sectarian affiliations may lack relevance to a new generation that may not embrace or even recognize Deobandi or Barelwi identity. While in some countries where Barelwi institutions are well established, such as Britain, there seems to be more continuity of South Asian Sunni sectarian identities and practices, in the United States it may prove more difficult for a constituency that would support a figure such as Qadri to take hold. For example, Qadri was invited to Chicago and initially hosted by a small circle of Barelwi-oriented families. Some local Qādirī Sufis were eager to become his representatives, but they lacked any coherent circle of followers or institutions and subsequently no chapter of the organization took hold.

In terms of globalization and its impact on local (Pakistani) elements of Qadri's Barelwiism, one can visually trace transformations and adaptations in the Sufi elements of Qadri's career through his sartorial choices, as mentioned above. One may assess this shift in costume as signaling a move in identity from associating with local Pakistani *ṭarīqah*-based Sufism to the taking on the role of a transnational Islamic religious leader. Qadri's shift from *ṭarīqah*-based Sufism to global "traditional Islam" has enabled him to forge and maintain conceptual and cooperative connections with diverse scholars and Islamic institutions that espouse similar views, and he has increasingly faced Islamist and literalist opposition since. In the West, figures associated with this form of Sufism include American Hamza Yusuf Hanson and Yemeni Habib al-Jifri. Qadri globalized and vitalized his "brand" among diaspora youth by associating with such popular figures. As part of internationalizing and broadening his appeal, Qadri has increasingly placed emphasis on his qualifications and writings in the area of hadith studies and Islamic law. Morgahi has traced in detail Qadri's invocation of hadith knowledge and in particular his position as a transmitter of hadith within the *isnād* (chains of transmission). In some cases Qadri enhances his authority as a transmitter by invoking features such as the brevity of the hadith's chain of transmission reaching back to the Prophet.[51] The system of *ijāzah*—being granted authorization or permission from a respected scholar to be added to an existing chain—both positions Qadri within a chain as an authentic scholar and gives him the ability to link others to these chains. It is noteworthy that the Minhaj website, as well as a number of Qadri's publications, repeat these *isnāds* of authorization at great length.

Qadri both draws on and moves beyond South Asian Barelwi identity in the light of various contemporary factors impacting traditional Barelwiism, thus demonstrating that he represents a new sort of post-*ṭarīqah* mobilization, relying on public sources of "Islamic" authority outside of purely Sufi credentials.

Public Controversies Related to Barelwi Beliefs and Practices

The characterization of South Asian Muslims as being Deobandi, Barelwi, or Ahl-e Hadith has traditionally been associated with class and ethnic factors as well as doctrinal positions and specific religious ritual behaviors.

The increasing differentiation across Barelwis, Deobandis, and Ahl-e Hadith in South Asia was evidenced in nineteenth-century "fatwa wars" across these groups, often focused on particular points of doctrine or practice that could distinguish one group from another. These points of dispute were generally associated with perspectives on Sufi practices or beliefs, for example: Do the Prophet and Sufi saints remain alive in the grave? Did the Prophet have knowledge of the Unseen (*ghayb*)?[52] Despite this long-standing rivalry and contestation between Barelwis and other groups, Qadri is noted as having tried to avoid hostile characterizations of the other positions, as in this description of him by Ahmad:

> Qadri, a Barelwi *alim* (singular of ulema) by training and family background is, unlike most of his fellow Barelwis, quite tolerant and accommodative of other school's doctrines and practices. He is one of the few Barelwis who allows his followers to pray behind a Deobandi imam. His relatively tolerant views on Deobandis have caused a great deal of resentment against him by his fellow Barelwi ulema, who are also critical of his liberal views on the role and status of women.[53]

Still, in assessing representations of Qadri on Internet sites and YouTube, it is apparent that certain doctrinal positions that he has publically taken or practices that he has engaged in engender controversy and negative reactions from those affiliated with other groups, including other Barelwis who reject some of his positions.[54]

One instance is a "Sufi 'dancers' video" posted on YouTube and elsewhere. Critics reacted negatively to clips featuring Qadri and his associates listening to *qawwālī* musical performance and Turkish *nashīds* during sessions in which a few listeners make movements traditionally associated with the ecstatic Sufi *raqṣ* (dance).[55] Throughout the centuries the practice of ecstatic dance has been vigorously debated by both supporters and detractors, who may condemn it for an apparent lack of sobriety, or as being an innovation in religion that was not known in the time of the Prophet Muḥammad. The debate over whether Qadri had erred in attending and approvingly smiling and gesturing as some of his companions "danced" spilled onto YouTube, and a lengthy rebuttal video features Qadri giving extensive citations of "dancing" behavior among the early Companions of the Prophet as well as a famous hadith report where the Prophet approves of some of his Ethiopian followers dancing with happiness.[56]

In another point of doctrine disputed across rival groups, the Barelwi Sufi orientation of South Asia holds that the Prophet Muḥammad and the Sufi saints continue as living presences in their graves. There are quite a number of Qadri's discourses available on this topic. A related controversy surrounds a video that shows Qadri at the gravesite of a young man who has just been buried, apparently exhorting the deceased to answer questions affirming his faith as if he is still alive and can respond. Opponents challenge this as a misguided belief that contravenes the Quran itself.[57]

The third example of doctrinal dispute involves Qadri's dream life. In the Islamic tradition, dreams, and especially dreams of the Prophet Muḥammad, are very respected. There are, however, discussions about the propriety of publicly recounting such dreams and whether they should be seen as conveying some broader authority beyond the message intended for the individual dreamer. Qadri has written extensively about dreams and on numerous occasions refers to his own dreams. The most provocative of these is one that has been heavily criticized and commented on by his opponents. The original speech in which he recounted the dream is preserved in grainy footage and of course posted to YouTube as evidence of impropriety by more than one source.[58] The narrative of this dream, which occurred in January 1989, is that the Prophet had arrived in Pakistan and then expressed his displeasure with the state of affairs there, indicating that he wanted to depart. Qadri asked forgiveness on behalf of Pakistan and implored the Prophet to stay; after much pleading and weeping, the Prophet agreed on the condition that Qadri would become his host. This would include making all the arrangements for his visit, including buying the ticket. The elements of the dream that seem to most annoy critics of Qadri are an inflated sense of his own importance, the fact that this dream was publicly recounted to bolster Qadri's status and authority, and also the offensiveness of implying that the Prophet would require his assistance in purchasing a ticket. Of course, there were also those, whether secularist or anti-Sufi, who simply found the aspect of using dreams to make any sort of truth claims, metaphorical or otherwise, to be offensive.

In response, Qadri produced a lengthy rebuttal video, the gist of which implies that the context of the speech was for a private audience of members of Minhaj-ul-Quran and that he did not broadcast the speech to gain notoriety or support.[59] In addition, Minhaj spokespersons have posted multiple responses,[60] and a publication of some one hundred pages presents written responses by Qadri and others to criticisms of this dream and of dreams in general.[61]

Tahir-ul-Qadri as a "Good" Muslim

The call for a promotion of certain interpretations of "moderate" Islam by U.S. think tanks for national security and ideological reasons has often cast suspicion on the sincerity and neutrality of Muslim actors who are viewed and even praised as being "moderate."[62] This includes, in particular, Sufis whose support was encouraged in at least one post-9/11 Rand report as a counter to radicalization.[63] Rosemary Corbett, in chapter 1 of this volume, treats such promotions of Sufism as motivated by American strategic interests.

Evidence of Qadri's "moderation" is his openness to interfaith and intra-Muslim dialogue. Qadri has taken more of an interest in interfaith than most of his Pakistani counterparts among religious leaders. According to Ahmed, Qadri has been the only religious leader in Pakistan who has initiated serious efforts toward reaching out to the Christian community and sharing its concerns. He founded a Muslim-Christian dialogue forum that facilitates regular contacts between the two communities and organizes discussions on matters of mutual concerns. Furthermore, Minhaj-ul-Quran is the only group in Pakistan that organizes Christmas celebrations, inviting Pakistani Christians of various denominations to an annual Christmas party.[64]

Qadri's relationship to the Pakistani blasphemy laws, which have disproportionately been used to target Pakistan Christians by accusing them of making defamatory remarks about Prophet Muḥammad, is controversial. This is a very sensitive issue among all Pakistani Muslims, and especially Barelwis, for whom devotion to the Prophet is a paramount tenet. The specific issue related to Qadri is his stance regarding the blasphemy laws, which plays very differently across multiple constituencies. For some Pakistani Barelwis, upholding these laws, whatever their consequences, is a badge of honor. Thus, when the assassin of Government Minister Salman Taseer, Mumtaz Qadri, was hung for this crime in 2016, a segment of Barelwis mounted violent demonstrations across the country and subsequently they have made his grave into a shrine since they view his action as worthy of praise and even veneration for its supposed defense of the Prophet. In late 2018, rumors that a Christian woman, Aasia Bibi, who had been accused of blasphemy and was ultimately acquitted by the Pakistan Supreme Court, had been released, led to further Barelwi-organized demonstrations and rioting.

There are claims that Tahir-ul-Qadri helped write the original blasphemy code for former president Zia-ul-Haq. On the other hand, Qadri is on record declaring before human rights groups in Europe that he was not directly involved in developing the blasphemy laws, since Zia-ul-Haq eventually abrogated the consultative elements of the process at which Qadri had simply given testimony as a scholarly advisor.[65]

In terms of intra-Muslim relations, Qadri is also considered to be in favor of Sunni rapprochement and eschewing the usual criticism of other Muslims, such as Deobandis, who are viewed as opposing certain practices associated with Sufi shrine veneration as well as specific doctrines favored by Barelwis. A more detailed discussion of some of the religious issues that distinguish Barelwis from Deobandis may be found in chapter 4 of this volume, by Brannon Ingram. Some Barelwi scholars, who, in turn, distance themselves from Qadri, may do so on the basis of his rulings on doctrinal fine points and to some extent on his less hostile attitude to other factions.

Further evidence of Qadri's "moderate" position are his more recent campaigns against suicide bombings, terrorist attacks, and radicalization. These activities represent a new platform for global outreach for Qadri as a moderate Muslim scholar condemning extremism. In March 2010 Qadri issued a historic six-hundred-page-long fatwa (religious opinion) against suicide bombings and terrorism. This work, which features an introduction by American scholar of Islam John Esposito, compiles references from the Quran, hadiths, and Islamic legal writings providing Islamic legal proofs that suicide bombings are strictly prohibited in Islam and that persons who indulge in such practices are equivalent to nonbelievers.[66]As is usual with Qadri's publications, the book is largely a compilation of citations from authoritative Islamic sources, in particular the Quran and hadith, with little commentary or analysis. Among the topics covered are sections on the unlawfulness of various aspects of terrorism, the illegality of rebelling against the Muslim state, and the need to employ peaceful methods of social and political struggle. Classical sources containing a brutal condemnation of the Kharijite sect, disassociating them from Islam and calling for their extirpation, are taken to apply to contemporary Muslim proponents of violent secessionism. Some Sufi background is hinted at by Qadri's early citation and discussion of the "Hadith of Gabriel," according to which the religion is progressively based on Islam (submitting to God's commands), *īmān* (faith), and *iḥsān* (doing things beautifully) through remaining constantly aware of God. The *iḥsān* component referred to in the hadith is often taken to refer to Sufi traditions within the Islamic faith.[67]

The career of Tahir-ul-Qadri can serve to illustrate a number of issues raised by reconsidering Sufi Islamic identity and democracy in South Asia. Qadri's role, both in the Pakistani context and internationally, reflects changing roles of Sufism, both locally and globally. Various Pakistani regimes and political actors have appropriated Sufism and its shrines and saints since 1947.[68] In 2006 the Pervez Musharraf regime set up a formal body, the National Council for the Promotion of Sufism,[69] to advance aspects of the Sufi mystical tradition as an antidote to violent extremism and terrorism in the aftermath of 9/11. In 2009 this body was reconstituted as the National Sufi Council under Asif Zardari's government.[70] In Pakistan today provincial governments, such as that of Sindh, continue to sponsor Sufi conferences that promote the cultural aspects of Sufism, such as music and shrine visitation, but often do little to engage contemporary Sufi leadership or representatives, focusing rather on academic papers and artistic performances. Interestingly, the Indian government sponsored a World Sufi Conference in March 2016 at which Prime Minister Narendra Modi himself offered a keynote address, surrounded by the heads of various Indian shrines and Sufi orders as well as global representatives of Sufism. Qadri was one of the prominent international representatives at this event.[71] As expected, the discourse at this meeting was about Sufism as the "good" Islam that could counter violence and extremism while promoting peace and pluralism.

As Qadri became more directly engaged in Pakistani politics, his remarks and activities came under remarkable media scrutiny. Notable are the extensive efforts taken by his organization to respond to criticisms across media platforms, including robust social media initiatives. Part of the role of being a public post-*ṭarīqah* Sufi leader is managing a tension between populism and authority. Maintaining charisma in a disenchanted, complex, and contested public sphere clearly strains traditional expectations of Sufi behavior. For instance, classical Sufism formulated a category of the elite (*khwāṣṣ*), that is, those who might be exposed to utterances or actions of the Sufi leader that would be beyond the comprehension and appreciation of the masses. Today, however, nothing can be assumed to be "private."

In the new "authenticity Sufism," branded as "traditional Islam," authority claims shift to proofs anchored in classical Islamic sources rather than in the personal charisma of the *shaykh* or even the routinized charisma of a Sufi order. After all, the name of Qadri's social movement, Minhaj-ul-Quran, translates as "The Quranic Paradigm"—not the "Qādirī Sufi order."

In the development of global Sufism, the role of information in creating and sustaining a global Sufi community that is distinct from Islamist movements yet draws on many of the some textual sources is vital. The fact that media have such a large presence can work both for and against a message, for instance, making Tahir-ul-Qadri a household name in Pakistan but also exposing him to unprecedented vituperation and even ridicule. The posting of videos on YouTube allows the proliferation and wide dissemination of negative publicity against Qadri emanating from "Wahhabis," Deobandis, disaffected Barelwis, and skeptical secularists. This, in turn, generates a veritable flood of response videos. These debates continue on Tumblr, Twitter, and other platforms, with significant public engagement and participation.

Religion is very public and very contested in Pakistan, and its elements, whether Sufism or Islamic laws, have proven very susceptible to being coopted by successive regimes. The Pakistani government has been criticized for policies that bow to the pressure of conservative groups in order to increase regime legitimacy through an appeal to the "Muslim masses." Major historical examples include the condemnation of the Ahmadis during the Bhutto (Zulfiqar ʿAli) period, or passage of the Islamization laws (Hudood Ordinances) during the Zia-ul-Haq period.

Thus, regarding the role of Sufism and democracy in Pakistan, we might ask whether the religious identity of Tahir-ul-Qadri and its projection through the media to a broad Pakistan public is a phenomenon that at least exhibits, and perhaps even encourages, democratic debate, engagement, and ideally, praxis, or whether the role of this religious actor is in fact cynical and a threat to public order, if not to the democratic system itself.

Commentary on Part I

Ambiguities and Ironic Reversals in the Categorization of Sufism

CARL W. ERNST

Any consideration of the politics of Sufism brings into question the coherence of applying a category from the study of religion (i.e., Sufism) to particular social and political contexts. There are inevitable tensions between the use of Sufism as a category in scholarly argument, and the role of that term (or the insider term it purports to represent, e.g., *taṣawwuf*) in any given social context.

The case of Sufism is a notable example of category formation with a strongly Orientalist agenda. Originally based on a romantic reading of Persian poetic and philosophical writings, the category of Sufism was proposed by Sir William Jones and others at the end of the eighteenth century as a universalist teaching, ultimately derived from Hinduism, which could safely be separated from Islam. This vision of the misguided mystic East, which built on prejudices articulated by seventeenth-century travelers such as Chardin and Bernier, used marginalizing terms like "quietism" and "pantheism" to assign Sufism an outlier role for modern European thought.[1] This romantic notion of Sufism as mysticism of private experience probably hit its high water-mark by the middle of the nineteenth century, with the 1847 publication of a deeply flawed English translation of the *Dabistān-i madhāhib*, a text that found Sufism and universalist mysticism everywhere.[2] In contrast, the naked mendicants (*faqīrs*) and unruly dervishes found in Asian streets mostly aroused disgust in European observers, who saw no connection between such figures and classical Sufi texts. Yet like other categories of religious identity, the concept of Sufism too would eventually be affected by the anthropological turn of the late nineteenth century. As Jonathan Z. Smith has argued, this expansion of the term "religion" made it "an anthropological, not a theological category."[3] This emphasis on society meant that phenomena such as the Sufi orders and shrine pilgrimage would come up for consideration, although by no means always with clear results. All this would take place during a time when internal Muslim critiques of Sufism multiplied both from reformist and secularist perspectives. The normal gap between scholarly terms and social reality has therefore been more confusing than usual in the case of Sufism. Certainly, the chapters in this volume by Rosemary Corbett, Verena Meyer, and Marcia Hermansen provide numerous examples of deployments of the word "Sufism" in ways that can seem perplexing and even contradictory.

Gaps and mismatches in the scholarly understanding of Sufism are abundant in the examples adduced by Corbett, particularly in the way she describes the efforts of the Ford and Rockefeller Foundations to advance liberal causes through projects focused on Sufism, which was assumed to be unconnected to politics or violence. She points out that French scholars of North Africa gave greater attention to the social dimensions of Sufism than did British scholars with regard to India, so the British might have learned something from considering the North African material. French studies on Sufism (or "maraboutism") included the work of colonial administrators like Octave Depont and Xavier Coppolani, co-authors of a massive 1897 survey of Sufi orders based on close political surveillance.[4] This was hands-on research based on experience attempting to manage Sufi politics; Coppolani was actually killed in 1905 by a rebellious Qādirī Sufi group in Mauretania. But British scholars of Sufism, like A. J. Arberry, remained resolutely focused on classical texts, and indeed Arberry regarded the popularity of Sufi shrines and orders as clear evidence of its "decay," a process that in his view began centuries ago.[5] If there had been a more vigorous social scientific body of research on Indian Islam, the political dimension of Sufism in South Asia could have been explored, for it certainly existed. Just to give one example, recent research has highlighted the importance of charismatic *faqīr*s for Indian military units, including the role they played in the 1806 Vellore mutiny against the British.[6] But in the eyes of the handful of British scholars specializing in Sufism, neither such anti-colonial resistance, nor the co-opting of shrine custodians into the colonial bureaucracy, was seen as relevant.

So, when the Rockefeller Foundation began to formulate an approach to Muslim societies, the scholarship they drew upon came from Islamicists making sweeping generalizations in which Indo-Persian Sufism was prominent. But neither H. A. R. Gibb nor W. C. Smith had ever done any research relating to Sufism, either in its textual traditions or its social manifestations; moreover, both were Arabists who lacked expertise in Persian. So, this account of American foundations and their relations with Islamic studies scholars raises a number of questions. If the foundations hoped to obtain from scholars a key to liberalizing Muslim societies, did they really expect that (for example) reading Rūmī would turn fundamentalists into liberals? Did the scholars actually believe the sketchy, perhaps opportunistic claims presented in their grant applications? How did the foundations measure the impact of these grandiose experiments in ideological intervention? The disjunctures between scholarly research and development programs, and the different assumptions about how to define Sufism, contribute to the obscurity of this episode.

Another form of problematic use of religious studies categories occurs when academic terminology is taken up in the public sphere in unexpected ways. This phenomenon is demonstrated in the chapter by Verena Meyer, which focuses on the articulation of the concept of "Neo-Sufism," a term initially proposed by Pakistani scholar Fazlur Rahman, and then later adapted by the Indonesian thinker Nurcholish Madjid. The term was coined by Rahman to designate a reform of Sufism undertaken by the fourteenth-century Ḥanbalī scholars Ibn Taymiyyah and Ibn Qayyim al-Jawziyyah, which, according to Rahman, led to "a puritanical, moral meaning and an orthodox ethos," in short, a truly Islamic Sufism as opposed to the un-Islamic Sufism that had compromised with local cultures.[7] It is noteworthy that Rahman's concept of Neo-Sufism was not defined primarily as a description of modern movements, though it implicitly accepted the genealogy going back to Ibn Taymiyyah that was claimed by the Wahhabis and other critics/reformers of Sufism. For Rahman, the transformative work accomplished by the prefix "neo-" was to subject Sufi practices and institutions to a rigorous legal and ethical standard, so that "the medieval *ṭarīqas* or brotherhoods are essentially rejected as aberrant . . . [but] Sufism is affirmed."[8]

With the Indonesian thinkers, however, the evaluation of Sufism and its reformulation rested on a much larger adaptation of a central concept of modern European thought, that is, society. Charles Tripp has shown how Arab thinkers more than a century ago began to grapple with the systematic theories of social thinkers like Herbert Spencer and Karl Marx.[9] The term "society" was quickly adapted into Arabic in the mid-nineteenth century, usually through the term *ijtimāʿ* or some variation upon it. What is remarkable is the success of this import, as the notion of "Arab society" or "Muslim society" began to take on the aura of naturalness, so that every Middle Eastern intellectual was expected to hold forth on these topics; the same process was undoubtedly occurring also in South and Southeast Asia. The adoption of the concept of "society" went hand-in-hand with the appropriation of master concepts like "culture" and "religion." The analytical reflection to which each of these concepts was subjected necessarily contributed to the objectification and reification of religion, which in turn led to instrumental reflections on religion as a means to other ends. This is the context for the fascinating observations of Indonesian Muslim thinkers such as Hamka and Nurcholish Madjid, reflecting on how Sufism could be calibrated for the benefit of society. Rather than treating Sufism as a self-evident path to the moral improvement and spiritual realization of a small elite, these thinkers felt bound to consider Sufism as a force that could be harnessed for the social benefit of the masses, within the frameworks of democracy, modernity, and civil society. It is as if Max Weber were to be channeled to expound upon "the Sufi ethic and the spirit of capitalism." Such are the parameters that lie behind their re-articulated concept of "Neo-Sufism" as a social project.

As an aside to the actual deployment of the term "Neo-Sufism," it will be helpful to pause briefly to consider the structure of this neologism. By combining the prefix "neo-," which means "new," with a historically established category such as Sufism, one creates several different rhetorical possibilities. "The new" may have the connotation of "new and improved," in which case the new compound basically replaces the now outmoded original term. Alternatively, "neo-" may carry connotations of the novel, the untested, and the inauthentic, making the compound a derogatory reference. Scholars of literary history and political science have drawn attention to the ambiguities that go along with the introduction of prefixes such as "neo-."[10] Again, there is an irony in the use of this term by Rahman. Like his role model, Iqbal, Rahman was deeply critical of historical Sufism, both in its theoretical expressions and its social embodiments. Apart from his critical edition of the letters of Aḥmad Sirhindī,[11] Rahman did not do any focused research on Sufism as such, and his interest in Sirhindī undoubtedly had to do with the latter's sharia-minded agenda. As a committed reformer dedicated to the restoration of Islamic ethical normativity, Rahman had no confidence either in the gnostic speculations of Ibn ʿArabī nor in the social and political domination of the Sufi orders. His portrait of the creation of a new form of Sufism, adhering to the critical legal judgments of fourteenth-century reformer Ibn Taymiyyah, has been criticized on historical grounds as an implausible hypothesis and a considerable oversimplification.[12] Indeed, it sounds like wishful thinking to imagine a purified Sufism, devoid of superstitions and innovations—but such is the power of a prefix like "neo-." Yet these prefixes have other possibilities as well, which are completely unconnected to Rahman's normative project. Some scholars employ the term "Neo-Sufism" to describe esoteric movements adopted by non-Muslim Europeans and Americans with no reference to Islamic normativity.[13] Others have defined the same term as a broad description for all the colonial permutations of institutional Sufism, ranging from new Sufi orders to post-*ṭarīqah* movements like the Nurcus and Gulenists as well as non-Muslim groups.[14] I tend to agree with Hermansen, in her chapter in this volume, that "post-*ṭarīqah* Sufism" offers greater analytical clarity than the ambiguous "Neo-Sufism."

Hermansen's discussion of the career of Tahir-ul-Qadri raises the issue of Sufi identity apart from the institutionalized orders that were so prominent in Muslim societies from the thirteenth through the nineteenth centuries. It is often presumed that Sufism is defined by *ṭarīqah* orders, an assumption that takes one particular phase of the history of Sufism as an essential characteristic, despite its lack of ubiquity. The formative period of Sufism in fact did not display any kind of formal organization that resembles the *ṭarīqahs* that emerged in the thirteenth century, such as the Naqshbandīs, Chishtīs, and Qādirīs. Prominent Sufis from before that time did not belong to Sufi lineages, but later interpreters often incorporated early figures into the genealogical charts that were used to construct retrospective histories of the transmission of authority. And contemporary data on saints' shrines indicate that *ṭarīqah* affiliation is not in fact the norm. A list of festivals held at 255 shrines in the Punjab supervised by the Pakistan Ministry of Charitable Trusts indicates that half of the shrines had no affiliation with any Sufi order, while the other half were split among orders classified as Qādirī, Chishtī, Suhrawardī, Naqshbandī, mixed orders, and other.[15] All this suggests that taxonomic essentialism is a mistake. The assumption that scholars (or administrators) have access to uniquely authoritative lists of bullet points that define unchanging religious identities does not stand up to historical analysis. The notion of a fixed definition for a religious adherent has to be nuanced by fuzzier realities, like the "sympathizer" who does not formally join a religious group.[16] It is for such reasons that one may prefer to employ categories from a polythetic or "family resemblance" perspective, in which some but not necessarily all of the characteristics associated with the definition may be applicable in a given case.

Tahir-ul-Qadri has indeed dispensed with some of the seemingly characteristic markers of the typical Barelwi Sufi master, including initiation rituals and even customary apparel. Yet he retains connections with the Qādirī order and partakes of its charisma both through his name and his life story. His adoption of a personal style associated with traditional Islamic learning and authority seems calculated to appeal to a global audience far wider than the normal clientele of a Pakistani Sufi order. So, in this respect, it is appropriate to consider Tahir-ul-Qadri in the category of post-*ṭarīqah* Sufism. He does not conform to the model of the local Sufi *pīr*, nor indeed does he share the exclusionary zeal of the modern Barelwis against non-Muslim minorities. It is arguably the political vision of Qadri that drove him to expand his religious profile while retaining a modest connection to Sufism. In the instances discussed by Corbett and Meyer, the political stakes can be high, especially when Sufism is identified as a force for the transformation of society. In the case of Qadri, the difference is that institutional Sufism is viewed as a political liability. In all these examples, Sufism continues to resist definition, even as it is reified and instrumentalized.

PART II

Sufis, Sharia, and Reform

4

Is the Taliban Anti-Sufi?

Deobandi Discourses on Sufism in Contemporary Pakistan

BRANNON D. INGRAM

The previous decade has witnessed a spate of attacks on Sufi saints' shrines in Pakistan, many carried out by the Tehreek-e Taliban Pakistan (TTP) and affiliated movements.[1] These events date at least to March of 2009, when the tomb of the Pashtun poet Rehman Baba, on the outskirts of Peshawar, was bombed during his *ʿurs* (the celebration of a saint's death anniversary).[2] Shortly thereafter, in June 2009, the Barelwi mufti Sarfraz Naeemi, who had publicly criticized Taliban suicide bombings, was killed in a suicide attack claimed by TTP leader Beitullah Mehsud.[3] These events were followed by one of the most brazen strikes against Sufis in Pakistan: the July 2010 bombing of the tomb of the patron saint of Lahore, al-Hujwīrī, popularly known as Dātā Ganj Bakhsh.[4] Then, in October 2010, there were strikes against, first, the shrine complex of a saint of equal stature, Bābā Farīd Ganj-e Shakkar in Pakpattan,[5] and subsequently, the ʿAbd Allāh Shāh Ghāzī complex in Karachi, for which the TTP claimed responsibility.[6] Just a few months later, in April 2011, Taliban affiliates attacked the *ʿurs* celebration of Sakhī Sarwar in Dera Ghāzī Khān. Ehsanullah Ehsan, a spokesperson for the TTP, told Reuters it was revenge for a government offensive against the TTP.[7] Finally, in December 2011, the Bahādur Bābā shrine was dynamited and the Shaykh Nisā Bābā shrine was set on fire, with speculation that the TTP was responsible.[8]

Media and policy analysts have attributed these attacks to what is assumed to be a deeply seated hostility toward Sufism among the Taliban. Such approaches understand these events as part of a perceived clash between an intrinsically irenic Sufism and an intrinsically violent fundamentalism—a dichotomy whose genealogy stretches back to eighteenth-century Orientalist discourses on Sufism, if not earlier, but which has gained a new political valence in the aftermath of the War on Terror.[9] Thus, as a 2010 *Time* story understood these events, the Taliban attacked Sufis because they "deem Sufism . . . a heresy," which in turn has prompted Sufis, "typically nonviolent and politically quiescent," to begin "preparing for battle."[10] In academic studies as well, we are often told simply that the Taliban is "hostile to Sufism as well as the veneration of shrines and saints."[11]

When such studies do attempt to explain Taliban hostility to Sufism, they usually do so with reference to the Taliban's emergence from seminaries affiliated with the Deoband movement, the network of Islamic institutions that originated with the famed Dār al-ʿUlūm Deoband seminary in 1866.[12] This chapter seeks to complicate that narrative and challenge its explanatory efficacy. What the narrative ignores is the deep ambivalence toward Sufism, Sufi saints, and their shrines throughout Deobandi history; indeed, the Deobandi critique of Sufism is, in fact, best characterized as a critique of Sufism *by Sufis*.[13] Deobandis' critics often deny that they are Sufis at all, which arguably says much more about the contemporary politics of defining Sufism than it does about the Deobandis' place within it. But more importantly, it also overlooks the extent to which this ambivalence informs even those institutions linked directly to the Taliban. This chapter explores that ambivalence among a specific group of Deobandi scholars affiliated with the Dār al-ʿUlūm Ḥaqqāniyya (also commonly spelled Darul Uloom Haqqania) in northwest Pakistan, where many of the leaders of the Taliban studied. In taking this approach, I do not intend to conflate the Pakistani Taliban with the Afghani Taliban, or either group with its leaders. In this sense, the question in the chapter's title—is the Taliban anti-Sufi?—is not just rhetorical but unanswerable: There is no one view proffered by the Taliban on Sufism or any other subject, nor do Ḥaqqānī scholars necessarily "represent" the Taliban. Nevertheless, I contend in this chapter that the teachings and writings of that institution's leaders do offer insights into the broader institutional and intellectual genealogy of the Taliban and its contested relationship with Sufi piety. Indeed, by the estimate of Samīʿ al-Ḥaqq (d. 2018), the Dār al-ʿUlūm's director from 1988 until his death in 2018, "nearly 90 percent of Taliban leadership graduated from Darul Uloom Haqqaniyya."[14] Its alumni include the founder of the Afghan Taliban, Mullah Omar, as well as the leader of the Ḥaqqānī terror network, Jalaluddin Haqqani.[15]

Specifically, this chapter makes the case that "ideological" explanations for Taliban attacks against Sufi saints' shrines are limited. While Ḥaqqānī scholars have criticized some devotional practices at Sufi shrines, they have not called for violence against the shrines or their devotees.[16] On the contrary, their stance fits within Deobandi approaches to Sufism generally: that Sufism is an integral, if not essential, aspect of Islamic piety, that it ought to be centered around self-reformation rather than saintly devotions, that the companionship of a Sufi master is the best means of effecting this self-reformation, that Sufi saints ought to be revered as moral exemplars rather than intercessors, and that many of the practices that have coalesced around the shrines of Sufi saints are illicit innovations in religious practice, known as *bidʿah*, and invitations to associate God's divinity with the saints interred there, known as *shirk*.[17]

Some readers, by this point, will ask: Surely in the "ideological" violence of the Deobandi discourse on *bidʿah* and *shirk* lay the seeds of real violence? This may be the case, in this context as in others. At minimum, however, this chapter makes clear that there is no reflexively anti-Sufi stance among Deobandi antecedents of the Taliban, let alone in Deobandi thought as a whole. More broadly, in much the same way that Brian Bond's contribution to this volume (chapter 6) proposes that we situate debates about the Sufi musical assembly, the *samāʿ*, within local understandings of space, my chapter proposes that we view recent attacks on saints' shrines through the lens of local politics rather than purportedly inherent anti-Sufi antipathies.

The Dār al-ʿUlūm Ḥaqqāniyya

The Dār al-ʿUlūm Ḥaqqāniyya has featured in nearly every journalistic indictment of Pakistan's madrasas in the last two decades. Thus, as the *Philadelphia Inquirer* opined as early as 1998, "Darul Uloom Haqqania is to the Taliban as Harvard was to the Kennedy administration."[18] Christina Lamb, writing for the UK's *Sunday Times*, called it the "Eton of budding Islamic warriors."[19] Such analogies with renowned Western academic institutions are meant to convey its unparalleled importance among Pakistan's seminaries. It is, indeed, one of the first madrasas to be founded in the wake of Partition. Despite the coverage Dār al-ʿUlūm Ḥaqqāniyya has received in newspapers and policy studies, it has received almost no attention from scholars of Islam and South Asia, and its collection of legal opinions (*Fatāwa-e Ḥaqqāniyya*) in particular—on which this chapter is largely based—remains virtually unexamined in any scholarly context.[20]

The Dār al-ʿUlūm Ḥaqqāniyya was founded in 1947 by Mawlānā ʿAbd al-Ḥaqq (d. 1988). He established the madrasa in his birthplace, Akora Khattak, part of what was then the North-West Frontier Province, now Khyber Pakhtunkhwa.

Born in January 1909, ʿAbd al-Ḥaqq studied in madrasas in Meerut and Amroha, and entered the Dār al-ʿUlūm Deoband in 1928 or 1929. At Deoband, like any student there, he focused on mastering the six canonical collections of Sunni hadith, and in fact studied hadith with one of the towering personalities of Deobandi history, Ḥusain Aḥmad Madanī, a relationship that would prove formative for him. He also studied with Muhammad Shafīʿ, who would become, after Partition, the founder of the Dār al-ʿUlūm Karachi and arguably the most important Deobandi scholar in Pakistan.

Mawlānā ʿAbd al-Ḥaqq graduated from the Dār al-ʿUlūm Deoband in 1933 or 1934, and later taught there from 1943 until Partition in 1947.[21] Connections to the Deoband movement and the reformist currents out of which that movement grew are cited as inspirations for the establishment of the Dār al-ʿUlūm Ḥaqqāniyya, which locates its ultimate origins in the thought of Shāh Walī Allāh as channeled through Sayyid Aḥmad Barelwī (d. 1831).[22] Ḥaqqānī scholars narrate a story in which Sayyid Aḥmad's armies were attacked at the site where Dār al-ʿUlūm Ḥaqqāniyya would later be built, the "sacred blood of martyrs" being "imbibed" by the soil.[23] These currents reached their apex in the founding of Dār al-ʿUlūm Deoband. Hence, one scholar would later describe Dār al-ʿUlūm Ḥaqqāniyya as "a spitting image of [Dār al-ʿUlūm] Deoband."[24]

During Ramadan of 1947, ʿAbd al-Ḥaqq was at home in Akora Khattak and could not return to Deoband because of the tumult associated with Partition. He established the Dār al-ʿUlūm Ḥaqqāniyya in Akora Khattak to accommodate students who could no longer travel to Deoband. A department for issuing fatwas, a Dār al-Iftāʾ, was established soon thereafter, where ʿAbd al-Ḥaqq served as the primary mufti.[25] Outside of his role in directing the madrasa and composing hundreds of fatwas over the course of his career, ʿAbd al-Ḥaqq, like most Deobandis, was a student of Sufism. He was the pupil of Hājji Ṣāḥib Turangzai,[26] after whose death he became devoted to Ḥusain Aḥmad Madanī, with whom he "completed all the stages of the Sufi path."[27] But like other Deobandi Sufis, "he successfully waged jihad, in a sage-like manner, against innovations (*bidʿah*) and customs (*rusūmāt*), the consequences of which were that illicit customs in Ahora Khattak and surrounding regions were ended."[28]

Upon ʿAbd al-Ḥaqq's death in 1988, ʿAbd al-Ḥaqq's son Samīʿ al-Ḥaqq was appointed chancellor of Dār al-ʿUlūm Ḥaqqāniyya, where he served until his death in 2018. Born in 1937 in Ahora Khattak, Samīʿ al-Ḥaqq graduated from Dār al-'Ulum Ḥaqqāniyya, completing his hadith training in 1957, and his study of Quran commentary (*tafsīr*) in 1958 or 1959.[29] He began teaching at the Dār al-ʿUlūm in 1958, and founded the monthly journal *Al-Ḥaqq* in 1965, where many of his fatwas first appeared.[30] Samīʿ al-Ḥaqq's works included a two-volume commentary on Muḥammad ibn al-Tirmidhī's *Shamā'il Muḥammadiyya* (also known as *Shamā'il al-Tirmidhī*), a compilation of hadiths on the character of the Prophet Muḥammad,[31] several anti-Ahmadi polemics and, most recently, political tracts on the War on Terror.[32] He also had an active political career. In 1974, Samīᶜ al-Ḥaqq addressed the Pakistan National Assembly on the "problem" of the Ahmadis, and was a member of the Senate of Pakistan from 1985 to 1991.[33] But above all, Samīᶜ al-Ḥaqq is known for his support of the Afghan mujahideen against the Soviets and his close relationship with the Taliban leadership. As Mukhtār Allāh Ḥaqqānī, editor of the *Fatāwa-e Ḥaqqāniyya*, puts it, "In the Afghani jihad and Taliban movement, Mawlānā Samīᶜ al-Ḥaqq's key role is not hidden. He played a leadership role in this jihad." He was "patron of the movement, and thousands of students and ulama of Dār al-ᶜUlūm Ḥaqqāniyya were involved."[34]

Sufism, Saints, and Sufi Devotions Among the Ḥaqqānīs

The remainder of this chapter draws from the writings of ᶜAbd al-Ḥaqq and Samīᶜ al-Ḥaqq, and especially the collected fatwas of the Dār al-ᶜUlūm Ḥaqqāniyya, to understand Deobandi approaches to Sufism, Sufi saints, and saintly devotions in contemporary northwest Pakistan broadly, and within the Dār al-ᶜUlūm Ḥaqqāniyya specifically. I show that these scholars regard Sufism as not only legitimate but as a *necessary* means of cultivating piety and a life in accord with the Prophet Muḥammad's sunna.

Like any fatwa collection, most fatwas in the six-volume *Fatāwa-e Ḥaqqāniyya* concern mundane aspects of religious belief and practice: prayer, fasting, charity, and the like. They rarely provide detailed legal rationales for their verdicts, but they do typically cite wide-ranging sources in Ḥanafī jurisprudence.[35] They are almost all undated and do not indicate the identity of the individual who requested the fatwa or the mufti that answered it. But the collection does state that most of the queries came from the region near the Dār al-ᶜUlūm.[36] Significantly, most of the fatwas that expound on Sufism derive from a book within the second volume, the Book of the Sufi Path (*Kitāb al-Sulūk*), whereas most of the fatwas that are critical of Sufi practices derive from the first volume, the Book of Belief and Faith (*Kitāb al-ᶜAqāʾid wa-l-Īmāniyyāt*), which discusses not just "right" belief but attempts to correct erroneous belief as well. This distinction is suggestive of how these scholars conceptualize Sufism: "innovations" such as visiting saints' graves, for example, are not regarded as an error within Sufism *per se* but as an error in belief more broadly.

On Sufism, Sufi Masters, and Meditative Practice

Like the Deoband movement as a whole, the *Fatāwa-e Ḥaqqāniyya* regards Sufism as an essential part of Muslim piety. In one fatwa, citing Aḥmad Sirhindī, the collection reiterates the common trope that Sufism and sharia are simply the internal and external manifestations, respectively, of the same truth. "In reality, the two are the very same thing. Thus any person who says they are separate has been overtaken by deviation."[37] Another fatwa substantiates the validity of the four major Sufi orders of the subcontinent (Qādirī, Suhrawardī, Chishtī, Naqshbandī),[38] which ʿAbd al-Ḥaqq reiterates elsewhere as well.[39]

On the level of Sufi ethics, the fatwas are clear that all Muslims must purify their lower selves (*tazkiyat-e nafs*), something best done under the tutelage of a Sufi master, who is the principal means of achieving a "union with God" (*wuṣūl ilā Allāh*).[40] How does one go about choosing a master? He must be a scholar (*ʿalim*), pious (*muttaqī*), and an ascetic (*zāhid*) in his sensibilities. He must enjoin the good and forbid evil, he must be available for companionship (*suḥbat*),[41] and he must shun illicit innovations (*bidʿah*).[42] Likewise, Samīʿ al-Ḥaqq asserts that spiritual training with a Sufi master is an essential part of becoming a complete Muslim, but cautions that one must train with a "perfected master" (*kāmil shaykh*), not with a "sinful *pīr*."[43] One individual inquires about the nature of pledging allegiance (*bayʿah*) to a Sufi master, stating that "some people understand *bayʿah* only in the context of jihad and say that the *bayʿah* between master and disciple is not its true form. Is this the case?" The mufti responds: "[Attaining] the stage of spiritual excellence (*iḥsān*) and purification of the lower self are necessary for all Muslims. In this age, one can attain the stage of spiritual excellence and purify the self through Sufism . . . and taking *bayʿah* is substantiated by the Prophet Muḥammad and the Companions."[44]

Numerous fatwas clarify Sufi meditative practices (*zikr*) and other spiritual techniques. The collection endorses, for example, the Chishtī *zikr* practice known as *zikr ḥaddādī* with reference to Niẓām al-Dīn Awrangābādī's *Niẓām al-Qulūb*, the first Chishtī manual on *zikr*.[45] Citing Shāh Walī Allāh and others, it also assuages one individual's concern about the legal status of the forty-day meditative retreat, known as *chillah*, stating the practice is "permissible without any doubt."[46]

On Saints and Their Shrines

On the subject of saints and sainthood, similarly, the *Fatāwa-e Ḥaqqāniyya* reasserts positions that it shares both with Deobandis and non-Deobandi Sufis.

Citing the Ḥanafī legal scholar Ibn ʿĀbidīn (d. 1836), the collection regards miracles (*karāmāt*) as a fundamental feature of sainthood and how saints establish their saintly status: "A deed arising from a pious, sharia-abiding person that is contrary to the normal course of things is called a miracle (*karāmat*), though it may appear strange to the common folk. But miracles are not necessary to become a saint."[47] The fatwas define a saint capaciously, and solely in terms of personal piety, in accordance with how most Deobandi texts have defined it: "Every Muslim who conforms to the sharia, is sober and abstemious, and avoids sins both major and minor is one of the saints of God and among God's friends."[48] And yet, the collection also ratifies the hierarchy of saints, answering one inquiry about the legal status of saintly ranks—*ghawth* (helper), *quṭb* (pole), and *abdāl* (substitutes), in particular—by confirming their attestation in early Sufi sources and, at least for *abdāl*, in the hadith itself.[49]

Insofar as much of Deobandis' anxiety about popular understandings of the saints revolves around their graves, the Ḥaqqānī muftis, notably, believe saints perform miracles (*karāmāt*) while alive and continue to do so after their deaths.[50] It is even possible to form a spiritual connection (*nisbat*) with a deceased saint.[51] It is only in believing that saints have the power independently of God to intercede on behalf of their followers that one begins to tread dangerously close to unbelief (*kufr*).[52] Similarly, asking any entity other than God for help (*istimdād*)—with the understanding that such an entity, "whether a prophet or a saint," has independent power to alter events—is "impermissible and forbidden."[53] One can call upon the Prophet Muḥammad, but to assume he is omnipresent when one does so is unbelief. Overall, therefore, believing in the intercession of other beings, living or dead, is acceptable, so long as it is clear that the entity who has the power is God alone, not the intermediary, just as, it says, the second caliph ʿUmar implored for rain through the mediation of the Prophet Muḥammad's uncle, ʿAbbās ibn ʿAbd al-Muṭṭalib.[54]

Popular misconceptions about the power of the saints make the masses prone to *shirk*, associating the saints with God's divinity. One individual inquires whether a person who prostrates toward a tomb is a mere sinner or an unbeliever. The mufti replies that prostrating oneself in the *vicinity* of tombs is "extremely undesirable" (*makrūh taḥrīmī*), whereas "prostrating oneself directly toward the tomb, in an attitude of veneration, is forbidden. And to consider it an act of worship is associating in God's divinity [*shirk*]."[55] It states elsewhere, even more categorically, "The whole *ummah* is in agreement that bowing before anyone besides God is impermissible and is in fact unbelief [*kufr*] and associating God with other entities [*shirk*]."[56]

Still other fatwas condemn other common devotional acts with little legal explanation, aside from the oft-cited analogy with normative Islamic ritual practice, as in the following: "It is forbidden to wipe, touch, or kiss the grave of a saint (*buzurg*), or to put stones or dust on the body. They are vile innovations. In the same way, circumambulating graves is forbidden because circumambulation is an act of worship reserved for the house of God."[57] Or they condemn a practice because of its ostensible similarity to a non-Islamic practice, as in the following: "Kissing tombs is unbelief [*kufr*] if done to honor them, and a major sin [*gunāh kabīra*] if done unwittingly. It is a practice like that of Jews and Christians."[58]

Additionally, they explain, some Sufi beliefs and practices are acceptable within elite Sufi circles but must be kept from the purview of the uninitiated or unlearned, precisely because they create opportunities for associationism (*shirk*) if misunderstood. One individual asks about the permissibility of believing in the materialization of spirits (*tajassud al-arwāḥ*), a concept most commonly associated with the Sufism of Ibn al-ʿArabī, denoting how the spirits of saints and prophets dwelling in the World of Imagination materialize in the corporeal world.[59] The mufti responds: "The spirits [*arwāḥ*] of the prophets and saints are able to materialize in the world [*dunyā*]. The writings of Rashīd Aḥmad Gangohī, Qāżī Sanāʾ Allāh Pānīpatī, and Shāh Walī Allāh approve this,[60] but it should not be part of the beliefs of the masses because such things are conducive to *shirk*."[61] Similarly, numerous fatwas endorse the practice by which a Sufi master expends spiritual force (*taṣarruf-e shaykh*) to assist disciples on the Sufi path. It is permissible to believe that a Sufi master can invisibly help initiates overcome a personal struggle or spiritual ailment, but "this should not become part of the masses' belief because it engenders the belief in [the *shaykh* having] knowledge of the unseen [*ʿilm-e ghayb*] which, in turn, leads to *shirk*."[62] Saints, too, can use such powers to help individuals, in a way analogous to *taṣarruf-e shaykh*. But, once again, the muftis caution that such a notion can be easily misunderstood by the uninitiated. God alone enables the power of the saint to wield such spiritual energies, but if the belief is that the saint exercises power himself, this likewise necessitates belief the saint has knowledge of the unseen (*ʿilm-e ghayb*), which God alone has, thus opening up the door to *shirk*.[63]

Finally, a question about "knowledge of the unseen" (*ʿilm-e ghayb*) prompts the sole reference in the *Fatāwa-e Ḥaqqāniyya* to the Barelwis, which I quote in full:

> The Barelwi sect was founded by Aḥmad Rażā Khān, who said many incorrect things about the Deobandis and other ulama, which I will not repeat here. Additionally, based on a selective omission of the statements of the Deobandis, he acquired fatwas declaring unbelief [upon the Deobandis] from ulama of the Ḥaramayn, on the basis of which many simple-minded Muslims

> have avoided the true ulama. He has also caused many innovations [*bidʿah*] and illicit customs [*rusūmāt*] to become widespread. In spite of all this, the true ulama have not declared unbelief [*takfīr*] against Khan or his followers, though one who espouses the ideas of knowledge of the unseen [*ʿilm-e ghayb*] and the notion of [the Prophet Muḥammad's] omnipresence and omniscience [*ḥāżir o nāẓir*] is certainly worthy of it. As God says, "Say [Prophet Muḥammad]: 'I am only a human being like you, one to whom it has been revealed that your god is one God'." [18:110] Or as he also says, "Say: 'Glory Be to my Lord! What am I but a human messenger?' " [17:93][64]

The stance toward Aḥmad Rażā Khān is nothing if not hostile, though the stance toward the Barelwis in general is cautiously conciliatory. They are not, it points out, to be regarded as non-Muslims. And, I have argued elsewhere, Deobandis and Barelwis have far more in common than their battle over Sufi devotionalism would suggest. Like the Deobandis, Barelwis see their movement as an expression of their commitment to the sharia, as Usha Sanyal makes clear in chapter 5 of this volume. Like the Deobandis, they, too, have critiqued *bidʿah*. And they, too, believe certain shrine-based practices lead to *shirk*.[65]

A Return to Politics

The status of the Barelwis in the *Fatāwa-e Ḥaqqāniyya* brings us full circle to the contemporary contestations with which I opened this chapter. It is clear that the muftis of Dār al-ʿUlūm Ḥaqqāniyya are conversant with, and supportive of, core Sufi ideas and practices, even as they critique others. But while this is the case, there is little interest in Sufism beyond the fatwas. Across numerous works by ʿAbd al-Ḥaqq and Samīʿ al-Ḥaqq, one finds little more than passing references to Sufism. They did not, to be sure, author any treatises or guides on Sufism, nor are there references to either figure taking Sufi disciples under their tutelage.[66] These two observations go hand in hand: The scores of treatises, guides, and commentaries that a Deobandi like Ashraf ʿAlī Thānawī (d. 1943) composed were done primarily for the benefit of his disciples, as well as to clarify issues concerning Sufism for the general reader.[67] Compared to Thānawī, at least, there is simply little concern for Sufism outside of the fatwas—which, themselves, are responses to the interest of individual Muslims in Khyber Pakhtunkhwa and elsewhere, rather than expressions of the concerns of their authors.

What might this suggest? The legacy of Ḥusain Aḥmad Madanī, rather than Ashraf ʿAlī Thānawī, towers over the works of the Ḥaqqānī scholars.[68] As Muhammad Qasim Zaman has noted, referring specifically to the Taliban, "Madani is . . . held in considerably higher esteem in militant Deobandi circles today than is Thanawi."[69] Barbara Metcalf noted the irony in this, citing a letter written in praise of Madanī by none other than Samīʿ al-Ḥaqq, "known today for his role in educating the Taliban, whose politics could not, of course, differ more dramatically from Madani's."[70] But it's also ironic given Madanī's fierce opposition to the creation of the state of Pakistan.[71] In the letter mentioned above, Samīʿ al-Ḥaqq praised Madanī's immense knowledge and unassailable virtue, conceding that even though there was discomfort within some Deobandi lineages about Madanī's "political tack" (*siyāsī maslak*), there was absolute consensus about his stature as a scholar and teacher. But nowhere in the letter does he mention Pakistan.[72] Nonetheless, Madanī has become, for many Deobandis in Pakistan, the paragon of the politically engaged activist scholar who stood up to the British, and Ashraf ʿAlī Thānawī has become his foil, the hermetic mystic-scholar who actively shunned politics and critiqued ulama who did not, especially under the aegis of Indian nationalism.[73] For the Ḥaqqānīs in particular, the "Madanite" lineage came to exert far more influence than the "Thanawite" lineage.[74] This may help to explain why Sufism is not a central concern of theirs, but it is not sufficient to explain it fully.

Is this indicative of something larger? Whether, and to what extent, Deobandis' relationship with Sufism has changed in recent decades is an open question. Beyond the Ḥaqqānī scholars I have discussed here, there is evidence to suggest that Sufism is no longer as central to Deobandi thought as it was for Deobandi scholars from Gangohī to Thānawī and beyond, and that Deobandi Sufism has become preoccupied with its own "discourse of decline."[75] But other evidence belies such a notion. To take just one example, Muḥammad Rafīʿ ʿUsmānī, president of Dār al-ʿUlūm Karachi and among the most prominent Deobandis in Pakistan today, has recently argued not just the standard trope that Sufism is an indelible part of Islam, but indeed that knowledge of Sufi principles is incumbent on all Muslims individually (*farz-e ʿayn*) and that mastery of Sufism is a duty of Muslims collectively (*farz-e kifayah*).[76] At the least, we must keep in mind the ongoing internal complexity of Deobandi thought: While we may be able to discern overarching contours, there is no one "Deobandi" stance on any given subject, Sufi or otherwise.

Let me conclude by returning to the theme with which I opened: the politics of contemporary contestations over Sufi saints' shrines. Referring to the Wahhabi anathematization of "saint worship," Carl W. Ernst has noted, "While the language of the polemic is theological (saint worship equals idolatry), the form of the struggle is distinctly political."[77] In a similar vein, Zaman observes that Taliban attacks on saints' shrines cannot be separated from the Pakistani government's highly politicized embrace of Sufism after 9/11, a period in which Prime Ministers Pervez Musharraf and Yusuf Riza Gilani set up a "National Sufi Council" and a "Sufi Advisory Council," respectively, to combat "extremism and fanaticism."[78] The Taliban were all too aware of the West's embrace as well. In 2010 the U.S. ambassador allocated nearly $150,000 for the preservation of three Sufi shrines in the Punjab. Zaman concludes, "Insomuch as venerated Sufi shrines have become associated with the War on Terror, it is not surprising that some of that terror has come to visit these shrines."[79]

In the wake of the Taliban's destruction of the Buddhas at Bamiyan, scholars such as Jamal Elias and Finbarr Flood called for seeing this act not as some primordial expression of "Islamic" iconoclasm, but as a context-specific power struggle with precedents throughout the medieval and early modern periods.[80] We would do well to approach the destruction of Sufi shrines in the same light, as A. Afzar Moin has argued.[81] Accordingly, I have argued that we should resist the temptation to regard attacks on Sufis and their shrines simply as a "weaponized" version of the Deobandi critique of Sufism. That critique, surely, informs the hostility toward these shrines, but that hostility cannot be reduced to it. While we can debate the extent to which deeming a practice to be *bidʿah* or *shirk* is tantamount to endorsing violence against those who engage in it, we must be cautious in assuming that one leads, necessarily and inexorably, to the other.

5

Sufism Through the Prism of Sharia

A Reformist Barelwi Girls' Madrasa in Uttar Pradesh, India

USHA SANYAL

As is well known, Sunnis in South Asia self-identify not only in terms of the "path" or "way" (sunna) of the Prophet Muḥammad but also—in many cases, though by no means universally—in terms of subgroups within this overarching category. The frequently used Urdu word *maslak*, another word for "path," is derived from the Arabic *sulūk*, which means "comportment" or "behavior." This multiplicity of terms testifies to the fact that, for Muslims in South Asia, there are paths within paths. More specifically, Anwar Qureshi writes, a "maslak organizes a spiritual genealogy to which an adherent belongs, while also providing a hierarchy of authorities and teachings through which one engages the Islamic tradition. Related to this,. . . the maslak is characterized by a variety of practices that its particular discursive constellation authorizes that fashion and shape the adherent."[1]

The Barelwi *maslak*, so named after the nineteenth-century Islamic scholar (*ʿalim*) Mawlānā Aḥmad Rażā Khān Barelwī (1856–1921), is one of the major South Asian *maslaks*.[2] Sufism in the Barelwi case has, from the inception of the movement, coexisted with the category of *ʿilm* (or knowledge, specifically knowledge of the sharia). On the one hand, Aḥmad Rażā Khān Barelwī had numerous Sufi disciples in the Qādirī order who took disciples of their own and added the word "Riżwī" (sometimes spelled "Rażwī") to the end of their names to indicate their Sufi affiliation with him. On the other hand, Aḥmad Rażā Khān was more interested in writing fatwas and scholarly rebuttals of his Deobandi and other contemporaries than in writing poetry or *malfūẓāt* (Sufi discourses), though he did the latter as well. His followers recognized his scholarship by giving him the title *mujaddid* (renewer) of the fourteenth Islamic century, and referred to him as Aʿlā Ḥażrat ([his] eminent presence). In the next generation, his eldest son, Mawlānā Ḥāmid Rażā Khān, was known by the title Ḥujjat al-Islām (proof of Islam) and his younger son, Mawlānā Muṣṭafā Rażā Khān, as Muftī-e Aʿẓam-e Hind (India's great jurisconsult). These titles refer to the Islamic legal tradition, not to Sufism. They are an important indicator of the self-image of the Barelwi movement, which regards itself first and foremost as a *Sunni* movement, one which takes the Prophet Muḥammad's practice or "way" (sunna) as its model of behavior, and only secondarily as Barelwi, Riżwī, and so on.[3] In practical terms, and in contrast to what many people assume about Barelwis, this means that Sufism coexists with and *is subsidiary to* the sharia as interpreted by Aḥmad Rażā Khān and others.

As an example of this arrangement, I present in this chapter ethnographic data from a Barelwi girls' madrasa in Uttar Pradesh (U.P.), India, which, I argue, not only prioritized sharia over Sufism but also inculcated reformist practices and perspectives in students while positioning itself firmly within the Barelwi tradition. Working from the opposite (Sufi) end and from the ground up, I start by presenting a powerful performative tradition in the madrasa that signals its Sufi identity. This allows me to place the madrasa within a Sufi genealogy that traces its descent from Aḥmad Rażā Khān through his younger son, Muṣṭafā Rażā Khān. I then turn to the ways that the madrasa is not just Sufi but reformist. In doing so, I am positioning the Barelwis within the same Islamic tradition as the Deobandis,[4] rather than as antithetical to them, as is common in the scholarly discourse, while recognizing that Barelwis and Deobandis differ from one another in ways that each *maslak* considers significant.[5] In this, my argument echoes that of Brannon Ingram in chapter 4. Ingram's examination of the Dār al-ʿUlūm Ḥaqqāniyya, which has Deobandi roots, shows that, like the Deobandis, this "Taliban" madrasa regards the practice of Sufism as an integral part of Muslim piety. My chapter also shows that failure to recognize that there are internal distinctions within the Barelwi movement results in an oversimplified and inaccurate picture of this movement, which is a complex and historically important part of the South Asian Muslim landscape.

A Performance Tradition: The Weekly *Anjuman*

Every Thursday night, between the evening (*maghrib*) and night (*ʿishāʾ*) prayers, or about 7:00 to 9:00 p.m. in the summertime, the students of Jamiʿa Nur al-Shariʿat girls' madrasa (Jamiʿa Nur, for short)[6] in Shahjahanpur, U.P., participate in a student-led program called an *anjuman* in which they recite Quran verses (*qirāʾat*), poems in praise of the Prophet (*naʿt*) and saintly figures (*manqabat*), or give sermons (*taqrīr, waʿẓ*) based on hadith on a variety of themes (prayer, fasting, the importance of the mother, and so on) that reinforce the lessons learned at the madrasa.[7] Every student is called upon to do this a few times in the course of the year. At the end of the program, each participant's name is called out by the student MCing the program, and she is given one of three grades (high [*aʿlā*], middle [*awsaṭ*], or poor [*adnā*]) on her performance and told what mistakes she made. Then, the following week's participants' names are announced, along with the category in which they must perform. Because sermons are the most difficult and praise poems are the least so, newcomers and junior students are more likely to be assigned the latter. Each time a girl's name is called out, she is required to stand up.

In August 2015 I was present at an *anjuman* in which a student recited a poem in praise of a Sufi saint (*manqabat*). Interestingly, the "saint" was none other than Mawlānā Aḥmad Rażā Khān. The poem was written by a young poet (*shāʿir*) from Bareilly whose name was not known to the student reciting it.[8] The poem had a strong rhythm and sound alliteration, lost in English translation, which made it a delightful listening experience for the audience. The student's delivery was spirited and highly effective, holding the attention of her audience throughout. As Mareike Winkelmann has noted, student performances at madrasa events show the distinct influence of popular culture such as Hindi films, although students did not listen to Hindi films or music directly.[9] Yet the reformist tone of the madrasa was evident in the fact that student performers had no instrumental accompaniment (on this debate, see Brian Bond's arguments in chapter 6). Students came to the front of the hall when called upon, recited from memory without the help of written notes, and returned to their seats in the audience when they had finished. There was no clapping or audience response, though the MC delivered a formulaic note of appreciation before calling on the next speaker.

The words of the poem made explicit the Barelwi identity of the madrasa. Allusions scattered throughout the poem gave ample evidence of themes such as Aḥmad Rażā's love of the Prophet, which is a signature Barelwi refrain.[10] However, unlike the well-known flagship Barelwi boys' madrasa, Madrasa Ashrafiyya in Mubarakpur, eastern U.P., the girls at the Jamiʿa Nur al-Shariʿat did not engage in open denunciation of other Sunni groups. The difference between the two madrasas may be understood in terms of the histories and ethos of the two institutions. As Arshad Alam explains, "It [was] mandatory for all officials of the [Madrasa Ashrafiyya], including the members of the general committee and working committee, to take a pledge of loyalty to the madrasa. This pledge includes the statement, 'I am a true Sunni Muslim and I believe in every word of *Hussam al-Haramain*.'"[11] In this 1906 fatwa, which received signatures of approval from several ulama of the Haramayn, Aḥmad Rażā declared that several Deobandi ulama and the founder of the Ahmadiyyah movement were *kafirs* (infidels). Given the fatwa's strong denunciation of several eminent Deobandis, it has been a source of friction between the two *maslaks* ever since, and the fact that the Madrasa Ashrafiyya consequently requires such a declaration is extraordinary. The madrasa was also founded in a spirit of deep rivalry with the Deobandis of Mubarakpur, indicated in the use of the word *akhāṛā* (wrestling arena) by the parties involved.[12] Such is not the spirit animating Jamiʿa Nur.

To return to the poem I heard at the *anjuman* in 2015,[13] some of its verses were:

He who is the lifeblood of Sunni identity
Leader of the community
He who is the slave of the Prophet
His name is Rażā
Refrain: My Rażā, my Rażā . . .

The beloved of the Prophet
Who is a mountain of knowledge
You are the roar of the lion
The one of whom the Wahhabis are afraid
Many of them were thoroughly reformed [changed]
He is the leader of love
Refrain: My Rażā, my Rażā . . .

After Rażā, Mustafa Rażā
was gifted to us
Who made it possible for every Sufi seeker
to meet the pure Helper [ʿAbd al-Qādir al-Jīlānī, founder of the Qādirī order]
Now where could one find such a Sufi master
Other than in Azharī Miyāñ?
He gave us fame
His name is Rażā
Refrain: My Rażā, my Rażā . . .

He who, all his life
Has been breaking the hearts of those who are false
He in whose veins flowed
His love of the Prophet

He refuted the Wahhabis
And gave [us] the *Fatāwā-e Riżwiyyah*
He who fulfills all needs
He is the imam of love
Rażā is his name.
Refrain: My Rażā, my Rażā . . .

What ties the madrasa to the people mentioned here? First, as I noted above, it makes specific references to Aḥmad Rażā Khān as an "imam," leader of the community, not in the Shiʿi sense of the term, but in the Sufi sense as "a leader of love" (*ʿishq ka imām*), because it was "He in whose veins flowed his love of the Prophet." In keeping with the dual focus of the Barelwi *maslak* on Sufism and sharia, with the latter taking precedence over the former, he is also referred to as the author of the *Fatāwā-e Riżwiyyah* and the rebutter of "Wahhabis," namely, Deobandis in this context. So, the two go together, the Sufi and the religious scholar, or *ʿalim*. The poem mentions Aḥmad Rażā's younger son, Mustafa Rażā Khān, who was Sayyid Sahib's Sufi *pīr*. And the reference to Azharī Miyāñ is also significant, as it signals the intra-Barelwi politics rife in contemporary Bareilly (to which I turn below) and indicates that Sayyid Sahib had aligned himself with the scholarly mufti rather than the caretaker of the Sufi shrine.

The poem also makes clear, however, that these men ultimately derived their spiritual legitimacy from their descent from Aḥmad Rażā Khān, as he is its primary subject. It is, in effect, an abbreviated spiritual genealogical tree (*shajarah*) linking Sayyid Sahib to Mustafa Rażā Khān, and through him to Aḥmad Rażā, and through him to ʿAbd al-Qādir al-Jīlānī, the founder of the Qādirī order, and from there directly to the Prophet Muḥammad. Given that some of the girls at the Jamiʿa Nur al-Shariʿat were Sayyid Sahib's disciples, it was also their spiritual genealogical tree. The poem matches to an extraordinary degree—although it did not emanate from anyone at the madrasa—the lines of spiritual authority that Sayyid Sahib recognized as his own and that linked him to the worldview he and fellow Barelwis know as "Sunni."

Jamiʿa Nur al-Shariʿat, Its Founder, and the Qādirī Sufi Network Through Muṣṭafā Rażā Khān

Located in the small West U.P. town of Shahjahanpur, in 2015 Jamiʿa Nur had about four hundred girls in the boarding school in addition to about forty who studied there during the day but returned home at the end of classes. Two distinctive features of the madrasa were its sectarian affiliation and its rural, largely working-class background. In sectarian terms, as noted already, the founder and students self-identified as Barelwi Muslims, rather than one of the other major Sunni schools of thought, such as the Deobandis, with a wide following in South Asia. Also noteworthy was the fact that most of the students came from either rural families in western U.P. and neighboring Indian states, or from small towns such as Shahjahanpur, with a small number from larger cities. In many cases, the girls' parents had not studied beyond primary school. However, they had invested heavily in the education of their children, both boys and girls.

The madrasa was founded in 2003 by Sayyid Muhammad Ehsan Miyan, affectionately known as Abbā Ḥużūr ("respected father") by the madrasa students and as Sayyid Sahib by the adults around him. Sayyid Sahib was a tall, bespectacled man in his fifties with a wiry frame and energetic manner, and excellent posture. He wore a long white kurta with white pajamas, and a white cap or turban on his head, depending on the formality of the occasion. His manner was direct, informal, and open, with a touch of humor, and his language was simple, even colloquial. Originally from the western U.P. district of Kannauj, he had lived all his life in different western U.P. districts. After traveling to Bareilly to study at the Madrasa Manzar-i Islam for two years, he taught at a boys' madrasa in Pilibhit district for fifteen years. His move to Shahjahanpur was the result of his *pīr*'s perception of the need for a Barelwi presence in the area, given what he saw as an educational "desert" sorely in need of Barelwi institutions of learning for boys and girls.

In 2015, after I had known Sayyid Sahib for about three years, I came to think of him as a man in a hurry, as he had a full agenda of self-appointed goals. After 1999, when he founded the boys' madrasa, he founded a number of other schools as well: the girls' madrasa, as noted, in 2003; an English-medium school in Shahjahanpur in 2005 that taught the U.P. state-approved syllabus and had boys up to class V and girls up to the end of Indian high school education); a smaller Hindi-medium school in the same building that operated on an afternoon shift; a CBSE-approved public school,[14] in 2010, for about eight hundred boys and girls just outside Bareilly (about fifty miles north of Shahjahanpur) that was housed in a large building surrounded by open land and fields; and a girls' madrasa for about two hundred on the top floor of the same building. The mix of religious and secular schools was deliberate, as Sayyid Sahib firmly believed that Muslim students needed to have both kinds of education, though the emphasis between the one and the other would vary in accordance with students' personal goals and aptitudes.

Like many Barelwi scholars (ulama), Sayyid Sahib was both a teacher (*muʿallim*)—in his case, of prophetic traditions (hadith), Islamic law (*fiqh*), and occasionally Sufism (*taṣawwuf*)—and a Sufi guide and master (*murshid*) to his disciples. Also, like most Barelwi scholars, he belonged to the Qādirī Sufi order. In the nineteenth century the Qādirīs, like the reformist Chishtīs and Naqshbandīs, prided themselves on their adherence to sharia norms while at the same time maintaining a firm commitment to the ties of the "*pīrī-mūrīdī* bond, the shrine, and the ʿurs."[15] Sayyid Sahib belonged to the Sufi chain (*silsilah*) known as Riżwī Barelwi after Mawlānā Aḥmad Rażā Khān Barelwi. His Sufi master was Rażā Khān's son Mustafa Rażā Khān (d. 1981), who he and others always respectfully referred to by his title "Muftī-e Aʿzam." Mustafa Rażā's tomb was in Bareilly, and his descendants had built a Sufi center in the same area. His *pīr* was the true kind, Sayyid Sahib said, one who was spiritually pure and didn't seek fame and glory.

According to Sumbul Farah, there were two main competing centers of power in Bareilly, as well as a number of "satellites."[16] One main authority was Mawlānā Akhtar Rażā Khān (known as Azharī Miyāñ), who held the office of mufti (jurist who issues fatwas) and was the only one of Aḥmad Rażā's descendants with a reputation for scholarship. A great-grandson (third-generation descendant) of Aḥmad Rażā 's through his older son, Ḥāmid Rażā Khān, he was in his seventies when I met him (unfortunately he died in 2018, which leads to an uncertain dynamic going forward). His house in Bareilly was at the center of a vast network of disciples and followers from all over the world. In 2000 he inaugurated a large and modern educational center in Bareilly called the Centre of Islamic Studies Jamiatur Raza. Financed through donations from wealthy foreign Barelwi admirers of Akhtar Rażā, it was set on a large, well-maintained campus.

The second center of spiritual authority was Subḥān Rażā Khān (known as Subḥānī Miyāñ), a fourth-generation descendant of Aḥmad Rażā. He was the head (*gaddī nashīn*) of Aḥmad Rażā's shrine and, as Azharī Miyāñ's nephew, was considerably younger than him. He managed the Madrasa Manzar-i Islam but seemed to have fewer financial resources. Sayyid Sahib respected the authority of Azharī Miyāñ, though he had not received any financial help from him, and he was on close terms with Mawlānā Taḥsīn Rażā (d. 2007), a grandson of Aḥmad Rażā Khān's younger brother Ḥasan Rażā Khān.[17]

The politics of the descendants of Aḥmad Rażā Khān in Bareilly, particularly between the scholar-mufti (Azharī Miyāñ) and the *gaddī nashīn*, the spiritual successor to the shrine (Subḥānī Miyāñ), have been explored in great detail by Farah. She writes: "The sense of entitlement that marks the family's attitude coupled with the veneration of the believers serves to characterize the

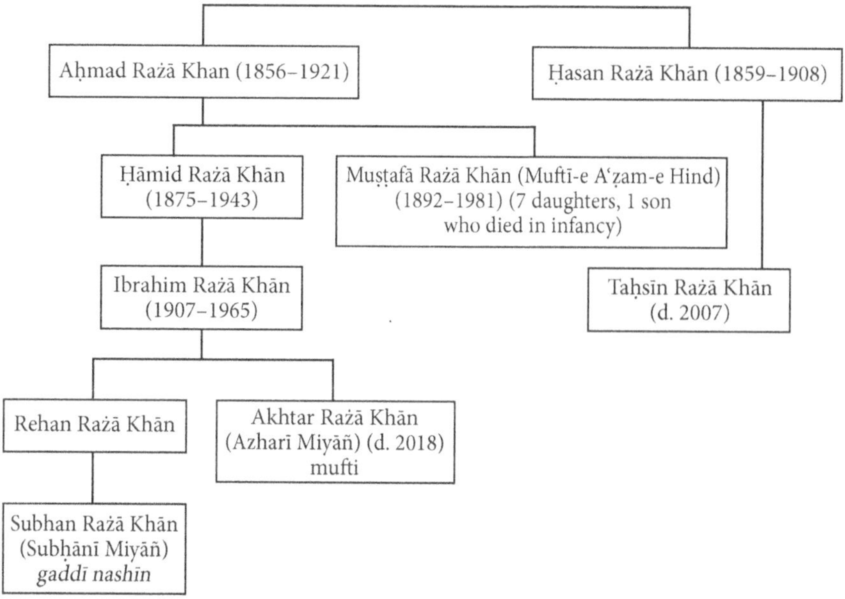

FIGURE 5.1 Abbreviated genealogical tree of Aḥmad Rażā Khān and his descendants.

descendants of Aḥmad Rażā Khān as the religious elite of Bareilly. They wield much power over the masses and occupy . . . high ritual status. The metaphor of royalty can therefore be aptly evoked in this context."[18]

Sayyid Sahib's comments to me indicated that he had distanced himself from active involvement in the affairs of the Barelwi ulama in Bareilly, choosing instead to build his own networks through travel, teaching, and Sufi ties with men in different U.P. districts. In effect, what we have here is a Sufi network that traces its spiritual roots back to Mawlānā Aḥmad Rażā Khān through his son Mawlānā Mustafa Rażā Khān, while simultaneously distancing itself from the spiritual lines that go through Aḥmad Rażā Khān's older son Ḥāmid Rażā Khān and his sons.[19] Because Mawlānā Mustafa Rażā Khān had daughters but no sons, his spiritual lineage has been overshadowed by that of Ḥāmid Rażā Khān. However, to his disciples, of whom there are many, his presence in their lives is real, even more than thirty years after his death. In many cases, the people who revered him were young boys when they took their oath of loyalty (*bay'ah*) at his hands. They ascribed small, everyday strokes of good fortune in their lives to the blessings of their *pīr*, Mustafa Rażā Khān, who is watching over their affairs.[20]

The people who had helped Sayyid Sahib build his schools from scratch were small business owners, townsmen, and villagers from the districts of Shahjahanpur and other parts of western U.P. Many were his Sufi disciples.

Bricks for the buildings had been donated by owners of brick factories that dot the landscape on the highway from Shahjahanpur to Bareilly. Cement had also been donated, while the land was purchased in small increments as finances became available.[21] This network of discipleship was a loose one, as Sayyid Sahib did not keep track of the names, physical whereabouts, or phone numbers of his disciples, and thus he was unable to tell me how many there were. He thought they numbered in the thousands. He was willing to accept as disciple any Muslim man or woman who sought to become one, telling me that, since he himself was an imperfect seeker on the spiritual path, he did not feel qualified to judge the spiritual readiness of others.

The process of becoming a disciple was simple: The would-be disciple clasped the master's hand (women did so by holding one end of a long cloth, which could be the master's turban [*ʿamāmah*] or a woman's scarf [*ḍupaṭṭā*]), recited the Muslim testament of faith (the *kalimah* or *shahāda*), and agreed to abide by certain personal standards of daily conduct. These included regular observance of the daily prayers, doing good deeds (including always telling the truth), and avoiding bad ones. Sayyid Sahib then gave the new disciple a personal supplication (*duʿāʾ*) from God—again, this varied from a general, well-known Quranic verse to a particular supplication—for his or her protection. This sealed the relationship. Subsequently, further interactions between the disciple and Sayyid Sahib occurred at unpredictable intervals, often by phone if the disciple wanted to get his advice on a personal matter.

With regard to the power dynamics in Bareilly, Sayyid Sahib was very circumspect and never directly criticized the descendants of Aḥmad Rażā Khān, who trace their lineage through Ḥāmid Rażā Khān (see fig. 5.1). He often, however, expressed his frustration with the state of the Muslim community, saying that the Muslims were their own worst enemies. Blaming the Barelwis specifically for many practices which amount to "the *dunyā* (world) entering the *dīn* (religion), instead of the *dīn* coming into the *dunyā*,"[22] he laid the responsibility on the Barelwi ulama, who he said had made a business out of their religion. On another occasion, he said:

> A Muslim has to follow the sharia, the first step of which is to offer prayer [*namāz*] regularly. If you don't take the first step, how can you climb the ladder? Likewise, Sufism [*pīri-murīdī*] also has to be conducted within those limits. But they have made it into a business. They have become egotistic and self-important just because they are descendants of Aḥmad Rażā Khān. They make you wait hours on end in their waiting rooms before they see you, then they want you to bow to them. I am not willing to do all that.

Comments such as these came up periodically in our conversations. Clearly, despite the importance of Sayyid Sahib's Sufi practice and the ways his relationships to others were deeply structured by Sufi traditions and networks, Sayyid Sahib prioritized sharia observance over Sufi practice and fealty toward *shaykhs*. This was an attitude he brought into the madrasa, which sometimes gave instruction in the madrasa a distinctly reformist aspect.

Inculcating Islamic Values in Madrasa Students

The new madrasa student is seen as a person in need of reform. Like a potter shaping clay, under Sayyid Sahib's watchful eye the madrasa shapes the contours of a new personality with the active involvement of the student herself. The process is multifaceted. To start with, some habits must be cast out. In one of his sermons on the afterlife, Sayyid Sahib admonished his listeners that "love of the world" (*dunyā kī muḥabbat*) was at the root of all sins (*gunāh*), and if allowed to grow unchecked would lead people to forget the afterlife and the path to heaven. He said:

> According to Imām Ghazālī, [love of] the world refers not only to wealth, but to everything which causes you to become forgetful [of the afterlife] before your death. . . . Every man wants his drinking water to come from a fridge, he wants cool air to blow from a cooler or AC, a double bed with good mattresses to lie on, a sofa set to sit on, fine chairs and tables, a Maruti car and a Tata vehicle, women of loose morals [*ʿuryān aur faḥḥāshī ʿawrateñ*], servants to wait on him, twenty changes of clothes, one in the morning and one in the evening, and all sorts of foods to eat. . . . All these things are the desires of the lower self [*nafs kī khwāhish*]. The one who stops these desires is on the path to heaven.[23]

The lesson, clearly, was that one must limit one's worldly desires, discipline one's lower self (the *nafs*), and keep one's eye on the long-term goal, namely, that of earning a place in heaven. But note also that the specific everyday goods that Sayyid Sahib disdains in the above passage are associated with a Western lifestyle. This is not to say that he himself never sits on a chair, or uses a car, or enjoys cold water from a fridge. Rather, as he saw it, the Muslims around him were so caught up in getting ahead in the world that they didn't think of the things that *really* mattered, namely, the life of religious observance, of *dīn*.

Elsewhere he admonished parents for getting angry with their children when the children neglected the family business, but not for watching television, playing video games, or gambling, because they themselves did these things:

> When your son enjoys himself playing chess or cards, telling lies, or neglecting his prayers and fast, do you say even once, Son, what are you doing? Think about it, have you ever upbraided him? When he neglects the shop or his responsibilities at work, how hard do you try to do something about it, supplicating God and getting amulets [*taʿwīz*] in order to make him improve his behavior?[24]

Reform of the children—sons and daughters—necessarily entailed reform of the wider Muslim community as well, in Sayyid Sahib's view. And the madrasa he directed was organized to effect just that.

Life at the Jamiʿa Nur, as in any typical South Asian madrasa, was very community-oriented.[25] Students shared living quarters, often twenty or thirty to a room, and the living space doubled as a classroom during the day. Students slept on thin cotton mattresses on the floor, rolling them up and stacking them neatly against the walls during the day. While this was one indication of financial hardship (together with the rather basic fare provided during meals), the shared living quarters fostered camaraderie and friendship among both teachers and students. I have observed teachers oiling, combing, and braiding each other's long hair every morning, laughing together, eating their meals together, sitting in their room. Being just a few years older than the senior students, most had studied in this madrasa, and some had known each other for many years. Private space and time were limited. Nevertheless, each student and teacher was held personally responsible for her compliance with the madrasa's expectations of daily prayer, religious study, respectful behavior, observance of veiling (*pardah*) practices, and so on, in a way I take to be reflective of the reformist bent of the madrasa. In this way, a pious habitus was gradually built up over the course of time, part of whom the students learned to become.[26]

Gail Minault writes that one of the hallmarks of the Muslim reform movements of the late nineteenth century was the "idea of emotional control. . . . To lead a moral Muslim life, self-control and discipline are necessary; reason must control the senses."[27] I believe that self-discipline and self-control were central to what students learned at the madrasa. When I asked students what they had learned at Jamiʿa Nur and how their educations had changed them, they told me:[28]

Student #1: The biggest lesson I learned . . . is that we should deal with everyone in a good way and we should deal with all our elders with respect, and we should deal with those who are younger than us with kindness, and we should never backbite against others. And the most important thing is that we should never stray from the truth. . . . The thing I like best about Jamiʿa Nur is that here there is great insistence on doing things according to regulation [*qānūnoñ par*], and when one is in difficulty no one leaves their side. . . . Had I not come here, I would have been lost in the pleasures of . . . worldly things,. . . and I would not have been blessed with *pardah*.

Student #2: The greatest lesson I have learned . . . is that together with our worldly lives, we must also take care of our afterlife. We must deal with others well, respect our elders, fulfill our promises, and be patient during hard times. And what we want for ourselves, we should want the same for others as well. . . . I like the fact that in Jamiʿa Nur every principle [*uṣūl*] is followed with great attention [*sakhtī, achchhī ṭaraḥ*], and all my teachers have good character, which is dear to all our hearts. And when we read, I feel I never want to stop reading. I really like to read.

Student #3: I like the rules [*qānūn*] here and [the fact that] these rules are implemented with rigor [*sakhtī ke sāth*]. The teachers here interact with us with great love. When someone is feeling unwell, others don't leave their side, and we receive a very good education. . . . When I leave here, I will teach my brothers and sisters good ways, like telling the truth, respecting our elders, offering *namāz*, keeping the fast, and so on. . . . Had I not come to Jamiʿa Nur, my life would have been incomplete without religious knowledge.

I received a number of student responses along these lines. Their responses made it clear that the religious and the social went hand in hand: Parents and teachers in particular must be respected, those younger than them cared for, and moral virtues such as truth-telling and refraining from speaking ill of others must be cultivated. So must the practice of female seclusion (*pardah*) from nonrelated males. Living a religious life thus went beyond individual religious practice—although of course the madrasa insisted on the daily performance of religious duties, particularly prayer—to encompass the social relationships in which the students were embedded. This was how the madrasa effected change and brought about socioreligious reform. It began with the self-discipline and self-control exercised by the students to fulfill their obligations as students, daughters, sisters, and practicing Muslim girls preparing for motherhood and adult responsibilities toward their families, neighborhoods, and communities.

What social impact the changes in lifestyle and mental attitude among the madrasa students will have down the road remains to be seen.

I have laid out two arguments in this essay. First, being a Barelwi school whose founder was linked to the Qādirī network of Sufis, the madrasa promoted the view that adherence to the sharia took precedence over Sufi teachings and practice. As Aḥmad Rażā stated, a *pīr* should fulfill four exacting standards: He should be a Sunni Muslim of sound faith (*ṣaḥīḥ ʿaqīdah*); he should be a scholar with sufficient knowledge of the sharia to be able to consult the sources directly without recourse to anyone else; the chain of discipleship should be unbroken between him and his spiritual master all the way back to the Prophet; and he should be a person who leads an exemplary life, and is thus a model for others to follow.[29] This was the tradition in which Sayyid Sahib operated. Simultaneously, while the madrasa did not explicitly teach about Sufism in the academic syllabus, it encouraged one to have a Sufi *pīr*, one who fulfilled the conditions set out by Aḥmad Rażā Khān, in order to be guided through the pitfalls of life. Sayyid Sahib's two daughters, who were teachers at the madrasa, were also his disciples, as were some of the older students.

In terms of everyday norms of conduct, the values that the madrasa sought to inculcate in students were the very same ones associated with Sufism, namely, a God-centered life dominated by piety, a simplicity of needs and wants, an emphasis on respect for authority, self-sacrifice, and love and service toward one's fellows. In addition, like other contemporary South Asian madrasas, this madrasa emphasized religious outreach, or *tablīgh*, seeing in the world outside a mass of Muslim men, women, and children in need of Islamic reform and education. Toward this end, it trained the students in public speaking through its weekly evening programs. However, the girls were not trained to be combative or aggressive in making their arguments. Rather, the emphasis was on quiet persuasion.

The second, related, argument I have made in this essay is that the madrasa falls within the tradition of reformist Islam, although it belongs to the Barelwi *maslak*. The Barelwis should not be viewed in monolithic terms. This essay has highlighted the internal differences between Barelwis who follow the main line of descent from Mawlānā Aḥmad Rażā Khān through his eldest son, Ḥāmid Rażā Khān, and those who follow his younger son, Mustafa Rażā Khān. In addition we need to recognize that while some Barelwis are predominantly rural, engage in customary local practices, and are not well educated, others are urban or semi-urban, engaged in small-scale private business, are educated to middle or high school if not beyond, and are part of the South Asian middle or working class. Thus, variety and complexity of socioreligious practice within the Barelwi *maslak* must be recognized as the norm, as it undoubtedly is in other *maslaks* as well.[30] Within the safety of the discursive space of the madrasa, students found the opportunity to study, learn, and gain the confidence and the self-respect of their fellows, and to think of ways of reaching out to others after they graduated. Even after they became wives and mothers, they hoped to find ways to teach the children in their neighborhoods and in the family. They wanted to become models of emulation for younger Muslim girls, just as they were at the reformist school in which they were educated.

6

Lives of a Fatwa

Sufism, Music, and Islamic Reform in Kachchh, Gujarat

BRIAN E. BOND

For generations, Muslims in Kachchh have sung and recited the Sindhi-language verses of Sufi poets, most notably those of Shāh ʿAbd al-Laṭīf Bhiṭā'ī (1689–1752). Sufi poetry performance, both with and without musical accompaniment, remains an important medium of Islamic devotion and knowledge transmission in the region. Over the past few decades, however, the increasing circulation of Islamic reformist discourses has led some Muslims to question the Islamic acceptability of performance practices that utilize musical instruments, such as *kāfī*, a Sufi song genre.[1] In the early 1970s, the Muftī-e Kachchh (jurisconsult of Kachchh) Sayyid Ḥājī Aḥmad Shāh Bukhārī-Qādirī (b. 1929) pronounced a fatwa (nonbinding legal opinion) stating that music is "impermissible" (*nājā'iz*) in Islam.[2] Aḥmad Shāh Bāwā (father), as he is respectfully called, is Kachchh's preeminent representative of the Ahl-e Sunnat wa-l-Jamāʿat (Barelwi) movement, and the region's foremost spiritual master of the Qādirī lineage of Sufis; he is a deeply influential figure who has shaped the character of Sunni Islam in the region since the late 1960s.

In this chapter, I examine the responses of two respected Kachchhi Muslim musicians to the mufti's fatwa, which has had diverse consequences for musical life in the region. I analyze their responses in relation to the moral pronouncements of the mufti and his younger relative, a popular reformist preacher. One of my aims is to show how the discourses of both musicians and reformists—regardless of their views on music's permissibility—are expressive of concerns about the ethical capacities of listening selves within spaces perceived to be beset by sexual and material desire—spaces that some of my interlocutors explicitly marked as "modern."[3]

While focusing on these men's shared concern with ethical audition, I develop a second strand of argument that examines ways in which my interlocutors' opinions about music diverge. My goal is not to rehash the "debate" about *samāʿ* (audition) and music's "status" within Islam, the finer points of which have been discussed elsewhere.[4] Rather, I am interested in how contemporary Muslims' views on music are linked to broader ethical and epistemological claims articulated within the Islamic tradition. In my analysis, I underscore the contestation of music's morality within a Sunni milieu shaped by and attached to Sufi discourse and practice. This is a phenomenon that, while acknowledged, is nonetheless partially eclipsed when "Sufis" are pitted against "legalists" and "orthodox" Muslims in literature on music and Islam. While Ahl-e Sunnat leaders in Kachchh remain committed to some practices associated with Sufi traditions, they challenge the legitimacy of other traditional practices such as Sufi song.[5] Like Brannon Ingram in chapter 4 and Usha Sanyal in chapter 5 within part 2 of this volume, this chapter lends nuance to our understanding of the ways in which Muslims in South Asia have conceived of and grappled with the relationship between Islamic legalism and aspects of locally embedded Islamic tradition and practice.

Objections to music in contemporary Kachchh are thankfully not accompanied by violence or intimidating threats, in contrast to Afghanistan and Pakistan.[6] As far as I am aware, social ostracization by other members of one's *jamāʿat* is the greatest potential consequence of publicly embracing music in Muslim communities[7]—such as the Khatrī, Memon, and Rāymā—that more uniformly refrain from including music at community celebrations such as weddings.[8] What one finds in Kachchh is intermittent objection to a practice that is otherwise well entrenched within Muslim social life. I therefore think of the differing ethical viewpoints I present here as constitutive not of a "battle" over music's role in a Muslim society,[9] but rather a conversation about how to live an ethical Muslim life.

An antimusic fatwa may seem unremarkable, a reiteration of an opinion that has been voiced for more than a millennium. But we should not presume that the assumptions and concerns underlying opposition to musical audition in modern Muslim contexts are wholly continuous with those of the past.[10] Since the late 1980s, in particular, significant socioreligious changes have occurred within Kachchh's Muslim communities for numerous reasons, including labor migration to the Gulf states, transnational ties with global Islamic reformist movements, social and political marginalization, and anti-Muslim violence and rhetoric.[11] As I discuss below, the difference between the Muftī-e Kachchh's position on music and that of his elder family members demonstrates that institutionalized Islamic learning has also played a significant role. In view of these processes and the novel contexts they have engendered, a careful examination is necessary to discern how older Islamic discourses about ethical audition—such as one finds in the eleventh-century writings of ʿAlī ibn Uthmān al-Jullābī al-Hujwīrī—converge with and diverge from similar ones in contemporary Kachchh.

Hussein Ali Agrama has argued that fatwas are not simply doctrinal imperatives, and that a fatwa can function as a mode of ethical self-cultivation for those who regard it as valid.[12] Seen in this light, a mufti's authority as an issuer of fatwas is derived from his ability to act as an ethical guide.[13] Agrama's emphasis on ethics helps us see a fatwa as something other than just a means of adapting Islamic tradition of the past to the modern problems of the present and future. It urges us to attend ethnographically to fatwa reception and take seriously the question: To what extent do individuals bring fatwas to bear on their lives? As I discuss below, the Muftī-e Kachchh's antimusic fatwa has been rejected or ignored by many Muslim musicians in the region, who have thus implicitly disputed his authority to act as an ethical guide in that sphere of their lives. In order to understand the circulation of diverse strands of Islam, it is vital to examine the kinds of "ethical work" that individuals undertake, and the processes, activities, and arguments by which ethical and epistemological positions are rendered authoritative or not.[14]

Historically, Islamic concerns with music making and audition constitute a set of themes of moral problematization.[15] These themes include: (1) music's potential to distract from one's incumbent duties, especially prayer; (2) the association of music, particularly string and wind instruments, with alcohol consumption and Satan; and (3) music's sensual power and its concomitant potential to lead one to engage in improper sexual behavior. In my conversations with reformists and musicians, it is this last theme—usually expressed as an anxiety about the lack of gender segregation in musical spaces—that arises most frequently. I submit that this stems from a concern, more acutely voiced by reformists, with the maintenance of Islamic forms of sociability in an era seen to be ridden with moral pitfalls that threaten to undermine patriarchal norms of gendered space. This differs subtly but significantly from the concerns one encounters in older discourses about *samāʿ* spaces, in which it is the aspirant's progress on the Sufi path that is at stake.

In addition to the themes outlined above, two more themes of moral problematization surface in my interlocutors' responses. They index concerns that, even if not uniquely modern, have perhaps acquired greater salience in contemporary Kachchh, a region that has undergone significant social upheaval since the 2001 earthquake.[16] The first theme is the commodification of musical performance and its deleterious effect on the ethical dispositions of performers. The second theme, more specific to reformist concerns, is the perceived association of certain musical practices with Hindus, which is one manifestation of a long-standing effort to rid South Asian Muslim communities of what are seen as locally rooted, un-Islamic customs.[17] In what follows, I reflect on what the surfacing of these themes in discourses about music in western India reveals about wider concerns with ethical Islamic practice, and where, or in whom, Islamic authority and knowledge can be located.

A Note on Islam in Kachchh

Kachchh is a border and littoral district of Gujarat, adjacent to Sindh, Pakistan. Muslims make up between a quarter and a third of Kachchh's population of about two million people, a large proportion compared to most regions of India. Most Muslims in the district identify as followers of the Ahl-e Sunnat.[18] There are also adherents of the Tablīghī Jamāʿat missionary movement, as well as Shiʿi communities like the Dawoodi Bohra and Khoja Ismaili. The Ahl-e Hadith movement has been influential in pastoralist communities in the Banni and Pacham areas of northern Kachchh since the 1960s.[19] My focus here is on Muslims who identify as followers of Ahl-e Sunnat wa-l-Jamāʿat and claim the identifier "Sunni."[20]

Kachchh has historically had strong social and cultural connections with Sindh, which were continually renewed through trade, migration, pilgrimage, and cattle-grazing routes. Although India's Partition in 1947, the more decisive closure of the India-Pakistan border after the 1965 and 1971 wars, and the incorporation of Kachchh into the state of Gujarat in 1960 have contributed to the obstruction of these social and cultural linkages, Muslims in Kachchh continue to see Sindh as a fount of valued cultural production, especially poetry, music, and textiles.[21] Most people in the district speak Kachchhi, a southern dialect of Sindhi, and Sindhi Sufi poetry is an important medium through which Muslims engage with the Quran and hadith. Shāh ʿAbd al-Laṭīf Bhitāʾī, the most revered poet of the Sindhi language, embedded phrases from the Quran within his verses and conveyed foundational Islamic ideas through locally meaningful symbols.[22] Like other Sufi poets of the Indus Valley, he employed vernacular tragic romances (Sindhi-Kachcchi: *qiṣṣā*, sing. *qiṣṣo*; also *dāstān*) as allegories for the human soul's longing for reunion with God. Among Muslim poetry enthusiasts in Kachchh, Shāh's poetry is seen as brimming with symbolic references to Islamic history, cosmology, eschatology, and soteriology. Sindhi Sufi poetry, especially when sung and recited, is an affectively potent and deeply localized form of engagement with the Islamic discursive tradition.[23]

Sung Sufi poetry historically played an important role in the process of producing Muslim religious subjects in South Asia,[24] and poetry performance in contemporary Kachchh continues to be a medium for the transmission of Islamic knowledge in rural Muslim communities. Performers of *kāfī*, the region's most popular Sufi genre, interweave their melodic renderings of poetry with storytelling (*dāstān*) and explication (*bayān*) to ensure that their listeners understand the "real" (*ḥaqīqī*) meanings of metaphorical poetic texts. Poetry performance, both sung and recited, thus functions as a form of Islamic pedagogy that imparts knowledge of how one should conduct oneself in the world, and what sort of relationship one should aim to cultivate with God. In this way, it enables the cultivation of disciplined sensibilities that sustain locally embedded Islamic tradition.[25] Crucially though, for some Muslims in Kachchh, incorporating musical instruments into poetry performance—which, in Islamic terms, transforms "recitation" into the morally problematic "music"—has the potential to detract from its ethical value.

The Ethical Auditor

Islamic reformism in Kachchh today extends the project—continuous in South Asia since the late eighteenth century—of revising Islamic practice.[26] In the late nineteenth century, Aḥmad Raẓā Khān Barelwī (1856–1921) initiated the Ahl-e Sunnat wa-l-Jamāʿat movement, which defended shrine-based practices, especially the practice of requesting deceased Friends of God (*awliyāʾ Allāh*) to intercede with God on the devotee's behalf.[27] As a reaction to the Deoband school and the scripturalist Ahl-e Hadith movement, the Ahl-e Sunnat might be best described as "traditionalist" rather than "reformist." Nevertheless, as a socioreligious movement participating in the conscious (re)definition of Islam in colonial India, it too can accurately be placed under the rubric of Islamic reformism.[28]

Although Aḥmad Raẓā and his followers defended practices associated with Sufism, Aḥmad Raẓā was opposed to *qawwālī* musical performance at shrines and during *ʿurs* festivals.[29] Contemporary Ahl-e Sunnat leaders appear to be divided over the question of whether or not musical instruments are admissible in *samāʿ*. While Sufi practice is often linked with musical performance, Sufis have never unanimously supported its use. Members of the Naqshbandi order famously have not,[30] though one can of course find exceptions to this position in practice.[31]

The writings of the eleventh-century Lahore-based Sufi ʿAlī ibn Uthmān al-Jullābī al-Hujwīrī (d. 1077), whose *Kashf al-Maḥjūb* is the oldest surviving Persian treatise on Sufism, are useful for considering how modern Islamic discourses about music differ from older ones. Al-Hujwīrī's highly ambivalent but ultimate acceptance of *samāʿ* (audition) as a *potentially* ethical practice makes his writing amenable to this project. In contrast to Abū Ḥāmid al-Ghazālī (1058–1111), who wrote of the benefits of *musical* audition,[32] al-Hujwīrī's approval of *samāʿ* seems to have been limited to melodically recited poetry *without* instrumental accompaniment, a practice not considered "music" or often even "singing" in Islamic terms.[33] This crucial difference is obscured at times in Reynold Nicholson's English translation, in which he occasionally glosses "*samāʿ*" as "music."[34] This is a significant slippage: While *samāʿ* can in certain contexts denote practices employing instruments besides the human voice, this is not always the case.

In his chapter on *samāʿ*, al-Hujwīrī notes that "the obligatoriness of knowing God is ascertained by means of hearing . . . and for this reason the Sunnis regard hearing as superior to sight in the domain of religious obligation."[35] The recognition of audition as the most powerful component of the human sensorium has led countless legal scholars, theologians, and spiritual leaders to engage in a debate concerning the "admissibility" of music and dance.[36] While conceding that *samāʿ* could have potential spiritual benefits, al-Hujwīrī emphasized that this potential depends on the dispositions of listeners and performers.[37] In his view, no absolute judgment can be made on the moral propriety of audition: "Its lawfulness depends on circumstances and cannot be asserted absolutely: if audition produces a lawful effect on the mind, then it is lawful; it is unlawful if the effect is unlawful, and permissible if the effect is permissible."[38] Moreover, he does not conceive of the self as a static entity; one's ability to listen ethically is determined by one's location (*maqām*) on the Sufi path.

Despite acknowledging the potential benefits of *samāʿ*, al-Hujwīrī implored aspirants not to make a habit of practicing it, lest one "cease to hold it in reverence."[39] Beginners should be especially careful: The spaces in which *samāʿ* is practiced may bring one into close proximity with objects of sexual attraction, namely women and male youths.[40] Such concerns are not confined to worm-eaten treatises; they have echoes in contemporary Kachchh. Just as different spaces determine the character of a sound's reverberations, these echoes resound differently in the discourses of musicians and reformists, who have distinct views about the ethical capacities of modern selves.

Samāʿ in the "Modern" Era

The Muftī-e Kachchh Aḥmad Shāh Bāwā returned to Kachchh in the mid-1960s after completing his formal Islamic education in Dhoraji (Saurashtra, Gujarat) and Bombay, and appears to have first issued his antimusic fatwa in the early 1970s. A written version of the fatwa's initial pronouncement has proven elusive, but anecdotal evidence suggests that news of it was published in a Bhuj-based Gujarati newspaper aimed at a Muslim readership. One iteration of Aḥmad Shāh Bāwā's position can be found in his popular 1986 Gujarati translation (reprinted ten times) of the Urdu text *Jannatī Zewar* (Heavenly ornaments, 1979).[41] *Jannatī Zewar* was written by Aḥmad Shāh Bāwā's teacher, the mufti ʿAllāmah ʿAbd al-Muṣṭafā Aʿẓamī, as an Ahl-e Sunnat answer to the influential Deobandi text *Bihishtī Zewar* (also Heavenly ornaments).[42] In this text geared toward youth, Aʿẓamī states that the following activities are "impermissible": dancing, clapping, singing/listening to songs, and playing instruments such as the *sitār*, harmonium, *chang*, *tanbūr*, and *dhol*.[43] One is permitted to play the *daff* frame drum on Eid days and at weddings, but only if one does not follow the "rules of music" (*mūsīqī ke qawāʿid*)[44] and uses the drum only for the purposes of announcing the celebration.[45]

In a recently published fatwa collection in Gujarati, the Muftī-e Kachchh provided two music-related fatwas. In the first, he states that it is "forbidden" (*ḥarām*) for a Muslim professional musician to donate his earnings to a mosque or madrasa because singing with instruments is *ḥarām*.[46] The second fatwa is given in response to a question that asks, "If Shāh ʿAbd al-Laṭīf Bhiṭāʾī sang to the accompaniment of the *tanbūro* drone lute, why do ulama object to people doing so today?"[47] The mufti answers:

> It is not proven anywhere that Shāh ʿAbd al-Laṭīf Bhiṭāʾī, mercy of God be upon him, himself played *tanbūro* and sang. It is only said that this was so. If it is true, this is permitted [*mubāḥ*] only for those Sufis . . . who are people of the heart [*ahl-e dil*], who become intoxicated with love of Prophet and love of God, in whose heart the light of God burns along with the sound of the playing of the Sufi's *tanbūro*'s string. But if someone like me sits in a gathering like this that is going on, it becomes *ḥarām* for everyone. This matter is only a matter for blessed Sufis; for us people this is impermissible and prohibited [*manaʿ*]. (Fatāwā-e Razwīyā Jild–10)[48]

In this response, the Muftī-e Kachchh cites the Ahl-e Sunnat's main fatwa collection to affirm that he—the head of the Qādirī order in Kachchh, a man who has thousands of devotees who revere him as a living Friend of God and come to him for healing through his supplicatory prayers—has not reached a spiritual station sufficient to qualify him for ethical audition. While one might interpret this as a Sufi performance of self-effacement, it is also a savvy rhetorical move: by placing himself in the category of "us people," the mufti puts ethical musical audition beyond the pale for the average Muslim. He deftly redraws the ethical boundary integral to the widespread Sufi position that certain practices are acceptable for advanced, learned (*khwāṣṣ*) Sufis but impermissible for less-learned, ordinary (*ʿawām*) Muslims (see Ingram in chapter 4 of this volume for a discussion of another application of the elite/ordinary distinction).

In 2015 I interviewed Aḥmad Shāh Bāwā's middle-aged relative Rashid,[49] who has assumed many of the duties of the elderly mufti. Rashid travels around Kachchh constantly, giving sermons at weddings and on Islamic holidays in an effort to teach people how to become better Muslims. As I spoke with Rashid about *samāʿ*, he echoed the opinion of the mufti and al-Hujwīrī, stating that if one could keep oneself completely absorbed in contemplation of God, then *samāʿ* with musical instruments would theoretically be permissible. But he argued that modernity has ushered in a state of moral precariousness such that Sufis who could participate in musical audition without moral infractions no longer exist, and that in contemporary times music will inevitably lead to dancing and the mixing of genders. Rashid said:

> The *danbūrā* [drone lute] is not *ḥarām*.[50] The instruments which are around these days, and the ones like them in the old days, what's wrong with them? There is no *adab* [propriety] in them. And that music is *ḥarām* in which "ladies" are present, to which "ladies" might dance, in which they might sing.[51] If one maintains *adab*, then it is permitted to listen to *danbūrā*, but that *adab* should be there. . . . But at this time, in this era [*zamānah*], no one can maintain that *adab*. Only some Sufi [will be able]. Nowadays it's the "modern" era. If a youth comes [to listen], the first thing he will look at is the "ladies." Right? We know![52]

For Rashid—indeed, for all of my male interlocutors, including musicians—the moral questionability of musical performance stems from a concern about the intrusion of females into male homosocial spaces. This is neither surprising nor novel. Al-Hujwīrī warned that women might slyly watch dervishes engaged in *samāʿ* from roofs or elsewhere.[53] But for Rashid the problem is particularly acute in the "modern" era. He said of the past, "In those days . . . 'ladies' weren't included. There were only 'gents.'" Rashid continually referred to an indeterminate earlier period in which "real" (*aṣlī*) Sufis listened to music while observing the restrictions that *adab* entails. According to him, such Sufis hardly exist today: "And where could one find a Sufi like that these days, who listens to music with *adab*?," he asked rhetorically. Rashid's response suggests a discomfort with modern spaces, in which women supposedly circulate more freely than they once did. His critique of *samāʿ* with musical accompaniment is undergirded by this concern, as he casts doubt on the sustainability of ethical selves within a modern order in which *adab* is impossible to maintain. In this fragile moral landscape, the possibility of ethical musical audition is negated because musical contexts are seen as inevitably compromised by gender mixing and therefore the potential of sexual desire.

It is crucial to emphasize that Rashid and the Muftī-e Kachchh wholly embrace Sufi poetry and its performance. But like many Sufi predecessors, they advocate for performance in homosocial contexts without musical accompaniment, in which performers do not "sing" but melodically "recite" verses. In their view, Sufi poetry performance is an ethically and spiritually valuable practice but only when unencumbered by the moral baggage of "music." I attended a few "music-less" *kāfī* performances, which were hosted by men who abide by the mufti's teachings and had requested the invited performers—some of whom otherwise perform as singers with instrumental accompanists—to melodically recite poetry unaccompanied. Such performances are rare, however, and a consequence of Sunni reformists' efforts is that many Muslims have stopped hiring Sufi poetry performers for community occasions such as weddings, which previously were an important venue for *kāfī*. At weddings in reform-oriented families and communities, the portion of the occasion that once featured Sufi music now features sermons by preachers like Rashid, along with Urdu-language *naʿt* recitation. As another contributing factor to the decline in Sufi music performance opportunities, *kāfī* singers cited the parallel phenomenon of decreasing interest in Sindhi poetry in the younger generation of Kachchhi Muslims, who prefer to hire dance-music ensembles or DJs for their weddings if they include music at all. Sufi music thus occupies an uncomfortable position, caught between the currents of modern Islamic reform, music-stylistic trends, and the declining knowledge of and interest in Sindhi in Muslim Kachchh.

Music in the Mosques: Bāwā Turk Responds

The late *kāfī* singer Bāwā Abdullah Husain Turk (1950–2015) was deeply respected in Kachchh for his commitment to the transmission of Sindhi Sufi poetic knowledge. In recent years, Turk founded an organization called Khuddām-e Ṣūfīyyat (Servants of Sufism, henceforth KMS) with local Sufi singers and their drummer accompanists. One purpose of initiating KMS was to unite Sufi musicians in order to set fair fees for performances. Another goal was to protect Sufism from reformist forces, and from its perceived commodification in India in recent years, such as the use of Sufi themes in Hindi film songs.[54] When I met Turk in July 2014, he was fighting a losing battle with throat cancer. We met for a second and final time a couple of weeks later on Eid al-Fitr, at his village home in southern Kachchh. Despite his obvious pain, he spoke for hours about Sufism and musical life in Kachchh. I was fortunate for the opportunity: Turk passed away on March 23, 2015.

For Bāwā Turk, music and Sufism were "one" (*ek haiñ*). He saw the history of Islam in Kachchh as tied to musical practice. He recounted how men used to sing *kāfī* songs to the accompaniment of the *tanbūro* drone lute inside of mosques after ritual prayer (*namāz*). According to Turk, this was practiced in every mosque in Kachchh until about fifty years ago. The practice declined after Partition, he claimed, and particularly in the last decade. Although local adherents of the Ahl-e Hadith had opposed musical performance long before that, he made it a point to say that, in the past ten years, even those within his own community ("Sunni") had begun to object. He attributed this to the fatwa of the Muftī-e Kachchh,[55] and said of the mufti's followers, "If he says 'It is daytime,' they will say 'It is daytime.' If he says 'It is nighttime,' they will say, 'It is nighttime.' Now he has said that daytime is nighttime." Bāwā Turk did not question the morality of Sufi music; he claimed it was through Sufis that Islam was spread in Kachchh, and that half of the Friends of God buried in its myriad shrines were singers. He pointed out that Aḥmad Shāh's own father and paternal uncle were talented *kāfī* singers: "His whole family sang . . . [but] he studied at a madrasa, and then came back and said, 'no.' "

Turk hoped that KMS would increase people's understanding of Sufism and knowledge of what Sufis have done for the world, which he saw as a necessary effort to resist the corrupting authority of mullahs (Islamic teachers). To underscore and lend authority to this position, he recited a verse by Shāh Bhiṫā'ī in which the poet likens mullahs to hunters and says, "They'll exchange a precious jewel for a wild animal's meat" (*mirū sandī māh*^{u} *tāñ māṇak*^{u} *maṫā'īñ*). Turk understood this to mean that scholars manipulate Quranic verses and hadith for selfish ends. Using poetry as his critical entry point into the Islamic discursive tradition, he laid claim to a vision of Islam in which legalists are not the final arbiters.

The Benefits of the Fatwa: Nazar Ustād Responds

Nazar Ustād is a member of the Laṅgā community of Muslim hereditary musicians who perform mainly on *dhol*, *shehnā'ī*, *tablah*, *dholak*, and *naqqārah*.[56] They perform at Sufi shrines, especially at ʿ*urs* (death-anniversary) festivals; Muslim, Hindu, and Jain weddings; Hindu and Jain religious festivals; and as accompanists for Hindu *bhajan* (devotional song) singers. A handful of especially skilled Laṅgā *dholak* players accompany *kāfī* singers from agriculturalist and pastoralist Muslim communities at Muslim weddings and ʿ*urs* festivals.[57] Laṅgā families live in villages and towns throughout Kachchh, but in recent decades many have moved to Bhuj, the district's administrative center and historically its seat of royal power. At weddings, Laṅgā musicians perform in ensembles consisting of multiple *shehnāʾī*s and *dhol*s, and sometimes on stages with electronic drum pads, keyboards, and drum sets. During a long interview in which Nazar Ustād smoked innumerable *bīṛī* cigarettes, I asked him his thoughts on Aḥmad Shāh Bāwā's objections to musical performance. Nazar Ustād's response revealed that he understands moral disagreement to be an unavoidable natural phenomenon. But, echoing al-Hujwīrī's emphasis on perception and intention as contingent factors in the ethics of audition, he argued, by way of a musical demonstration, that music is permissible in Islam:[58]

> My belief is that there is no question of whether or not [music] is impermissible. Now, look. If we hear Sindhi *dholak*, what meaning can we pull out of it? [Plays a rhythm on his *dholak*.] It has spoken: "ḥaqq Allāh ḥaqq Allāh ḥaqq Allāh ḥaqq." [Recited in the same rhythm he played on *dholak*.] What is forbidden [*ḥarām*] in this? Everyone has his own thinking. One person says of the sun, "It's good, it should exist." But there are two creatures that have said that it should not exist. I don't know what you call this bird in English, but in our language it's called *hūwar*. It comes out at night and does not come out during the day. The second bird is small. It's called *cīcī camṛā* [a kind of bat]. It comes out at night; it never comes out during the day. So according to both, the sun should not exist. Now for this bird [Aḥmad Shāh], there should not be *rāg* ["song," or "music" in Sindhi].[59] Some will say music is "ḥaqq," [Truth, God] and some will say "ḥarām."[60]

Nazar Ustād initially agreed with Bāwā Turk's claim that Sufi musical performance has declined in recent years due to the efforts of Islamic reformists. But he soon backtracked from this position by emphasizing the fault of musicians, whose misguided intentions and material desires have attracted reformist opposition to musical performance at tomb-shrines (*dargāh*s): "When people used to play and sing in *dargāh*s, their goal was in the 'word,' and was connected to the *dargāhwāle* [buried holy men]. Now, people have become such artists (*fankār-kalākār*) that their goal is in money. So that [spiritual] effect is finished."[61] Nazar Ustād's concern with the spiritually diluting presence of morally inferior participants at shrine performances recalls al-Hujwīrī's claim almost a millennium prior: "[In] the present age some persons attend meetings where the wicked listen to [*samā*ʿ], yet they say, 'We are listening to God;' and the wicked join with them in this audition and are encouraged in their wickedness, so that both parties are destroyed."[62]

Shrine performance aside, Aḥmad Shāh's fatwa—which Nazar Ustād claimed was issued in 1972—did significantly impact the presence of Laṅgā musical ensembles at Muslim weddings, specifically *shehnāʾī-dhol* ensembles. Nazar Ustād first claimed that the mufti's fatwa had no effect on the Laṅgā community's livelihood, but then blurted out, "Things got better!" I laughed out of confusion: How could a hereditary Muslim musician possibly welcome an anti-music fatwa? But Nazar Ustād assured me, "I'm telling the truth! We benefited because of Aḥmad Shāh's fatwa." Prior to the fatwa, he explained, Laṅgās were "bound" (*baṅde huʾe*) to Muslim patrons in their villages and were expected to remain in the village at all times in case a need for their services arose. Aḥmad Shāh's fatwa effectively deprived them of these patrons when Muslims began to refrain from hiring Laṅgā musicians to play music at weddings. The Laṅgās began to play more at Hindu and Jain events, which were often attended by nonlocals who extended invitations to play outside the village, and even outside of Kachchh.[63] For the Laṅgās, then, the fatwa had the indirect effect of improving their reputations as wedding musicians and extending their geographic reach.

Aḥmad Shāh's fatwa and similar activities on the part of Ahl-e Sunnat scholars and preachers can be seen as contributing to a larger, longstanding reformist effort to eradicate from Muslim communities those "customs" (*rusūmāt*) perceived to be un-Islamic, which in the South Asian context often effectively also means "Hindu." In the case of music at Muslim weddings, the quintessentially auspicious *shehnāʾī* is for reformists a potent sonic signifier of local, un-Islamic customs. Unsurprisingly, though, Aḥmad Shāh's efforts to discourage Muslim involvement with music have not made inroads within the Laṅgā community, which relies for its livelihood on musical performance in diverse religious and social contexts.

Debates about the morality of sonic performance practices in the Islamic tradition stem from the acknowledgment that sound, musical and otherwise, is an emotionally powerful sensorial force with which the listening self must reckon. Al-Hujwīrī is helpfully straightforward on this as usual: "Anyone who says that he finds no pleasure in sounds and melodies and music is either a liar and a hypocrite or he is not in his right senses, and is outside of the category of men and beasts."[64] But how can one listen ethically? For Bāwā Turk and Nazar Ustād, to pronounce a fatwa proclaiming music's impermissibility within Islam is to deny local Islamic history and music's potential to be an ethically formative practice that brings Muslims closer to God. For Bāwā Turk, this truth appeared self-evident, proven by the historical interconnectedness of Islam, Sufism, music, and poetry in Kachchh. Nazar Ustād's response is more ambivalent; his emphasis on the ethical dispositions of individuals in determining music's moral propriety invokes the Hujwīrīan notion of the fundamentally contingent nature of ethical audition. Yet, unlike reformists, he maintains hope in Sufi music as a path of Islamic devotion and knowledge acquisition that is suitable for average Muslims, and it is precisely this possibility that is contested when reformists make blanket proclamations about the danger that music poses to the Muslim self in an era of perceived moral fragility.

Strikingly, both musicians employed metaphors invoking the binary of day-night, in which day appears to represent a world where music is seen for what the two musicians believe it is: a practice that can be utilized for positive, moral ends, the good of which is attested to by local tradition. Night is contrastingly invoked to portray a world in which music does not exist—a world in which even the good of sunlight is not recognized. Muslim musicians in Kachchh respond in creative and articulate ways to the claim that their preferred mode of Islamic devotion is immoral and un-Islamic. They take action, even initiate formal collectives, in the face of change that they perceive as threatening to their vision of locally rooted Islam and its practice. In so doing, they declare the propriety of Islam's embeddedness within song, and of song's embeddedness within Islam. But despite their differences of opinion with reformists, they too grapple with the problem of moral degradation in modern spaces, where sexual and material desire, and the commodification of Sufi symbols, appear to threaten the sustainability of music as an ethical practice oriented toward achieving closeness with God.

Commentary on Part II

Sufis, Sharia, and Reform

MUHAMMAD QASIM ZAMAN

Reform is a frequently encountered but fraught idea in Muslim societies and in the study of Islam. It is common for Muslim scholars and activists of different kinds to claim the mantle of reforming Islam or this or that aspect of Muslim life and practice. Taking such claims seriously, as indeed they should, academic and other observers of Islam and of Muslim societies have sought to understand what the reform in question amounts to; its intellectual, religious, cultural, social, and political contexts; the claims to authority that underlie and accompany them; and the success or failure of such projects. Much important work has been produced on questions relating to reform in South Asian Islam and in other Muslim societies.

Yet the idea of reform is fraught with ambiguity and contestation. It involves questions of authority—who decides what is in need of reform and how it is to be accomplished. More fundamentally, the contestation has to do with the fact that Muslims, no less than adherents of other religious traditions, have had varied understandings of their faith and its imperatives. Traditions, furthermore, can undergo significant change over time and from one place to another, which means that what is considered unremarkable at one time or place might be perceived as deeply problematic at another. Historical amnesia has often also had a role to play: Scholars and Sufis who have come to be viewed by later generations as embodiments of reformist aspiration may have held views on particular matters that would not necessarily pass muster by the standards of those later generations. All this is to say that, like Islam itself, reform and the need for it or its modes can mean quite different things to different people.

The academic study of reform can pose its own problems, and not only for the reasons just mentioned. Scholars of Islam have tended to view law as lying at the core of the religious tradition, with the result that efforts to foreground adherence to Islamic law have been seen as reform proper, and a resistance to such efforts, even when elaborately reasoned, as connoting something akin to an opposition to the idea of reform itself. Calls for a strict adherence to the Islamic foundational texts—the Quran and the reported traditions of the Prophet Muḥammad (hadith)—are likewise prime candidates for what reform should look like, with the result that efforts to anchor practice in other sources of norms can be relegated to the realm of the religiously inauthentic or as lacking the requisite authority.[1] In the heyday of modernization and secularization theories in the 1950s and the 1960s, the success of Islamic reform tended also to be judged by the degree to which norms and institutions of a modern Western provenance had found a home in Islamic thought and Muslim societies.[2] At the same time, there was much uncertainty about whether Islam could really be adapted to conditions of modernity. From a different but not unrelated angle, there continue to be questions about how well the imperatives of Islamic law and the practices and institutions of Sufism can go together.

In focusing on Sufism in relation to the sharia, the three chapters in part 2 problematize scholarly and other assumptions about reform in some illuminating ways. They demonstrate that Sufi devotional piety, at its broadest, is anything but irreconcilable to the sharia and, as Usha Sanyal shows in chapter 5, that adherence to sharia norms took precedence over all else in the thought of Aḥmad Rażā Khān, the founding figure of the Barelwi doctrinal orientation. It is not just that the sharia was, and is, deemed to be paramount by the Barelwis, however; it is also that Aḥmad Rażā Khān, a Qādirī Sufi master revered as a saintly figure by his followers, gave a great deal of his attention to the kind of writings, such as legal opinions (fatwas), that are often seen as residing at the core of the ulama's legal and scriptural concerns. As Brannon Ingram notes in chapter 4, many among the Deobandis have continued, for their part, to regard Sufi piety as an integral part of Islam. Rather than viewing the sharia and Sufism as discrete entities that might need to be reconciled to each other, many Deobandis and Barelwis see Sufi ethics as helping to cultivate properly Islamic norms and virtues. Even the leadership of the Dār al-ʿUlūm Haqqāniyya, the madrasa in Khyber Pakhtunkhwa (the former North-West Frontier Province bordering Afghanistan) more closely associated with the Taliban than any other, has tended to allow in its fatwas considerable space for Sufi ethics. Scholars of Islam in modern South Asia have long demonstrated that Sufi norms were part of Deobandi thought and practice from the very beginnings of this doctrinal orientation and that the Barelwi religious leadership has had a shared investment in guiding people's lives in accordance with the sharia. Yet stereotypes about a Deobandi aversion to Sufi piety and a Barelwi embrace of it to the neglect of everything else have continued to persist not just in journalistic accounts and policy analyses but sometimes also in academic writing. The chapters in this section perform a useful function in debunking those stereotypes.

There is no denying, however, that attitudes toward Sufi ideas and practices can vary widely. One end of the spectrum of Sunni Islam in modern South Asia is occupied by those, notably the Ahl-e Hadith (or Salafis) and many Islamists, who have often characterized the veneration of Sufi saints as tantamount to associating partners with God, *shirk*, the gravest of sins in Islam. The other end of the spectrum is represented by those, notably the Barelwis, who find nothing un-Islamic in the idea of holy men and women interceding with God on behalf of common believers or in their performing miraculous deeds not just in their life but also after death. The idea, moreover, that one could prostrate at a Sufi shrine rather than exclusively to God is anathema to many people, for it denotes nothing less than polytheism; the self-appointed task of many a Muslim reformer is precisely to stamp out such polytheistic practice from within the Islamic fold. Devotional music, the subject of an illuminating discussion by Brian Bond in chapter 6, can likewise create strong antipathy in particular reformist circles to those engaging in or enjoying it.

Yet, it turns out that it is not just the practice but even the theory that is considerably more complex than reformist rhetoric might suggest in some of its expressions. So far as the practice is concerned, a wide latitude can be created by arguing that the permissibility or otherwise of devotional music depends on the ethical sensibilities that one brings to it: As Bond shows, some of the musicians opposing a fatwa on the impermissibility of music based their position precisely on "the ethical capacities of listening selves." Likewise, as Ingram observes, even Deobandi muftis can authorize belief in the miraculous powers of dead saints provided that the powers in question are believed to be dependent on God rather than thought to be exercised by the saint unaided.

So far, however, as the theory is concerned, even the question of prostration to living Sufi masters or at their shrines is far from unambiguous. Shāh Walī Allāh, the eighteenth-century North Indian hadith scholar and Sufi who has come to be viewed as a paragon of Islamic reform, had stated that going to excess in the veneration of shrines was a very grave sin but that it was not unbelief.[3] On a visit to the Hijaz in 1926, the Deobandi stalwart Shabbīr Aḥmad ʿUsmānī had cautioned Ibn Saʿūd—whose Wahhabi followers were then engaged in the destruction of revered shrines in the Hijaz and elsewhere—against treating people as polytheists for prostrating at such shrines. Such practices were reprehensible, he had said, but they did not constitute unbelief. The worship (*ʿibādah*) of anyone other than God was forbidden, but people prostrating at shrines were not necessarily "worshipping" those buried there; such people could be punished at the king's discretion, but they could not be dealt with as though they were idol worshippers.[4] In a fatwa from 1975, Muftī Muḥammad Farīd, the leading jurisconsult at the Dār al-ʿUlūm Haqqāniyya, had stated that desecrating a grave because of the illegitimate practices that took place at it was unlawful. He had characterized such desecration unfavorably as the way of "the Salafi-Najdī group," that is, the Wahhabis.[5] In a later fatwa, dating from 1989, he had rejected the idea that it might be permissible to kill the caretaker of a shrine where un-Islamic practices laden with *shirk* took place or to burn down his living quarters.[6] Other fatwas emanating from those associated with the same madrasa characterized prostration to a shrine by way of veneration (*sajdah-e taʿẓīmī*) to be prohibited, and prostrating to it by way of worship (*sajdah-e ʿibādat*) to be the grave sin of *shirk*.[7] Even such fatwas did not, however, advocate the destruction of the shrines in question. It is also to be noted that a proof text this latter fatwa had adduced, from the late Mughal-era *Fatāwā-e ʿĀlamgīrī*, discusses this question with reference to prostrating before the sultan, not a shrine, and it states that the preferred opinion is that doing so is a grave sin but *not* unbelief. The same passage in the *Fatāwā-e ʿĀlamgīrī* does, however, adduce an opinion, also quoted in the Dār al-ʿUlūm Haqqāniyya fatwa, according to which prostrating to the sultan is unbelief, even when it is not intended as worship.[8]

In Deobandi circles, the space for distinctions between prostrations meant only to show respect versus those that amount to worship has arguably become narrower. Those engaging in the destruction of Sufi shrines probably have local muftis who authorize and commend such deeds. The foregoing views on prostration suggest, however, that even among the Deobandis—and even among those most closely associated in Pakistan with the Taliban—the question is not a settled one. As the authors of the three chapters in this part demonstrate, doctrinal orientations such as the Deobandis and the Barelwis are not monolithic in the positions their adherents espouse. There is in fact considerable debate and contestation *within* these orientations and not just between members of rival orientations. The question of prostration is one telling example. Music is another.

As Bond shows in his contribution, there is resistance among the musicians of Kutch in Gujarat to a fatwa issued sometime in the early 1970s by a leading Barelwi mufti on the impermissibility of musical instruments. These musicians have responded by emphasizing the ethical sensibilities by which the question of permissibility ought to be judged, and they have drawn attention to what music can do by way of facilitating a devotee's sense of mystical fulfillment. It is significant, however, that learned Barelwi opinion has come down on the side of impermissibility and that at least some of those arguing *for* permissibility have had to do so by challenging the very authority of the ulama. Yet the ulama have had nuanced views on the matter. A scholar of the stature of Shāh ʿAbd al-ʿAzīz (d. 1824), a son of Shāh Walī Allāh and a key figure in the genealogy of Deoband, is said by one of his late nineteenth-century biographers to have had "complete mastery in the science of music."[9] He had also written a treatise on the subject. In late colonial Punjab, an initiative to outlaw singing and dancing by women in Sufi shrines to the accompaniment of music was enacted into law, though not without strong opposition.[10] Such legislation notwithstanding, devotional music has continued, of course, to be part of many a shrine's life in South Asia. Attacks on Sufi shrines in Pakistan, by groups associated with the Taliban and with ISIS, have occasionally been timed to target such performances, which incidentally serves to suggest the militants' recognition of the continuing hold of such practices on the local culture.

As might be expected, family politics, too, can fuel some of the contestation among those belonging to a particular doctrinal orientation. Despite the Barelwis' shared devotion to the Prophet, Sufi saints, and other holy personages, the privileges claimed by descendants of Aḥmad Rażā Khān have bred, as Sanyal shows, some resentment in sections of the Barelwi leadership in Uttar Pradesh, India. There are rivalries within the founding father's family, too, and intra-Barelwi politics has sometimes taken the form of people pointedly attaching themselves to one rather than another of the family lines. Enterprising Barelwi leaders have also charted their own paths, which are often beholden only in name, if even that, to spiritual blessings received from key members of Aḥmad Rażā Khān's family. Something similar could be said of the Deobandis, not only in terms of rivalries among leading Deobandis, or between prominent families of scholars, but also by way of resentments among less-privileged members of the ulama community vis-à-vis those who are more affluent.

A final point worth highlighting with reference to the studies in this part is the importance of understanding the multifaceted contexts in which particular formulations of Islam, the sharia, Sufism, and reform are articulated. It should be no surprise, given the different political frameworks in which Islam has developed in postcolonial India, in Pakistan, in Bangladesh, or in the United Kingdom, for that matter, that there can be considerable variation in Barelwi or Deobandi or Sufi practice from one country, region, or locale to another. What Deobandi Islam signifies in, say, the tribal areas of Pakistan's Khyber Pakhtunkhwa can differ significantly from how muftis in Karachi or in the Indian town of Deoband itself understand their legal or mystical heritage. As Ingram observes, the Pakistani Taliban's attacks on Sufi shrines have a local political context, too, and we need to take account of it in trying to analyze such actions. At the same time, the interaction among local and wider—transregional, even global—trends ought also to be brought into our purview. Sufi orders, the Ḥanafī and other schools of law, and the Deobandi, Barelwi, and Ahl-e Hadith orientations have a global presence, and it is worth examining how the discourses of major past and present Barelwi or Deobandi scholars are "translated" in particular local contexts. Through what intermediate channels, what loci of authority, are such discourses passed down, reworked, contested? Conversely, how does a course of events in particular contexts bear on wider debates or developments elsewhere? For instance, how do the Taliban's widely reported efforts to implement what they take to be sharia norms shape a national conversation in Pakistan on the question of the sharia's implementation? How do Taliban attacks on shrines in Khyber Pakhtunkhwa impact Sufi thought, institutions, and politics in Pakistan at large, in South Asia, even globally? The studies by Ingram, Bond, and Sanyal provide an important basis on which to explore these and related questions further.

PART III

Sufis and Politics in Pakistan

7

"A Way of Life Rather Than an Ideology?"

Sufism, *Pīrs*, and the Politics of Identity in Sindh

SARAH ANSARI

In the context of twenty-first-century Pakistan, Sindh is often described as the "land of Sufism" (and sometimes also of secularism). According to a newspaper report entitled "Can Sufism Save Sindh?"—published following an attack on an *imām bārgāh* (Shiʿi congregation hall) in Shikarpur in 2015—Sindh's "Sufi ethos" has "long been cherished as the panacea for burgeoning extremism in Pakistan."[1] Such bold statements, however, need to be assessed in the light of the place of the province's *pīr* families—the *gaddī nashīns*, or guardians of long-established Sufi shrines—within the province's religiopolitical life. As Noor Zaidi describes so vividly in chapter 9, Pakistan's sacred landscape remains dominated by the physical presence of shrines, both large and small, whose inescapable material presence testifies to, and reminds us of, the enduring significance that Sufism and its "saintly" representatives hold for millions of people living there.

As elsewhere in South Asia, *pīr* is the title given in Sindh to spiritual guides or religious preceptors adhering to Sufi traditions within Islam. They can be either practicing Sufis themselves or simply the descendants of earlier Sufi saintly figures fulfilling the role of guardian of their ancestors' often lavish tombs. The latter, who make up many of the province's *pīr* families, are—in the main—the hereditary custodians of local Sufi shrines, and not necessarily Sufi guides in their own right from a spiritual point of view. In other words, while individual Sindhi *pīrs* may not necessarily fit the image of a religious leader, nor more specifically that of a "saint," taken en masse they and their forebears have wielded huge influence over the lives of their *murīds* (followers) for generations. To those who revere them, they are regarded as physically embodying, or personifying, the Sufi tradition, irrespective of their personal spiritual credentials. Thus, in Sindh—as in neighboring Punjab—leading members of *pīr* families remain firmly ensconced as powerful religious figures—"living saints"—whose enormous popular, religiously sanctioned authority, combined with the influence that flows from being landowners of huge estates, endows them with substantial political clout. Indeed, in many ways, the situation in Sindh mirrors closely similar patterns observable elsewhere in Pakistan, such as in the Punjab, where the potent mix of landed power and spiritual leadership has led local *gaddī nashīns* (also known as *sajjādah nashīns*) to involve themselves in politics at the provincial and national levels, both before and since the creation of Pakistan.[2] Where the two contexts differ, however, is the extent to which the politics of identity in Sindh has complicated the political role assumed by these powerful families, injecting an important political distinction that needs to be acknowledged.

The following discussion accordingly examines what in practice has proved to be a far from straightforward relationship between *pīr* families and the politics of identity in Sindh, contextualizing and complicating debates about the potential role of Sufism as an ideological and practical means of combatting extremist intolerance and violence, whether in this part of southern Pakistan or elsewhere. Crucially—now as in the past—"Sufism" for many people in Sindh tends not to operate so much as an *ideology*—informed by an acute sense of the spiritual beliefs that make up this strand of Islam—but, rather, as a deeply embedded *way of life*, thanks to the deeply personal bonds that exist between *pīrs* and their followers, and the ways that local Sufi *dargāhs* (shrines) and the rituals that take place there fit into everyday Sindhi understandings of what being a Muslim means in practice.

"The Sufis always worked for the promotion of love and one-ness of humanity, not for disunity or hatred," or so claimed General Pervez Musharraf when he established his National Sufi Council in 2006 as part of a wider drive to counter extremism.[3] As Alix Philippon explains in chapter 8, Sufism, bolstered by the country's Sufi saints, became symbolic of the government's efforts to stem the tide of "talibanization." But if we wind the clock back to the same year, we would find that in Sindh ("the land of Sufism") the media were arguably more absorbed in a lengthy discussion about the impact on the province of the proposed Kalabagh Dam (which was to be constructed on the River Indus, one hundred miles southwest of Islamabad in the Punjab and intended to tackle threatening water shortages and Pakistanis' increasing demands for electrical power). Sindhi apprehensions ranged from worries that the project would turn Sindh into a "desert" to concerns about its adverse impact on cultivation in the province, to fears that seawater intrusion in the Indus estuary would restrict and contaminate drinking-water supplies in Lower Sindh.[4]

These reactions among Sindhis to the implications of the Kalabagh Dam for the province highlighted three important aspects of the political life of Sindh since Pakistan's creation in 1947. First, they pointed to the enduring significance of identity in Sindhi politics—Sindhi nationalist sentiment—since for many Sindhis this project represented the latest in a long list of efforts made by the federal Pakistani state to undermine Sindhi interests. (Apart from the economic consequences, reducing the flow of the Indus was tantamount to the devastation of Sindh's five-thousand-year-old cultural heritage.) Second, Sindhi reactions to this dam, long in the planning, underlined the centrality of water to political discussion in the province. While this is an issue that has played a key role in Pakistan's internal affairs and foreign relations, it resonates in Sindh particularly because locals often believe that their interests have lost out as a consequence of federal government decisions regarding who gets what water and when. Third, and perhaps less obviously, the 2006 media debate—thanks to the high-profile involvement of one of the province's leading "spiritual leaders," the Pīr Pagāro—also drew attention to the powerful involvement of local *pīrs* in Sindh's political life.

While an idealized Sufism has come to be regarded by Sindhi nationalists as a defining element of their province's identity, the reality is that *pīrs* themselves have had an ambiguous relationship with Sindhi nationalism.[5] Following his well-publicized enthusiastic support for the Kalabagh Dam's construction, the Pīr Pagāro was strongly criticized by Sindhi nationalist spokesmen for failing to represent, and by implication to defend, the province's interests.[6] So, while in the decades since Pakistan's creation individual *pīr* families—like that of the Pīr Pagāro—have proved a very active component of Sindh's political life and flexed considerable political muscle, it is debatable how far they, as opposed to the Sufi traditions with which they are associated, have engaged with or supported the politics of Sindhi nationalist identity.

Pīrs, Sindhi Nationalist Politics, and All-Pakistan Political Developments

To understand the relationship between *pīrs* and Sindhi nationalism, it is first necessary to place Sindhi nationalist politics in a broader political perspective. Despite Sindh's reputation as "a hotbed of various kinds of nationalism ranging from separatists and right-wing autonomists to socialist intellectuals and left wing political groups,"[7] the hard truth is that Sindhi nationalist parties have only ever won few (if any) legislative assembly seats at the provincial, let alone the federal, level. Like Islamist parties, which have routinely failed at the polls despite considerable street support, Sindhi nationalist groups have proved very vocal, but as yet they have not achieved significant electoral gains. Poignantly, the veteran Sindhi nationalist politician G. M. Syed has been widely reported as commenting, after one of the many elections in which the nationalists did badly, "They sing and dance for me, but they don't vote for me."[8] Since 1970, when the first national elections were held in Pakistan, Sindhis have tended to vote for federalist or all-Pakistan political parties, in particular the Pakistan People's Party (PPP).[9] In November 1988, for instance, when the PPP under Benazir Bhutto won 67 out of 141 seats in the Sindh Legislative Assembly (mostly from rural constituencies where the majority of voters were so-called ethnic Sindhis), not a single seat was won by Sindhi nationalists, and this was despite the fact that, only a few years earlier, in 1983, the Movement for the Restoration of Democracy (MRD), which achieved high levels of popular support in Sindh, had derived a great deal of its appeal from being able to tap Sindhi resentment of Zia-ul-Haq's Punjabi-dominated military regime.[10]

As for Sindhi *pīrs*, while their spiritual reputation, or, perhaps more accurately, that of their forebears, is central to understanding the leverage that they have exercised in Sindh's political arena, their day-to-day relationship with ordinary people of the province has not necessarily always been based simply on their "spiritual powers" alone. Instead, in practice, this relationship has frequently been mediated through leading *murīds*—namely, powerful landlords, village-level faction leaders, and government officials who consider each other as *pīrbhā'īs*, or *pīr*-brothers, and who co-operate accordingly.[11] In addition, *pīrs* are often large landowners in their own right, which means that, in such cases, they are able to influence and control the political decisions of their own followers. Either way, though, it might be argued that their politics—while linked to their role as religious leaders—functions on a distinctly non-spiritual basis.

By the time of Independence in 1947, *pīr* families possessed a long-established tradition of functioning as intermediaries, or mediators, in the Sindhi countryside. This role was recognized, for instance, by the British colonial state that sought very early on to draw *pīr* families, along with other landed interests, into its system of imperial control.[12] Some steadfastly maintained a tactful or discrete distance from politics (some even went as far as opposing British rule during the all-India Khilafat Movement of 1919–24), but many others took advantage of the new opportunities offered by the British to consolidate their local power and influence by accepting honors, joining district boards, and eventually participating in the system of political representation that the British established in the province as elsewhere in the subcontinent. In the run-up to Independence, the All-India Muslim League likewise recognized the usefulness of *pīrs* as local political power brokers, and much of the party's electoral success in Sindh before 1947 (as in the Punjab) can be attributed to the fact that many *pīrs* there instructed their followers to vote for the league in the decisive provincial elections of 1945–46.[13]

In addition to the above history and dynamics, other factors need to be taken into account when considering the political role of *pīr* families in post-1947 Sindh. These include the impact of Partition-related migration on demographic patterns in the province as well as its redrawn geopolitical borders. After the exodus of most of Sindh's non-Muslim population from its towns and cities, migrants from India arrived to fill this vacated urban space. Simultaneously, refugees from the Punjab were shifted in large numbers to the Sindhi countryside. As a result of these population shifts after Independence, there was a far greater presence of "outsiders" in Sindh than before, and this played a part in stimulating Sindhi disquiet at how the province's resources were subsequently distributed. This concern was exacerbated by the separation of the then-federal capital, Karachi, from Sindh in 1948, a move that locals described in terms of Sindh being "beheaded."[14]

Before the Independence and partitioning of British India, it would be fair to say that Sufism—in the popular form that it took in this region—had had a tradition of bridging differences between different religious groups. Modes of religious worship in Sindh were fairly syncretic, to the extent that observers would often talk in terms of the province's "Sufi-indoctrinated way of life" and the blurred religious distinctions that existed between Muslims and Hindus who could worship at the same shrine. After 1947, however, Sufism came to play a somewhat different role. Now, differences *between* communities—"old Sindhis" and "new Sindhis" (as the central Pakistani government of the day tried to call them)—tended to be reinforced by new kinds of religious distinctions among Muslims. Unsurprisingly, migrants from India felt little loyalty toward the province's traditional religious leaders and tended either to venerate saintly figures associated with places left behind in India or actually to reject the style and content of religious leadership offered by the representatives of *pīr* families in favor of more reformist scriptural traditions. Moreover, the fact that these urban-based migrants were not tied into the web of reciprocal relationships that existed in the Sindhi countryside meant that local *pīrs* had far less to offer newcomers by way of mediation or intercession, important "currency" in Sindh's religious "marketplace." At the same time, however, contemporary observers acknowledged the key role that the members of certain *pīr* families were playing in the political life of the province, such as drumming up support for the controversial vote in favor of One Unit that was passed by the Sindh Legislative Assembly in 1955. The Pīr Pagāro, for one, lent his support to this political amalgamation of the provinces making up West Pakistan.[15] While the rationale for One Unit from a West Pakistan perspective was linked to the need to justify the new federal arrangements being built into the forthcoming 1956 constitution, the move to consolidate Pakistani identity threatened to sublimate regional differences in the western wing.[16] Moreover, since, during Pakistan's early years, the federal authorities actively promoted a modernized form of Islam as the basis for national identity, "the infamous one-unit scheme [. . . also] went hand in hand with efforts to purify Islam from what was condescendingly seen as regional folk traditions, superstition and non-Islamic elements."[17]

It was against this polarized backdrop in the period following Partition that the politics of identity in the form of a more self-conscious Sindhi nationalist ideology and rhetoric emerged, and when Sindh's close identification with Sufism was deliberately articulated. In 1953 G. M. Syed formed the Jeeye Sindh Mahaz (JSM), which called for recognizing the de facto existence of separate nationalities in Pakistan. The JSM demanded full provincial autonomy, leaving only defense, foreign affairs, and currency with the federal government, and also called for the re-merger of Karachi with its Sindhi hinterland. It was the first political organization to oppose One Unit and, together with other regional parties, formed the anti-One Unit Pakistan National Party.

Syed, who was himself from a family with long-standing spiritual authority, chose to associate Sindhi identity with mystic Sufi traditions, in the process seeking to disconnect the ideology of Sufism from the temporal power of the *pīr*s themselves, as well as to distinguish Sindh from Pakistan as a whole. In Syed's words, "a Sufi Sindh and an Islamic Pakistan cannot coexist, [just] as you can't put two swords in one scabbard. If Pakistan continues, Sindh will die. If, therefore, Sindh is to live, Pakistan must die."[18] Hence, according to Oskar Verkaaik, Sindhi nationalist intellectuals designed their own version of Islam, which allowed them to argue for a separate Sindhi national identity based on what they claimed was Sindh's unique experience with Sufism.[19] Syed, for one, wrote a great deal about the history of Sufism in Sindh, including his (at the time) provocative *Religion and Reality* (1967), in which he labeled Sindh the "cradle of mysticism," with a long history of religious tolerance and revolt against the supposed tyranny of ulama and mullahs.[20] Sindh's Sufi poets, in particular the eighteenth-century Shāh ʿAbd al-Laṭīf Bhiṭāʾī, as well as "socialist Sufis" such as Shāh ʿInāyat of Jhok (c. 1655–1718), were held up as potent symbols of

Sindh's separate cultural, spiritual, and political identity. Syed's efforts "on the cultural front" also included the establishment of the Sufi Society of Sindh.[21]

By the late 1960s this emphasis on the combination of "ethnic" identity and Sufism was proving very attractive to student activists and others belonging to Sindh's burgeoning middle classes, who, critical of Pakistan's military rulers, took to the streets in the late 1960s to call for free democratic elections.[22] Though Sindhi intellectuals such as the "leftist" Ibrahim Joyo were influenced by Marxist ideas, and so roundly condemned *pīrs*, along with other big landlords, for exploiting the peasantry in feudal fashion, personal loyalty to Syed (as well as Syed's own opposition to the uncritical following of spiritual guides) meant that, despite his privileged status, they accepted him as the leader of their Sindhi nationalist struggle. As Verkaaik has further explained, "GM Syed encouraged his new friends and 'comrades' not to restrict their activities to the university campus and schools. He sent them to the many shrines of local holy men in the rural areas, especially on the annual *urs* celebration. . . . [In] the interpretation of GM Syed and his group, [these] holy men were martyrs for the cause of mysticism, Sindh and the liberation of the peasant."[23] All the same, reinterpreting holy men as social reformers in such a populist and challenging manner must have seemed like a potential (and potent) threat to many of the province's *pīrs* and *sayyids*. Not surprisingly, this helped to alienate the vast majority of them from Syed's Jeeye Sindh movement that was founded in 1972 (in the wake of Bangladesh's secession) and demanded the creation of a separate Sindhu Desh (Sindhi nation).[24]

But, while condemning *pīr* families for various class-related reasons, Sindhi nationalists have also attempted to harness the charisma of the spiritual traditions that *pīrs* represent to the wider Sindhi nationalist cause. In this they have not been alone, however, for since the 1950s other political interests at work in the province have done precisely the same thing. As Philippon similarly points out, successive Pakistani regimes have attempted to redefine Sufism and Sufi saints so as to manipulate them for their own political benefit. Hence, while official government policy from the late 1950s may have been to reduce the power of *pīr* families on the grounds that this was incompatible with the political and religious goals of successive administrations, consecutive leaders such as Ayub Khan, Zulfikar Ali Bhutto, and Zia-ul-Haq all sought to exploit the legitimizing power of the *dargāh*, albeit in somewhat different ways, as part of their wider programs to restructure Pakistani society. For Ayub, the goal was "modernization" combined with development; for Bhutto, greater "democracy" or "Islamic socialism"; and for Zia, a more consciously Islamic state. For all three regimes, these priorities involved (at least to some extent) confronting existing power holders, of whom *pīrs* represented a significant section.

Ayub's modernizing policies incorporated land reforms that threatened their economic interests, Bhutto's populist rhetoric seemed to reject their political role, and Zia's stress on scriptural Islam appeared to undermine the basis of their religious authority. In practice, however, these governments were never really able to stamp their authority fully on the institution of the *pīr*, but what they were able to do was to seek to harness the popularity of the shrine to their own purposes.[25]

Recasting Sufism for Federal Purposes and the Changing Role of *Pīrs* in Sindhi Politics

As Katherine Ewing has described, in 1959 Ayub established the Auqaf Department (i.e., a branch of the provincial government devoted to the upkeep of endowments and trusts, including shrines and mosques, facilities for pilgrims, and the resolution of disputes over possession of a religious site) and assigned to it the day-to-day task of running shrines in order to demonstrate that the *gaddī nashīns* themselves were not essential for their upkeep. The conspicuous attendance of government bureaucrats at *ʿurs* celebrations symbolized this within a ritualized context. Shrines were also used as a way of introducing change to the countryside, by being recast as social welfare centers or spreading awareness of new agricultural techniques at the time of their festivals. But the fact that Ayub was pursuing a similar strategy elsewhere in Pakistan during this period underlines the artificiality and, some might suggest, futility of attempts to link Sindhi identity to its Sufi-informed *pīr* traditions.[26] As in the case of Bībī Pāk Dāman in Lahore's Old City, explored by Zaidi in chapter 9, the factors that drove the government decision to take control of key shrines under the authority of the West Pakistan Waqf Properties Ordinance of 1961 were complex, and often motivated by the desire to resolve conflicts over claims to authenticity and authority in ways that worked to the state's advantage.

With Bhutto, it was much the same story, with, if anything, greater emphasis on government participation in the shrines' rituals. The fact that Bhutto, a Sindhi himself, came from a Shiʿi family may in part explain his distance from some of the province's hereditary *pīrs* (though equally many Sindhi *pīr* families are Shiʿi themselves) and helped fuel his project to co-opt *dargāhs* into a populist mode of social organizing. Either way, *dargāhs* there (as in Punjab and in other parts of Pakistan) became evermore translated into national cultural symbols for the glorification of the nation, and, increasingly, of Islam: the

ʿ*urs*es of important saints were converted into occasions of national celebration, inaugurated by national political figures. Permanent research centers and libraries were planned for the shrines of Sindh's famous Sufi poets. Like Ayub, Bhutto recognized the need to show that the mediation of a *pīr* was becoming largely superfluous in changing social linkages operating in the Pakistani countryside. Bhutto thus made a conscious effort to draw parallels between the Sufi and the social reformer, and between their goals and his own. Though not belonging to a Sufi family background himself (his branch of the Bhutto "clan" had been large landholders since colonial times), Bhutto understood the importance of using a vocabulary that ordinary Sindhis would understand, and with which they might empathize. Hence, in the 1970 elections, as Verkaaik has pointed out, Bhutto "too went to the rural shrines, sat down to talk to the peasants and pilgrims, and called himself a *faqīr*."[27] Official and semi-official publications from this period presented a picture that stressed the *piety*, as opposed to the *miracles*, of individual saints, as well as the reconstruction work carried out by the authorities.[28] In the view of some commentators, the Bhutto years represented a tough time for *pīr* families: "People started shifting their loyalties. They chanted slogans like "*na pīr jo, na mīr jo, vote aa żamīr jo*" (we will not vote for *pīr*s or *mīr*s, but according to our conscience).[29] But once Bhutto had been deposed in 1977, many *pīr* families quickly regained lost ground.

The Zia period marked something of a change in direction in that, instead of the *symbolism* of the Sufi, it was the *language* of the ulama that pushed forward the government's program of Islamization. Religious festivities during the annual ʿ*urs* in many shrines were now carefully monitored for supposedly un-Islamic practices such as dancing and drumming, and in Friday prayers, devotional attendance at shrines was discouraged. Even so, Zia's government made deliberate efforts to profit from an association with the region's Sufi legacy by incorporating representatives of this brand or branch of Islam within its own ideology. Government officials continued to make long speeches to commemorate the birth or death anniversaries of saints, emphasizing that the original saints had also been religious scholars who could be fitted into the ulama mold. Zia's government also maintained its predecessors' policies of investing in improvements in the physical conditions of the tombs themselves, and took care to ensure that no antagonism on the part of the regime toward the Sufi tradition was discernible at the popular level.[30] More generally, as Seyyed Vali Reza Nasr has argued, Zia hoped to promote certain Islamic traditions, as opposed to using concrete action, to quiet political demands from among the province's increasingly vocal migrant (*muhājir*) communities (supporters of the so-called ethnic political party, the Muhajir Qaumi Mahaz, established in

1984) while he rewarded Sindhi cooperation.[31] And the same practice continued under Musharraf, who—Philippon reminds us in chapter 8—referred repeatedly to Sindh, like Punjab, as the "land of Sufi saints" when seeking to promote his own later "war" on extremism.

But despite these policies aimed at undermining their power bases in the Sindhi countryside, *pīr* families remained central to the religious and political life of Sindh, and continued to wield enormous influence at the provincial level. As Zaidi argues, state attempts to impose sectarian secularism failed in practice. The actual number of shrines that the Auqaf Department controlled in practice remained relatively small. Apart from major shrines and cultural centers—such as those of Lāl Shāhbāz Qalandar, Shāh ʿAbd al-Laṭīf Bhiṭāʾī, Sachal Sarmast, Makdūm Nūḥ of Hala, and the Pīr of Luari (supervised by the Auqaf Department for reasons linked to the controversial re-enactment of the hajj that had "traditionally" taken place there until the shrine was closed during the British period)—most of those under government management were fairly minor *dargāhs*, and the vast majority of shrines did not fall under Auqaf Department control. Land-reform measures from the 1960s onward had, in practice, a similarly restricted impact on many *pīr* families, who, like their secular counterparts, often found creative ways of evading official ceilings on land ownership. The benefits of this popular religious authority also meant that they could receive additional support from *murīds* to compensate for any losses that they incurred. And this same combination of resources enabled *pīrs* to carry on playing a prominent role even where they had lost full control over the *dargāh* itself. Their large followings provided these local power brokers with a continuing constituency of support that politicians needed at times when democracy was in operation, and which could be just as crucial when it was not. Undeniably, the failure of the Pakistani state to penetrate the countryside effectively throughout most of this period reinforced the mediating functions of local power holders, including *pīr* families. It was precisely the access to rural Sindh that *pīrs* still provided that explained why governments (sooner rather than later) came to terms with their enduring existence.

Sindhi *pīrs* themselves displayed a continuing readiness to be flexible when confronted with changing political circumstances. The extension of the franchise at the time of Independence encouraged them to participate more directly and in relatively larger numbers at all levels of the political process, all the way up from local councils to the National Assembly and the Senate. One of the most important *pīr* families to become much more actively involved in politics (as compared with its role before 1947, when its representatives maintained a deliberate distance from overt political activity) was that of the Makhdūms of Hala. The incumbent Makhdūm Ṭālib al-Mawlā was first a supporter of Ayub and later of Bhutto, on whose PPP ticket he was elected in 1970 and 1977. Once in political "retirement," his place in the party was taken by his sons, two of whom became PPP central and provincial ministers. In such positions, *pīrs* still often fill the role of key intermediaries or mediators, in political as well as spiritual ways.

As the examples of Pīr Pagāros and the Makhdūms of Hala underline, *pīrs* frequently function as "go-betweens," linking ordinary Sindhis with those who control the state and vice versa, while on occasion taking on a role at a national level themselves. As a consequence, Sindhi identity politics, in practice, has had relatively little to offer them, for all the talk of a reformed Sufism associated with it by its leadership. Inevitably, some *pīrs* may take a pro-"Sindh" stance if the conditions or timings are right, such as the Makhdūm of Hala's involvement in the anti-Zia MRD agitation of the early 1980s. That particular *pīr* family, however, which had become a leading force within the PPP in Sindh, could hardly have supported Zia's military regime. Likewise, the Pīr Pagāros, with substantial numbers of *murīds* living across the border in the Punjab, are unlikely to view themselves, in political terms at least, as "Sindhis" pure and simple.

When considering the politics of Pakistan it is always advisable not to confuse rhetoric with reality. Sindh, for all its apparently Sufi-friendly history and present-day landscape, is characterized by deeply unequal relationships that divide those who enjoy power and those who are powerless. Since the beginning of the twenty-first century, it has been argued that Sindh has experienced

> a significant rise in the power of the wadera [large landholder]. . . . Many people in Sindh believe General Musharraf's devolution of democracy plan was flawed as it patronized the local wadera and provided him more money and power. . . . There were more and bigger vehicles, weapons and a lust for more power, [and] the democratic rule of more recent years has witnessed not a reduction but an extension of that culture. . . . Not unrelatedly, honor killing and karo-kari [Sindhi for honor killing] have increased.[32]

A 2006 World Bank report, *Securing Sindh's Future: Prospects and Challenges*, similarly noted that Sindh had the narrowest distribution of land ownership in Pakistan, with 1 percent of all farmers there owning 150 percent more land than the combined holdings of 62 percent of small farmers: "Given its feudal traditions, progressive ideas and reforms have always taken more time to take roots in the interior of Sindh than in most other areas of Pakistan. Sindh has the highest incidence of absolute landlessness, highest share of tenancy and lowest share of land ownership in the country."[33] *Pīr* families, in general, continue to operate as fully signed-up members of Sindh's privileged provincial elite, and hence benefit collectively (just as their nonspiritual counterparts do) from the range of inequalities that underpin and sustain their place in Sindhi society, whether in terms of the province's spiritual rhythms or its more worldly operations. While acknowledging that a central theme of Sindhi politics since 1947 has been Sindhi nationalism/separatism versus Pakistani nationalism—which is sometimes construed as an "Islamic" counter to "Sufi Sindh"—it is clear, on the one hand, that the Sufism associated with *pīrs* there symbolizes what is taken as unique about the province, while on the other hand, in practice they have often tilted toward "Pakistan" and use their declining power strategically to maintain local influence. In turn, federal governments, from the time of Ayub onward, have sought to manipulate shrines to their own ends.

So returning to the reference at the beginning of this chapter to Sindhi "nationalist" responses to statements on the Kalabagh Dam in 2006 proffered by the province's leading *gaddī nashīn*, the Pīr Pagāro, it could be argued that his stance represented a logical reaction on the part of a local power broker who had—for the previous fifty years—consistently kept his eye focused on the broader state of Pakistani politics, with the aim of playing an all-Pakistan role, albeit as a religio-political leader who hailed from the minor (and arguably marginalized) province of Sindh. Sindhi nationalists, belonging as they often have to more recently emerging urban-based Sindhi middle classes—who have often challenged the social and power relations that underpin the relationship between *pīrs* and their *murīds*—tend to be perceived by many *pīr* families as more of a threat to their position than a potential source of support. Clearly, the impact of Musharraf's Sufism policy (and subsequently that of his PPP successors who have their own focus on Sindh's religio-cultural heritage[34]) on the role of *pīrs* in the life of Sindh has yet to be quantitatively and qualitatively measured. On the other hand, as recent election results have indicated, powerful and well-entrenched interests in Sindh can now be challenged, if and when the circumstances are right. Spiritual veneration is no longer necessarily the automatic guarantor of victory at the polls, and Sindhi politics, like politics elsewhere in the region, should not be viewed as mired in tradition, whatever this means for the struggle between "toleration" and "extremism." In the words of one 2014 commentator, "Even makhdooms must supplant power with patronage, because their constituencies are changing, and including those that are no longer willing to blindly hand their spiritual masters their votes."[35] Whether such shifts in electoral support represent a change in the loci of power and patronage at the provincial level or reflect changing wider attitudes toward Islam in the region, however, remains to be determined. What does seem clear is that—like their predecessors—many *pīr* families in Sindh today appear willing and able to deploy the same kind of political flexibility that allowed them to respond positively to earlier challenges to their authority, whether during the British colonial period or since Independence and the accompanying creation of Pakistan.

8

Sufi Politics and the War on Terror in Pakistan

Looking for an Alternative to Radical Islamism?

ALIX PHILIPPON

Since the beginning of the War on Terror, Sufism, the Sufi shrines, and the Sufi saints in Pakistan have gradually become the symbols of the fight undertaken by the governments against creeping "talibanization," which is deemed to threaten the very fabric of the nation. The number of initiatives, often financed by the government, aimed at promoting Sufism have indeed proliferated. In order to elevate it to the rank of pillar of national identity and antiradical ideology, a massive diffusion policy has been undertaken through editorial activities, the production of CDs, TV or radio programs, and the organization of Sufi music festivals and conferences. Sufism has indeed been overwhelmingly politicized through a process of culturalization. It has been officially defined and promoted as a fundamental element of Pakistan's heritage and culture, and its value has been enhanced in different art forms (mainly poetry and music) and cultural products. It has been enshrined as a harmless and apolitical cultural patrimony that could help legitimize the authority of the state. It has thus been to some extent "folklorized,"[1] as these cultural elements have been instrumentalized by authoritarian powers. Simultaneously, Sufism has been presented as an essential part of Islam, or even as the "true Islam" that Pakistan needs to embrace to counter the terrorist wave threatening the Pakistani nation and the world. This promotion of Sufism as "culture" and as "true Islam" has formed a two-pronged strategy aimed at delegitimizing the radical Islamist galaxy, which is notably hostile to popular Sufism but also to art and entertainment. "Sufism" and "radical Islamism" have thus been constructed as two mutually exclusive concepts and two rival entities fighting each other for the soul of Pakistan. Sufism has thus become an instrument of the process of identity demarcation undertaken by the state against its main challengers.

If "Muslim politics" pertains to the use of normative codes and their symbols to rework the boundaries of civic debate and public life,[2] this chapter is dedicated more specifically to "Sufi politics" in Pakistan in the shadow of the War on Terror. In founding the National Sufi Council in 2006, President Pervez Musharraf (1999–2008) was not the first Pakistani leader to manipulate Sufi symbols for political ends. Every Pakistani ruler has tried to redefine Sufism and the Sufi saints, and instrumentalize them for his or her own political benefit.[3] But the extreme tensions to which Pakistan has been subjected since 9/11, especially since the rise of radical Islamist groups who generally contest the legitimacy of the U.S.-allied government in the War on Terror, constitute a major political and cultural crisis. These developments contributed to a vigorous ideological reformulation of Sufism in order to defend positive values but also create a collective consciousness. Sufism was thus erected, or even reified, as an "Islam of peace and love," and presented as an integral part of Musharraf's "enlightened moderation" and of the "soft face of Pakistan." The main objectives of this "new paradigm" of enlightened moderation included the protection of women and their better representation in Parliament, the promotion of the arts, culture and entertainment, and the creation of new private TV channels.[4] But before all, it was meant to promote to Pakistanis as well as Westerners a tolerant, open, and progressive image of Pakistan and of the version of Islam that is practiced on its soil. It was about engaging once again in the old symbolic struggle over the nature of Islam, in the name of which the country had been created, but also about projecting a reassuring image of Islam to the West and restoring foreign investors' confidence. Indeed, Sufism enjoys the reputation of being a quietist mystical tradition and can also boast of a rich artistic heritage, two qualities that might be perceived as allowing more points of commonality with the West than other Islamic expressions, especially the Islamist one. It can thus appeal to many Westerners,[5] but also to American think tanks such as the Rand Corporation, the Heritage Foundation, or the Nixon Center that have published reports advocating an approach based on Sufism to counter extremism, which have been very influential in Pakistan. Furthermore, the recourse to Sufism was an attempt at legitimizing the principles and actions of Musharraf's "enlightened moderation" with reference to the Islamic heritage of Pakistan. Sufism has been used by secular leaders of the country as a religious authority to legitimize themselves and their policies.[6] Musharraf, who was indeed a secular and liberal-minded politician, is no exception. When he inaugurated his diplomatic mission to India on April 16, 2005, by offering his prayers at the shrine of the Sufi saint Hazrat Khwaja Muʿīn al-Dīn Chishtī in Ajmer, he claimed, "I have come from Pakistan with a message of peace and solidarity." The "symbolic" is indeed "real politics."[7]

The president was known to be a great admirer of the Turkish nationalist leader Ataturk, who had launched an authoritarian secularization and Westernization of Turkey, as well as a drastic reformation of Islam marked as early as 1925 by a ban on Sufi orders and shrines. Despite this official reprobation, Sufism, notably that of the Mevlevi order, founded after the death of the great poet and mystic Jalāl al-Dīn Rūmī, has been used as a cultural showcase for Turkey. In the 1950s, the ceremony of the whirling dervishes was authorized again, but only as a cultural heritage. Since then, the organizers of such Sufi ceremonies have "had to clarify that it was not a religious service but a cultural event."[8] It is no surprise that a tour of Turkish whirling dervishes was organized by the Pakistani government in 2007. Just as in Turkey, the official performances resembled folkloric shows more than devotional rituals.[9] In both countries, Sufism was thus promoted more as cultural heritage than religion per se. This process of patrimonializing religion has elsewhere been described as "the discursive, material, and legal ways in which religious symbols, artefacts, and practices are sacralized as secular elements of the nation and its history."[10] The historian Thierry Zarcone has noticed, in the case of the Mevleviyya in Turkey, a dilution of Sufism into a mere artistic and philosophical product. The "true ascetic practice with its rules, trials, sufferings and spirituality" within a structure of transmission has thus gradually disappeared.[11]

Musharraf never rejected Islam as a whole, nor did he try to erase it from public life as Ataturk did. Conscious of the fact that Islam is the pillar of national identity, he tried to give it an alternate interpretation to that of the Islamists, with their brand of political and puritanical Islam. Under his reign, the long despised "popular" aspects of Islam present at shrines were revivified and became part of the "soft face" of Pakistan. Many Sufi actors (known as *pīrs* or *gaddī nashīns*[12]), who are often descendants of Sufi saints, custodians of their shrines, and often now the targets of contempt by both Islamist and modernist elites, were discreetly involved by the government in that new promotion of Sufism. Confronted by a new wave of violent activism, the PPP-led coalition government that came to power in 2008 more actively co-opted and supported Sufi-based groups (Barelwis) than Musharraf ever did, through a Sufi Advisory Council launched in 2009. As Clifford Geertz would put it, ideological wars are not only fought with ideas, but also with the social groups that carry them in society. For ideas to have powerful social effects, some relevant social groups need to be empowered.[13] However, these Sufi policies have had counterproductive results, as we shall demonstrate. The laws and rules of the state might have unexpected results, both for the state and for the society it is intent on ruling. The implementation of public policies may have had effects that were not foreseen in the initial project. Successive governments have implemented "eclectic strategies" according to their own ideologies and political imperatives that might have produced paradoxical results as far as combating extremism is concerned.[14]

On the basis of ethnographic fieldwork, including observations and interviews conducted in Pakistan since 2005, I discuss here some of the ways Sufi saints and shrines have been politicized by the government, and then turn to the creation of the National Sufi Council aimed at institutionalizing that new Sufi ideology of peace and love. I then show that this master narrative of "good Sufi Islam versus radical Islam" has been severely contested before concluding with the idea that the official promotion of Barelwi politico-religious actors (perceived as "good Sufis") has deep ironies built into it, thus making "Sufism" more of a moving symbol than a consistent entity able to ensure political objectives.

The Enrollment of Sufi Shrines and Saints in the Fight Against Extremism

In Pakistan, unlike Turkey, Sufi orders and shrines have never been banned. But it was partly as an engine against the hierarchical system of meanings and practices centered around these places of devotion, and especially their custodians, that the Ministry of Religious Endowments (Auqaf) was created in Pakistan under the regime of the modernizing President Ayub Khan (1958–69), following which many shrines were nationalized.[15] At that time, the path to "progress" was thought possible only once these alternative loci of power had been harnessed by the authorities and their powerful religious appeal channeled into allegiance to the state. As influential religious but also political actors, the *pīrs* were delegitimized in modernizing discourses, and their authority was also meant to be curbed and replaced by that of the bureaucracy. They were deemed to be the main vectors of a politico-religious system of domination and considered as backward leaders preventing the emancipation of Pakistanis into modern citizens. Indeed, Pakistani Sufi orders are often run by the biological descendants of past Sufi saints, who inherited the title of *pīr* without undergoing any special spiritual initiation. Their authority is generally a blend of traditional authority and of hereditary charisma—their families were often affiliated with the order for generations—and they also inherited their disciples. Jamal Malik thus argues that the nationalization of shrines amounted to a secularization process, as shrines had to be represented as "worldly" (and no longer religious) institutions run by secularly legitimized bureaucratic agents.[16] However, if living *gaddī nashīns* were combated to impose a new "cosmology,"[17] dead Sufi saints kept being celebrated and redefined to suit each government's imperatives and objectives.[18] This is a typical dynamic of postcolonial states: "With the view of insuring a proper foundation for its legitimacy, the State should, on the one hand, appropriate a field of solidarity which transcends it in order to neutralize it and, on the other hand, activate it to benefit from the reception of its symbols."[19] Under Musharraf, *gaddī nashīns* ceased being viewed as challengers and started being relegitimized by the government. A clear sign of that change was the nomination of a *gaddī nashīn* as Punjab minister of Auqaf and Religious Affairs, Pir Saeedul Hassan Shah, from 2003 to 2007 (and then again since September 2018 after the *pīr* joined the Pakistan Tehreek-e Insaf party currently in power).

Shah is the *gaddī nashīn* of the shrine of Chiragh Ali Shah located in the Punjab. When I went to the shrine of Data Sahib in Lahore to meet him in 2006, his secretary introduced him to me before his arrival as a descendant of the Prophet, a *sayyid*, "not only by blood but by activity, adopted from father to son. Sufism has been passed on. He is a *pīr* himself, in the Naqshbandiyyah and the Qādiriyyah." The Auqaf employee who served us tea seemed excited to be working under the mandate of a *pīr*, as if the Ministry itself had been turned into a bureaucratized Sufi order. When I asked him about Sufism, the minister stressed the newfound interest of foreigners in this topic, as many American officials had already come to visit him. He emphasized the Sufi power of uniting different religions and bringing about harmony to humanity as a whole, in a sharp, yet implicit, distinction with "extremist" views of Islam:

> It is one thing that actually unites or brings together in the same harmony not only a tribe or a caste or a religion, it is something that combines other religions to it. If you visit Nizāmuddin Awliyāʾ in India, you'll see Sikhs being there, Hindus are there and Christians are there, and they all have the same feelings for the *pīr* who is there, they all have the same devotion, they are all devoted to the same man. So, it is a platform for humanity, it has a power to unite and bring harmony even between religions, because it doesn't differentiate between religions. It is not like . . . it is only this type of people who will enter paradise and the others won't enter paradise, we don't have this authority to decide, it is Him who decides.[20]

These words echo those uttered by Musharraf in 2006 when the National Sufi Council was first established: "The Sufis always worked for the promotion of love and one-ness of humanity, not for disunity or hatred."[21]

After decades trying to curb the power of *pīr* families, the state thus remains dependent on the shrines and on their custodians, as both still continue to function as political resources. As Sarah Ansari shows in chapter 5 of this volume, *pīrs* are still prominent actors in the political field, notably in the Sindh province but also in the Punjab. Their role as local power holders, mediating between the population and both the state and God, has been weakened but definitely not erased. Until today, even if being a disciple does not mean being completely subservient to the wishes of one's master, the *pīrs* still enjoy the political benefits of turning their spiritual following into a vote bank in times of elections. Each administration has tried to control them without ever succeeding fully in that endeavor. Each government, however, has successfully tapped into the symbolic reservoir of legitimacy that the shrines and saints associated with the local spiritual traditions represent for the population.

Since the beginning of the War on Terror, the Sufi saints have indeed been once again officially redefined as metaphors of the ideal Pakistani nation and of the "true" Islam the country was created to embody. They have been promoted as the hallmarks of indigenous identity, who ostensibly incarnate the positive values characteristic of Pakistan that Pakistanis are exhorted to emulate. If the redefinition of Sufi saints undertaken by President Ayub emphasized their role as social reformists, that adopted by Musharraf envisaged their role more as promoters of peace and tolerance. If, under President and Prime Minister Zulfikar Ali Bhutto (1971–77), the great patron saint of Lahore ʿAlī ibn Uthmān al-Jullābī al-Hujwīrī was presented as the precursor of "Islamic socialism,"[22] he became under Musharraf the herald of the patience and intercommunal harmony Pakistan needs to progress.[23] Indeed, during his trips to Sindh or Punjab, Musharraf exhorted the populations of this "land of Sufi saints" to "promote tolerance, liberalism and a moderate culture in order to eliminate the destructive forces of extremism" and to pray "to protect the country against the misdeeds of extremists and fanatics who are trying to damage it."[24] This discourse endowed past Sufi saints and the shrines that prolong their moral reign, which already embody an ethical order and social values that make sense in the provinces of Sindh and Punjab, with an Islamic authority. These saints are thus projected and perceived as symbols that have to be exalted to defeat the extremists' designs. As Shah, the Auqaf minister, put it: "The teachings of the saints are essential for love with each other, for tolerance, for sacrifice. Therefore, the saints love the public. . . . They love the public only for Allah. They have no enemy, no . . . and Allah loves those persons."[25]

The commemorations of the saints' deaths (*ʿurs*), which generally draw huge crowds to shrines, have also been used by the government and its administration to promote and popularize the philosophy and poetry of the great Sufis.

As places of huge communal gatherings, Sufi shrines have become cultural centers but also platforms for the state to relay its ideology to the masses and, by showing allegiance to the saints, find a source of Islamic legitimacy for its own authority. Therefore, this revivification of shrine culture by the government allows a reciprocal legitimization process. By celebrating pilgrimages, government officials have indeed relegitimized a practice that has been heavily criticized both by secular modernists and Islamists, and thus allowed popular Sufism to be promoted as a central element of national identity. Conversely, the recourse to shrine culture and actors helped the government to inscribe "enlightened moderation" into the national territory and history.[26] These Sufi shrines have been promoted as a collective heritage and culture that can be claimed by everyone in Pakistan.

Celebrating Sufi Culture: The National Sufi Council and Other Initiatives

Consistent with this vision, Muhammad Iqbal's grandson, the famous socialite and musical producer Youssaf Salahuddin, has been the advocate of a version of Sufism defined as the "liberal," "tolerant," and almost "secular" trend of Islam. This vision was at the very same time promoted by the South Asian Association for Regional Cooperation (SAARC) in a conference organized in Delhi.[27] Salahuddin's idea of a National Sufi Council (NSC) aimed at promoting Sufi music, poetry, and philosophy was swiftly appropriated in 2006 by Musharraf, who was willing to inject a specific religious referent into his "enlightened moderation" so as to counter extremism. In September 2006, Salahuddin met Musharraf to put forward his concept of a Sufi Council, and Musharraf gave him carte blanche to form a think tank aimed at rethinking the programs of the state television channel, PTV. Salahuddin, who thinks of himself as a "true Sufi," wished to transform the connotation of "Westernization" attached to "enlightened moderation" into a nonconservative, endogenous modernization. However, his discourse betrays the same strong modernist tendencies his grandfather was famous for. In Iqbal's eyes, the expressions of institutionalized Sufism had all been corrupted in his time and were unable to assist Muslims on their way to progress. Salahuddin echoes this idea, turning Sufism into markers rooted in the past and no longer defining a community of believers: "I never look for Sufis, I don't, I have no faith for Sufis today. The true ones are gone, it is their message that you have to get."[28] He believes both mullahs and *gaddī nashīns* have been exploiting the people. "The *gaddīs* are everything that the Sufis did not preach. You think the Sufis wanted that their children to sit on the grave and make money?"[29] Salahuddin argues that most Sufi poets have denounced the hypocrisy and empty ritualism of religious specialists, quoting the famous Punjabi poet Bābā Bulle Shāh: "Bulle Shāh says that praying, fasting, going to Mecca is meaningless if your intentions are not good. If you do that without love of God, just for fear of heaven, it is not good, just love God because God is to be loved. Like Iqbal says, the real love is when you don't expect anything in return."[30] This distancing from living Sufis, and from Sufism as an organizational force of religious life, allows for Sufi poetry, music, and other artifacts "to be recognized as a common good that everyone, believer or non-believer, can appropriate as a piece of shared history, culture and values."[31] Indeed, Salahuddin does not think of Sufism so much as a form of religiosity than as an important element of Pakistani cultural patrimony and national identity that needs to be promoted: "This council is going to promote Sufism and the Sufi thought and music. In our country, we need to bring that tolerance.... We want our children to know about their history and their roots, we have a very rich culture and history. We don't want to lose that, when other countries are trying to protect their culture, their music. I think we have a very good chance."[32]

The type of Sufism that was promoted then by the Musharraf administration did not include any sort of orthodoxy or orthopraxy in its definition. It was a liminal, cultural, and slightly heterodox Sufism. This is best illustrated by a book offered by the CIA mission chief in Islamabad to Salahuddin at a party organized in November 2006 at the leader of the party in power's house: *Sacred Drift: Essays on the Margins of Islam*, by an American Sufi and anarchist, Peter Lamborn Wilson (also known as Hakim Bey).[33] Quite a departure from promotion of the (mostly Salafi) mujahideen back in the 1980s by the U.S. administration.

Besides Salahuddin, the NSC was composed of Musharraf (chief patron); the leader of the then ruling Pakistan Muslim League (Quaid-e Azam), Chaudhry Shujaat Hussain (the chairman, who was given a turban at the Punjab House in Islamabad by Pīr Sarwar Chishtī, the *pīr* of the Indian shrine of Ajmer, in a symbolic bid to promote him as a "Sufi"); as well as other high-profile politicians and intellectuals: the chief minister of Baluchistan, Jam Mohammad Yussuf; the chief executive of Dawn Press Group, Hameed Haroon; an ex-senator and ex-federal minister for North West Frontier Province and Northern Areas, Abbas Sarfaraz; and the president of the Senate Committee for Foreign Relations and general secretary of the party in power, Mushahid Hussain. In 2006, during the launching ceremony of the Rumi Forum aimed at spreading the teachings of the great mystic poet, Hussain declared that "the mystic literature of Islam is a source of inspiration and following its universal values of love, peace, harmony and tolerance can bridge the gap between East and West."[34] What struck him most as far as Rūmī's poetry is concerned is precisely "his influence on the thought, literature and forms of aesthetic expression in the world of Islam."[35] And it is worth noting that UNESCO "designated the year 2007 as the year of Rumi to develop inter-faith dialogue and spread his message of humanism throughout the world."[36] Meanwhile, the Pakistani army was attacking "insurgents" in Waziristan (since 2004) or in the Swat Valley (since 2007). Obviously, military action was then considered a more efficient means to eliminate terrorism in the short term than promoting Sufism.

The NSC was launched by Musharraf in a grand ceremony, attended by numerous indigenous elites and diplomats, in the historical heart of Lahore on the occasion of Iqbal's birthday in November 2006 and during which a musical CD of his poetry was released under the NSC label. The same month, an international conference called "Sufism, the Way to Peace" was organized by the Punjab Institute of Language, Art, and Culture (PILAC) under the direction of the chief minister of the province, Pervaiz Elahi, the cousin of the leader of the party in power, Chaudhry Shujaat Hussain. Elahi and Hussain are the two main political actors Musharraf leaned on after his coup to give reality to his newly founded party, the Pakistan Muslim League (Q). This conference aimed at legitimizing them both, and they were guests of honor at the opening and closing sessions. The same Sufi ideology of love and peace was promoted to combat the expressions of "mullah Islam," and the shrine of the Qādirī saint Miāñ Mīr in Lahore was also invested for the occasion. The American officials in Pakistan, in their endeavor to find harmless expressions of Islam and to fund the renovation of Sufi shrines, showed a keen interest in all these manifestations. For instance, the public affairs officer of the American Consulate in Lahore, Kathleen Eagen, visited PILAC's director, Shaista Nuzhat, to express her interest in the conference. The American consul also visited the minister of Auqaf and Religious Affairs, Shah, who explained to the consul that there are two types of Islam: "Mullah Islam" and "the Islam of the saints," the latter being defined as a "blessing": "Regarding terrorism, we should emphasize the education of the saints, the bombs are not the solution. Nobody likes bombs. The consul agreed."[37] Sufism has clearly become the new force in which Westerners are putting their hopes. Salahuddin is aware that Sufism has a great market value and is symbolically powerful for mystic-hungry Westerners eager to consume exotic religious resources:

> Basically, I have always thought that in today's world where every culture is being promoted by governments, the things that Pakistan can sell are Sufi

> music and Sufism!... Music is so powerful and it is so deep, so meaningful.... Look at the West, they are very few people who actually have faith, and I think those people are looking for something spiritual, which speaks of universalism, of humanity, which speaks of tolerance, which speaks of love, of equality, I think this is a very good message to spread.[38]

The NSC, which monitored the famous singer Abida Parveen's recording of the whole poetic work of the saint Shāh ʿAbd al-Laṭīf Bhiṭāʾī, as well as the recording of *qawwālī* songs composed by Nusrat Fateh Ali Khan's uncle, seemed to agree.[39] But the latter was not the only organization to partner with the government in promoting Sufism and Sufi music. Several cultural organizations also got involved, providing Musharraf with a way of folding artistic endeavors into his program of "enlightened moderation." Hence, the Musharraf administration seized the opportunity to promote festivals of Sufi music. As early as February 2005, the cultural organization Rafi Peer Theatre Workshop (RPTW) was approached by Musharraf to celebrate the "soft face of Pakistan." Later that year, in November, the president was the chief guest of the annual World Performing Arts Festival organized by RPTW. The international media widely reported on the event, such as in a December 2005 article in *The Guardian* entitled "Sufi's Choice": "In Pakistan, one festival is defying Islamic hardliners—but delighting the president."[40] After attending an evening organized at the residence of the governor of Punjab, where all the artists of the festival performed, Musharraf went to the festival the following day to see the musical fusion between local pop stars and Western and Pakistani groups of spiritual music. The British press described "the mystical Sufi movement" as "one brand of Islam that actively encourages music and approves of musical collaborations that help promote the lyrics of Sufi poets."[41] Musharraf even urged the *qawwālī* singer Shehr Miandad to sing his song, written by the poet Bulle Shāh and attacking the mullahs, to the Muttahida Majlis-e Amal.[42] The president thus used reference to a great Sufi poet as a resource to legitimize himself religiously in the face of the Islamist opposition. As Dale Eickelman and James Piscatori have observed, "Rulers... routinely invoke Islamic imagery and ideas to legitimize their rule and to defend themselves against Muslim critics."[43]

The first international festival of Sufi music was organized in April 2006 by RPTW in Lahore, then the second in Karachi and Multan the year after in collaboration with the government of Sindh. They were resounding successes. The president of RPTW, Faizaan Peerzada, had become famous in Pakistan for the promotion of the arts and the organization of numerous festivals. For him, as for Salahuddin, Sufism pertains before all to *culture*: It is embodied in a rich poetic and musical patrimony. And it is in this cultural field that Peerzada chose to fight the "mullahs." He believed the promotion of Sufi music could help "counter the extremism of the mullahs who use the mosques to spread ill-will against the west. In the mosques they talk about hell, and scare people, but Sufism is about divine love. Sufism can be used against the mullah culture. The fundamentalists created a hardline Islam, but we want to promote the softer side."[44] These cultural actors were not the only ones to mobilize for the promotion of Sufism. Sufi actors themselves got involved. In April 2006, the two representatives of Sufi Order International in Lahore, then in empathy with Musharraf's doctrine of "enlightened moderation," organized an international Sufi conference in collaboration with RPTW's music festival.[45] Entitled "Universalism and Islam," the conference wished to address the "war within Islam between those who take religion hostage . . . and those who believe in a religion of peace and tolerance."[46] The two organizers, Ayeda and Naeela, addressed the problems linked to radical Islam in an exclusively religious way. In a decontextualized fashion, the manifestations of radical Islam were analyzed only as a deviant interpretation of the "authentic" message of Islam.

In such a perspective, the identification of the problem, as well as the proposed solution, pertained, above all, to hermeneutics. For these Sufis, and their Sufi guests from around the world, the Quranic message encapsulated a universalist philosophy presented as antithetical to the sectarianism of the "literalists" and the "radical reformists." Hence, Islamism appears as a "heresy,"[47] to quote Faouzi Skali, who, in the context of Morocco, presents obvious similarities with these Pakistani actors. Skali is an anthropologist who has authored numerous books on Sufism and is a disciple of the Qādriryyah Bouchichiyyah. In April–May 2007, he presided over the first Festival of Sufi Culture in the city of Fès, gathering numerous artists, scholars, and intellectuals from Morocco and abroad.[48] With the theme of "Sufism and Human Development," this festival sought reconciliation of conflicts but also promoted spiritual and cultural tourism. King Muhammad VI, who supported the rediscovery of Sufi artistic and spiritual patrimony and the potential of Sufism to combat extremism, was the festival's patron. The themes of the roundtables, such as "Sufism and Human Rights" or "Sufism and Diversity of Cultures," showed the desire to equate the values of Sufism with those of liberal democracy. Every night, Sufi groups were invited to perform for the audience on stage, thus partially transforming their religious rituals into cultural shows.[49]

Whether in Morocco or Pakistan, the entrepreneurs of such initiatives mostly belonged to the Westernized, cosmopolitan, and liberal fringe and were inscribed in common networks of sociability. In Pakistan, many had been co-opted by the government or supported it unconditionally. Indeed, the liberal bourgeoisie's support of the "enlightened" general was a widespread phenomenon in Pakistan before Musharraf started becoming unpopular from 2007 on, due to the judicial crisis that shook the country in the wake of the sacking of Chief Justice Iftikhar Chaudhry, and of the red mosque crisis that led to the emergence of the Movement of the Taliban of Pakistan. Gilles Boquérat and Nazir Hussain have observed that 85 percent of the scholars, intellectuals, journalists, analysts, and politicians they interviewed in the course of their research believed in the sincerity and authenticity with which Musharraf promoted his "enlightened moderation," but that it was above all a program directed at the West.[50] This has led to many criticisms.

A Contested Master Narrative: Sufis Versus Islamists

Many religious and political actors, as well as journalists and intellectuals, criticized the government's "Sufi venture" as the latest effort to manipulate the symbols of Sufism in order to paint the military dictatorship in mystical colors. Others denounced it as a bid to use a "sweetened" Sufism as a neocolonialist tool, providing Islam with harmless content that would be acceptable to Western powers. As expressed by a civil servant who helped organize PILAC's conference:

> We are here to please the king. We try different colors on his dress, and we stitch what looks best. This National Sufi Council is bullshit. Why is the West so interested in Sufism? Because Sufis are being projected as subservient goodie-goodie Muslims, who don't complain and don't resist. This new interest for Sufism in the Pakistani establishment is before all a message to Westerners in a package that includes the promotion of the arts and entertainment.[51]

According to a leader of the Barelwi Islamist party Jamiat-e Ulama-e Pakistan (JUP), this promotion of Sufism equals the promotion of a new Islam: "Do you know who the president of the NSC is? Youssaf Salahuddin!! Do you realize? They are doing that to alter Islamic values. Promote Sufism . . . but that is not Sufism!!"[52] In some issues of the Urdu newspaper *Nawa-e Waqt*, the promotion of Iqbal by his grandson in the framework of the NSC was notably contested as a mere takeover of Sufism for imperialist ends.[53] Iqbal's Sufism was interpreted as being emptied of its original content and filled with all the deviations that he had precisely denounced, just to sedate Muslim masses. The "propaganda" in favor of Sufism has been perceived as a way to delegitimize rightful political struggles in the Muslim world and as a confiscation of the very interpretation of Islam by actors who are perceived as illegitimate, notably Westernized Sufis. Being a "moderate" Sufi Muslim is clearly understood by many as being a supporter of U.S. foreign policy. In point of fact, since 9/11, the distinction between "moderate" and "radical" has taken on a specific meaning, linked to security concerns. Moderates are those with whom the West can negotiate, whereas radicals are generally those who are reluctant to cooperate.[54]

The definition of Sufism given by government representatives is very selective and tends to make ideological use of some traditional cultural elements in order to offer answers to the challenges of extremism. In this process, the history of Sufism is often reinvented in order to erase, wittingly or unwillingly, all the elements that might go beyond the bounds of the ideological mold and master narrative promoted by government powers. That reinvention is not necessarily strategic. Many actors deem it impossible for Sufis to be politically active or militarily involved, and they simply ignore the historical evidence of such profane activities carried out by many Sufi orders. Thus, although Sufism is invoked as an endogenous identity linked to the past, this ideology manifests deep dynamics of reinvention, "cultural extraversion," and "transfer of meaning."[55] This recourse to Sufism among the Pakistani political or cultural elite is tantamount, to use Jean-François Bayart's terms, to a "fabrication of authenticity," a "process of cultural elaboration in the ideological and sensitive realms."[56] As the ideologization of Islam since the nineteenth century demonstrates, arguments in favor of a "tradition" are constructed and defended once the tradition's legitimacy has been questioned. This recourse to Sufism does not constitute a return to a naive traditionalism but is rather an "ideological re-traditionalization."[57] This ideological re-traditionalization is evident in comments made by the Punjab secretary for culture involved in PILAC's conference, who stated that

> the Sufi culture and teachings have always been a part of our rural scene. . . . All our folk culture is based on Sufi teachings. That is why people of these areas, especially the rural ones, are more secular, or if I want to use another word, more tolerant. This wave of extremism, this radicalism, has never existed before today. It has gradually come about because of the domination of extremists in our society who have indoctrinated people and made them more radical, less tolerant of other religions and sects. . . . There was a necessity to revive, or at least recall to our people what our culture and our system were in the past. That is why we think the renewal of Sufism is a necessity. . . . The extremists are a minority. The majority of Pakistanis are Barelwis. They believe in shrines, in Sufis and in their tolerant teachings and message. The

others are Shiʿa and Deobandis. All the extremism we can witness today, Al Qaeda, the Taliban, all of them are Deobandis.[58]

It is interesting to note that the Barelwi identity has found a new relevance in the power ratios structured by the War on Terror in Pakistan. In this discourse, the term Barelwi has become synonymous with the majority religiosity centered on the cult of the saints and of the Prophet. This very religiosity has long been the target of modernist as well as Islamist attacks, and Barelwis have long been deemed by the secular political elite to be the most backward segment of the religious class. Since 9/11, in a context where Sufism has been idealized, Barelwis have been equated with a Sufi, "tolerant," and "secular" Islam . . . and have been promoted by the PPP-led coalition government from 2008 on. However, we see the ironies of such a promotion: Barelwi groups and actors who have mobilized to defend this identity can also be considered part of the Islamist field.

As for the Deobandis that the secretary of culture holds responsible for all the extremism plaguing Pakistan, they have always counted Sufis in their ranks. Since its inception in colonial India in the nineteenth century, the Deobandi movement has been very much connected to the tradition of Sufism, notably to the Chishtī order. It is a Chishtī Sufi, Ḥājī Imdād ʿAlī, who actually inspired the nascent Deobandi movement and became the *shaykh* of Rashī Aḥmad Gangohī (1829–1905) and Muḥammad Qāsim Nānatwī (1833–1877), the leaders of the first Deobandi seminary founded in India in 1867.[59] However, even if the Sufi dimension of the Deobandi movement has been explored by historians, little is known of its manifestations in today's Pakistan, in a troubled time when religious identities have been radicalized and where Sufism is more surely associated with the Barelwi movement. One of the most notable examples of a Sufi order rooted in the Deobandi movement is the Naqshbandiyyah Owaysiyyah (NO), founded by a Deobandi scholar, Allāh Yār Khān, in the 1960s. This order has been promoting a Sufism that many who are sympathetic to Sufism would consider "orthodox," and that some might even see as Islamist. It is elitist, as the order mainly recruits from the urban middle and upper middle classes, notably among the pious bourgeoisie of the city of Lahore. The implementation of sharia and the setting up of a "real" Islamic state are part of the ideology of its political branch, the Tanzeem-ul Ikhwan (the organization/movement of the brothers), founded in 1992. Most of the cadres of the Tanzeem are retired soldiers, officers, brigadiers, or generals.[60] Many of these military men were disciples of the order before they retired. For several decades the order has established strong networks within the military, and this influence might partially explain the latter's gradual Islamization.[61] It is mainly these military men who formed the contingent of disciples who gathered at the headquarters of the Tanzeem in 2000 and threatened to launch a march to Islamabad if General Musharraf, then in power, did not implement the sharia. Furthermore, as Brannon Ingram aptly shows in chapter 4 of this volume, Sufism is still considered today by the scholars of the famous Dār al-ʿUlūm Ḥaqqāniyya in the Peshawar province, from which many Afghan Taliban leaders graduated, as a legitimate means of leading a life in accordance with the Tradition of the Prophet. And although some convergences between Deobandis and the Salafi-jihadi transnational al-Qaeda movement have been noted, we should remember that these two traditions are theologically very different.

When viewed in light of these complexities of Sufi politics in Pakistan, the hegemonic, yet reductive, "Sufi Islam versus mullah Islam" narrative appears as one ideology among others. It is also reminiscent of the differentiation between "good" and "bad" Muslims Mahmood Mamdani analyzed when he denounced the essentialist prism of "culture talk."[62] The latter is a tendency "to read Islamist politics as an effect of Islamic civilization," and "it dehistoricizes the construction of political identities."[63] In addition to being overly focused on "culture," such an approach completely conceals from the West the responsibility of its own policies in the production of terrorism. So, the "good Sufi Muslim" can only be made possible through a negative contrast with the other "bad Islam" embodied in the Islamists. All this tends to anesthetize the reality of power struggles and to ignore the sociopolitical dynamics of sectarian radicalization in Pakistan and elsewhere.

Under the "culture talk" framework, the Taliban insurgency in Pakistan is understood above all as a religious phenomenon. This interpretation aims at opposing and reifying the "Sufi" and "extremist" expressions of Islam. Consequently, Sufism is interpreted as a solution to extremism in all its forms. This definition of Sufism is a *specular one*, an inverted reflection of a religious definition of "extremism" as a "violent and sectarian" Islam. But this way of defining Sufism is not harmless, as it attempts to define some Muslims as inherently prone to violence and others as more predisposed to tolerant and moderate attitudes to the world because of different theological orientations, a claim that cannot be scientifically confirmed.[64] Furthermore, such a perspective tends to portray Sufism and the various forms of Islamism as abstract and rival entities, thus obfuscating the numerous forms of interactions between the two throughout history, as well as the social and political factors that might explain, among other things, their modes of action, organization, and transformation. Hence, this ideological approach to Sufism and its nemesis ignores the complex religious sociology of Pakistan. Sufis have not all been as "secular" or "moderate" as they are currently being portrayed.

The Ironies of the Official Support for "Sufi Islamists"

In the framework of the War on Terror, mainly targeting Deobandi and Ahl-e Hadith groups, the Barelwis, identified as "good Sufis," have enjoyed governmental support, financing, and promotion. The Musharraf regime and its successor have used sectarian dynamics that set these different movements in opposition to underpin and give teeth to their fight against terror. In the official narrative portraying the current war as an ideological conflict between "moderate" and "extremist" forces within Islam, the Barelwis have indeed been identified as falling into the first of these categories.

According to Olivier Roy, Islamism involves the emergence of new organizations, whether activist religious associations, Sufi orders, or political parties, perceiving Islam both as a "religion" and as a "political ideology."[65] In point of fact, the Barelwi movement has played a widely ignored role in the Islamist politics of Pakistan.[66] Given such convergences between Sufi and Islamist groups, it seems important to sharpen our understanding of these various and often invisible interactions, especially in the framework of a state where the religious, political, and identity referents are tightly intertwined. Sufism has taken on an ideological dimension among new organizations formalizing their doctrinal differences in order to transform their specific religious identity into a political resource and a sectarian stance. The Barelwi leaders define Sufism as the tolerant aspect of Islam and present themselves as peace-loving people who have never been responsible for the violence plaguing Pakistan. And, indeed, the majority of Pakistani radical groups, whether sectarian or jihadis, are not Barelwi. Hence, the "Wahhabis" are denounced as the "real culprits," the only actors of the current wave of "terrorism." However, the Barelwi groups have also evolved different strategies to defend their version of Islam and fight for an Islamic state, an endeavor they call "the system of the prophet" (Niẓām-e Muṣṭafā). As such, they could be considered Sufi Islamists, thus challenging the ideological redefinition of Sufism undertaken since 9/11.

Since the start of the War on Terror, which triggered a process of radicalization among mainly Deobandi and Ahl-e Hadith groups, sectarianism between Sunnis has grown increasingly violent. The Taliban Movement of Pakistan is mostly inscribed in Deobandi Islam and promotes a version of faith that is extremely hostile to the Barelwis, who are considered *mushrik*.[67] And, since 2005, with Sufism increasingly brandished as an official mascot and an effective bulwark against terrorism, Sufi shrines and Barelwi actors have been more specifically targeted for attacks by militants. The latest official endeavors to promote a "state Sufism" may have further solidified the sectarian divide. Debates between Sufis and anti-Sufis are far from new in South Asia. What is new, however, is the systematic targeting of Sufi places of worship, and this cannot be explained solely by rising Deobandi or even Salafi influence, which already existed throughout the 1980s, well before the violence became more common. When the state, particularly an authoritarian state, tries to co-opt a given Islamic movement for controversial political ends, it can leave the movement vulnerable. In this context, we can ask whether the aggressive promotion of Sufism in the framework of the War on Terror, and potential interpretations of it within the jihadi galaxy as a neo-imperialist tool, explain partially why it was only beginning in the 2000s that shrines were actually attacked and Sufis killed by radical militants. Similar questions arise elsewhere in the Muslim world:

> What happens when Sufis come to stand in for an American proxy, when the Americans themselves are so out of reach? This is a question we must also ask of Mali, when among the first objects to be attacked in Timbuktu on its occupation by Ansar al-Din in 2012 were those sites that were both Sufi and classified as UNESCO World Heritage sites, a message that clearly had more than one intended recipient. . . . Might the internationalization of these sites within inter-government projects explain why it was only now that they were destroyed?[68]

On June 12, 2009, the Barelwi mufti Sarfraz Naeemi, the director of a madrasa in Lahore, was killed in a suicide attack claimed by Beitullah Mehsud, the leader of the Taliban Movement of Pakistan. From Bernard Kouchner to Barak Obama, condemnations were unanimous. The former (and future) prime minister of Pakistan, Nawaz Sharif, among many others, deplored a national tragedy. A harsh opponent of the Taliban and the author of a fatwa condemning suicide attacks as un-Islamic, Naeemi had become a target for those he denounced as the enemies of Islam and of Pakistan. Indeed, he supported the government and the military operation in Swat. After his death, he became a martyr, the symbol of a modern, moderate, and tolerant Islam that Pakistan had to defend to confront the terrorist threat. The unusual agitation provoked by Naeemi's death in official circles was yet another clear sign of the political change in the perception of the government toward Barelwi actors, who had long been marginalized.

As explained by Naeemi's son, "these days, the government has a soft corner for Barelwis."[69] This opinion seems to be shared by numerous observers, who all agree that government support for the Barelwis is not only rhetorical, even though the precise nature of official "encouragements" (funds, ammunition?) remains difficult to assess.[70] However, the institutional signs of an official cooptation of Barelwis are plentiful. As early as November 2008, just two months after the new government led by the Pakistan People's Party came into office, a prominent Barelwi leader, Syed Hamid Saeed Kazmi, was appointed federal minister for Religious Affairs, succeeding Ejaz-ul Haq, the fundamentalist General Zia-ul-Haq's son. Kazmi quickly mobilized his networks in Barelwi circles to support the government's policies. The minister appointed Hajji Hanif Tayyab, the leader of the Barelwi party Niẓām-e Muṣṭafā and a disciple of Kazmi's father, as the president of the new Sufi Advisory Council. This body seems to be more than just a resurrection of the NSC. At the time of its creation, the council was lauded by foreign officials in Pakistan but subject to harsh criticisms from all Islamist groups. If Musharraf tried to build Sufism as an alternative ideology to "extremism," his bid mainly remained a rhetorical one, popularized through the media and cultural events. For Minister Kazmi, there has been a change of strategy since the election of the new government, especially since 2009: "The Barelwis are encouraged by the current government, who wishes to mobilize public support against Taliban. They are helped in organizing conferences, and they have the opportunity to meet with the prime minister and the president. They benefit from their moral support, and they can accede more easily to jobs in the civilian bureaucracy."[71]

In August 2009, Kazmi survived an attack on his car, during which his driver was killed. In May 2009, the Council of the Islamic Ideology, which is a constitutional body aimed at advising provincial and national assemblies on the conformity of laws to Islam, was subject to a dramatic increase in its members: initially eight, the members shot up to twenty, including six Barelwis.[72] They are appointed by the president of Pakistan and enjoy a similar status to that of members of the National Assembly. According to Riaz-ur Rehman, the council secretary: "It is a political gesture to incorporate a few members from the Barelwi sect."[73] At the International Islamic University of Islamabad, which was founded by Saudi Arabia, it is a Barelwi *pīr*, Sajid-ur Rehman, who was appointed in June 2009 as director of the Dawa Academy (preaching academy) of the university. This choice has amazed many within the institution, as Saudi Arabia is known for its opposition to Sufism.[74]

However, besides being Islamists in their own right, Barelwi actors are not all as "tolerant and peaceful" as they would wish to be seen in the current context. That is notably the case of the sectarian outfit Sunni Tehreek (ST), known for its radical modes of action aimed at defending Barelwi actors and institutions. The founder, Saleem Qadri, recognized the political plight of Barelwis in Pakistan and wanted to commit more actively, and more violently, to defend his school of thought. That is the main influence of the ST on the way of thinking of Barelwis, who had been perceived by Qadri and his followers prior to the ST's creation as too accommodating, and too unconscious of the real danger of disappearance threatening them. Hence ST is not exactly what one might objectively call a "moderate" group. However, at the very start of the military operation against the Taliban in May 2009, Pakistan's foreign minister (the hereditary *pīr* from Multan Shah Mehmud Qureishi) mentioned the group in a speech in order to officially announce during the *ʿurs* of the Sufi saint Shah Rukn-e ʿAlam the mobilization of the Barelwis against the "talibanization" of the country.[75] Several government meetings had already taken place with the leaders of ST and other Barelwi groups to encourage the latter to lead a social movement against Taliban-affiliated insurgents in the country's northern Swat Valley (the Taliban Movement of Pakistan, or Tehreek-e Taliban Pakistan),[76] who were suspected of having ties to al-Qaeda. The insurgents wanted to impose a judicial system founded on Islamic law, the sharia. If the Taliban succeeded in becoming popular for a time among the young in Swat, it was indeed because they had become a mouthpiece for the concerns of working people and because their struggle to implement the sharia had taken on the task of class warfare against a feudal elite. The radicalization of the insurgents in the Northwest is not merely the result of a certain "extremism" in interpreting Islam but because of multiple factors (including social injustice, the alienation of masses by a predatory elite, state failure, U.S. strikes in Afghanistan and Pakistan, collateral damage, etc.). The day after Qureishi's speech, the first demonstration of Sunni Tehreek in Peshawar took place, which was then followed by the launching of the "Save Pakistan" campaign by Barelwi forces, just before a Barelwi eight-party alliance was formed. Feeling their very existence threatened by the Taliban phenomenon, the Barelwi leaders have tried to organize themselves around a common platform to forward their views. The Taliban insurrection in the North has hence allowed the convergence of Barelwi sectarian interests with those of the government and of the military establishment.

Sufi Violence in Pakistan

The latest developments of the War on Terror in Pakistan have intensified intra-Sunni sectarianism and clearly manifested the Barelwi potential for radicalization. Indeed, it was a member of Sunni Tehreek who killed Salman Taseer, the governor of Punjab, in January 2011. Taseer wanted to amend the law on blasphemy that required the death penalty for any offender against the Prophet Muḥammad, who is venerated by Barelwis. Taseer's killer, Mumtaz Qadri, was his bodyguard, and shot Taseer with dozens of bullets. He instantly rose to fame after the murder and became a hero. He was glorified by large segments of the population including lawyers. Some of them welcomed Qadri's appearance at his murder trial with rose petals and fought to have the honor to defend him in court. This appeared to many observers to be a clear sign that the current radicalization of Pakistani society is to be blamed not only on the Taliban but paradoxically also on what some might call an overzealous interpretation of certain basic Sufi tenets, like the veneration of the Prophet. With his execution in February 2016, Mumtaz Qadri became a martyr and then a saint. A Sufi shrine has indeed been erected by his family members above his tomb in Barakahu, near Islamabad. And a pilgrimage has already started.

While specific acts of Sufi violence in Pakistan may be uncommon, violent sentiments are not. In September 2018, I was traveling in Pakistan with a colleague on a night train heading back to the city of Lahore from the province of Sindh. We made friends with fellow travelers in the compartment. All of them emphasized the fact that Sindh is indeed the "land of the Sufis" and that Sufism is all about "love for humanity." We fell asleep rocked by that consensual definition of Sufism that we had heard from just about everyone we had met during the trip. But in the morning, we were woken by one of our companions, who was shouting: "We should kill them all! They all deserve to die because they don't respect the Prophet Muḥammad! We have such love for our Prophet!" One expression, coined by the anthropologist Ida Sofie Matzen, suddenly flashed in my mind: "extremists of love."[77]

The man, named Afzal, was referring to the Ahmadis, a sect founded in the nineteenth century by Mirzā Ghulām Aḥmad (1835–1908) and declared non-Muslims in 1974 in an amendment to the 1973 constitution. The Ahmadis have been the target of much contempt, criticism, and violence in Pakistan. This is notably the case because the founder of the Ahmadi movement declared in 1889 that he was given by God the mission to revive Islam as a renovator (*mujaddid*), before calling himself a messiah, a guide (*mahdī*), and the reincarnation (*burūz*) of the Prophet Muḥammad.[78] This last claim is often interpreted as an unforgivable breach to the finality of Muḥammad's prophethood, considered to be the best and the last of the Prophets, and as a provocation severe enough for many to advocate death in the name of love. Ghulām Aḥmad is thus considered an apostate by mainstream Muslims, for whom converting to the Ahmadiyyah amounts to blasphemy. "They are worse than infidels," Afzal told us. There seemed to be no cognitive dissonance in his mind between a definition of Sufism centered on love for humanity on the one hand, and the promotion of death for blasphemy on the other.

I asked Afzal what he thought of the most virulent religious group currently mobilizing to protect the honor of the Prophet and to fight against blasphemy against him, the Tehreek-e Labaik Pakistan (TLP). He went on to talk with admiration about the "special powers" of the TLP leader, Khadim Hussain Rizvi. The latter is indeed considered a *pīr*, endowed with great authority by his followers, as is often the case within the Barelwi movement to which he belongs. The TLP became the fifth-largest vote-getter in the 2018 general elections (and the third for the province of Punjab). The recent acquittal by the Supreme Court of Asia Bibi, a Christian woman accused of blasphemy in 2009 and imprisoned ever since, led in November 2018 to the TLP bringing the country to a standstill through massive nationwide demonstrations. The party called for mutiny within the army, threatened to kill the judges, and pushed for Bibi to be hanged. The government met this new threat from Sufi Islamists with a massive countrywide crackdown against thousands of TLP workers and leaders. The latter have been booked under sedition and terrorism charges. These developments appear as the latest, and most eloquent, indicators that Sufis are not always antidotes to radical Islamism.

In this chapter, I have tried to show how the different political dimensions of Sufism are intertwined in often contradictory ways: the official narratives and public policies concerning Sufi actors and institutions, the role of hereditary Sufi leaders in the local power structure and national politics, and the activism of neo-Sufi orders. In other words, I attempt to understand the social and political underpinnings of the various discourses and practices that Sufism has inspired in different actors mobilized within the Pakistani arena of "Muslim politics." "Sufism," as a reservoir of symbolic resources and identity referents, has long been the locus of debate between competing groups within the public sphere. Determining the nature of Sufism, as the Pakistani state has tried to do, is an act of power—of trying to impose norms and meanings and adding to the already existing power relations that have marked the very definition of the term. Since 2001, Sufism has been aggressively promoted in order to solve the one legitimate political problem of that decade: fighting radical Islamists. Sufism was idealized and positive elements attributed to it (love, brotherhood, peace, tolerance, moderation, harmony, secularism, etc.) with the intention of defining a "true Islam" in opposition to that propounded by radical groups. But throughout history, Sufism has diversely proved efficient in structuring social issues, offering a repertoire to articulate political claims and mobilize for collective action. As such, it is probably best analyzed as a symbol.[79] It has never possessed a single meaning. Rather, it is uncertain, fluid, ambiguous, and gives way to competing interpretations. It is a signifier that is efficient in mobilizing powerful emotional projections, a "sublime object of ideology."[80]

9

"Our Vanished Lady"

Memory, Ritual, and Shiʿi-Sunni Relations at Bībī Pāk Dāman

NOOR ZAIDI

Pakistan's landscape is dotted with hundreds of shrines, in massive complexes and small villages, marking the sacred landscape of a country where ties to Sufism and its saints run deep. These shrines have at various times been positioned as examples of a syncretic, moderate Islam, as sites of critical political influence, or as spaces that need to be monitored and controlled. Yet perhaps no site so fully captures the range of competing ideologies and tensions about the proper role of religion in society that has emerged in the process of nation-building in Pakistan than the shrine of Bībī Pāk Dāman, nestled among the crumbling colonial construction and bustling narrow streets of Lahore's Old City. Hundreds of thousands of devotees flood the shrine throughout the year, and the shrine has been portrayed in official discourse and in the media as a unifying space for its visitors. "Of all the shrines and holy places across the city, there is a single place where differences among all sects simply vanished," one newspaper article proclaimed in 2008.[1] Another journal mused in 2017 at the peaceful Sufi environment at the shrine: "While sectarian conflict overshadows Shia-Sunni relations elsewhere, these distinctions blur away at the shrine of Bibi Pak Daman, as all become devotees."[2] Yet despite these characterizations, and amid the bustling crowds, a tense ambiguity pervades the small inner sanctum and courtyard of the site, where conflicts over claims to authenticity and authority have simmered for decades.

The shrine is said to house the graves of six women from the Prophet Muḥammad's household and has long been subject to a range of theories regarding its origins. Despite the popularity of *ziyārat*, or "visitation," to Bībī Pāk Dāman, uncertainty over the actual identities of the women buried at the shrine has been a source of some controversy in the years following Pakistan's Independence. The most widely disseminated claim about the shrine is that the main mausoleum in Bībī Pāk Dāman belongs to Ruqayyah bint ʿAlī, daughter of ʿAlī ibn Abī Ṭālib, the first Shiʿi imam and the most revered figure in Sufi ritual and theology, considered the first Muslim saint (*walī*). ʿAlī occupies a profound dual importance for both Sufi and Shiʿi communities, and this devotion imbues shrines to his family with particular significance. Hagiographies written about Bībī Pāk Dāman vary in the details about how Ruqayyah might have traveled to what would become present-day Pakistan, yet all imply that it was a preordained fate for her to arrive in Lahore. Some attest that, on his deathbed, ʿAlī instructed Ruqayyah to travel to those distant lands, since he foresaw that she would be the one to convert the masses to Islam.[3] Other narratives assert that she was present with Ḥusayn ibn ʿAlī on the plains of Karbala, where the army of Yazīd, the Umayyad caliph, slaughtered Ḥusayn and his male family members and companions in a formative moment in Shiʿi sectarian understandings. According to these narratives, on the night before the massacre (known as the day of ʿĀshūrā) Ruqayyah was sent away with companions to head toward her destiny in Lahore, bearing witness to the tragedies that had befallen her family along the way.[4] Thus, Bībī Pāk Dāman became a powerful symbol for its Shiʿi devotees, proof that they could claim a stake in the central moments of Shiʿi martyrology.

The contention that a daughter of ʿAlī was buried at the shrine is not undisputed, however, especially among the shrine's Sunni and Sufi visitors. An alternate explanation is that this Ruqayyah was the daughter of Sayyid Aḥmad Tokhta, a twelfth-century Sufi saint. Yet the natural conclusion of this belief is that the shrine of Bībī Pāk Dāman was thus no different spiritually than the many other revered sites across Pakistan, with no unique connection to the Prophet's family. For Shiʿa in particular, denials that this is actually Ruqayyah bint ʿAlī have continually been interpreted as yet another slight to negate the importance of ʿAlī's lineage, which resonates with their belief in the historic tragedies faced by the Prophet's family.[5] These debates over hagiography, narrative, and meaning have had a real impact on the physical space of the shrine, creating and exacerbating the conflicts that have emerged in on-the-ground practice and in the administration of Bībī Pāk Dāman.

As part of the state of Pakistan's federalization of *waqf* properties in the 1960s, the shrine was taken over by Department of Auqaf in 1967, which ushered in a new period of tension over narrative, ritual, and identity.[6] Government bureaucrats initially professed a desire to maintain the continuity of daily life at the shrine to avoid destabilizing religious harmony. Indeed, the government's wariness of the charged nature of Bībī Pāk Dāman was not unfounded. The physical space of the shrine was constrained, often overflowing with pilgrims, and the spiritual investment and political implications potent. There were real divides in historical and religious perspectives between various groups at the shrine, but they had been mediated on an individual and community level; the state's takeover of the space led to the escalation of the conflict between Sunni and Shiʿi pilgrims and leaders, and Auqaf officials soon found themselves thrust into arbitrating divisive issues surrounding practice at the shrine.

This chapter traces how officials sought to nonsectarianize the shrine and to construct conditions that would neutralize the space of underlying conflicts—reinforced by the government's desire to retain order in a chaotic urban space set within a charged political environment. Nevertheless, devotees at the shrine often resisted the restrictions that were placed on their behavior, as sectarian claims still provided an effective language for articulating a range of concerns—land rights, gender questions, and religious rituals—in the political context of the tumultuous 1970s. This increase in sectarian meaning belies the claim (sometimes issued by state authorities) that Sufi shrines in Pakistan transcend religious differences and are sites of peaceful syncretism.

Managing Communal Conflict

On September 9, 1967, the government took control of the administration of Bībī Pāk Dāman and the surrounding land through the authority of the West Pakistan Waqf Properties Ordinance of 1961, ending centuries of ambiguity over the control and ownership of the shrine. The shrine was registered as a Sunni shrine, likely because, over the centuries, Sufi *gaddī nashīns* (hereditary administrators of the shrine) in the surrounding environs had claimed their descent from Ruqayyah and had thus managed the affairs of the shrine. The notice of federalization, Notification 1(71)-Auqaf/63, was published in the West Pakistan *Gazette*, stating that the chief administrator of Auqaf had "taken over and assumed the administration control, management, and maintenance of the Shrine," including the attached mosque and graveyard.[7] Simultaneously, Muhammad Asghar, the assistant manager of Auqaf, Lahore Central District, was dispatched to the shrine to take possession of Bībī Pāk Dāman. The process was a remarkable marshaling of the state's nascent bureaucratic capacity, with meticulous attention given to the site now under the government's purview. The assistant manager's assessment of the shrine provided minute detail on its state of affairs so that the government could continue daily life there, assuring the chief administrator that all surveying was done with "full respect to the ladies who reside at the shrine and specially [*sic*] the veiling of women, in reference to your requests."[8] Immediately following the state takeover, there was an acknowledgment of the particularity of Bībī Pāk Dāman—the predominance of female visitors to the shrine and the Shiʿi claim of Ruqayyah's importance as ʿAlī's daughter—which would have to be reconciled with a male-dominated state authority inserting itself into the site's ostensibly mixed public space, where Sufis and Sunnis frequented the shrine in large numbers.

The letters between Auqaf officials in the early stages reveal an attempt to maintain the general rituals at the shrine, especially with regard to female devotionalism and its unique relationship to Ruqayyah, even as they injected themselves into the shrine's management and formalized structure.[9] Yet from the beginning, the Auqaf administrators, likely influenced by the changing political climate on a national scale, also seemed preemptively alert to any potential discord among the Shiʿa. From the chief administrator of Auqaf of West Pakistan came the directive that Auqaf officials at Bībī Pāk Dāman were required to "adopt a suitable line of action to which all the parties might be agreeable. [He] further desired that Shiʿi Leaders should be taken into confidence" in all matters.[10]

On a national level, while President Ayub Khan's government had tried to clamp down on right-wing religious parties in the preceding years, sectarian tensions had increased, making the state sensitive to signs of discord. In 1963, for example, two separate attacks on Shiʿi Muslims had raised the specter of a growing spiral of sectarian retaliation. In response, the government had attempted to persuade the Shiʿa to restrict Muḥarram processions and created new impediments to obtaining permits for these public displays. Prominent Shiʿi ulama (clerics) had protested these restrictions, demanding at the All-Pakistan Shia Ulema Convention that the government provide adequate security for these public rituals to continue and for the self-administration of Shiʿi trusts, shrines, and *waqf* properties.[11] The combination of outbursts of religious violence, new Shiʿi leadership in the political and clerical classes, and the state's broader attempts at Sufi shrines to harness the popularity of these shrines while regulating religious behavior would eventually facilitate new ways of understanding what it meant to be Shiʿi in Pakistan.

The state rhetoric of restrictions on shrines for the good of public safety and sectarian protection was echoed in the guidelines put forth after the government's takeover at Bībī Pāk Dāman, another site that had clear potential for conflict over the use of public space. The most immediate conflict that emerged focused on the control of the *masjid* (mosque) attached to Bībī Pāk Dāman and the issue of religious ornamentation—calligraphic depictions of revered figures or Quranic verses—of the shrine itself. The competing Sunni and Shiʿi claims on Bībī Pāk Dāman would be marshaled to influence these disputes, forcing the government to become a reluctant arbitrator in an increasingly volatile situation.

As part of their initial information gathering at the shrine, Muhammad Asghar and other local Auqaf officials had observed the designated prayer times of both Shiʿi and Sunni devotees to avoid any conflict. However, tensions over different prayer timings regularly led to confrontations between members of both sects and local officials. In 1969 the Auqaf Department divided the *waqf* properties of Bībī Pāk Dāman and gave up rights to portions of the shrine's adjoining lands. The *masjid* attached to the shrine, which had been recently renovated by devotees, was relinquished, and the salary of the imam, or head of the congregation, was passed on to local leaders.[12] This relinquishing again signaled the state's initial reluctance to become too deeply involved in daily religious functions at the shrine.

Despite the Auqaf Department's desire to remain out of explicitly religious disputes by returning the *masjid* to private ownership, just months later they were compelled to reassume "the administration, control, management, and maintenance of Masjid Hanfia" to restore order to a chaotic situation that had emerged from regulating and then deregulating this space so quickly.[13] The existing staff members—the imam and the *muezzin*, who calls the daily prayers—were again placed on the Auqaf payroll.[14] The consequence of this decision, however, was that for bureaucratic purposes, the *masjid* was designated in the same manner as the shrine—officially a Sunni religious site, albeit one where the rights of the minority communities could not be prejudiced.

Through this act, the government reengaged in the attempt to neutralize divisive matters but in a manner that would ultimately affirm a sectarian framework for regulating dispute. An ensuing conflict, for example, soon came to the forefront of Auqaf and Punjab Secretariat records. In July 1970, an Auqaf official at Bībī Pāk Dāman alerted the central office of a crisis that was brewing. For the previous two years, Sheikh Abdul Majid, a member of Bībī Pāk Dāman's Religious Purposes Committee (RPC), had been commissioning work and construction on the shrine from his own private finances.[15] The construction had been on the government's radar, but it had not been a matter that elicited enough reaction among devotees to require interference. Once completed, however, the official noted with alarm, "Inside the dome, Sheikh Abdul Majid is having the names of the *Aʾimmah Kirām* (*Ahl al-Bayt*) [members of the Prophet Muḥammad's immediate family that are revered by Shiʿi Muslims] inscribed in glass-etch work. On this issue, the *Ahl al-Sunnat* [Sunnis] and their followers are raising objections that along with the names of *Ahl al-Bayt*, the names of the Prophet's Companions should be inscribed."[16]

As a result of their explicit desire to mediate potential religious strife, this dispute at the shrine was now firmly an Auqaf matter. Notably, the government itself labeled the divide over inscription a Shiʿi-Sunni conflict, despite the wide range of devotees who visited the shrine. The content of these inscriptions drew an immediate reaction from high-level Auqaf authorities; because members of the shrine's official RPC were involved, the government ultimately stepped in to act as an arbitrator. In reference to the above memo, the chief administrator of the Auqaf ordered local officials "to take immediate measures to avoid the sectarian clash, by stopping the construction immediately. Further construction should not be started until a gentleman [*sic*] agreement is reached between the two parties."[17] This message was then passed on in a handwritten note to Sheikh Abdul Majid, requesting him to "stop further construction immediately to avoid sectarian clash at the shrine."[18] The context was set—these were sectarian divides that required government mediation.

In this particular instance, however, there were financial considerations at play alongside purely devotional concerns. Sheikh Abdul Majid had undertaken a much-needed renovation and aesthetic upgrade of the shrine, financed completely through private funds and donations. In response to the crackdown on his construction, he claimed it was not intended as a religious or sectarian confrontation, but rather a tribute to the family of the women commemorated at the shrine. The government, too, was ever resistant to increase their financial commitment to any one shrine, especially one as contentious as Bībī Pāk Dāman. As a result, they sought to mediate a solution that would not impede the renovation entirely. The chief administrator of Auqaf sent new instructions to officials on site, those who had had numerous dealings with the involved parties. He directed, "You were directed to stop the construction ~~personally~~ [*sic*] immediately. . . . Now it is desired that you should try to settle the dispute between the two sects at your personal level, say by calling a meeting of the two sects and persuade them in a reasonable manner and tacts [*sic*]."[19]

One can easily see how the Auqaf's directors sought to protect its financial interests by refraining from involvement in this situation, although they claimed they could not prevent renovation due to the need to protect minority rights. In fact, in terms of the shrine's importance, the government's interest clearly aligned with that of the Shiʿi pilgrims in refuting the idea that this was the daughter of a twelfth-century Sufi saint. The presence of Ruqayyah bint ʿAlī in Pakistan lent a critical validation to the historic presence of Islam in the subcontinent, an Islam intrinsically tied to the early history of the faith—a fact that government pamphlets routinely emphasized.[20] It was also the second-largest shrine in the Punjab in annual donations and revenue; the peak periods of donations to the shrine came on important dates in the Shiʿi calendar of mourning.[21] While there had previously been disagreements among members of the Shiʿi community represented on the RPC over where funds should be directed, following the government's lead, pilgrims and religious authorities, too, would engage within a sectarian framework, despite the government's larger intentions.[22]

The Continued Impossibility of Neutrality

In 1971, there was once again danger of "serious conflict" breaking out among devotees at the shrine.[23] The struggle began on July 27, 1971, when a group of Sunni pilgrims commissioned the engraving of the four Rāshidūn caliphs (the Prophet's companions as claimed by Sunnis) on one of the internal structures in the shrine. Honoring the Rāshidūn is objectionable to Shiʿa, who believe that the three earlier caliphs had usurped ʿAlī's legitimate claim as Muḥammad's successor. Inscribing their names on the shrine for one of ʿAlī's daughters was seen as a deliberate provocation in this context. The conflict over ornamentation reveals how deeply aesthetics and sectarian devotion were linked at this site and the importance of the choice of textual references for devotees. As a result of the brewing conflict, on October 25, 1971, the RPC and the chief administrator of the Auqaf again called Shiʿi and Sunni representatives together and discussed a compromise on the use of Bībī Pāk Dāman, to neutralize the warring division of space that had evolved.

A joint ruling sought to pacify both parties. Men were barred from the inner sanctum of the shrine, a concession to Shiʿi beliefs that respect for the piety and veiling of Ruqayyah and her family must continue even in their physical absence (as one of the most important tropes in Shiʿi history is related to the forcible de-veiling of its Shiʿi women). This rule had been shared with the female attendants at the shrine in 1967, when government employees arrived to take control of the shrine; now, it was brought into these discussions as a part of a formalized and routinized religious conduct.[24] Rather than a debate about men simply following proper traditions of *adab*, or respect, as it had been addressed previously, it became inserted into this sectarian framework.

To pacify Sunni devotees, it was decided that no *majālis* (or religious lectures on the topic of Shiʿi mourning) would be held inside the space of the shrine. This was interpreted as a significant blow to Shiʿi organizations around Bībī Pāk Dāman, as *majlis* gatherings were a critical component of

Muḥarram rituals and had historically been an important tool in reinterpreting the Karbala narrative into the local context, placing the shrine within a particular sacred geography. Most importantly, the *masjid* located inside Bībī Pāk Dāman—the one the government had so recently reacquired—would no longer issue the *adhān*, or call to prayer, of either sect, so as to neutralize it. Thus, all people could pray inside, but it would no longer function as a mosque where devotees could congregate for collective prayers.[25] This was a dramatic step—Muslims are required to recite Friday afternoon prayers in congregation. The mosque was seen as a living institution. Now this site would be emptied of doctrinal rituals, and the blessings attached to praying together would be deactivated from collective public use in order to avoid conflict.

That the government would take such an aggressive approach at Bībī Pāk Dāman is not surprising. In March 1971, the Awami League announced the declaration of Independence of East Pakistan, beginning a nine-month armed struggle against West Pakistan. On December 16, 1971, East Pakistan was officially separated from Pakistan and replaced by the new state of Bangladesh. The pervasive sense of loss this event precipitated cannot be overstated. The impact of the war and the dismantling of Pakistan was "the most traumatic event in Pakistan's short life as an independent nation."[26] The material losses were also tremendous—Pakistan lost over half its population, a significant portion of its territory, and its second-most economically productive province. The new Pakistani government of Zulfikar Ali Bhutto, called to take over on December 20, 1971, would play on the shame of the war. "Desperate men who were blinded by their lust for power and seemed to have been possessed by death had first destroyed and then surrendered half the country to an aggressor. The other half was in imminent danger of destruction. The people of West Pakistan were lost and completely demoralized. . . . An appalling defeat and disgrace had been inflicted on our unprepared people," Bhutto lamented in 1972.[27] Worse than the shame, however, was that the destruction of the territorial integrity of Pakistan dramatically undermined a central ideal of the Pakistan movement—that Islam was enough to create and hold the new nation-state together, even with its sectarian, ethnic, and linguistic divisions and discontiguous geographic reality.[28] The lesson was that political dissent and minority discontent could create a powerful platform to articulate grievances that could turn into the roots of dissolution. With trouble simultaneously brewing in Baluchistan and the Northwest Frontier Province and growing Sindhi nationalist agitation, in the eyes of the state any additional conflicts—including sectarian conflict—had to be mitigated.

The struggle with East Pakistan and the social ruptures it revealed provides an illuminating, albeit complicated, lens into the debates at Bībī Pāk Dāman. It is no surprise, then, that the government so swiftly acted to bring the parties together and neutralize the Sunni-Shiʿi conflict at the shrine. Their perception of the threat of sectarian conflict undermining Islamic unity was real, and they acted to regulate behavior in a way they believed would temper these tensions. However, though officials agreed on the new terms, the prohibition on men entering the inner spaces of the shrine caused great unrest among the Sunni population, leading to a collective letter of protest to the governor of Punjab. On March 15, 1972, a new notification was issued in response to these agitations. The new guidelines stated that there would be no limit on the recitation of the Quran in the inner shrine by any pilgrim, that the names of the Rāshidūn were allowed to remain, and that *majālis* would not to be allowed inside the inner courtyard of the shrine, "so that no person of one faith will commit an act that will wound the other side."[29] However, the notification reiterated that the shrine was acquired as a Sunni shrine and would continue as such, even though the Sunni majority could not obstruct the Shiʿi faithful from carrying out personal religious rituals. Once again, the state's attempt to promote a sectarian secularism and neutrality favored one of the communities over the other.

This amended compromise reveals the uneasiness with attempts to categorize the shrine and the difficult balance the government sought to keep as a perceived neutral party. It is striking that both Sunnis and Shiʿa appealed to officials to negotiate their spiritual and ritual differences and segment the physical interior of the shrine, illustrating the ways that devotees appropriated the government's takeover of the shrine as a new way for asserting their preferences, creating a channel through which grievances could be aired. The state was now an active force on the ground at Bībī Pāk Dāman. The Auqaf Ordinances that federalized the shrine through the 1960s and 1970s created a framework in which the use of space would be contested and divided—a development that affected the ways in which different communities related to Bībī Pāk Dāman.

The trust in government intervention, however, remained tenuous, as mistrust existed on all sides. For national purposes, the Auqaf Department had displayed an investment in affirming that the graves at Bībī Pāk Dāman belong to Ruqayyah bint ʿAlī and her companions, yet the majority of the members of the RPC and the government authorities of the Auqaf Department were Sunnis and Barelwi Sufis. Once that became the lens through which these incidents were viewed, official interference, once tolerated and manipulated, was never greeted with total welcome. Indeed, the extent to which the government was able to exert control over day-to-day practice varied.

Attempts to Circumvent Sectarian Secularism

The distance between official judgments and daily ritual was illustrated on March 24, 1972, when another petition from local Shiʿi leaders, led by retired Lahore Court judge Sayyid Jamil Hussein Rizvi, to the chief administrator of Auqaf led to an amendment permitting *majālis* to be held a few times a year in Bībī Pāk Dāman, with advance notice.[30] Despite the limited number of official gatherings allowed, however, Bībī Pāk Dāman remained a hub of activity throughout the year, with *majālis* held daily throughout the holiest month of Muḥarram and on most important dates in the Shiʿi calendar, making clear the distance between law and practices. Bībī Pāk Dāman provided a space in which these opposing frameworks were negotiated on the ground. Auqaf officials recognized the potential for conflict that free expression of rituals would ignite at Bībī Pāk Dāman. Their solution was to regulate and restrict activities so as to have minimum impact on the opposing sect. Rather than allow devotees to fill the space with meaning through narrative, prayer, and ritual, the government sought to empty the shrine of all contention.

Yet Bībī Pāk Dāman was not a settled site, and it continued to provide space for asserting identity. Maulwi Muhammad Bakhsh Shah Qureshi, the Shiʿi representative on the RPC, remained unsatisfied with the compromises on ceremonies at the shrine. He noted that the chief administrator of Auqaf, Punjab, had mandated a limit on Shiʿi expressions of piety and that if any devotee "gets carried away by love and emotion and begins to recite a lamentation or weep, they are forcibly removed [from the site]." During *chehlum* ceremonies in Lahore, commemorating the fortieth day after the martyrdom of Ḥusayn, a rider-less *zuljanah* (horse symbolizing Ḥusayn's sacrifice) had traditionally led a procession through the streets and ended at Bībī Pāk Dāman. Such evocative symbolism had now been prohibited by the compromises of the past months and the government's desire for moderation in religious practice. For Qureshi, there was a disparity in regulation that had real implications on the lived experience of devotees. He charged, unhappily:

> It was to my astonishment that I saw that in this holy and blessed shrine, when the Sunnis arranged the yearly *ʿurs* under the auspices of the Auqaf within the boundaries of the shrine, not only did arrange a *mīlād* [celebration of the Prophet's birth] and *naʿt khānah* [rhythmic poetry], they organized a full musical evening with drums and chants. The *chādars* [sheets] were spread by men on the holy grave. . . . If a Shiʿi devotee is moved by the presence of his Bibi and begins to cry or recite a lament, it is not permitted, but the Sunnis can play music and engage in revelry—why is there such a difference?[31]

Qureshi's anger at these Shiʿi rituals being curtailed can be understood through Clifford Geertz's model of what ceremonies entail and why they matter. According to Geertz, ceremonies contain two distinct aspects—they provide a "model of" and a "model for" reality.[32] The *zuljanah* horse was seen as a symbolic model of the reality of Ḥusayn's rider-less horse returning to the camps to inform the women of the sacred imam's martyrdom. It was a way to access the emotional trauma of the moment in collective grief. Yet the imagery of Karbala also provided Shiʿi Muslims an ideal paradigm for organizing the world, to make sense of their minority status and the injustices of their history. Prohibiting the *chehlum* procession from entering Bībī Pāk Dāman was a direct challenge to the reality of Shiʿi experience and their attempts to impose meaning through ritual. For Qureshi, the latitude that was granted to Sunni devotees or to Sufi visitors, whose *ʿurs* celebrations mirrored those of Sufi shrines across the country in their carnivalesque affect, exacerbated the matter.

These attempts to neutralize the space were, of course, continuously negotiated, managed, and often disregarded by the involved parties. They also existed within a national political context in which Shiʿa were galvanizing to assert collective action. In May 1972, the Imamia Students Organization (ISO) was founded in Lahore, with the aim of advocating for Shiʿi needs through religious and social outreach. Membership in the ISO spread rapidly through much of Pakistan, and its students became increasingly vocal about the need for Shiʿi voices to be heard in textbooks, public religious rituals, and Islamic charities. Those assertive attempts were mirrored at Bībī Pāk Dāman. A letter written in late 1973 from the manager of Waqf Properties to the head of Auqaf, Central Zone, detailed multiple escalating events within the shrine that had challenged the neutrality of the site. The manager reiterated the Auqaf rules: "Other than fixed occasions of dates and hours, members of Shiʿi and Sunni communities are not allowed to congregate for religious rituals."[33] Pilgrims to the site regularly disregarded these schedules, conducting rituals and reciting prayers at all times of day. Yet in periods where tensions were heightened, as they were in the early 1970s, these rules become the default, and Auqaf officials recommitted to a strict division of space. Any actions, even on the individual level, that challenged that order were seen as real threats.

In one case, concerns were raised over a female devotee, Asma Kaneez, who had been chanting *nawḥahs*, or poetic lamentations about Karbala. This was a danger, it was reported, because "while listening to her the Shʿi ladies begin *mātam* [beating of chests in lamentation], which is a violation of the restrictions and cause of tension. While watching the Shiʿi ladies do *mātam* inside the shrine makes the Sunni ladies angry, it can also lead them to retaliate as they have threatened. This matter can be prolonged and become a cause of conflict."[34] Asma Kaneez protested that she was merely exercising her right to practice her faith at a public space, a ritual that was directly related to the story of Karbala. The official insisted, "If this is agreeable then the following notification should be publicly posted inside: 'Inside the shrine's inner grounds, after offering basic salutations and prayers, kindly restrict yourself to reciting the Quran; other than that, *majlis, mīlād,* and *nawḥah* can only be practiced in the allotted space and time.' "[35] Interestingly, the Auqaf manager does admit that these rituals were viewed as necessary religious expressions that "refresh" faith, yet when they carried such emotional resonance as to move listeners to collective action, they became a threat at a site like Bībī Pāk Dāman. The take-over of Bībī Pāk Dāman did not give the government legal license to dictate explicitly what religious expressions were practiced or what emotional affect would occur, but they were able to enforce negotiated schedules under the threat of sectarian violence.

Bībī Pāk Dāman's Auqaf manager goes on to relay in this 1973 letter another brewing conflict, one that again revolved around the highly charged question of ornamentation and how a particular holy site can be read: the inscription of a particular Quranic verse that Shiʿi Muslims believe refers to the Prophet's family. In Sūrah al-Shūrā, verse 23, Allah instructs Muḥammad, "Say: no reward do I ask of you for this except the love of those near of kin." For the Shiʿa, this is a clear reference to ʿAlī, Fatima, and their children, known as the *Ahl al-Bayt*, and a legitimization of the Shiʿi line of succession; Sunnis contest this claim. At Bībī Pāk Dāman, this verse had a clear connotation, as Ruqayyah is the immediate link to the *Ahl al-Bayt.* The manager of Waqf Properties related the following narrative about the conflict:

> Sayyid Ahmad Hussain Shah, a member of RPC, has installed a black stone plaque inscribed with this *āyat* [verse] for which he received permission Oct. 25. Two other members [of RPC] . . . confirmed that no one had any objections to the installation of this stone. However, upon further inquiry, it was found that the installation was delayed for some time because the *ayāt* was engraved with the Urdu translation. Many Sunni devotees had objections to the translation. It was decided through negotiations that if this *ayāt* was installed without translation, there would be no objections. As a result, on this plaque, only the Quranic *āyat* is written, without any translation.[36]

The calculation made here is striking. There was no justifiable reason to remove a verse of the Quran from a sacred site, even one as polarizing as Bībī Pāk Dāman. Negotiations between members of the RPC had led to a settlement, yet outcry from pilgrims prompted a change. An Urdu translation would involve making particular choices and allow pilgrims to understand a particular interpretation. For a site like Bībī Pāk Dāman, translations, narratives, and understanding threatened the balance of what could be allowed and managed. Only Arabic, which few could understand, would be permitted.

The Failure of State-Imposed Sectarian Secularism

Auqaf officials and the government managed the tense space of the shrine by ordering behavior in a sectarian context. Although pilgrims, religious leaders, and local residents often ignored Auqaf orders, the bureaucratization of religious representation and the segmentation of rules and rituals constructed a formal sectarian secularism at Bībī Pāk Dāman, one perpetuated by government attempts to neutralize the space from conflict. The Auqaf takeover in the 1960s was not without opposition, nor did these ordinances create uniform standards. Indeed, as seen in these instances, those rules continued to be negotiated, as devotees repeatedly appealed against and to the government in their attempts to assert autonomy over their religious practice. In these instances, devotees displayed a considerable degree of sophistication, playing various branches of the government against one another to receive the desired ruling and utilizing the language of constitutional rights to continue their devotional routines. Yet these contestations over space, finance, and ritual also created a new way of being Shiʿi at the Bībī Pāk Dāman shrine. Being Shiʿi once required a public acceptance of the narrative of Ruqayyah bint ʿAlī and the practices that corresponded to those beliefs; it was now equally defined by the government as a structure of behavior to be regulated. These constructs were increasingly mirrored in public spaces across Pakistan.

The Auqaf's failed attempts at enacting neutrality recall a larger problem inherent in state attempts to regulate religion: Although secularism is thought of as the refusal of government to take sides in religious disputes, laws and governmental agencies—in Pakistan and elsewhere— impact religious communities in myriad ways. Popular narratives about Sufism in South Asia often depict Sufi shrines as spaces that transcend religious divisions. As other authors have demonstrated in this volume, that ideal is not always enacted in practice. Nor can sectarian divisions—ones that take on meaning in the context of larger political developments—be so easily eradicated. If anything, the Pakistani government's attempts to do that by denuding the shrine of sectarian meanings so as not to exacerbate larger national sectarian conflicts only intensified its importance for local sectarian communities.

Commentary on Part III

The Problems and Perils of Translating Sufism as "Moderate Islam"

SHERALI TAREEN

While the chapters in part 3 engage multiple themes, sites, and questions, they all in one way or another address the problem of "the moderate Muslim" discourse, especially when mobilized in the context of South Asian Sufism. The discourse of religious moderation is among the most powerful and equally insidious features of the new global politics of religion. This discourse seeks to produce "moderate" religious subjects at ease with the aims and fantasies of liberal secular politics. Certainly, liberal secular thought and practice takes varied trajectories; secularism is indeed a complex and variegated phenomenon the precise texture of which depends on specific contextual and historical dynamics. However, as anthropologist Saba Mahmood powerfully argues, while the precise trajectory of secularism is historically specific to each context, the inextricability of secularism from liberal political rule is derived from analogous conundrums and paradoxes involved in the modern state's management of religious difference.[1] The regulation and moderation of religion as a category of life represents a touchstone of secular thought and politics. But defining "good, moderate" religion constitutes not only a matter of much ambiguity. The ideal of the moderate is also highly fluid, one that absorbs and ingests varied and often variously conflictual qualities as it travels from Euro-American settings to the Global South. The collection of chapters in this part shows the multiple yet overlapping ways in which demands for religious moderation have shaped the contours of Islam, especially Sufism, in Pakistan. The pressure and anxiety to carve a moderate Islam has deeply affected contemporary Muslims around the world, especially in Euro-American Muslim-minority contexts.

But what makes the moderate Muslim discourse particularly potent and pungent in the Pakistani context is the dominant tendency—in international politics, media, and even some scholarship—to view Pakistan primarily in terms of a perpetually simmering threat crying out for containment. Since the specter of religious extremism and violence always hovers over the country, so this problematic yet powerful narrative goes, the threat of fundamentalist violence must be mitigated by the liberal prophylactic of moderation. The preceding chapters bring this narrative into serious doubt by providing more nuanced accounts of the tensions and contradictions generated by the equation of Sufism and moderate Islam. They also admirably attend to the specificities of the local micro-politics involved in the appropriation and at times confrontation of Sufism's packaging and promotion as moderate Islam in Pakistan. Therefore, taken together, these chapters allow readers to view both Sufism and Pakistan as complicated constructs unavailable for generalized narratives or caricatures. But before I engage specific elements of these chapters, as a way to frame my comments, let me first highlight some major conceptual and political problems reflected in the desire to moderate religious subjects, especially Muslims.

Moderation Talk

For Muslim communities around the world, and especially in South Asia, few expectations and pressures have carried more weight and urgency than that of passing the test of moderation. Indeed, the search, often taking the form of a demand, for moderate Muslims seems at once ubiquitous and yet wholly undefined. There is no clear answer to the question of what precisely a moderate Muslim subject looks like. This question inspires a staggering variety of answers. The moderate can include an ally in surveillance against the radical "internal other." She often represents the pursuer of a suburban American dream simulating white Protestant ideals of progress.[2] The moderate is someone who prioritizes loyalties of citizenship over his religious identity and commitments, with a conviction in Abrahamic American exceptionalism a bonus virtue. Or the moderate is someone who favors seemingly mild, private, and more "spiritual" articulations of religion over its harsher and more legally oriented forms as represented by the monstrous specter of the sharia, or Islamic law. The chapters here engage this last modality of moderation most directly. But regardless of how moderation is conceived, it cannot escape certain irresolvable contradictions.

The demand for moderation is intimately connected to a larger secular politics of critique that seeks to domesticate and purify religion so as to make it more appetizing for liberal secular governance. As Ananda Abeysekara has pointed out, the word "moderate" is derived from the Latin *moderare*, meaning to "tame," "control," "reduce," and "restrain."[3] Moderation is a discursive strategy to tame and regulate religion so that it is rendered amenable to the protocols and expectations of liberal secular reason. For religion to be acceptable, it must first be baptized in the moderating force of secular critique. But no attempt to neutralize, humanize, regulate, and moderate religion can resolve the irresolvable contradiction of seeking to retain the name of religion while also differing from that name, of having religion without religion. As Abeysekara brilliantly sums up, "At the end of the day, [critique] can only have religion without religion, religion emptied of the fanatical, the superstitious, the not so religious. Emptied of its substance, still named religion, this 'religion' remains itself by not being itself. The name religion is substituted for its own (same) name!"[4]

It is this irresolvable contradiction of seeking to retain the name of Islam while also differing from that name that plagues moderate Muslim discourse, especially when employed with regard to Sufism. Sufism in this scheme represents Islam that is not really Islam; it is the softer, innocuous, and neutered Islam at peace with liberal secular expectations of what religion in the modern world should look like, namely, religion that is apolitical, ritually lax, consigned to the domain of inner private piety, and unencumbered by external institutional authority. Even the most elementary understanding of the Sufi tradition mitigates against this caricatured representation. Nonetheless, as the chapters in part 3 amply show, the Orientalist and more recently neo-imperial translation of Sufism as moderate Islam has engendered powerful political consequences.

Islamic Vocabularies of Moderation?

The skeptic may object to this analysis with the rejoinder that moderation represents a value and normative aspiration indigenous to Islam and not a foreign Western imposition. To further this counterargument, one may point to categories such as *wasaṭiyyah*, *iʿtidāl*, *mayānih-ru*, or *mayānih-rawī* in Arabic, Persian, and Urdu as examples of Muslim categories corresponding to the notion of moderation. The most iconic Quranic reference one may cite here of course is verse 143 of chapter 2 (titled "The Cow"/"al-Baqarah"), the beginning words of which read "we have made you a balanced community [*ja'alnākum ummatan wasaṭan*]." There are three major ways in which these categories are massively different from the modern secular discourse of religious moderation.

First, Muslim categories such as *i'tidāl* and *wasaṭiyyah* carry more the meaning of "balance," "justice," and "virtue." They signal the promise and aspiration of a disciplined life conducive to the cultivation of a just and balanced individual and body politic. They do not involve the moderation of a subject in the sense of compelling her to abdicate, soften, or tame her everyday religious life. Exactly the opposite, in traditional Muslim formulations, it is precisely the intensity of a subject's piety that ensures balance, probity, and justice. Second, these categories are not tethered to the power and sovereignty of the modern state. In stark contrast, the liberal discourse of religious moderation is inextricably entwined with political secularism, or the state's management and regulation of religion and its limits as a category of life. And third, in Muslim thought, the ideal of achieving a balanced disposition does not involve succumbing to the logic of an inverse relationship between Sufism and the sharia or Islamic law. In contrast, the moderate Muslim discourse thrives precisely on the law-Sufism binary. According to this binary, becoming more moderate means jettisoning one's attachment to legal demands and strictures while embracing a vision of Sufism far removed from if not opposed to the troubling shadow of the sharia. Such a framing makes a mockery of Sufi thought and practice. Abiding scrupulously to the dictates of law represents a prerequisite and gateway to embarking on the Sufi path and eventually to the realization of divine truth. This hierarchical arrangement is best captured by the rhyming formula sharia (Islamic law), *ṭarīqah* (the Sufi path), and *haqīqah* (divine truth/reality). A hierarchy is not a binary. Thus, searching for Islamic equivalents for the modern liberal discourse of moderation represents an exercise as politically problematic as it is conceptually clunky.

Sufism and Moderation in Pakistan

The preceding chapters demonstrate that the translation of Sufism as the "tolerant" and "moderate" form of Islam, both by actors within and outside Pakistan, has shaped the religious and political topography of the country in profound ways. Sarah Ansari in chapter 7 and Alix Philippon in chapter 8 both show the versatility of Sufism as an object of political mobilization. As their analyses makes clear, political leaders of different stripes and generations in Pakistan have sought to dye Sufism in the colors of their own political aspirations and agendas. So, for instance, in the populist Zulfikar Ali Bhutto's hands, a Sufi reformer was equivalent to a socialist reformer. For the Sindhi nationalist G. M. Syed, Sufi and Sindhi were synonymous, as he attempted to position Sindh as the cradle of a "tolerant" Sufi heritage. Similarly, more recently, Pervez Musharraf, the former president and military dictator, outsourced the "War on Terror" post-9/11and framed Sufism as quintessentially "anti-extremist" and the ideal antidote to "radical Islamism." All these actors translated Sufism in the image of their own political interests. But, this operation was often messy and far from seamless. Particularly telling in this regard were the attempts by players such as Bhutto, and the contrasting military dictators Ayub Khan and Zia-ul-Haq, to downplay mystical elements such as miracles, saintly authority, and so on, in their presentation of Sufism. The quest to excise the mystical from the mystical tradition in Islam was bound to engender some profound ironies. Their political ideologies may have ranged from populist socialist (Bhutto) to neoliberal modernist (Ayub Khan) to ostensibly Islamist (Zia-ul-Haq), but these leaders were united in the modernist push to render Sufism compatible with a liberal rationalist sensibility.

However, as Ansari's chapter clearly shows, the encounter between state power and Sufi charismatic authority has hardly constituted a one-way street. Rather, the political mileage afforded by the latter has attracted every successive government, at the federal and provincial levels. The ambivalent power dynamics attendant on the relationship between the state and Sufism in Pakistan is perhaps best exemplified by the figure of the *pīr*, or charismatic spiritual guide attached to a Sufi lineage and shrine. Ansari's chapter shows with great clarity that *pīrs* represent both a promise and a threat. Deeply entrenched in the spiritual economy and power politics of rural areas in Sindh and Punjab, they are often seen disdainfully as stumbling blocks to modernization. And yet, even the most modernist of political rulers have seemed eager to extract the charismatic authority of the *pīrs* as part of their political calculus and calculations. For their part, *pīrs* have also shown ample adeptness at negotiating the political terrain by engaging with or dissociating from electoral politics according to their preferences and priorities at a given moment in time. I would suggest that Ansari's telling account of the shifting role and place of *pīrs* in Pakistani politics brings into view what one might call the "political theology" of the institution of the *pīr*. The figure of the *pīr* represents an intermediary in the political and theological realm, as the person who simultaneously connects the local masses to both the political and divine sovereign. Ansari's analysis highlights a striking symmetry in the political and theological mediation of the *pīr*. In the theological realm, the *pīr* provides the masses access to the vatic capital of a Sufi master, and through him, to the Prophet and God.

And in the political domain, he serves as a critical link between the worldly political sovereign and the vagaries of everyday life that occupy the members of a community. It is this political theology, or the mutual imbrication of the political and the theological, that lends the figure of the *pīr* its political and material power. It is a form of power that poses as both a promise and a peril.

Let me now turn to Philippon's chapter. She shows the conundrums and slippages found in the international and national valorization of the Barelwi orientation as the true banner-bearer of "moderate Islam" in Pakistan. Further, she highlights the catastrophic consequences of intervening in internal and ongoing intra-Muslim debates and contestations by deciding who gets to don the mantle of moderation and who gets consigned to the infamy of extremism. This is not to say of course that the Barelwis are not really moderate or that their rivals like the Deobandis are in fact the real moderates. The problem rather, as Philippon shows, lies in the very quest to identify and frame indigenous actors according to conceptual templates that are not of their choosing or making.

Take for instance the Barelwi-Deobandi polemic. This polemic, arguably the most long-running and bitter intra-Sunni rivalry in South Asia, with beginnings in late nineteenth-century North India, centered on competing imaginaries of Prophet Muḥammad. How should a community imagine the relationship between divine sovereignty and prophetic authority during the colonial moment when South Asian Muslims had lost their political sovereignty? This was the central question at the heart of this polemic. It animated bitter disagreement over such questions as the nature and scope of the Prophet's knowledge of the unknown (*ʿilm al-ghayb*) and the normative legitimacy of the Prophet's birthday celebration (*mawlid*). The Barelwi-Deobandi polemic, in other words, brought into view two competing political theologies articulated by rival groups of scholars who were both prominent jurists and Sufi masters.[5] The Deobandis, often caricatured as fundamentalist puritans, have always been steeped in Sufi thought and practice, as the chapters in this volume show. The Barelwis, for their part, are no populist Sufis either but are rather thoroughly grounded in Islamic legal discourses and traditions.

Thus, reading this polemic and the social imaginaries of its participants through the prism of binaries like moderate-extremist, Sufi-fundamentalist, or puritan-mystical is at once misleading and spurious. But this is precisely the sort of binary framing that has occupied actors ranging from neoliberal think tanks like RAND and the Heritage Foundation to champions of "enlightened moderation" within Pakistan like Pervez Musharraf. I should mention in passing that while not comparable, the tendency to approach intra-Muslim moments of contest, especially the Barelwi-Deobandi disagreement, through the framework of the law-Sufism binary, is often found even in otherwise serious scholarship.[6]

In any case, as Philippon argues, the privileging of Barelwis as the truly moderate brand of South Asian Muslims has had the paradoxical effect of catalyzing Barelwi militancy, as seen most notably in the late Barelwi activist Mumtaz Qadiri's murder of Salman Taseer in 2011, then governor of Punjab. Again, this does not mean that the equation of Barelwis with Sufi moderation was misplaced. Rather, it highlights the inherently violent and unsustainable nature of the very enterprise of translating Muslim normative discourses and imaginaries to satisfy the liberal secular appetite for moderation and moderate subjects. Collapsing the categories of Sufi-Barelwi-moderate has only confounded rather than resolved any alleged problem of extremism. In this regard, I find Philippon's neologism of "Sufislamism" a potentially useful conceptual tool to puncture the promise of approaching Islam as a neatly delineated spectrum ranging from militant fundamentalism to peaceful mysticism, whereby Muslim actors can be readily compartmentalized into either end of these categories.

Noor Zaidi, in chapter 9 on the Bībī Pāk Dāman shrine in Lahore—a shrine invested in competing sectarian histories and believed by many Shiʿa to be the burial place of Ruqayyah, the daughter of the first imam, ʿAlī ibn Abī Ṭālib (d. 661)—brings the paradoxical quality of the gesture and desire to moderate religion and Sufism into sharp relief. Zaidi's carefully historicized analysis of the Pakistani state's attempts at regulating the performance of ritual life at the Bībī Pāk Dāman shrine over the last several decades, especially during the 1970s, highlights the impossibility of resolving religious difference through state-sponsored moderation. Fraught with the possibility of sectarian conflict, the Pakistani state took control of the shrine in 1967, and has since constantly sought to manage and regulate its public use, as a way to check and control the potential for Sunni-Shiʿi tensions and violence. But as Zaidi demonstrates, such attempts at nonsectarianizing the shrine have only intensified and solidified a sectarian sensibility and outlook among both Sunni and Shiʿi stakeholders connected to the shrine. This phenomenon Zaidi aptly and astutely categorizes as an expression of what she calls "sectarian secularism." The seemingly paradoxical construct of "sectarian secularism" signals the process through which state projects of moderating religion by rendering it less sectarian generate the opposite effect of further exacerbating sectarian identities and conflict.

Secularism in the context of Zaidi's chapter refers to state interventions in the choreography of devotional life at Bībī Pāk Dāman to neutralize and empty it of any controversial or potentially incendiary ritual and affective traces, such as patterns of ornamentation laced with sectarian overtones, or rituals such as Shiʿi commemorative practices (*majālis*). In effect, moderation also entailed the regulation of religious life in a manner that privileged the sensibilities and normative priorities of the majority Sunni population. Therefore, Zaidi's examination punctuates an irresolvable contradiction at the heart of the secularizing gesture of state neutrality: neutralizing religious difference with the aim of maintaining public order can only produce a form of religion that conforms with majoritarian expectations and desires. Zaidi's chapter thus also amplifies Mahmood's argument, advanced in the context of Egypt, that the entwinement of political secularism and the contradictions of modern state sovereignty is not specific to Western contexts but is also found in non-Western and avowedly religious/Islamic states like Egypt and Pakistan. Again, while the specific trajectory of political secularism varies from context to context, its irresolvable contradictions are ineluctable to the condition of the modern state, as Zaidi's analysis of Bībī Pāk Dāman in Pakistan also underscores. Ultimately, I read Zaidi's chapter as a thoughtful and convincing meditation on the tensions between state sovereignty and the contingencies of everyday devotional life, tensions that simmer in especially dramatic ways when staged in populous urban centers like Lahore. The messiness of the everyday, even as it unfolds under the creeping shadows of the state, constantly frustrates the state's sovereignty, revealing the latent yet always imminent fragility of sovereign power.

Finally, and briefly, I found particularly fascinating the threat of affective excess that underlay many of the intra-religious protests and the state's attempts to contain the velocity of those protests at Bībī Pāk Dāman. Particularly instructive here, as quoted by Zaidi in chapter 9, are the words of Maulwi Muhammad Bakhsh Shah Qureshi, the Shiʿi representative on the Religious Purposes Committee, who piercingly bemoaned the unequal treatment by the state: "If a Shiʿi devotee is moved by the presence of his Bibi and begins to cry or recite a lament, it is not permitted, but the Sunnis can play music and engage in revelry—why is there such a difference?" Qureshi's lament at not being permitted to lament shows the intimacy of the body and the regulation of affect by state projects of religious moderation. It is not the passional per se but the expenditure of passions that might offend or disrupt majoritarian choreographies of religious life that is seen as a threat to public order. The carnivalesque Sunni celebration of the Prophet's birthday (the *mawlid*) therefore is not subject to state regulation in the same calculative manner as the public and passional display of Shiʿi rituals of lamentation or processions led by *zuljanah* (the horse symbolizing Ḥusayn's sacrifice). Moderating Sufism and religion thus also often involves regulating and moderating the body, emotion, and affect, through a disciplining calculus that invariably privileges majoritarian imaginaries of what constitutes a moral public order. This important theoretical insight opened up by Zaidi's chapter can be fruitfully explored in a number of other settings to examine the varied affective consequences and public reordering of the senses engendered by modern secular operations of religious moderation.

Here, let us pause to take note of the following: taken together, the chapters in part 3 underscore the tremendous elasticity of the idea and ideal of moderation. The expanse of this concept is remarkable: It can range from the valorization of the arts, entertainment, and poetry (Philippon) to a critique of feudalism and clerical authority (Ansari) to the state management of potential sectarian violence in Sufi/Shiʿi shrine spaces (Zaidi). What the collection of these essays teaches us then is this: Moderation is a powerful concept precisely because it is as vague as it is expansive. Much like the idea of the secular, the moderate coalesces a range of family concepts that, though fuzzy and intangible, are extremely powerful in terms of the normative pressure they collectively exert.

Concluding Thoughts and Questions

I want to conclude my commentary by raising a couple of broad questions that these chapters have pushed me to ponder. The first has to do with navigating the discursive, institutional, and technological mechanisms through which a normative ideal such as "religious moderation," especially as manifested in the translation of Sufism as moderate Islam, travels between the Global North and South. For instance, what are the precise ways in which Orientalist fantasies like Sufism representing the anticlerical and tolerant version of Islam become an active part of a twentieth-century Sindhi nationalist like G. M. Syed's normative imaginary? What are the micro-dynamics of this encounter between colonial power and indigenous thought and politics? To be sure, a normative ideal like moderation takes on multiple permutations and appropriations as it travels in different local settings. But how precisely does the normativity of a concept like "moderate Islam" encrust elite discourse (political and intellectual) and the stuff of everyday practice in settings like Pakistan?

The second question I wish to raise concerns the politics of scholarly critique. More specifically, what constitutes a generative practice of critique that might interrupt liberal secular narratives and projects of moderating religious lives? Clearly, mining the discursive resources of a tradition and, by so doing, presenting alternate logics of life that do not neatly fit liberal secular desires and expectations constitutes an important element of such critique. Such an attempt to disturb the universality of secular power and logics may not dissolve or overcome the disproportionate pressures of moderation impressed upon Muslim communities in Muslim minority or majority settings. However, it might at least open the possibility of imagining a political horizon that is not imprisoned to the impoverished assumptions and often-treacherous operations involved in fulfilling the mandate of moderating Islam and Muslim lives. But, there is a conceptual dilemma that awaits such a task. That dilemma is this: How does one acknowledge the pervasive yet often opaque power of secularity while also not cleansing a particular fragment of tradition from the stain of secular power by privileging its claim to authenticity? These are knotty and thorny questions. But there is little doubt that scholarship on South Asian Islam, Sufism, and on Islam more broadly cannot embrace or show apathy toward the insidious political operations involved in the mobilization of the "moderate Muslim" discourse. The preceding chapters, with their attention to the specificities of local and global power dynamics, and by virtue of their multidisciplinary foci, combining approaches from political studies, anthropology, history, and religious studies, present an excellent model for the curation of a politically productive and analytically enriching labor of critique.

PART IV

Sufism in Indian National Spaces

10

Is All Politics Local?

Neighborhood Shrines and Religious Healing in Contemporary India

CARLA BELLAMY

Courts and Contexts

The South Asian landscape is filled with places that are imbued with the charisma and healing powers of Muslim teachers, saints, and supernatural beings. While their lineages and histories vary, these places are united by their shared reputation for providing access to powerful personalities who help and heal devotees with physical, social, psychological, or financial afflictions. Shrines built in memory of Sufi teachers are often constructed over their graves, but shrines may also house a relic or mark places where Sufis once performed acts of asceticism or prayer. Other shrines are built by members of the Shiʿi community to honor the memory of martyred members of the Prophet Muḥammad's family,[1] and sometimes a local shrine will experience a miraculous manifestation of the charisma of a distant shrine. Finally, ruins or abandoned structures sometimes develop a reputation for being inhabited by jinn—supernatural beings with origins in Arab cultures.[2]

All shrines participate in local histories and are embedded in discrete networks of lineage-based and sectarian identity. However, because of these shrines' Islamic identity and shared ritual vocabulary, in India their devotees also recognize them as being of a similar type. This perspective is signaled by the term used by devotees to describe the shrines: *dargāh*, a Persian-derived Urdu word meaning "court." Indeed, the language of healing at a *dargāh* is legal: One registers a case with the saints by virtue of one's "presence" (*ḥāżirī*) at the *dargāh* and seeks a "ruling" (*fayṣlah*) from the saint. Devotees may also compose petitions that they attach to the shrines, in some cases even providing photocopies typically required by a state court.[3] From the perspective of devotees, therefore, religious courts of family law, courts of the secular Indian state, and *dargāhs* are all potential sources of justice. Of course, these three types of court are legitimated by different types of authority, and it is generally understood that problems caused by black magic can only be dealt with at a *dargāh*, but these differences are tempered by the underlying assumption that these courts are all legitimate sources of real-world, observable justice.[4]

While *dargāhs* are understood as manifestations of a similar type of court, there are nevertheless important differences between the cultures of small neighborhood shrines and large, famous *dargāhs*. These differences hinge on the extent to which petitioners who come to the shrines are able to maintain anonymity while they are there. While anonymity is an essential element of the healing- and justice-dispensing capacities of larger *dargāhs*,[5] for small neighborhood shrines, maintaining anonymity is impossible. Ironically, because of the lack of anonymity at local shrines, aspects of caste, gender, and religious identity that are verified by and legible to the Indian secular state remain operative within and in some cases amplified by local shrines even as these very shrines derive their authority in part from their reputation for transcending sectarian, gender, and caste divisions and hierarchies.

State intervention in the culture of *dargāhs* necessarily shifts the interplay between liminal identities that develop in the context of the shrine and the never-quite-forgotten state-sanctioned categories of identity. Outcomes of clashes between the state and *dargāhs* depend on the ways in which the boundaries between state and *dargāh* are articulated and enforced. In chapter 11 of this volume, for example, Helene Basu shows that state-sponsored attempts to reconfigure therapeutic practices at the *dargāh* of Mirā Dātār were ultimately unsuccessful because the state actively sought to displace the traditional healers who control the site. Specifically, she notes that the healing processes of pilgrims at Mirā Dātār operate within a worldview where scientific and ritual modes of healing function in ways that are complementary and occasionally overlapping. Religious healers affiliated with the shrines who initially welcomed the state-sponsored therapists saw their ritual practice and the clinical practice of the psychiatrists as complementary, with therapists treating the mentally ill with medication while religious healers worked to eradicate malevolent spirits through ritual. However, the therapists sent by the state to treat pilgrims did not share this view, and instead regarded the religious healers as part of a culture of uneducated superstition. Their attitude eventually provoked hostility and unwillingness on the part of religious healers to refer pilgrims to them, ultimately leading to the failure of the government-sponsored effort to provide access to mental health professionals at Mirā Dātār.

A state-shrine clash that took place while I was conducting ethnographic research at a neighborhood shrine in Mumbai in 2003 offers another perspective on what can happen when the quasi-state status of saint shrine culture—its functionality as a court—collides with the structures and disciplinary processes of the secular Indian state. A key difference between this example and that of Mirā Dātār lies in the nature of the state's interference. As we will see, at this neighborhood shrine, neither the state nor its agents actively sought to regulate the life of the shrine; rather, it was neighbors and devotees of the shrine itself who leveled accusations of abuse and manipulation against the family that operated the shrine and sought the protection and intervention of the state. The ensuing conflict forced both the owners of the shrine as well as their accusers to shift their experiences and arguments into the languages and phenomena that are readily recognized by the state: birth-based, clearly delineated religious and caste identity were foregrounded and discussion of magic or spiritual affliction—the reason devotees visit the shrine—were temporarily abandoned, as was the idea that devotion to Ḥusayn and ʿAli constitutes an identity that eclipses all sectarian and religious differences. The consequences of this conflict offer insight into the ways in which the Indian state influences locally held understandings and experiences of religious, gender, and caste identity.

The Politics of Everyday Religious Identity

The neighborhood shrine where the conflict arose was a home-based *imāmbāṛā*. *Imāmbāṛās* are typically maintained by Shiʿi Muslims and contain objects that represent revered members of the Prophet Muḥammad's family, including his grandson, Ḥusayn. This *imāmbāṛā* occupies part of an Ithnā ʿAsharī Shiʿi family home located in Santa Cruz East, a neighborhood in Mumbai. To access the *imāmbāṛā*, patrons must traverse a narrow alley. The alley was originally unmarked, but as the *imāmbāṛā*'s reputation for healing developed, the family put up a sign advertising a charismatic link between the *imāmbāṛā* and a larger set of shrines in Madhya Pradesh known as Husain Tekri, or Ḥusayn Hill. Built in memory of Ḥusayn, grandson of the Prophet Muḥammad, the shrines of Husain Tekri have an historic connection to the city of Mumbai; it was Shiʿi

Khojas from Mumbai and Surat who funded their construction after a miraculous series of events reportedly took place in the then Sunni Muslim princely state of Jaora (now part of Madhya Pradesh) during the Islamic month of Muḥarram in 1886.[6] Descendants of the Khoja Shiʿi community that funded the construction of the shrines remain involved in Muḥarram events at Husain Tekri, but they are unrelated to the Ithnā ʿAsharī Shiʿi family that operates the Santa Cruz East *imāmbāṙā*.

A connection between Husain Tekri and this neighborhood *imāmbāṙā* exists because sometime in the 1980s, a member of the family that maintains the *imāmbāṙā*—whom I will call Aisha—experienced problems with her health, the health of her newborn son, and her marriage. These problems eventually led to an extended stay at Husain Tekri, where Aisha engaged in the healing rituals typical of *dargāh* culture, including the inhalation of a type of incense commonly referred to in Hindi and Urdu as *lobān*, and the practice of *ḥāżirī*, a process by which the presiding saints of a *dargāh* force a malevolent possessing spirit to vacate the petitioner's body. *Ḥāżirī*—literally, "presence"—connotes both presence in the saint's court and a ritual process whereby the saints physically torture malevolent spirits understood to have invaded the petitioner's body. The presence of the petitioner in the court, in other words, precipitates the torture of the malevolent spirits present in the body of the petitioner. The resulting shaking, rolling, gyrating, and other rhythmic violent actions are understood to be the physical manifestation of the saints' disciplinary tactics. The goal of *ḥāżirī* is to elicit a confession from the spirit, after which the saint renders a verdict (*fayṣlah*) and the offending spirit vacates the body of the petitioner.

After Aisha was healed, she returned home, but like many who are healed at *dargāh*s, she needed a way to remain connected to the transformative experiences she had at Husain Tekri. Pilgrims meet this need by making regular visits to a local *dargāh* or, in some cases, by establishing a shrine or healing practice in their home. Shiʿi pilgrims like Aisha may already have home-based *imāmbāṙās*, which typically house a range of devotional objects, among them *ʿalams*, or battle standards associated with members of Muḥammad's family who were killed by rivals near the Middle Eastern city of Karbala. Ritual mourning of these "martyrs of Karbala" is a key marker of Shiʿi identity in South Asia. A common type of *ʿalam* features a *panje* atop a tall pole. Typically made from embellished metal, a *panje*—from the Persian term for "five" (*panjah*)—is shaped like an outstretched hand, the five fingers of which represent five important figures from early Islamic history: Muḥammad, ʿAli (Muḥammad's son-in-law and cousin), Ḥasan (son of ʿAli), Ḥusayn (son of ʿAli), and Fāṭimah (daughter of Muḥammad, wife of ʿAli, and mother of Ḥasan and Ḥusayn). These individuals, valorized in Shiʿi discourse as the "five pure ones," are particularly venerated in contemporary Shiʿi communities.

In Aisha's case, upon her return from Husain Tekri, a miraculous event gave her family *imāmbāṛā* the same healing properties associated with Husain Tekri itself. There are several versions of the miracle story, but all of them feature the appearance of mysterious lights that traveled down the alley, through the door of the family's home, and into two *ʿalams* located in the family *imāmbāṛā*. In Islamic narratives in general and Sufi traditions in particular, light—*nūr*—indexes divine or saintly presence; in Ithnā ʿAsharī Shiʿism, it is this same divine light that is understood to be the essential nature of the venerated twelve imams, including ʿAli, Ḥasan, and Ḥusayn. Thus, the symbolism of the miraculous events in the *imāmbāṛā* resonates across sectarian and lineage-based boundaries, and reinforces the notion that the underlying source of all *dargāhs*' power is the same.

At the end of the alley is a small shop operated by one of Aisha's brothers-in-law; here, visiting petitioners can purchase the supplies necessary for making an offering. On the right, just past the shop, is the door to the home and its *imāmbāṛā*. Passing through the entrance, the visitor is immediately confronted with the somewhat disorienting experience of entering a space that is simultaneously sacred and everyday. On the right is a bed, several wardrobes line the walls, and at the far end of the room members of the extended family can be observed engaging in various domestic tasks. A door on the right, at the far end of the room, leads to a small kitchen. On the left, dominating nearly the entire wall, is the *imāmbāṛā*, its space delineated by metal bars running from the ceiling to the floor. A doorway allows petitioners to enter the *imāmbāṛā* to make offerings of thanks and petition on the platform containing the *panje* and other venerated objects.

While the *imāmbāṛā* is open all day for petitioners to come and offer prayers, it is busiest when *lobān* is ritually offered. As at Husain Tekri, the offering of *lobān*, a form of frankincense that emits billowing clouds of sweetly scented smoke when burned, is the major ritual event at the *imāmbāṛā*. *Lobān* is commonly offered at Sufi shrines throughout South Asia, and on Thursdays it is also burned in portable containers carried by Muslim mendicants. Particularly on Thursdays—when the *imāmbāṛā*'s crowd is intense—the home overflows with petitioners of all religious backgrounds who partake of the smoke. Both inhaling *lobān* and being enveloped in it are regarded as therapeutic. At the *imāmbāṛā*, as at Husain Tekri, prayers and blessings upon the Prophet Muḥammad and his family are pronounced over the *lobān* as it is burned, and as individuals are exposed to the smoke, many of those waiting outside the *imāmbāṛā* engage in *ḥāżirī*. Their cries and gyrations, combined with nearly opaque clouds of smoke, create an otherworldly atmosphere.

At the larger shrine complex of Husain Tekri, this moment, during which so many of the petitioners lose normal consciousness, is one where everyday boundaries—including religious and gendered ones—are broken or radically reconfigured.[7] However, at the local Santa Cruz *imāmbāṛā*, this same moment of *lobān*, *ḥāżirī*, and loss of consciousness cannot break down boundaries of gender, religion, and sectarian affiliation in quite the same way. In part, this is because the geography of the *imāmbāṛā* itself is unofficially segregated. I say "unofficially" because nobody would claim that women, men, Hindus, Muslims, or Christians ought to be confined to one place or another. The *imāmbāṛā* is theoretically open to all, and this discourse of openness is an important element of the appeal and reputation of Muslim saint shrines. Indeed, as Rachana Rao Umashankar shows in chapter 12 of this volume, the idea of *dargāhs* being places where religious conflict can be resolved and national unity restored has become a popular trope in Bollywood film.

This ideal of cross-tradition unity is not exactly a fiction: The crowd that stands in front of the *imāmbāṛā*, in the main space of the home, is mixed in terms of caste, gender, and religious background. The lines that form outside are similarly diverse. The diversity of the crowd is such that, in an effort to defend the potentially suspect practice of allowing the sexes to commingle, one member of Aisha's extended family once explained that, just as the sexes are not separated on the hajj, so they ought not be segregated at the *imāmbāṛā*.

However, during *lobān* at the Santa Cruz East *imāmbāṛā*, an exclusively female Shiʿi group gathers in the home's kitchen to partake. For some Shiʿi women, it seems, what is acceptable for the hajj is, from their perspective, inappropriate at the *imāmbāṛā*. Another segregated group congregates just outside the front door of the home, across from the supply shop. While this group is also exclusively female, it is mainly Hindu, and, as it turns out, many of these women come to the *imāmbāṛā* from a nearby neighborhood. The majority of these women suffer from *ḥāżirī*, and, because of this condition, they say they are not permitted to enter the home itself. In this way, the *imāmbāṛā*'s policy resembles Husain Tekri's: Those with *ḥāżirī* are not permitted to enter the shrines themselves, and instead congregate in the courtyards that surround them. However, while at Husain Tekri, the segregated community of those with *ḥāżirī* is mixed in terms of gender, religion, and sectarian affiliation, at the smaller *imāmbāṛā*, the group barred from entry is mainly Hindu and exclusively female. This reality changes the healing experiences of pilgrims, and it also suggests that while many at the *imāmbāṛā* are invested in an ideal of ecumenism and openness, religious identity and boundaries remain sources of discrimination and also, as we will see, fear.

Locality Lost: The State, Religious Identity, and Conflict

While discriminatory statements and actions based on religion or caste are generally frowned upon in *dargāh* culture, distinctions can be openly made using the category of *ḥāżirī*. Thus, family members and *imāmbāṙā* visitors offered two rationales to explain why those with *ḥāżirī* were required to keep a certain distance. First, those with *ḥāżirī* were labeled "ritually impure" or "physically dirty" (the categories seemed to overlap—as though one was an indicator of the other), and second, they were understood to be violent and unpredictable. This type of behavior might result in disrespectful treatment of (or damage to) the venerated ritual objects themselves. In fact, this is why the two miraculous *panje* were veiled—family members explained that a person might inadvertently cause him or herself great harm if he or she looked at the *panje* disrespectfully or while in a ritually impure state. The powerful *panje*, in other words, were veiled to protect the masses.[8]

Disrespectful treatment of the *imāmbāṙā* and the complexity of religious identity and inter-religious interactions were both factors in an incident that took place during my research. The conflict at the *imāmbāṙā* took place at dusk. Popularly understood to be a time when the presence of Ḥusayn and his companions is most pronounced, sunset is recognized as a moment of particular efficacy and, therefore, deserving of particularly respectful behavior. As such, the family requires that petitioners stand away from the bars that demarcate the *imāmbāṙā* from the main room of the home. After the petitioners step back, officiating members of the family offer prayers in the *imāmbāṙā* undisturbed.

On the evening in question, a longtime patron of the *imāmbāṙā* refused to step back from the bars and, as a result, became involved in a physical confrontation with a brother-in-law of Aisha whose work at the *imāmbāṙā* typically involves managing the crowd and operating the ceiling fans. Though I did not see the confrontation, the family insisted that Aisha's brother-in-law had only physically restrained the woman, hitting her "no harder than a mother might slap a small child." Following this event, the woman went to the police and filed a report alleging that she had been attacked at the *imāmbāṙā*. When one of Aisha's cousins related this event to me, she added a telling detail: Although this woman had converted to Islam and taken a Muslim name, she had used her (former) Hindu name when filing the police report. Aisha's cousin inferred that the woman had used her Hindu name because "most of the police are Hindu."

The cousin's implication was clear: While conversion to Islam and cross-tradition devotion to the *imāmbāṛā* are all well and good, when push comes to shove, Hindus are more inclined to protect someone they perceive to be one of their own. Although this calculation may very well have been part of the reason this woman chose to use her Hindu name when she filed her report, her choice might also have reflected certain realities about the nature of conversion in contemporary India, and thus the larger issue of religious diversity at *dargāhs*. What does it mean to "convert" to Islam?

In theory, from an Islamic legal perspective, conversion requires nothing more than recitation of the *shahādah*. Awareness of this fact is widespread in South Asian Muslim communities. In practice, however, for all but the most elite Indian communities, religious identity is intimately intertwined with familial obligations and caste identity, both of which create the social and economic structures that sustain people throughout their lives. In the case of the *imāmbāṛā* convert-turned-accuser, though she may have accepted Islam, the implications of this conversion would differ depending on her life circumstances. If she were married to a Muslim, her outward religious life might appear more conventionally Muslim. If, on the other hand, her husband was Hindu, the choice and ability to neglect Hindu domestic rituals would be far more difficult and, therefore, unlikely.[9]

In any case, that the woman would register her complaint using her Hindu name is suggestive of what I have found in my research at Muslim saint shrines to be a widespread attitude not only among Hindus, but also Muslims, namely, that a person is born to his or her religious identity, and that identity can never be fully effaced. This attitude is reinforced by the way in which the Indian state categorizes identity, potentially placing religious identity as a legal status at odds with personal and local meanings. The highly politicized issue of conversion also discourages converts from registering their changed status with the state, and this structural disincentive is augmented by the pressures that converts may feel from Hindu right-wing volunteer organizations like the Vishva Hindu Parishad, whose propensity to attack non-Hindu minority communities is well known.[10] In short, conversion is a tricky business, and a personal declaration of faith is less likely to put the convert at risk if it remains private.

This was not the first time that the *imāmbāṛā* had been accused of corruption, manipulation, and abuse, and, as in the case of the convert's accusations, issues of religious identity were at play. According to another of Aisha's cousins, the same Hindu neighbors who in one version of the *imāmbāṛā*'s origin story witnessed the arrival of the miraculous light that heralded the power of the *imāmbāṛā* to grant the requests of petitioners also once accused Aisha and her family of using magic to manipulate people into coming to the *imāmbāṛā* in order to extract money from them. Ironically, this cousin felt that the motivation behind this accusation was the reason so many at the *imāmbāṛā* suffered from *ḥāẓirī*: jealousy. Elaborating, he noted that when the miracle at the *imāmbāṛā* happened, the Hindu neighbors had been better off than Aisha's family. As the *imāmbāṛā*'s fame grew and Aisha's family was able to make improvements to their home and purchase more desirable clothes, motorcycles, and other markers of middle-class status, the neighbors felt left behind and, consequently, envious.

In this instance, again, it is meaningful that the neighbors are Hindu. Initially, their Hindu identity bolsters the legitimacy and reputation of the shrine: Its miraculous power has been attested to by non-Muslims. Hindu endorsement of the shrine also strengthens its claim to a central trope of Muslim saint shrine culture, namely that it is a culture that welcomes everyone, regardless of religious identity. However, the same Hindu identity subsequently became an unstated but nevertheless effective marker of irreconcilable difference or fundamental untrustworthiness: later, as the *imāmbāṛā*'s reputation grew, it was a Hindu family that turned against their Muslim neighbors. Whether for good or for harm, because of the larger context of communalism and a lack of anonymity, the mere fact of the family's Hindu identity makes a statement.

Aisha's family had no choice but to take accusations of abuse or manipulation seriously. When the Hindu neighbors approached the police claiming that *imāmbāṛā* devotees were subject to abuse and manipulation, both magical and physical, the family responded by circulating a petition among pilgrims. In it, the signatories stated that they benefited from visits to the *imāmbāṛā* and came and left of their own free will. As it turned out, one the signatories of this petition was the woman who had accused Aisha's brother-in-law of attacking her at the *imāmbāṛā*. One member of the family speculated that the presence of her signature—using her Muslim name—on the petition significantly weakened her subsequent case with the police.

While the woman's signature on this petition gave Aisha's family some sense of security when she brought a case against them with the police, they ultimately took the exceptional measure of hiring a professional photographer to photograph daily events at the *imāmbāṛā*. Since, as the family said, "the police don't believe in magic," it was imperative that they produce proof that the goings-on of the *imāmbāṛā* were legitimate and, from their perspective, photographic evidence to this effect was a good strategy. In particular, as the family said, the majority of people visiting the *imāmbāṛā* were women, and this made the family particularly vulnerable to accusations of manipulation and otherwise improper conduct. During the period of my research in 2003, the legal case did not move forward, though it remained unclear whether or not the photograph file they produced helped their cause.

Although a complex mixture of factors was at play, it is nevertheless clear that both sides in the conflict—the family and the woman—were aware that religious identity can either bolster one's own case or call into question that of another. These events illustrate the limits of boundary-crossing at local shrines, places where by their nature individuals remain rooted in local communities and anonymity is not possible. Because crossing boundaries is an important element of the healing process of pilgrims, this distinction between local and regional *dargāhs* is important to recognize and acknowledge.[11]

With one potential problem with the law seemingly averted, Aisha's family was still faced with the challenge of ensuring that visitors to the *imāmbāṛā* remained at a safe and respectful distance during evening prayers. This was a particularly pressing concern as the Islamic month of Muḥarram approached, and the neighborhood Shiʿi community—including Aisha's family—was preparing for Shiʿi *mātam* practices. Throughout India, Hindus are often enthusiastic participants in Shiʿi-organized Muḥarram activities. While Hindu participation in Muḥarram rituals is relatively common and often welcome, in light of the altercation that had taken place several weeks earlier, Aisha's family felt compelled to preserve and protect a respectful atmosphere at sunset.[12]

In this context, the segregated group of mostly Hindu women with severe *ḥāżirī* became more threatening to the family, though the threat was articulated in the language of *ḥāżirī* rather than religious or gender identity. The caste identity of the women was never explicitly mentioned, though it is worth noting that descriptions of the lower castes as "dirty" often involve the same language as descriptions of those with *ḥāżirī* as "dirty."[13]

The solution to the problem of keeping *imāmbāṛā* visitors in check at sunset came, as solutions often do, in a dream. In the weeks following the altercation, Aisha had a dream in which Ḥusayn and his half-brother ʿAbbās, accompanied by two children whom Aisha did not recognize, appeared to her and suggested that the family should light a small white candle at sunset and place it outside the *imāmbāṛā*. Oddly enough, several days before Aisha told me about the dream, I noticed a small white candle burning just outside the door of the home. This seemed to be new, and so I asked one of Aisha's cousins about it. She explained that since evening is a time when Ḥusayn—accompanied by a retinue of heavenly creatures—comes to the *imāmbāṛā*, the candle acts as a sign to those outside the *imāmbāṛā*—and specifically, this group of Hindu women—to stay back until the candle has burned out.

The members of this group of mainly Hindu women were regulars at the *imāmbāṛā*; many of them had been coming for more than a decade, and many of them came from the same neighborhood. Although they suffered from *ḥāżirī*, they reported that their situations had improved significantly because of the time they spent at the *imāmbāṛā*. Their devotion extended to other Muslim saint shrines: They explained that if one of them felt called to a distant shrine, they would pool their resources to rent a car to take them there; some years earlier, for example, they had journeyed to Ajmer. It was clear that the company that these women enjoyed at the *imāmbāṛā* was of significant therapeutic value. Particularly for women of limited economic means, Muslim saint shrines provide one of the few socially acceptable places to meet friends, relax, and gain some perspective on the problems at home that bring them to the shrines.

Ostensibly, these women were excluded from the *imāmbāṛā* in general and especially at sunset because of the ferocity of their *ḥāżirī*, so it would not be accurate to say that they were excluded simply and solely because many of them were Hindu. In addition, it is also possible that Aisha's family may have regarded these women as low-caste. The family's need for privacy in their domestic space may have also been a factor—during my time at the *imāmbāṛā*, family members occasionally expressed frustration with petitioners who loitered after offering their prayers or taking *lobān*.

Still, when I finally got the nerve to cross the border, as it were, and sit in the alley with these women, none of Aisha's family members joined me. The brother-in-law who tended the shop seemed to find the situation awkward and funny. "Are you *trying* to enjoy yourself?" he asked one day, implying that to do so in such company would take quite a bit of effort. His joke upset the young women: They immediately defended themselves by saying that though they might suffer from *ḥāżirī*, they were still human, and worthy of courtesy. Why shouldn't the researcher spend time with them, too?

Contrary to the popular image of Muslim saint shrines as places where religious difference is subsumed by a devotional atmosphere presided over by a saint who does not distinguish between Hindu, Muslim, Christian, and Sikh, everyday life at the Santa Cruz East *imāmbāṛā* shows that differences shape not only how individuals experience a space, but also where they go in it and how they use it. While the desire to see *dargāh* patrons as a unified group is strong, the lived reality of religious diversity at the Santa Cruz *imāmbāṛā* is complex and constantly changing in response to national, international, and local events. On the one hand, if asked, petitioners at the *imāmbāṛā* happily volunteered sentiments that hew to a vision of a glowing, countercultural unity that grows from shared experiences of suffering. On the other hand, communities' perceptions of one another and the ways in which these perceptions shape conflict, conflict resolution, and the geography and use of a space demonstrate that on the local level, many boundaries and perceptions of difference endure. Furthermore, shared devotion to Imam Ḥusayn or personal conversion to Islam lack legal status, and, therefore, if conflict arises and state institutions like law enforcement and courts become involved, caste- and birth-based religious identities become the sole mechanisms for seeking justice and protection. Despite *dargāhs*' reputations as places that transcend religious boundaries, the culture of these local shrines is shaped by religious differences and fixed notions of religious identity that are reinforced by the administrative categories of the Indian state and, as this chapter has shown, amplified at small shrines during periods of conflict. This is a discouraging truth at odds with popular perceptions of *dargāhs* as places open to all.

There is, however, a more hopeful dimension to the culture of *dargāhs* that becomes discernable when local shrines are contextualized within the larger pan-Indian networks of shrines. Specifically, the anonymity possible at larger and famous *dargāhs* and the healing that happens at them is predicated on and experienced within a larger framework that includes patronage of local shrines. For devotees who leave their neighborhoods or villages to venture further into the realm of Sufi saint shrines, these very real and keenly felt experiences of religious difference—reinforced by state-sanctioned categories—have the potential to infuse the transformative cross-tradition alliances and friendships that form at the larger and more famous *dargāhs* with greater importance and strength by virtue of the fact that religious boundaries are being crossed. As a result of these experiences, pilgrims create a powerful counterculture: They become citizens of an alternative kingdom where, by the grace of the saint, they have overcome the discourses of religious difference that have tragically divided neighborhoods, communities, and the subcontinent itself.

11

Sufi Healing and Secular Psychiatry in India

HELENE BASU

In a storeroom inside a walled dargāh *in Gujarat a psychiatrist is sitting cross-legged on a mattress behind a low wooden table. He listens to a man talking about the constant chatter of spirit voices he is hearing in his head. Seated at the side, next to two assistants guarding huge bags full of medicines, a* khādim *(ritual servant) is present as an onlooker. While the patient elaborates on a female voice he is hearing singing beautifully like a nightingale, a long, piercing shriek cuts through the air from outside. The assistants crane their necks to watch a woman who is clad in a worn sari agitatedly yelling while pushing through the crowd hustling in the courtyard. The patient seems to take no notice of the commotion. When loudspeakers transmit the call for prayer, the psychiatrist instructs the assistants to give a handful of pills to the patient. The psychiatrist gets up and quickly makes his way to the exit gate.*

This scene illustrates the somewhat unusual setting of a psychiatric outpatient department (OPD) in the ritual space of a Sufi *dargāh*. In the first decade of the twenty-first century the community mental health care program "Dava & Dua" (medicine [*davā*] and prayer [*duʿāʾ*]) was introduced at the shrine of the saint Mirā Dātār in North Gujarat.[1] The program resulted from efforts made by mental health professionals to tap religious healing places as a potential resource for providing mental health care and education to rural and economically weaker populations in India.[2] Thus, a similar cooperation between faith healers and psychiatrists, "Rituals & Tablets," was launched at a Hindu temple in Tamil Nadu in South India.[3]

Psychiatry's entry into religious spaces raises questions about the local circumstances of cooperation and the attitudes mobilized in encounters between two very different kinds of healers attempting to operate within the same religious space. Furthermore, in the Rituals & Tablets (e.g., tablets of medication, or pills) program, Hindu priests cooperated with Hindu psychiatrists, whereas the Dava & Dua Program involved collaboration between Hindu mental health workers and Muslim representatives of the *dargāh*. The latter constellation challenged participants not only because providers used different classificatory models of mental illness and appropriate treatment methods but also because of religious differences. The shrine of Mirā Dātār is frequented not by Muslims alone but, as are many other Sufi shrines, also by pilgrims from diverse religious communities (especially Hindu and Jain). In contrast to these pilgrims, psychiatrists did not come for supplication but for reform—and that too at a time when communal violence loomed large in the state of Gujarat. Under these circumstances, the cooperative Dava & Dua Program brought tolerance and dynamics of toleration sharply into focus. These are the subject of this chapter.

Experimenting with religious and clinical cooperation is part of reforming the mental health care sector, which has evolved as an important site for the ongoing fabrication of modernity in India. This includes the narrative of psychiatry as a secular project of emancipation from religion, which also informs programs of therapeutic cooperation. Such programs commonly build upon secular ideas of religion as a private matter of belief and as separate from scientific knowledge. While scholars debating modernization have questioned the status of secularization as a signature of modern societies by acknowledging the persistence of public religions in a globalized world,[4] in contemporary India secularism and public religion have emerged as subjects of intense political contestation. These become manifest in practices conceptualized by Bruno Latour as "work of purification."[5] Dichotomous modeling, characteristic of modern thought, such as nature-culture, modern-traditional, human-nonhuman, religious-secular, and so on, Latour argues, is not descriptive but provokes and creates social realities that are constantly made, reshaped, or unmade in accordance with a logic of separation effecting asymmetrical positioning of actors in variable configurations. In modern India, for example, the Committee to Eradicate Superstition in Maharashtra, an offshoot of the Maharashtra Rationalist Association, engaged in purifying society from irrational "superstition" by debunking and ridiculing Hindu healers of spirit possession in public campaigns.[6] Hindu nationalist parties (such as the Bharatiya Janata Party [BJP], and Shiv Sena), on the other hand, accused the organization of anti-Hindu activities and led demeaning campaigns against "secularists." The founder of the antisuperstition committee, a leading psychiatrist, was assassinated in 2013 by unidentified gunmen.[7]

Efforts at modernization through practices of purification in the Latourian sense, however, are not always and necessarily driven by intolerance but may also work with dynamics of toleration. The work of purification conducted through programs of cooperation between psychiatrists and ritual healers actually depends on toleration. While the notion of tolerance enshrined in liberal, secular worldviews refers to values and attitudes of acquiescing to difference, "toleration" pertains to practical processes of handling difference. As Catriona McKennon points out, "Toleration can only be required in response to features of situations or persons to which the tolerator is opposed in significant ways, which the tolerator believes herself to have the power to alter, suppress, or eradicate, and which the tolerator—as a result of all this—is disposed to interfere with so as to alter, suppress or eradicate."[8] This nuanced consideration of features marking possible positions of a tolerator proves helpful for the analysis of the interactional dynamics that shaped cooperation between representatives of the *dargāh* and psychiatrists. As we see below, while psychiatrists and ritual servants share the feature of opposition to each other's approaches, they differ with regard to the features of alteration and eradication.

Toleration in this sense, then, is a specific mode of performing works of purification that give shape to modern forms. The separation of science from religion, for this matter, brings about asymmetrical relationships between "effective" scientific psychiatry and "ineffective" faith healing. Thus, the Ritual & Tablet program implemented at the South Indian Hindu temple successfully purified exorcist healing from Hindu rituals through enactments of toleration that made the priests accept the psychiatrists' claim to the "superiority" of psychiatric knowledge "over faith."[9] In regard to Islam and in the wake of a global concern with the spread of intolerant forms of Islamic reformism, Sufism has been promoted by many secular governments as the "tolerant" Islam (as discussed by Rosemary Corbett in chapter 1 of this volume), and thus a possible site for modernizing Muslim populations.[10] In a similar vein, the shrine of Mirā Dātār emerges as a target of purification in multiple constellations of modern subject positions: as "backward/un-Islamic" (Islamic reformers), "impure/superstitious" (some Sufi *pīrs* in Gujarat), and "traditional/uneducated/superstitious" (middle-class).

Mental health programs promoting therapeutic cooperation are distinctively secular middle-class projects of modernization. As Henrike Donner points out, "Middleclassness relies heavily on imagery and on the production and consumption of images of spaces, sites and practices that are not necessarily ever fully realized."[11] Mental health care is one such site where Indian "middleclassness" is produced. Dava & Dua was thus a program where two distinct projects—education and progress—of producing the modern, middle-class, tolerant Muslim and Indian citizen, converged.

This chapter explores the social process through which this project evolved. After introducing the shrine of Mirā Dātār, I briefly discuss tolerance as enshrined in the Indian secular constitution, followed by a section on the political circumstances in Gujarat as a background to the development of the Dava & Dua Program. The remaining parts of the chapter analyze the dynamics of toleration and nontoleration as they unfolded in the interactions between representatives of the *dargāh* and mental health professionals.

The Shrine of Mirā Dātār in Gujarat

The walled and fortified *dargāh* of the Sufi saint Mirā Dātār sits at the outskirts of a village dominated by Hindu Patidar farmers in North Gujarat. The hagiographic narrative situates Sayyid ʿAlī Mirā Dātār in the fifteenth century, when the first Muslim Sultanate was established in Gujarat, gaining supremacy over Rajput kingdoms. The saint is depicted as a military commander who defeated a king, who was a sorcerer. His reputation as a powerful healer of demonic illness and afflictions of sorcery rests on the miracle he was able to perform by the grace of God that resulted in overcoming his own death.[12]

The shrine is maintained by a kinship association of ritual servants (*khādim*). No single living *pīr* presides over the *dargāh*. The shrine is jointly owned by a lineage segmented into nine sublineages, which all claim descent from the saint's paternal brother. Agnates share the role of *khādim* (ritual servant) and claim equal rights in mediating the saint's powers. Such rights are distributed among the lineage segments, each of which occupies a spatially circumscribed "seat" within the shrine premises. At the time of fieldwork, almost 600 *khādims* from 150 households shared the right to perform daily ritual services for nearly 1,000 Muslim and non-Muslim clients who visited the shrine during a week. Although the language spoken at the shrine is Urdu, most pilgrims are Muslims, Hindus, Jains, and Sikhs from diverse social, geographical, urban, and rural backgrounds who are also followers of *khādims* and the *dargāh*. The shrine thus emerges as a cosmopolitan nodal point of extensive translocal and transnational social networks, which gives *khādims* political and business access beyond their ritual profession. The majority of pilgrims turn to the saint seeking treatment of afflictions related to demonic illness (*balā kī bīmārī*).

The *dargāh* is administered by a trust formed according to the rules of the Gujarat State Wakf Board installed in 1995–96.[13] It is composed of eleven members elected every four years, with nine ritual servants representing each sublineage and two drawn from the local Patidar caste. Presiding over the trust is an elected chairman who represents the *dargāh* to the government. Among the *khādims*, there is intense internal competition for trust positions, leadership, and authority over the affairs of the shrine.

Today, the *dargāh* of Mirā Dātār is one of several healing shrines in the region.[14] Historically, its healing practices build upon Sufi "holy healing," dealing with "madness" and possession by jinn, *al-siḥr* (Islamic sorcery), and *kālā jādū* (black magic) as one strand in the multistranded Islamic history of medicine.[15] Today, Mirā Dātār is popularly reputed as a center of countersorcery, offering healing of demonic illnesses (*balā kī bīmārī*). The place draws pilgrims from local, transregional, and transnational settings. Demonic illnesses become manifest in a range of afflictions of which madness is the most troubling one.[16] Most pilgrimages are undertaken because of an acute problem of demonic illness or out of gratitude for solving a past one. Although the majority of shrine visitors belong to the Muslim community, Hindus, Jains, and others also seek help in times of personal crisis. *Khādims*, however, do not refer to pilgrims in terms of their religious affiliation but categorize them as "guests" (*mehmān*, those with no immediate demonic problem) or "supplicants" (*sawālī*, those with immediate demonic problems).

The process of healing, the delivery from the effects of black magic and spirit possession, is framed as the saint's battle with demonic agents in the bodies and minds of the afflicted. It is enacted in performances of possession trance (*ḥāżirī*).[17] *Khādims* assist in the healing process governed by the saint communicating with *sawālī*s through dreams and trance. Healing is distributed over a network of practices linking sung congregational prayers (*duʿāʾ*) performances of possession trance (*ḥāżirī*), and the give and take of material substances (*davā*, or "medicine").[18] The *khādims*' role in this process is to help pilgrims make sense of their experiences by translating the "orders" (*ḥukm*) of the saint received in states of trance into concrete instructions to act (e.g., to take a bath in a pond) and by distributing Mirā Dātār's *davā* (washing water from the tomb, rose petals, oil, etc.).

The premises of the shrine encompass the main tomb of Mirā Dātār and minor tombs dedicated to male and female ancestors and a mosque. Tombs constitute arenas of ritual healing monitored by *khādims*, and also accommodations inside and outside the shrine (rooms and guesthouses) for pilgrims and long-term patients with their caretakers. In the past, the shrine had also accepted "psychotic" patients abandoned by their families who were unable to look after themselves.[19] Lone male patients who needed to be restrained were regularly fed and bathed by *khādims* but kept in chains in a separate room.

Differences of religion and gender between pilgrims as well as between their concerns are accommodated by circumscribing distinct spatial spheres of actions controlled by *khādims* on behalf of the sovereign power of Mirā Dātār. For example, arenas of ritual healing around a tomb are sites demarcated for *sawālīs*, that is, men and women of any religious community suffering from a demonic problem. *Sawālīs* are also accorded center stage during the daily *duʿāʾ* rituals in the evening when the congregation of pilgrims (guests and caretakers) gathers to offer sung prayers to the saint under the lead of a *khādim*. While the spaces in the immediate vicinity of the tomb mirror gender divisions, with men standing on the right side and women on the left, male and female *sawālīs* may freely cross these spatial boundaries while enacting possession trance. Daily shrine routines are organized around the five daily prayer times (*namāz*) called for by the imam from the mosque. Male Muslim guests of the shrine pray in the mosque, while Muslim women settle next to the tomb for praying. Non-Muslim guests do not take part in *namāz*, and neither are Muslim *sawālīs* required to pray five times a day.

The ways in which such distinctions become practically accommodated at the shrine reverberate with vernacular notions of "tolerance" (Hindi, *sahansilata, sahhishnuta*) and "toleration," translated as "enduring" (Hindi, *sahna*) and "a permissible difference; allowing some freedom to move within limits" and "respect for the ideals and institutions of others" (Urdu, *bardāsht*).[20] Whoever visits the *dargāh* must show respect to the saint through devotional acts and by conforming to the rules of conduct imposed by *khādims*; conversely, being different—mad, non-Muslim—is accommodated as permissible as long as certain limits are not breached.

Toleration Enshrined in the Indian Constitution

As with all Sufi *dargāhs*, the shrine of Mirā Dātār is protected by the constitution of the Indian state. Article 25 of the Indian constitution grants "freedom of consciousness and free profession, practice and propagation of religion" to all religions practiced in India.[21] In 1976, an amendment of the Indian constitution declared the Republic of India "secular." Secularism (*sarva dharma sama bhava*) in India is subject to intense debates revolving around interpretations of secularism in terms of the neutrality of the state toward religions (*sarvadharmanirapekstra*) or toward religious communities.[22] Within the context of these debates, "toleration" in the sense of sympathy and respect for all religions has been highlighted in some discussions.[23]

In the constitution, a religion is defined as a system of "doctrines and beliefs whose observances are conducive to the well-being of its adherents."[24] Freedom of religion, however, is subject to other constitutional provisions, such as public order, morality and health.[25] This principle gave rise to the introduction of psychiatric clinics at religious healing places such as the Dava & Dua Program, as I show below, and, as a corollary, to the legal division between "religion" and "psychiatry." However, while the secular law of the Indian state actively pursues the differentiation of religion from medicine, it treats Islam as undifferentiated—an issue that incenses those who seek to purify Islam from local translations.

Thus, some Indian Muslims are critical of the Indian state's professed secularism because, in principle, it grants freedom of religion to all forms of Islam. Tahir Mahmood, a prominent Indian legal scholar and chair of the Indian government's National Minorities Commission from 1996 to 1999, insisted that "true" Islam is restricted to the five basic precepts of Islam.[26] According to Mahmood, "Islam's purely religious tenets" are not protected by Indian public law.[27] His complaint was that "Indian law hardly makes any distinction between the so-called shrines, which indeed have no religious sanctity in Islam, and the mosque, which undoubtedly has a pivotal place in the Islamic system."[28] The Indian state, Mahmood asserted, did not limit its definition of Islam to "what the dominant Muslim majority across the globe regards as Islam," but "protects every brand of Islam—Indian or foreign."[29] According to Mahmood, the state should withdraw protection of freedom of religion from "heretic sects" (Ahmadiyyah, Daudi Bohra, Khojas) that disregard "practices . . . that the majority of Muslims view as un-Islamic" and "superstitious," but especially from shrines where people venerate "graveyards, saintly tombs and living *pīrs*."[30]

A similar logic that separates "true" from "tainted" Islam as applied by Mahmood (and other Muslim reformers) also underlies dichotomous constructions of "ineffective" healing rituals versus "effective" scientific psychiatric treatment performed by psychiatrists. Thus, the secular principles that Mahmood found lacking in regard to the protection of Islam in India supported psychiatrists in their struggle against "superstitious" healing practices performed at Sufi shrines and other religious institutions.

The modernization of Indian mental health care was accelerated by an accident that occurred at a Sufi healing shrine in South India in 2001. A fire killed twenty-eight mentally ill people who were chained to trees. This unfortunate incident sparked a middle-class-based mental health movement calling simultaneously for modernizing decrepit psychiatric institutions inherited from colonial asylums and for eradicating "superstitious" and "unscientific" ritual healing practices.[31] Psychiatrists and other civilians launched writ petitions at the Supreme Court of India demanding the protection of the human rights of mentally ill persons—as guaranteed by the Mental Health Act of 1987[32]—against "unscientific" and "superstitious" customs cast in "backward" understandings of religion.[33] Successful petitioning led to an order issued by the Supreme Court of India in the following year: "Both the Central and State Governments shall undertake a comprehensive awareness campaign with a special rural focus to educate people as to provisions of law relating to mental health, rights of mentally challenged persons, the fact that chaining of mentally challenged persons is illegal and that mental patients should be sent to doctors and not to religious places such as Temples or *dargahs*."[34]

The verdict made three important points: First, it assigned responsibility for mental health care education to the government; second, it confirmed the modern separation of secular psychiatry (medicine) from religion; and third, it declared chaining of mentally ill persons illegal, as this practice violates their human rights.

The Gujarat government was quick to take up the Supreme Court's order and soon after sent out a delegation, led by the head of the Department of Family and Health, himself a psychiatrist, and the superintendent of the largest mental hospital in the state, to inspect religious healing places. The main duty of the delegation was to find out if chaining was practiced anywhere and, if this was the case, to suggest measures to deal with it. The delegation visited the most well-known healing places in the state: the temple of the god Kashtbhanjan, "Crusher of Sorrows" (a form of Hanuman), which belonged to the Swaminarayan "sect" (*panth*), and the Sufi shrine of Mirā Dātār. In regard to the latter, the delegation reported:

> The *khādims* treat patients with ineffective religious rituals and beliefs. The treatment lasts from one day to sixty days or more. These patients are made to stay in the premises of the *dargah* for long periods of time. When the illness becomes chronic, patients are chained and kept tied in the premises of the *dargah*. This leads to further complications. We feel a very strong need to sensitize the *khādims* that mentally ill patients gain from scientific treatment with psychoactive medication. Therefore, we suggest to implement an innovative community mental health care center where patients are treated scientifically without disturbing their faith.[35]

Setting up a psychiatric clinic at the shrine required practices of toleration at a time when religious intolerance loomed large in Gujarat.

Religious Intolerance and Secular Toleration

Civil, professional, and legal pressures to reform the conditions of mental health care provision for the Indian public erupted at a time when the ruling BJP in Gujarat had proclaimed the state a "laboratory of Hindutva."[36] In the aftermath of a train burning in February 2002, which killed more than fifty Hindutva activists and for which Muslims were held responsible, a wave of violence was unleashed across the state against Muslim persons, property, and religious institutions.[37] Nearly two thousand persons died, more were injured, and thousands lost their homes. More than two hundred *dargāhs* and mosques were desecrated and destroyed.[38]

With its walls and massive wooden gates, the shrine of Mirā Dātār could provide shelter to fellow Muslims fleeing from their attackers, but a smaller *dargāh* of the saint's mother's brother placed at a little distance from the Mirā Dātār *dargāh* was burned down by a Hindu mob. As T. K. Oommen points out, "historical tombs of Muslim saints" were among "the first few targets of the mobs."[39] Green flags hoisted over large and small *dargāhs* that signaled Muslim spaces were torn down and replaced with the saffron flag of the Hindutva movement. Among the many grievances and complaints long voiced by Hindus against Muslims allegedly being "pampered" by the secular state,[40] Gujarati Hindus again claimed that Sufi shrines are sites where Hindus are converted to Islam. From a Hindutva perspective, Sufi shrines do not represent "tolerant" in contrast to "intolerant" forms of Islam; rather, the fact that Sufi shrines are open to Hindus and other non-Muslims is considered as intolerable as the sound of prayers emanating from a mosque. Thus, shrines such as the *dargāh* of Mirā Dātār, which thrive on providing Sufi healing to a multireligious clientele of sufferers, are challenged from two sides, both of whom put Indian secularism into question and promote intolerance. Challenges come from Muslim reformers such as Mahmood who advocate an Islam that is purified from "foreign" (Hindu) elements and from Hindu nationalists who call for armed struggle against perceived Sufi/Muslim threats to "Hindu identity." Both strands of intolerance, which pervade politics in Gujarat, have an effect on shrine visitors. Thus, quite a few Muslim suffering pilgrims, mostly women, concealed their pilgrimage to the shrine of Mirā Dātār from husbands and sons because the latter were adherents of the Tablīghī Jamāʿat and had prohibited family members from visiting shrines; similarly, some Hindu pilgrims stayed secretly at the shrine without letting relatives and neighbors know.

The mental health delegation set out only a few months after the violent outbreaks against Muslims had been brought under control by the army. Recalling how they went on their mission, the superintendent of the mental hospital pointed out that the team did not worry about inspecting the Swaminarayan temple but was wary of what kind of response to expect from the *dargāh* of Mirā Dātār.

The team first went to the Hanuman healing temple belonging to the Swaminarayan sect. Here, exorcism is practiced by one college-educated Brahmin priest, and the temple's clientele consists almost exclusively of middle-class Gujarati Hindus. Pilgrims suffering from mental problems were not allowed to stay overnight at the temple but had to attend fixed consultation hours offered by the priest. He diagnosed possession illnesses through vibrations he felt in his own body when sitting next to an afflicted person. If he did not feel vibrations, the priest explained, he knew that the patient suffered from a mental illness and thus sent him or her to a psychiatrist. The superintendent, himself sympathizing with Swaminarayan Hinduism, was impressed with the disciplined behavior imposed at the temple and the almost bureaucratic organization of ritual healing. As no patients were found in chains, the delegation left without any further demands.[41]

When the delegation arrived at the shrine of Mirā Dātār, they were met with various challenges. Memories of the recent violence and of not being protected by the state still fresh, *khādims* bolted the gates and denied them entry. At a second visit, the delegation was backed up by the police, who forced their entry into the shrine. Inside, they discovered the room where patients were chained. The officer of the Department of Family and Health announced to the president of the Dargah Trust that this was an illegal practice that made the shrine liable "to be shut down." This action seemed risky, though, as the BJP government in Gujarat at the time was already facing numerous allegations from human rights inquiry commissions of having been actively involved in the pogrom against Muslims.

The delegation therefore began to enter into negotiations with members of the Dargah Trust. The leading psychiatrists adopted a stance of toleration defined by the position of a tolerator with power to alter a practice opposed as different. Seeking to win the trust of *khādims*, they informed shrine leaders that the aim was not to disturb the religious life of the shrine but merely to see to the implementation of the new law, which prohibited the use of chains to restrain mentally ill persons in need of psychiatric care. As *khādims* themselves had already considered lone and difficult patients a burden, they agreed to their transfer to the mental hospital.

As a result of the inspection tour, mental health professionals decided to introduce a community mental health care center at the Mirā Dātār *dargāh* rather than at the Swaminarayan temple. In the psychiatrists' view, the temple organized healing in accordance with a modern distinction between religion and psychiatry. Swaminarayan Hinduism is firmly anchored in the Gujarati Hindu middle class. This religious community (*panth*) builds from a history of purifying Hinduism from "superstitions," "social evils" (e.g., consumption of alcohol), and "impure" rituals (i.e., animal sacrifices).[42] The *dargāh*, by contrast, was perceived as distinctly "backward." To introduce a community mental health care center at such a place, mental health professionals reasoned, offered not only an opportunity to reach out to mentally ill patients but also to educate *khādims* and Muslims more generally about the true nature of mental illness and thus contribute to the modernization of "backward communities" in the state.

Mental health officers and the superintendent of the mental hospital later suggested to the Dargah Trust the introduction of a psychiatric clinic offering mental health care services inside the shrine. The project was designed by professionals in accordance with a secular understanding of religion as a private matter that was in principle distinct from biomedical psychiatry. Religious traditions of the shrine would be left untouched, mental health professionals assured the Dargah Trust, while the project would combine "*davā*" defined as psychotropic medicine provided by psychiatrists, and "*duʿāʾ*," praying and religious solace provided by *khādims*. It was understood that the *khādims* would support psychiatrists running an OPD by sending their clients for diagnosis and reception of psychotropic medicine free of charge. The Trust agreed to the proposal against the resistance of sections of the community of ritual servants. The practical implementation of the Dava & Dua Program, however, presented challenges related to mutual toleration both by members of the mental health team and by those *khādims* who had initially been in favor of the program.

From Toleration to Nontoleration

The psychiatric clinic opened in 2007. A nongovernmental organization (NGO) mediated between the trust, psychiatrists, and the government, and organized the order, supply, and distribution of medicine. The NGO was run by a manager, a former bank employee from Mumbai, assisted by two young men from the Hindu caste of the village. While the control of the program rested with the superintendent of the public mental hospital that supplied the medicine, psychiatric consultations were offered by two psychiatrists from a nearby town taking turns in the OPD. Neither the practicing psychiatrists nor the other members of the mental health team, all of them Hindus, had previously been to a *dargāh*.

In order to accomplish what the Dava & Dua Program had been set up for, members of the mental health team had to show toleration toward the behavior and concerns of *khādims* and pilgrims in specific "circumstances of toleration."[43] These circumstances entailed, first of all, that psychiatrists and members of the NGO tolerated talk about mental and behavioral disturbances in an idiom different from their own, which they fundamentally disapproved of (spirits, black magic, possession, etc.). Second, the psychiatrists believed that gradually *khādims* and patients would accept that mental illness is caused by a malfunctioning of the brain and/or emotional conflicts rather than by spiritual agents and that it is therefore medicine that provides remedy and not mystical healing powers of a saint. A perpetual source of frustration, however, was the insistence of patients to continue with practices considered highly unhygienic such as bathing in the shrine's sewer water in obedience to an order of the saint (*ḥukm*) and their claim that, ultimately, they found more relief in possession trance than from taking psychotropic medicine. The project members then complained to the president of the Trust that *khādims* deliberately manipulated pilgrims so that they resisted complying with psychiatric treatment.

Khādims, on the other hand, neither disapproved of nor opposed psychiatric practices. They conceived of psychiatrists as specialists of a different system of medical knowledge: "Psychiatrists are knowledgeable of *their* diseases," the president of the Trust said, "but they know nothing of the illnesses the Mirā Dātār is curing. Both are different."[44] Ritual servants did not consider their worldview, their understanding of demonic illness, and their healing practices as something calling for "toleration" by others but as something that was morally true and tangibly real and therefore commanded respect.

The Dargah Trust accommodated the psychiatric clinic as another instance of difference. By accepting the OPD, *khādims* had not agreed that Mirā Dātār's healing power was ineffective but presumed that some pilgrims might indeed benefit from medicine if they or their families wished to try it out. Mistrust became rife when NGO workers demanded a list of the names of all ritual servants in order to monitor who among the *khādims* sent clients to the OPD and who did not. If a *khādim* was identified who missed out on sending patients, the

NGO approached the Trust to enforce his cooperation. Increasingly, *khādims* felt that mental health workers did not "move within limits" but trespassed boundaries circumscribing "permissible difference."

Toleration implies the mutual positioning of actors in terms of tolerator-tolerated. The psychiatrists saw their position as tolerators of ritual healing practices they disapproved of and they viewed *khādims* as the tolerated who would benefit from toleration as they learned to alter their practices by accepting the superiority of scientific knowledge over "false belief." Simultaneously, however, *khādims* also viewed themselves as being in the position of tolerators, although not of practices they abhorred but of practices that were different and could be given room under the overall condition that the saint's superior power and the authority derived from it by *khādims* was not put into question. Thus, the Dava & Dua team was viewed similarly to Jain, Sikh, or Hindu patrons, that is, as "guests of the saint," who, within the realm of "acceptable difference," were allowed to perform charitable acts such as sponsoring a communal meal (*niyāz*) or, as in this case, giving out free medication.

From psychiatrists, who were their guests in the position of the tolerated, *khādims* expected an acknowledgment of their own religious authority in matters of demonic illness and, overall, respectful behavior to the saint and the *dargāh*. Like every newcomer offered hospitality, the mental health team had been introduced by a *khādim* to the rule of paying respect (*salām*) to the saint when entering the shrine. From then onward, however, the members of the mental health team no longer behaved as guests should but as if they had more rights than *khādims*. After their first visit, members of the Dava & Dua Program stopped greeting the saint every time they came to the clinic. "We had to do this at least once," one of the psychiatrists said, "in order to gain the *khādims*' trust. Otherwise, I would not have done it. I don't believe in this or any other Muslim saint."[45]

Observing the behavior of psychiatrists and others involved in the program, *khādims* increasingly noted a general lack of respect. The members of the mental health team were oblivious of the fact that in the space of the shrine they were accorded the position of "the tolerated." Self-confidently performing a superior status legitimated by scientific knowledge and supported by the law and the government, the psychiatrists and NGO workers acted as if they were in a clinical space and *khādims* were some lower-order staff. In the psychiatrists' view, *khādims* had to acknowledge what was done for them rather than the other way around. For some time, members of the Trust and ritual servants who had opted for the program interpreted and tolerated the lack of respect shown by the team for the socioreligious environment they moved in as a "permissible difference." Other *khādims*, who had from the beginning opposed the

Dava & Dua Program, however, demanded that the Trust withdraw its permission for the clinic. Gradually, toleration changed into nontoleration on both sides.

The program faced other problems, too, which led to a further deterioration of the relationships between the mental health team and the *khādims*. As the majority of pilgrims came from Mumbai, Rajasthan, and other places beyond the state of Gujarat, most patients who received a psychiatric diagnosis and medicine at the clinic also lived outside the state. Often, patients disappeared without informing the psychiatrist or the NGO. Many treatment records therefore remained incomplete and could not be used to document the progress and success of the community mental health program. The funding of the project, moreover, was provided by the Gujarat government and was meant to improve local community mental health care services; but at the shrine, most of the patients who benefitted came from other states. For this, too, the team held *khādims* responsible.

The team then began to recruit patients from nearby villages, which unsettled *khādims*. For some time, a stream of Hindu patients appeared who completely ignored the environment of the shrine and went straight to the consultation room, as they would in a hospital. Many of the men, *khādims* alleged, were drunk, and women were menstruating. Rather than contributing to an improvement of the shrine, the therapeutic cooperation brought defilement to the *dargāh*. Alcohol and menstrual blood defined the limits of "permissible difference" tolerated in the *dargāh* space. The program received its final blow when one of the practicing psychiatrists had given an interview to a local newspaper in which he referred to *khādims* as a "superstitious lot." At this point, the Trust finally withdrew permission to conduct the Dava & Dua Program and told the team to leave.

Unlike the "Ritual & Tablet" program conducted at the Hindu shrine in South India, the work of purification performed by the Dava & Dua Program did not result in Sufi practitioners' accepting the superiority of psychiatry over ritual healing. But to view this outcome as an instance of the resistance of "traditional" Sufi healing against a "rational" modern understanding of mental illness would miss the point. Both parties drew on toleration enshrined in the modern constitution of the Indian state. Conflicts arose in a process of toleration that foregrounded divergent framings of the positions of the tolerator and the tolerated. Simultaneously, the secular meaning of tolerance as translated in vernacular languages emphasizing acquiescence and respect on the one hand, and limits to toleration on the other, also informed the ways in which difference was accommodated at the shrine. The psychiatric project emerged from the limits set to tolerance. The conception of the Dava & Dua Program was motivated by restricting freedom of religion as it came into conflict with health and associated human rights issues epitomized by practices of chaining mentally ill persons at religious healing sites. But once the human rights issue (chaining) was removed, the principle of tolerating different religious practices came back into play and defined the limits of what kinds of difference were permissible.

The psychiatrists' framing of their position as tolerator privileged the feature of toleration of assumed "power to alter"—in this case to purify the shrine from treating mental illness. But *khādims* also framed their position in terms of a tolerator, namely as "hosts" of those opposed. Although the Supreme Court order had said that mentally ill persons should be treated by medical professionals, this formulation left open the question of whether all types of mental and behavioral troubles such as those treated at religious healing places are "really" manifestations of mental illness. While mental health professionals are convinced that this is the case, *khādims* of Mirā Dātār distinguish between "mental" and "demonic" illnesses as two different types of sickness. Notions of demonic illness are embedded in religious constructions of human/nonhuman relationships defined as different from mental illness. Practices of ritual healing, then, come under the protection of freedom of religion guaranteed by the Indian constitution. Thus, *khādims*' claims to the position of the tolerator are derived from privileging religious authority legitimated by "holy healing" as part of Islamic medicine, whereas psychiatrists' claims to superior authority and to the position of the tolerator are derived from the scientific status of psychiatry. In this vein, competing framings of positioning "toleration" were at work, which turned therapeutic cooperation from mutual toleration to nontoleration.

Complicating matters further, the Dava & Dua Program was set up at a time in Gujarat when calls for intolerance against all Muslims shaped the political arena. Regardless of the kind of Islam promoted by different factions, Muslims advancing a reformist stance such as spelled out by Mahmood were as much affected as those whom he had declared un-Islamic, including Sufis. Significantly, though, Islamic reformers and secular mental health professionals found common ground in disparaging Sufi practices as "superstition." But while Mahmood opted to demand that the Indian state alter its conceptualization of the Muslim community by narrowing the definition of Islam, mental health reformers opted for engaging in the work of purification enacted through toleration aimed at altering understandings of *duʿāʾ* (praying) in terms of a pious religious act separate from medical treatment of mental illness. Even if the Dava & Dua team had sought to separate mental health care concerns from religious identity politics, the repercussions of the recent violence against the Muslim minority perpetuated by the Hindu majority still made themselves felt in first subtle and then more open mutual distrust, which finally led to mutual nontoleration. Analyzing the work of this "clinic" inside a shrine thus reveals the complex and historically contingent composition of the value of tolerance and of the processes of toleration evolving in a Sufi setting discursively associated with "tolerant Islam." The encounter between mental health workers and *khādims* reveals that tolerance and the making and breaking of boundaries are less shaped by ethical ideals than by pragmatic negotiations of political power, knowledge, and the approval/disapproval of difference played out in practices of translation and purification.

12

Sufi Sound, Sufi Space

Indian Cinema and the Mise-en-Scène of Pluralism

RACHANA RAO UMASHANKAR

There is a veil! A veil!
Behind the veil is the one who is hidden.
If I succeed not in unveiling the veiled one,
Then may I never be called Akbar!

As words on a page, with their evocation of the hidden aspects of the divine, one would not be remiss in thinking that these were arcane verses from a medieval Sufi treatise. In fact, they are from a Bollywood *qawwālī*,[1] where the singer is the male protagonist Akbar—tailor and *qawwāl* par excellence[2]—who sits on an extravagantly decorated concert stage, his feathered cap cocked at a jaunty angle, with a color-coordinated back-up troupe. What he proposes to unveil is not the hidden secrets of God and the nature of creation, but his beloved, who sits in the audience wearing a rather flimsy *niqāb*.[3] This iconic *qawwālī* is from the 1977 blockbuster film *Amar Akbar Anthony*.[4] This is clearly *qawwālī* sans Sufism, sans Islam.

Moving ahead a few decades to 2000, another *qawwālī* rings out, this time in the movie *Fiza*:[5]

God and his saints are of one mind,
That at this hallowed threshold you find exaltation.
Supplicate with sincerity, for this is Haji Ali,
The friend of God.

The singers here are *qawwāls*, old and young, dressed in black *sherwānīs*.[6] They sing their song to Haji Ali, the popular saint of Mumbai, in the courtyard of whose shrine they sit: This is not a back-lot set. The song begins with a view of the mosque minaret and then pans down to the *qawwāls*. Throughout the rest of the song the camera follows a supplicant, an older Muslim woman, as she makes her way along the rocky causeway that links the shrine to the mainland, and then into the shrine's inner sanctum. She eventually emerges and joins the *samā*ʿ in the shrine's courtyard.[7] The contrast between these two renditions of *qawwālī* in Bollywood cinema is evident.

It is striking to note that, until about the year 2000, *qawwālī* in Bollywood cinema was almost entirely nonreligious in its content and setting.[8] The language of love expressed by the mystic to his master, or to God, was relieved of its Sufi vestments and was clad instead in the regalia of earthly romance. The dialogic quality and intertextuality of Sufi *qawwālī* was often transformed into a flirtatious war of words between lovers or rivals, typically in a concert or party setting. Another important aspect of twentieth-century Bollywood *qawwālī*s is that they functioned purely as signifiers of Muslim identity; they were one among several motifs in the film that signaled to the viewer that particular protagonists were Muslim (as opposed to the default setting of Hindu). But as motifs, these older Bollywood *qawwālī*s became part of the cardboard-cutout façade of Islam and Muslim socioreligious life in India.[9]

All of this changed at the beginning of this millennium. Bollywood *qawwālī* is now being reinfused with its Sufi essence. The *qawwālī* from the film *Fiza* discussed above is typical of this turn (other examples are discussed below). The scenes of *qawwālī* performance in the films of the first decade of the twenty-first century move for the most part back to the Sufi shrine, the performers pictured are often traditional *qawwāls*, and the words sung convey the ideal of mystical, ecstatic love, and union with the divine.

However, even at this turn, we find that the co-option of the *qawwālī* has not ended, but shifted. Once bowdlerized of its sacred content, *qawwālī*—resituated as it has been within a Sufi context—is now used to promote the rhetoric of national integration and Indian pluralism, or to bring into focus interreligious violence. Even when love stories (the staple of Bollywood cinema) are central to the plot of the film that features a song or two with Sufi themes, these romances play out against the backdrop of interreligious harmony or strife. The task performed by these *qawwālī*s now comes in primarily two forms: (1) the *qawwālī* itself mentions these themes—the *qawwālī* from the film *Fiza*, for instance, features the line, "At this shrine Hindus, Muslims, Sikhs, and Christians receive the grace of God"; or (2) the Sufi theme of the oneness of humanity before a single God is set in contrast to the interreligious strife that is the running narrative of the movie.

Sufi Themes and the Love of the Other

The film *Fiza* tells the tale of a young Muslim man who is drawn into a terrorist network in the aftermath of the 1993 Bombay Riots (widespread interreligious violence that was associated with the destruction of the Babri Mosque in December 1992 by Hindu nationalists). The woman pictured in the *qawwālī* is his mother, who has no idea what has become of her son since his disappearance during the riots. The pictorializing of the *qawwālī* includes flashes of her memories of her youthful and handsome son.

Another intriguing example is the film *Anwar.*[10] Here the title character is a young Muslim scholar studying ancient Krishna temples. In what is a complex love triangle, he is besotted with a Muslim woman, Mehru. It is a love doomed for tragedy, as she elopes with a Hindu man. In the striking closing sequence of the film, the bedraggled Anwar is shot by the police in the ruins of an ancient temple on the presumption that he is a terrorist; the local Hindus and the police presume this because they can't imagine what else a Muslim man might be doing hanging around a Hindu temple.

As he lies in the mud in his death throes, rain pouring down, he imagines himself as Krishna—blue body paint, flute, peacock-feather-topped crown and all—romancing his beloved Mehru, who is dressed in the simple saffron sari of Meera.[11] And in the background plays a stylized *qawwālī*—a female voice sings: "Why does the candle hope to melt? / Why does the moth hope to burn?" A male voice answers: "Life is the ultimate test of this desire [for annihilation]." The layers of religious symbolism here are astounding. First, Anwar, in his mud-splattered and disheveled appearance, is reminiscent of the mad lover Majnūn of Islamicate lore, whose passionate love and longing for Laylā is symbolic of humanity's unrelenting love for the divine beloved in Sufi imagery. Layered onto this is the Meera-Krishna pairing, with the Hindu mystical poet Meera as the lover who yearns to be united with her beloved, the Hindu deity Krishna. Then we have the actual words being sung: The candle burning through itself and the moth's fatal attraction to the flame are prominent motifs in Sufi poetry. These are symbolic of the annihilation (*fanāʾ*) of the self into God, which is the ultimate goal of the Sufi journey. All these images of unrequited and self-annihilating love for the divine find resonance in Anwar's own self-destructive quest for the unattainable Mehru.

Other popular Bollywood *qawwālī*s from the '00s include the immensely popular song *Khwaja Mere Khwaja*, from the film *Jodhaa Akbar*,[12] which features the blossoming romance between the Mughal emperor Akbar, the darling of those who promote Indian religious syncretism as an ideal, and his Hindu wife, Jodha; and a *qawwālī* in the film *Delhi-6*,[13] which is about a young man of mixed

Hindu and Muslim parentage (with a Hindu love interest) caught up in interreligious riots in Old Delhi.

The past decade and a half has seen the inclusion of *qawwālīs*, Sufi-esque verses, and Sufi shrines in innumerable Bollywood films. I have mentioned previously that many of these films present interreligious tensions as an important plot element. As is clear from the examples above, another feature of many of these films is love across the boundaries of religion—something that is still quite uncommon and even taboo in contemporary India. Interreligious romantic relationships and marriage—especially between Hindu women and Muslim men—have been deeply politicized since the mid '00s. Hindutva groups have promoted the idea that these relationships are part of a "love jihad"—a purported plot by Islamists to convert Hindu women to Islam by drawing them into romantic relationships.[14]

Whereas, previously, the secularized *qawwālī* was appropriated for the service of pure Bollywood romances, the reinfusion of its sacred context in contemporary Bollywood cinema is now associated with the workings of national and religious identity in India. Even the romances that play out to these Sufi soundtracks serve as metaphors for the politics of interreligious relationships in post-Independence India, and the existential threats to the Indian nation in the face of divisive religious forces. Against a backdrop of interreligious animosity, these romances foreground the love of the Other; the self- and world-altering possibilities of such barrier-breaking love find expression in ecstatic Sufi verses. The double metaphors of mystical self-denying union and love that disregards the tired conventions of the world intertwine to form a helix that serves as a blueprint for a unified Indian nation.

This co-option of *qawwālī* (or Sufi music and poetry in general) for the narrativization of religion and nation has not been limited to Bollywood, nor to themes internal to India. The year 2010 saw the launch of a campaign titled Aman Ki Asha (A hope for peace) by two media houses: the Jang Group in Pakistan and the *Times of India* group. Part of this initiative was a series of concerts throughout India that brought together Indian and Pakistani musicians and performers. Nearly every Aman Ki Asha concert in the following couple of years featured a prominent *qawwāl* or other Sufi musician. In the context of the usually tense, and often bloody, relationship between India and Pakistan over the past seventy three years, these nonstate attempts at cross-border conviviality represent a love of the Other writ large.

This brings into focus the question of why the reinfusion of Sufism into Bollywood *qawwālī* and the resurgent popularity of nonsecular *qawwālī* is overlaid with themes of nation and religion. What is the undergirding relationship between the Indian nation and religious identity that allows songs about ecstatic love and achieving oneness with the divine to unfurl into metaphors of national unity and interreligious harmony? What has led to the transformation of the Sufi shrine from a sacred space to one brimming with political possibilities in the imaginarium of Bollywood cinema?

From Sacred Space to Political Panacea

In order to understand the change in depictions of Sufi shrines and themes, it is necessary first to explore the changing ways Indian bureaucratic and cultural elites have imagined the nation for citizen audiences. Srirupa Roy, in her book *Beyond Belief: India and the Politics of Postcolonial Nationalism*, has argued that "it is through repeatedly encountering rather than believing in the official imagination of nationhood, through recognizing the sights and sounds of the state rather than 'buying into' its mythologies, that the nation-state is formed and reproduced."[15] Focusing on the early decades after Independence in 1947, Roy identifies such arms of the state as the Films Division, responsible for the production of public service messaging that brought the newly conjured nation to life on the screen, and state-organized annual public celebrations of the nation, such as the Republic Day parade, with floats celebrating India's cultural diversity, military might, and agricultural and industrial progress. It is these avatars of India that citizens of the then newly formed Indian state encountered, thereby providing a template for an imagining of the nation.

I agree with Roy that constant encounters with such an imagining of a nation—encounters engineered by state institutions—enabled the reification of the Indian nation for the citizens of the newly created Indian state. However, Roy frames her thesis squarely in the context of the years directly following India's Independence in 1947, when the project of nation building was still incipient. And while her argument rings true in these early post-Independence years for the generation that saw the creation of the Indian state and the generation that came of age soon after, subsequent generations have lived through a different experience of the nation.

I suggest that, reproduced often enough and for a sustained period of time, the institutional reminders of the nation that Roy outlines have the capacity to engender an internalization of the mythologies of nationhood, of national identity, and the identity of the nation. In an earlier era, the concept of nationhood was, as Roy suggests, "beyond belief" and more about state-structured encounters with national templates. For subsequent generations, however, the ubiquity of these institutional reminders of nationhood did in fact translate to certain convictions about the nature and reality of the Indian nation. In the context of the United States, for instance, phrases like "God Bless America" may have for an earlier generation evoked a Pavlovian response of patriotism; but for many contemporary Americans, there is certainly a deep-seated belief in American exceptionalism as an inalienable and God-given attribute of their nation. Similarly, the mega-projects of the early twentieth century—from the iconic New York skyline and the Hoover Dam to the Social Security system—constructed an image of a great, powerful, and wealthy nation in the midst of the ravages of the Great Depression; these attributes are now sacrosanct for many Americans. The contemporary twenty-first-century realities of crumbling infrastructure, inherited poverty, and failing state systems have resulted in fear and anger at the political establishment for betraying what many in the United States believe to be the fundamental truth of America's greatness.

Similarly, it may be true that a nationalistic response was elicited from earlier generations of newly minted Indians through the continual reproduction of the "nation" by state institutions and institutional memes. But for those born well after Independence, who came of age in the 1980s and 1990s, this process has gone on for so long that the construct of the "Indian nation" is something that is arguably reflexive for them. It is not just that the idea of the Indian nation itself is now very real for most Indians, but that there is a certain *ideal* of the nation that has been established. What is this ideal? What constitutes that which to many is the unquestioned ethos of the Indian nation?

In the decades after Independence and Partition (1947–70s), in the face of the wars with Pakistan and China, the existence of the state seemed ever more precarious; the fear of territorial loss and national disintegration was real. Thus, it is in this era—the late 1940s through to the early 1970s—that we find that state-produced messaging aimed to nurture a sense of unified nationhood and citizenship: celebrations of the state's strength through displays of military pageantry and regional products and resources in national parades,[16] documentaries that showcased massive development projects undertaken by the state,[17] and poster campaigns for family planning and public hygiene. These state-sponsored initiatives were geared toward nurturing civic virtue and the ideal citizen, for whom the needs of the nation-state were to be the priority. This was the first era of nationalistic messaging.

With the advent of nationally broadcast television programming in 1982,[18] and its rapid growth over the decade and through the 1990s, the state had the capacity to enter the homes of its citizens and to impact culture in a way not possible before. Public service messaging in this era came in the form of the inclusion of nationalistic themes in soap operas and other TV serials,[19] and through more obvious messaging in the form of pictorialized songs with nationalistic themes.[20] These were aired on the state-run Doordarshan, the only TV channel available to Indians until the early 1990s. These forms of media generated by the state focused on themes of "National Integration" and "Unity in Diversity": phrases that entered the vocabulary of nationhood and citizenship. These phrases suggest that the cohesion of the Indian nation depended on the capacity of those living within its territorial boundaries to look past their differences and find commonality as Indians. Purnima Mankekar proposes that Doordarshan programming aimed at the creation of just such a pan-Indian culture.[21] "Integration" implies the coming together of disparate parts; a theme echoed in the sister phrase calling for "unity in diversity." Following in line with the first era of messaging, the overarching suggestion in televised media was that the oneness of the Indian nation could be ensured through the rubrics of the Indian state.

Considering the religious fault lines that emerged and strengthened throughout the movement for Indian Independence and the creation of Pakistan, the religious diversity of India (even after Partition) could be seen as threatening the integrity of the newly independent nation. The media wings of the fledgling Indian state, emerging as they did in the shadow of India's bloody Partition, presumed that divisions and violence caused by religious difference were the primary impediments to the preservation of the Indian nation-state. From this perspective, India's religious diversity could be celebrated, but only in as much as the emphasis was on the unity of the Indian nation *in spite* of such diversity. Given the inertia of state-run institutions, this rather tentative attitude toward religion in state media continued well past the post-Independence years and into the era of televised messaging. An examination of the public service messaging produced by the above-mentioned Films Division or the Council for Public Service Communication (Lok Sewa Sanchar Parishad) well into the late 1990s reveals a striking elision: India's cultural and linguistic diversity are on full display; but religious diversity gets only a nod, and only superficially in the form of saffron-robed Buddhist monks and genuflecting Muslim men. It is hurried past, and one can almost hear a nervous bureaucrat say, "Move along, nothing to see here."

Take one of the most iconic of these public service shorts, *Ek Sur* (better known as, *Mile Sur Mera Tumhara*).[22] This approximately six-minute-long musical short features movie stars, sports figures, musicians, representatives from some of India's tribal populations, and ethnic and linguistic groups, all of whom appear sequentially on screen against the backdrop of India's diverse natural vistas. Running throughout is the song whose words give the film its more popular name: *Mile sur merā tumhārā, to sur bane hamārā* (The notes that you and I sing merge to create a harmony that is ours), and the film is clearly geared toward celebrating the diversity of India, while also emphasizing its unity—the harmony formed from the comingling of various notes. What is missing in this panoply of sounds and images is any engagement with India's religious diversity. Beyond the token appearance of a white-capped Kashmiri Muslim and a few turbaned Sikhs, religion is entirely elided in this film. This elision can be seen in most other state-created public service short films that aired on Doordarshan.

For many of the Indian cultural elite who dominate twenty-first-century Bollywood cinema, in stark contrast to those who elided religion in the first era of nation-building rhetoric, the greatest crisis experienced by the nation, and the greatest threat to its integrity, has been *domestic* interreligious violence. This is not particularly surprising, considering that these contemporary elites were bred on the institutional simulacra of the nation of which Roy speaks, including the all-pervasive narratives of India's founding fathers—Gandhian Satyagraha bringing peace at times of great religious violence, and Nehruvian visions of a diverse nation integrated by socialist five-year plans. These narratives were consumed by India's contemporary cohort of elites through media produced by the generations that preceded it. The national rhetoric that championed diversity but elided religion was produced by various monopolistic arms of the Indian state—the Doordarshan television broadcast service and All India Radio (Akashvani), the media arms of the Ministry of Information and Broadcasting, and school textbooks produced by state-run boards of education—but also Bollywood cinema from the 1940s to the 1970s, which echoed state rhetoric. It is at this table that the contemporary cultural elite of India has supped.

Many of these twenty-first-century cultural elites have internalized the ideal of the Indian nation as a unified whole. But this class of India's elites is also part of the generation that witnessed the destruction of the Babri Mosque by militant Hindu nationalists and the ensuing interreligious violence in 1992–93, the massacre of close to two thousand Muslims in Godhra by Hindu mobs as the state stood by, the attacks in Mumbai in 2008 at the hands of Islamist terrorists, and the resurgence of Hindu nationalism and the global spread of radical Islamism. Thus, we have a scenario here where members of the cultural elite find that their much-cherished ideal of a diverse yet unified Indian nation is in peril.

It is important to note that there is no agreement on the specifics of what this ideal of a diverse but unified Indian nation actually looks like. One major fault line is the way in which Indian Muslims are imagined: either as perpetual outsiders, and therefore conditional citizens of a primarily Hindu nation (the Hindutva perspective), or as a fully integrated and assimilated part of the Indian nation (a perspective held predominantly by India's secular elites). Even with the latter position, however, there are forms of Muslimness that are deemed more Indian (and safer) than others, and the onus of showing assimilation falls to the Muslim. Sufism is certainly imagined as a more syncretic, and thus more palatable, form of Islam by India's secular elites.[23]

Whatever the ideal may be, however, the sense of crisis over the endangerment of the nation has been accompanied by a steady and growing disillusionment with the Indian state and its capacity to reify the ideals of the nation. The common element that seems to be rending apart the nation is interreligious violence, something that for decades was never confronted openly in state-produced media that purported to be providing the true narrative voice of India, and something institutions of the state have failed to prevent. The silence of an older era of media on the issue of religion in the face of endemic interreligious violence is jarring.[24] And so, while the pluralistic yet unified character of the Indian nation has been internalized as valid and valuable by many members of the cultural elite (who now produce a significant portion of contemporary popular media), and also by a large swathe of the Indian public, the state is seen to have failed in nurturing these values and bringing them to fruition. What happens when the state accomplishes its goal of making nationhood real for its citizens but then fails to maintain the illusion that the state *itself* is the only viable means for the sustenance of this nation? This contrast is starkly rendered when one considers that the reins of the state, in the past decade, have been increasingly taken up by the Bharatiya Janata Party (BJP) and allied Hindutva groups.

I propose that this is what we have playing out in India over the past two decades. The imagination of pluralism-minded citizens is left unsatisfied by the failures of the state. It is to fill this lacuna that we see the emergence of Sufism—Sufi spaces, Sufi sounds—as a panacea for India's religious woes, a setting and soundtrack for this cherished ideal of religious pluralism.[25] As I discussed above, considering that religion and the public expression of religion is such a vital and ever-present part of Indian public culture, it is significant to note that state institutions acknowledge this only in a cursory manner, and there are very few state-instituted venues that satisfy this need. The Sufi shrine, and Sufi music, such as the *qawwālī*, fill this void.

Images of Sufi Shrines in Multireligious India

Sufi shrines in India are shared sacred spaces.[26] Sufism is one of the oldest and most widespread forms of Islamic practice in India, and Sufi shrines certainly attract large numbers of Muslim adherents. In addition, Sufi saints are revered as charismatic and spiritually elevated figures by non-Muslims in India, especially by Hindus. It is not uncommon to find as many non-Muslims as Muslims at the shrines of popular Sufi saints in India. A typical Thursday evening at a prominent shrine will find this religiously diverse following gathered around the *qawwāls*, who saturate the air with exuberant and moving renditions of centuries-old *qawwālīs*.

These familiar *qawwālīs* too exhibit an internal diversity in form and content.[27] They are often macaronic in nature—a mix of Arabic phrases from the Quran and the hadith and Sufi verses in Persian, Hindavi, Punjabi, Sindhi, and any number of other regional languages. To add to this intertextuality is the abundant use of Indic images in complement to Islamicate ones. A hallmark of Sufi poetry is the presentation of the Sufi as the lover, and God (or the Sufi Master) as the beloved.[28] *Qawwālīs* from the subcontinent feature verses that bring together lover-beloved imagery from both Islamicate and Indic sources. The traditional repertoire of *qawwālīs* heard at Sufi shrines in India today features such familiar Islamicate pairings as the moth and the flame, or Laylā and Majnūn, the lovelorn couple. Also present in these songs is imagery of Radha and Krishna, the lovers of Hindu lore; and *qawwāls* will also weave into their renditions verses by the medieval Hindu poet-saint Mīrabai, or by Kabīr, the iconoclastic poet of Medieval India.

For these reasons, Sufi shrines are frequently regarded as unique spaces in the Indian public sphere, where people of all classes, castes, and religions can gather. And this gathering at Sufi shrines is often concomitant with the performance of Sufi music, especially *qawwālī*. In this shared sacred space, the *qawwālī* offers the language of oneness before God and in God, of the unity of humankind regardless of creed or caste, the promise of comfort and succor to all who shelter within the shrine and seek closeness to the divine. It is language that is powerfully reminiscent of the language of Indian pluralism; a parallel that is further reinforced by the multilingual verses, and their cross-religious imagery.

For many, the *qawwālī* provides the appropriate language for the expression of national ideals—and in a space where these ideals are not corroded by the rust of the seventy three-year-old Indian state; one hears the promise of oneness sung in a multivocal and complex format, and this imagery of unity is echoed by the diversity (religious, social, class, and gender) among those present together at the Sufi shrine.[29] During my own fieldwork at multiple Sufi shrines in India, I found that my interlocutors saw few other spaces and few other sounds that evoked the reification of the ideal of the Indian nation. It is no surprise then that Bollywood cinema—the dreamworld for a billion

Indians—has come to embrace the narrative that the Sufi shrine and the *qawwālī* provide the mise-en-scène of national healing.

In chapter 11 of this volume, Helene Basu discusses the ways in which psychiatrists and Muslim reformists in India have turned into strange bedfellows in their criticism of Sufi shrine practices. Here, the Sufi shrine practices are the object of criticism, identified as antithetical to modernity and needing to be purified of practices that (depending on which party is asked) are deemed to be unscientific or un-Islamic. What we see in Indian cinema is the co-option of shrine-based Sufism by another community of modernists—the pluralistic Indian cultural elite. For them, the shrine space and its practices are not objects of derision, but rather of praise: They embody the vision of an internally plural but unified Indian nation. Basu uses Bruno Latour's conceptualization of "purification" as a key process in establishing modernity. Following this conceptual thread, we can see the same processes in action in contemporary Indian film, but in a different context, and with differing outcomes. Indian cinema of the twenty-first century has positioned the Sufi shrine as a rarified space where a purer national identity is able to rise above other (read "less-important") markers of identity; Sufi music and verse are similarly co-opted.

In the films that feature *qawwālī*, interreligious violence nearly always constitutes the backdrop against which the protagonists play their parts. Bollywood cinema of yesteryear stayed away from themes of violence among Indian citizens on religious grounds (Indo-Pak violence, yes; caste-based or class-based inequities, yes; but not internal interreligious strife) for the reasons I discussed briefly above. But, over the past two decades, an emboldened generation of filmmakers has increasingly taken on this deeply distressing issue through the vehicle of commercial Bollywood cinema. And in these films, Sufism (as voiced through *qawwālī* and Sufi-esque verse) is offered up as a counterpoint to interreligious violence.

This new configuration in the perception of India's pluralistic cultural elite toward the state and its capacity to reify the ideals of the Indian nation is lyrically presented in the final scenes of the film *Anwar*. As life ebbs out of the title character, his mud-splattered body drenched in blood and rain, the scene cuts to the crowd that has gathered around him. A policeman in khaki is flanked by a glowering Hindu mendicant wielding an ominous trident, and by a man in priestly saffron robes. Beside the mendicant is a man in a casual white shirt, but wearing a saffron stole around his neck that marks him as a Hindutva volunteer. Then, a young boy pushes through this rain-drenched wall of state authority and religious nationalism. He wears a simple T-shirt bearing three broad stripes of saffron, white, and green—the tricolor of the Indian flag. The youthful Indian citizen stands amid state-sanctioned, religiously motivated violence. All who stand behind him are implicated in the violence that confronts him. The soundtrack to this charged scene is a song brimming with Sufi themes.

In the face of the failed structures of the state that had long produced memes of unity and pluralistic nationalism, the use of these same tired tokens of the nation-state perhaps seems inadequate to the contemporary viewer, especially when these tokens now have been co-opted by Hindutva politics. One can imagine that, in a film about a young man drawn to radical Islamism as a consequence of post-Babri mosque violence, or a lovelorn Muslim historian mistaken for a terrorist and shot in a temple, the resounding tones of the Indian national anthem played without any sense of cynicism may seem mawkish and hollow. On the other hand, images of such violence *in tandem* with emblems of the nation-state allow for the suggestion of collusion and betrayal on the part of the old gods of nationhood and patriotism. How stark and poignant, then, the overlay of words that evoke the desire to be one, to be unified with a power that is eternal, that is morally higher, that renews the promises that the Indian state has failed to keep.

Commentary on Part IV

Sufism in Indian National Spaces

BRUCE B. LAWRENCE

In the introduction to this volume charting new approaches to Sufism, Islam, and politics in the South Asian context, Katherine Ewing, one of the co-editors, notes how important it is to understand "the split of Sufism as mystical philosophy from local practices associated with shrine networks." Grounding Sufism in local practices also requires looking at the relationship of various Sufi actors, as well as scholars of Sufism, to the global order (part 1), while also acknowledging key terms and categories within Islam that either qualify or challenge Sufism (part 2). The shadow of the state looms especially large because the two major postcolonial nation-states of South Asia, Pakistan and India, reflect divergent views of Sufism and Sufis, both their proponents and opponents. While Pakistan occupies part 3 of this volume, Sufism in Indian national spaces is the topic of the final section, part 4.

The Indian nation is itself, however, vastly complex—regionally, linguistically, and socially—and so Part 4, in turn, has to be circumscribed. It does not encompass all of modern-day India but instead focuses on developments in West India, the state of Gujarat, and the mega-cosmopolis of Mumbai. Indeed, the distinctive trajectory for Part 4 is to look at two sites of shrine activity (Carla Bellamy in chapter 10 and Helene Basu in chapter 11) and one site of commercial activity (Rachana Umashankar in chapter 12) in order to localize and exemplify themes that pervade the volume as a whole.

Each of the three chapters considered in part 4 has a distinctive West Indian color, two (Bellamy and Basu) projecting aspects of rivalry and contestation among the committed denizens of shrines near Mumbai, while the other

(Umashankar) concerns citizens of the nation as a whole, that is, the Republic of India, as projected through Bollywood, also in Mumbai.

All three essays provide answers for two central queries of this volume: Is Sufism in fact antipolitical or does it instead provide a forum for politics by other names? And related to this query: Beyond the invocation of harmony as the dominant Sufi ideology, how are other less-harmonious forces—at once rival and competitive—at work through Sufi agents, spaces, and activities?

While all three chapters in part 4 address these broad questions, they do so through discrete analyses that coordinate thematically even while differing topically. Bellamy's focus in chapter 10 is on a Muslim saint shrine that functions as a small neighborhood *dargāh* rather than a large, heavily trafficked central site. It is a Shiʿi *imāmbāṙā* that is actually located in a home behind a mosque in Santa Cruz East, a working-class and middle-class neighborhood in Mumbai. Even access to the shrine is difficult, requiring visitors to traverse a narrow, unmarked alley. Yet the site thrives on its connection to a larger sectarian symbol, in this case not directly to the family of the Prophet but to a complex of shrines remote from Mumbai known as Husain Tekri, or Husain Hill.[1] And far from being an historical connection, the link between this local *imāmbāṙā* and its remote symbolic node is very recent, dating only to the 1980s. Its connective agent is a local woman, here named Aisha, who experienced healing through a ritual practice called *ḥāżirī* (literally, "presence"), which Bellamy defines as "a process by which the presiding saints of a *dargāh* force a malevolent possessing spirit to vacate the petitioner's body" (p. 190). The story could have ended there except that Aisha, on returning to Mumbai and to Santa Cruz, participated in other healing rituals, as did her family members, in the space that served as both home and shrine for them. It was at an intense evening ritual gathering in this confined space of the local *imāmbāṙā* that a member of Aisha's family, her brother-in-law, had a confrontation with a female visitor, herself a frequent patron of this site. After the woman experienced not only disrespect but effrontery, she reported the incident to the local police. Again, this would not be extraordinary, except for the further disclosure from one of Aisha's relatives, a cousin: He reported to Bellamy that the woman claiming offense issued her report with her *Hindu* name. Not only the woman's "hidden," alternative religious identity but also other layered elements of conflict, either hidden or subsumed within the complex of relationships at the *dargāh*, then occupy the rest of this intense local narrative.

I relate the detail of these intimate interactions because they are the core elements for Bellamy's astute analysis of how healing takes place. Precisely because this home *dargāh*/*imāmbāṙā* is so small, its participants are all known to each other, despite their differing backgrounds, worldviews, and identities.

"Crossing boundaries is an important element of the healing process of pilgrims" (p. 196), observes Bellamy. But how to leave the door open for such healing while also retaining the protection of domestic space in this Santa Cruz *imāmbāṛā*? Hindu women—that is, women who were openly Hindu, not clandestinely Hindu yet outwardly Muslim like the affronted visitor—would come to the *imāmbāṛā* when they were seeking cures, but the inner part of the shrine would remain closed to them during high ritual moments. In short, one can emphasize either unity—all come together and seek/find healing in a shared space that crosses boundaries—or difference/opposition—collective notions of difference based on religion, class, gender, and location continue to matter, especially when disputes arise. The role of the state, as in the case of the police above, is always hovering, sometimes directly but more often indirectly influencing how pilgrims behave.

In the case study provided by Basu, the author examines not just an incidental but a frontal intervention of the state, and asks how that unprecedented and bold state intervention influences the way her Sufi subjects experience healing. Here we visit a rural shrine that is located in Gujarat and traces its origins to the fifteenth century. Unlike the local Mumbai *imāmbāṛā* of Bellamy, we encounter in Gujarat a Sufi tomb shrine, Mirā Dātār, teeming with both people and potential conflicts. Basu observes that "almost 600 *khādims* from 150 households shared the right to perform daily ritual services for nearly 1,000 Muslim and non-Muslim clients who visited the shrine during a week. Although the language spoken at the shrine is Urdu, most pilgrims are Muslims, Hindus, Jains, and Sikhs from diverse social, geographical, urban, and rural backgrounds who are also followers of *khādims* and the *dargāh*. The shrine thus emerges as a cosmopolitan nodal point of extensive translocal and transnational social networks, which gives *khādims* political and business access beyond their ritual profession" (p. 202).

Despite the difference in location and scope, there are crucial resemblances between the purposes of both the Santa Cruz *imāmbāṛā* described in Bellamy's chapter and the Gujarati Sufi *dargāh* described by Basu. As was the case with Bellamy, Basu sees healing or methods of seeking healing as the crucial element mapping activity at the shrine and also the valence of the shrine itself. Basu, concerned with the making of madness and mental disease within the ritual arena of healing of a Sufi shrine in Gujarat, sees ideology as inextricable from institutions, so much so that ideological asymmetries between "dominant" psychiatry and "subaltern" ritual healing depend on the spatial separation of two institutions: government directed mental health care workers (on the one hand) and Sufi-motivated custodians, with "magical" cures (on the other). When both are examined in the same locale, however, those who visit the shrine, that is, the pilgrims, see their interests served, their health secured, better by the local officiants than by government overseers. Despite the modernist, reform rhetoric of both Sufi shrine opponents who are Muslim, like the Tablīghī Jamāʿat, and largely non-Muslim government employees, "the encounter between mental health workers and *khādims* [at the shrine of Mirā Dātār] reveals that tolerance and the making and breaking of boundaries are less shaped by ethical ideals than by pragmatic negotiations of political power, knowledge, and the approval/disapproval of difference played out in practices of translation and purification" (p. 214).

What is of historical import here is the connection of government intervention to larger political forces. It is the threat of recurring Hindu-Muslim riots (summer 2002), after thousands had lost their lives in Hindutva-orchestrated mass killings (winter–spring 2002), that shapes state response to religious conflict: The national inquest to provide "mental health" at the Mirā Dātār shrine was intended to placate rival factions and make Sufism an instrument fostering national harmony.

Ironically, one of the practices curtailed at Mirā Dātār was the centuries-old tradition of music. In response to Muslim reformers, *qawwālī* was no longer performed inside the Gujarati shrine, and Basu herself made an ethnographic film of this site,[2] projecting how these changes happened, and what was the significance of seeking health, specifically of looking for remedies from black magic, at Mirā Dātār.

The third and final chapter of part 4, by Umashankar, not only highlights the importance of film but also foregrounds the practice of *qawwālī*, abandoned at Mirā Dātār, as itself the vehicle for national therapy. It is therapy required because the post-1947 Republic of India cannot, and did not, deliver on the promises made to its citizens. Huge rifts—in class and language, politics and gender, health, education, housing, and, of course, religion—persisted into post-Independence India. With the new pressures unleashed by a new millennium, post-2000 India saw the reinscription of religious imagery and values into a musical form—*qawwālī*—that had been emptied of its original spiritual thrust for nearly half a century. Bollywood *qawwālī*, in Umashankar's view, became "reinfused with its Sufi essence. . . . The scenes of *qawwālī* performance in the films of the first decade of the twenty-first century move for the most part back to the Sufi shrine, the performers pictured are often traditional *qawwāls*, and the words sung convey the ideal of mystical, ecstatic love, and union with the divine. . . . Once bowdlerized of its sacred content, *qawwālī*—resituated as it has been within a Sufi context—is now used to promote the rhetoric of national integration and Indian pluralism, or to bring into focus interreligious violence" (p. 216).

But even as *qawwālī* has had its spiritual import reinscribed from the top down, its projection as a national icon raises new questions. Can *qawwālī* be an effective Bollywood pan-Indian ideology of ecumenical harmony when it attempts to project love across religious boundaries? In a footnote, Umashankar hints at one of the major obstacles to such an idyllic harmony: "love jihad." As she observes, "interreligious romantic relationships and marriage—especially between Hindu women and Muslim men—have been deeply politicized since the mid '00s. Hindutva groups have promoted the idea that these relationships are part of a 'love jihad'—a purported plot by Islamists to convert Hindu women to Islam by drawing them into romantic relationships" (p. 218). Even though Indian courts and a large segment of Indian elites support freedom of religion, including freedom of marriage, the backdoor, local threats of Hindu advocates for "marital purity" are hard to ignore, as a recent *New Yorker* article made clear.[3]

Umashankar's larger point is to understand two needs simultaneously at work but moving in different directions. On the one hand there is the need to understand how the Republic of India has constructed national integration through social media as well as the earlier public service films, but on the other hand one must recognize that the fear of *domestic* interreligious violence is well founded, with no signs of reduction or cessation. Umashankar's conclusion underscores the dilemma for Indian elites and for the nation as a whole: "Many of these twenty-first-century cultural elites have internalized the ideal of the Indian nation as a unified whole. But this class of India's elites is also part of the generation that witnessed the destruction of the Babri Mosque by militant Hindu nationalists and the ensuing interreligious violence in 1992–93, the massacre of close to two thousand Muslims in Godhra by Hindu mobs as the state stood by [in 2002], the attacks in Mumbai in 2008 at the hands of Islamist terrorists, and the resurgence of Hindu nationalism and the global spread of radical Islamism" (p. 222).

Because Hindutva and Islamism are opposing ideologies that can be confronted but not eliminated, "members of the cultural elite find that their much-cherished ideal of a diverse yet unified Indian nation is in peril" (p. 222). Moreover, since "there is no agreement on the specifics of what this ideal of a diverse but unified Indian nation actually looks like," the myriad forces at work within political Islam, or Sufi politics, will at best provide a weathervane of future challenges facing all South Asians, not just Indians and Pakistanis, but also their neighbors in Bangladesh and Sri Lanka.

It is hard to underestimate the collective value of these three chapters. They are grounded in careful research, often based on painstaking observation of local agents, activities, and processes, and then folded into an analysis that links Sufism as a trope to developments that shape its use across time and space. Three conclusions stand out. First, ideology is not incidental but integral to what happens in each domain. It is not national political agendas but their local appropriation or rejection that matters. For Bellamy's subjects, Hindu identity can be used to reclaim space denied them, while for Basu the tug-of-war over health practices depends on local actors and their resonance with patients/pilgrims. For Umashankar, the glossy apparatus of Bollywood does not obliterate, but instead contends with, acts of violence that instantiate violence as part of local as well as national memory. Second, the state deploys its agents but does not control their local impact. This is particularly evident in Basu's narrative. Her pilgrim subjects, despite the superior resources and "modern" approach of the state, see their interests served, and their health secured, better by the local officiants than by government overseers. Though the state may seem remote from Bellamy's subjects, it is not absent from their decision making. As noted above, it provides the background or shadow to what impels an offended woman, and others like her, to seek recourse from police officers for personal affronts. And in the case of Bollywood *qawwālī*, its tunes may evoke the musical legacy and mercurial memory of an alleged harmony between Muslims and Hindus, but it is heard against the background of modern-day rifts, often government induced or abetted, between different religious communities. Finally, various forms of Sufism, as also popular Shiʿism, are permeable but not erasable. Through local shrines and familiar agents, they provide an affective element that transcends inscribed identity, ideological forces, or state enforcement. The sacred site nurtures hope within the limits of performance, whether at a saint's shrine or a medical clinic or a movie theater. It is not the Sufism of literary eminence or philosophical acclaim, but it remains a liminal element in the intertwined destinies of both Pakistan and India.

Conclusion

Thinking Otherwise

ROSEMARY R. CORBETT

The collection of practices, relationships, beliefs, and institutions now grouped under the broad category of Sufism are, and long have been, wide and varied—both within the Indio-Pakistani subcontinent and beyond. The essays and commentary in this volume have shown the incredible diversity of Sufi forms and philosophies, practices and genealogies, while showing their inextricability from those ostensibly more normative Islamic traditions that Sufism was conceptually cleaved from when Orientalist scholars created and popularized the "Sufism" neologism. Some Muslim reformers have since attempted to excise Sufis from Islam, and various governments have recently integrated ideas about Sufism into War on Terror attempts to counter "extremism."[1] In documenting this diversity, contributors to this volume have also shown that, whatever else Sufi traditions have been over time and space, such traditions and those who practice them have rarely, if ever, fit the apolitical image now propagated by various governments.

Sufism, as an idea, and Sufis, as supposedly paradigmatic moderate Muslims, are currently deeply politicized by state and local administrations within India and Pakistan and beyond. Such governments, aided in their definitions by the work of academics, among others, attempt to operationalize certain notions of Sufism in their efforts at privatizing or otherwise "moderating" Muslims' traditions and practices. This larger politicization, the highly potent inaccuracies rife within narratives opposing apolitical Sufis to reformists (who are ostensibly overly political or violent and often labeled "Wahhabis" or "fundamentalists"), and the origins and effects of such dynamics have been the foci of this volume. In bringing to light the history, present, and possible futures of state politicization and its lacunae, however, our contributors have also offered insights into the power struggles that transpire within and across various Sufi communities and sites—not least as local Sufis and their supposed opponents grapple with simplistic War on Terror terms, including embodying them with the aspiration of bending national or international governments in support of their own particular agendas.

Like state politicization, local contestations and power dynamics refuse to proceed in uniform or predictable ways, our contributors prove. Such contests and developments are shaped by factors intrinsic to specific communities, as well as by—and as these factors intersect with—larger national and geopolitical trends. As the contributors to this volume have shown, state promotion of Sufism as the ostensibly apolitical, pluralist variety of Islam can have very different effects for and among Muslims in Indian contexts than it does among Muslims in Pakistani ones. Add to this the fact that the Sufi traditions and practices politicized for state purposes and promoted by various officials can and do conflict to some degree with the forms practiced, understood, and transmitted by nonstate actors, and we find ample opportunity for confrontation, reinterpretation, and reformulation of tradition on many levels, within and across communities, on a sometimes global scale only accentuated by increasing access to the internet and social media. Our authors have charted some of the many ways these changes and developments unfold while also pushing readers—be they students, scholars, foundation officers, or heads of state—to question the simplistic framings used in instrumentalist projects to police and produce "good" Islam, and even the very aim of regulating religion, itself.[2]

Thinking Outside Instrumentalist Narratives

In South Asia and elsewhere, some of those identified as Sufi may be or have been proponents of pacifism, but others are and have been just the opposite. Alix Philippon demonstrates as much in chapter 8 with her examination of how, in patronizing some Barelwis as the face of Sufi moderation, Pakistani politicians may have overlooked one faction's drive to shape an Islamic state in their own image, consequently helping to spark Barelwi militancy that exemplifies what Philippon calls "Sufislamism"—a kind of practice in which Sufism and militant political action cohere.

Similarly, in contrast to tropes about the ostensible difference or division between mystical Muslims and legalistic ones, contributors here (particularly

Brian Bond, chapter 6; Brannon Ingram, chapter 4; and Usha Sanyal in, chapter 5) show how groups identified as Sufi or engaged in Sufi practices have also been as dedicated in their focus on sharia adherence as members of movements known as "reformist" for their desire to purify Muslims' traditions of non-Islamic elements. What's more, our contributors have demonstrated that even those practitioners who operate within the same shrine spaces have circumstances in which they are pluralist and ones in which they are not, moments when they are tolerant of sectarian or other differences and times when they are not (see especially Carla Bellamy, chapter 10; and Helene Basu, chapter 11). These dynamics effectively counter both the romanticized image of nonsectarian Sufi harmony propagated by Indian and Pakistani state governments and media corporations (which sometimes work in tandem, see Rachana Rao Umashankar in chapter 12 of this volume) and the ideas of administrators who create state projects to enforce nonsectarianism (see Noor Zaidi's contribution, chapter 9).

Ultimately, as our authors and commentators show, what Sufi traditions and those who practice them have *always* been is political—be it as local power brokers navigating regional politics and successive state regimes (see Sarah Ansari, chapter 7), figureheads vying simultaneously for national standing and international audiences and support (see Marcia Hermansen, chapter 3), or scholars determined to shape Muslim-majority societies (see Rosemary R. Corbett, chapter 1; and Verena Meyer, chapter 2). What Sufis have not been is political in uniform or predictable ways—thus the need for some interpretive flexibility, as Bruce Lawrence recommended in the course of contributing to this volume.

Attempts to instrumentalize Sufism as a tool in governmental administration are hardly new. Particularly in the context of South Asia, such attempts—profoundly dependent on the work of academics—began when British colonial scholars and officials created Sufism as a category, although the meanings ascribed to Sufism have changed greatly over time and differed even within the colonial period (see Katherine Pratt Ewing's introduction to this volume). One thing that remained fairly uniform for most of the many decades between then and the early twentieth century is that Sufi practitioners (philosophers and poets sometimes excepted) were regarded as "less." Less than civilized in their superstitious devotion to popular saints, less than enlightened in their ritualistic adherence to traditions, certainly less than modern in their "mystical" excesses, and no example of anything anyone would consider calling "moderate." These varying discourses of insufficiency have had myriad implications. This has particularly been the case as such discourses were enfolded into existing intra-Muslim political debates about practice and tradition (debates waged under very different assumptions and terms than those set by colonial officials), and then refracted through the politics of Muslim societies facing or fighting off colonial invasion and subjugation.

Many important developments have transpired since those inauspicious colonial engagements, several of which were sparked in part by pressures on Muslim-majority nations to prove their modernity in the face of imperial or neo-imperial advances. Among these things is the growth of state secularization programs that pushed Sufis to present their traditions as cultural practices rather than religious or political ones, as happened in as officially secular a state as Turkey and as officially religious a nation as Pakistan.[3] Also crucial has been the involvement of U.S. private foundations, along with government officials, in investigating and promoting particular forms of "modern" religion (which are political only in limited, liberal, pluralist ways).[4] Perhaps unsurprisingly, these two trends have culminated in another development: the late twentieth-century association of "good Muslims" with those subscribing to privatized, or supposedly "cultural," apolitical traditions. Such Muslims are ones who, if they couldn't be modern liberal secularists, could at least be religiously "moderate" and, therefore, politically moderated.[5]

It might seem almost ironic that practices, relationships, beliefs, and institutions as political as those described in the preceding pages of this volume could ever be deemed the global standards of apolitical religious moderation. Even more surprising is that the North Americans and Europeans involved in funding Sufism-as-moderation could settle on any Muslims as moderates after (initially borrowing from European political tradition) U.S. elites mobilized the specter of immoderate Muslims for the purpose of galvanizing policy makers and public opinion at multiple points over the nation's history—a trend that continues to the present.[6] The very category of religious moderation, however, particularly as employed by governments and imposed on Muslims, is born of the same political parents as that of the "Sufism" with which it is popularly conflated: colonialism and religious reformism.[7] And whether in the colony or the metropole, the demand for state coercion and even violence to enforce moderation has long been common, perhaps making it unsurprising that we find both tacit and explicit acceptance of this idea of state enforcement now.[8] What is ironic, then, is not the association of Sufism with religious moderation (in that both constructs were created in the crux of colonial encounters and for the purpose of enforcing colonial power dynamics), but the ways state governments operationalize this association as a means of countering insurgent violence and domesticating dissent, thereby attempting to reserve the right to exercise violence for themselves. With such high stakes, is it any surprise that the categories of both Sufism and religious moderation have been reinterpreted continuously, with those targeted for moderating later deploying the concept in novel, but equally political, ways and making new allies and enemies in the process?

Thinking Otherwise About Moderation and Its Opposites

As alluded to above, the politics of religious moderation are manifold, ramifying through different religious communities differently since the sixteenth-century expansion of European empires. Contemporary discourses about Muslim moderation, in particular, have been formulated as extensions of the earlier twentieth-century debates about Muslim modernity mentioned here. (See Tareen, this volume, for a discussion of how Quranic concepts now often associated with contemporary calls for moderation actually differ in origin and effect.) As noted, until relatively recently, officials in many South Asian and European contexts took it for granted that modern Muslims couldn't be Sufis, the denizens of superstitious devotion. But in the perpetually grinding crucible of imperial dynamics, some Muslim elites, in conversation with Christian missionaries and colonial scholars and officials, reinterpreted select Sufi traditions. These Sufi traditions were shorn of any seemingly irrational elements such as gnostic philosophy or popular devotions, and were thus available to be presented as prototypically modern. We can see this dynamic particularly well in South Asia with Muhammad Iqbal and those, such as Fazlur Rahman and his students, who were later inspired by him.[9] Iqbal was important to mid-twentieth-century Muslim modernists and Orientalists, Rahman and Wilfred Cantwell Smith included, because they perceived him as inveighing not against Sufism, per se, but against the "medieval technique of mysticism" of the ostensibly premodern, unenlightened variety.[10]

The imperative to respond to the forces of modernity, however that term has been understood by various actors over time, is evident in many, perhaps all, of the essays in this volume.[11] It is tempting to assume, as many mid-twentieth-century Orientalists did, that the pressure to modernize emanated from countries and continents that claimed modernity as their own—as synonymous with all things of "the West." Yet we can also see from the contributions to this volume that such pressures were exerted and campaigns conducted by elites within Muslim-majority societies, generally in ways explicitly or implicitly at some variance from the conception of modernization promoted by many North Americans and Europeans. This was certainly true of Muslim scholars who were invited to the McGill Institute of Islamic Studies to participate in projects of documenting and directing the shape of modern Islam, and it seems no less true for those now (such as Tahir-ul-Qadri) entangled in projects to promote Sufism as Islamic moderation.

Muslim scholars brought to the post–World War II United States did not simply parrot the ideas presented to them by their Orientalist hosts. Even though selected because of their sympathy to Orientalists' preexisting ideas, for example, those who studied and worked at McGill came with their own intentions and agenda and were participants in numerous other strands of local and global discourse. Verena Meyer vividly demonstrates the ways this kind of complexity continued into later projects in chapter 2 with her examination of Nurcholish Madjid, who Rahman and Leonard Binder brought to the University of Chicago to study modern Islam with them after local Ford program officers in Indonesia suggested his candidacy and the larger Ford Foundation provided him with funding. As Meyer argues, scholars must move away from a "one-dimensional model of influence" that would render Madjid's or other Muslims' endeavors as "reducible to Western interests"—something contemporary foundation officers and government officials, like their predecessors, still seem to struggle with as they rely on such models of influence to drive projects promoting moderate Islam around the world.

Yet while influence is a difficult thing to accurately chart and impossible to anticipate, impact is sometimes more apparent. We can see this with the extension of American Protestant metaphors to non-Protestant contexts across the globe, particularly with the terms now most frequently deployed in discourses about moderation. It is worth wondering whether Rahman ultimately would have promoted the historical narratives that juxtaposed Sufis to legal scholars and reformers—narratives then taken up in later projects to identify Muslim "moderates"—had he not studied with H. A. R. Gibb, a primary purveyor of such narratives in English, and later worked with another of Gibb's students, Wilfred Cantwell Smith. If these framings were nascent in Rahman's thinking prior to his studies with Orientalists, it is still worth exploring whether he would likely have adopted the American phrases his commonwealth hosts used to describe such dynamics (ones he later disseminated among students, scholars, and officers of state) had not he been pushed in that direction.[12]

In presenting select Sufi traditions as the potential precursor to or missing ingredient of modern or moderate Islam, Rahman and other scholars and sympathizers had to counter the kind of revisionist history that divorces Sufi practices and philosophies from the larger Islamic tradition. It is now quite common to lay blame for this severing of Sufis from the global Muslim fold at the feet of a category of people (and all of the problems of heuristic categories apply here) whom Rahman juxtaposed to Sufis. The name given to that ostensibly coherent contingent is not one any Muslims use to describe themselves; it is an American Protestant metaphor first mapped onto Islam by Gibb and Smith and then echoed by Rahman for very different reasons than those that structure War on Terror programs. That name, of course, is "fundamentalist."[13] While we certainly do not mean to imply here that no reformists have actively attempted to amputate Sufis from the Muslim family tree (because, indeed, many have), we find it necessary to pause at the use of this broad fundamentalist label and consider some of the unintended consequences of deploying it.

Blaming so-called Muslim fundamentalists for the inaccurate heuristic divide between "revivalist" Sufis and more "reformist" Muslims, is a losing strategy, even if executed in hopes of countering ahistorical narratives. At the very least, doing so hides the Orientalist history behind the counterposed categories of "Sufi" and "fundamentalist" that the chapters in this collection show to be not merely overly schematic but entirely inaccurate—not to mention laden with Euro-American Protestant assumptions. Worse, it does so by reifying those very categories, leaning on one of them ("fundamentalist," or "Wahhabi," with which the term is often conflated[14]), and thus lending credence to the ostensible division between the two. Lending credence to the division then, however indirectly and unintentionally, lends conceptual weight to the strategies of governmental bodies that attempt to manipulate intra-Muslim differences for their own agendas, deploying one ostensible faction against the other in some way. The imperialist history of the categories, including academic involvement in perpetuating them, comes full circle, with the categories being appropriated and taking on new lives in the political contexts of Muslim societies, sometimes at the cost of life itself.

Through deep ethnography and close readings of history, engaging at length with practitioners and sifting tirelessly through archives, authors of the chapters and commentary in this volume have uncovered the ways that even a heuristic bracketing of Muslims into the oppositional categories of mystic and legal reformer, moderate Sufi and supposed fundamentalist, is impossible. Such a move is as descriptively inaccurate, analytically useless, and even as intellectually elitist as attempting to bracket "popular" practices of Islam off from "normative" tradition, or bracket shrines and music from law and theology. This, too, hides the politics—local and global—inherent in such designations, while also obscuring how such politics can shift and change, taking on new resonances and involving new stakes in local arenas and beyond, as they ramify outward.

Thinking in Other Configurations

The directors of the workshop that led to this volume were initially tasked by foundation officers with gathering together scholars who could demonstrate the utility of Sufi traditions in producing modern, liberal, democratic publics. Instead, the directors gathered together scholars who could, as Ernst put it in one draft of his work for this volume, measure "presuppositions about an idealized Sufism . . . against the concrete situations that comprise its politics." What the research of these scholars has demonstrated is the inutility of government attempts (often fueled by the work of contemporary academics, as well as earlier ones) to produce properly instrumentalized religious subjects. Such attempts freight religion with, among other things, the responsibility of subduing—of rendering private, or "moderating"—the political grievances of populations subjected to infringements of sovereignty, citizenship, or even livelihood by their own states and/or by the expansive reach of neo-imperial political and economic regimes.

While the editors of this volume have grouped its contents to bring to light some of the politics of interpolating Sufi practices and traditions into state mechanisms in South Asia and beyond, this was not the only way we could or did think otherwise than instructed about the subject matter we were funded to explore. The arrangement we have created reflects many of our interests and understandings of salient dynamics but by no means all of them, and we know that reading the work of contributors across this volume will yield many more analytical insights than we have given space to here.

When read together, for example, the contributions of Basu, Bond, and Zaidi testify to how contestation over shrines and the activities within them involves not just states operationalizing theology or ideology but also state attempts to regulate affect as various registers of it are deemed enhancing of or inimical to larger projects of modernization. Relatedly, reading Bond and Zaidi with Bellamy and Sanyal illuminates how class-inflected gender constructs are often the ledger on which such affect is indexed, while putting Basu and Bellamy together with Ansari and Philippon gives insight into how economic factors can combine with political ones, among others, to influence understandings of how bounded, porous, or flexible religious identities can be.

On a different note, reading Hermansen's investigation of new trends in global Islam, as embodied by Tahir-ul-Qadri's intercontinental endeavors, in light of Sanyal's discussion of Barelwi genealogy highlights the fact that the spread of Sufi ideas outside of local networks is nothing new, nor is the fact that Sufis have traveled vast distances in pursuit of trading opportunities and expanding their influence. The new global Sufism that Hermansen discusses is novel less because of the geographic distance Sufi figures personally trek than because of the expansion of influence through social media and the relocation of authority, as Hermansen documents, from proof of affiliation with previous institutional networks to proof of certain kinds of interpretive strategies and epistemological frameworks. For this reason, the post- *ṭarīqah* professor is now sometimes prized over the *pīr*, the scholar over the *shaykh*, the latter of these identity pairs associated—in a discourse dripping with the colonial assumptions on which modernization projects have been based—with ignorance, superstition, and provincialism rather than with the elite status of those possessing modern knowledge, proximity to orthodoxy, and/or cosmopolitan universality. (On the long shadow of such colonial-turned-"modern" epistemologies and the ways they have structured changing state attempts to co-opt Sufism, one could also productively put the contributions of Ansari, Basu, Bellamy, Corbett, and Ingram in conversation.)

The inability, in myriad ways, to direct the outcome of programs designed to change or operationalize religious sensibilities has now been amply documented. Nevertheless, the modern conceit of treating heuristic conceptual categories (metaphors, at base) as factual records—as ideas that do not just have verisimilitude to complex lived realities but ostensibly capture them in an enduringly accurate way—continues to haunt the endeavors discussed throughout this collection and more contemporary ones. The lessons here for scholars and students and officers of state bears repeating. Even if it were possible to cleave philosophical and theological traditions from situated practices and institutions, one cannot simply collect conceptual samples, analyze them under a slide and tinker with their elements in a lab, and then release them with any predictable outcome back into the chaos that is life actually lived. More than the inefficacy, however, it is the ethics of such attempts to treat subjects as specimens and politics as experimental protocols that requires ardent rejection.

Making these points is not to argue that scholarship on such topics should cease—far from it. It is no doubt crucial to chart variety and differentiation among Muslims over time, particularly if one is to disrupt the vapid and even destructive narratives that depict Sufis as apolitical or juxtapose Sufi moderation with reformist intransigence and "fundamentalist" violence. Now that we know how extensively governing ideas about apolitical Sufis and hyper-political Islamists have been instrumentalized for selective purposes, and how deeply such stories can fuel new conflict, however, how do we account for the ways—economic and political—these narratives gain traction? And how much do we examine our own role, as academics, in their perpetuation? For just as there is hardly the possibility of an apolitical saint, particularly in the post-9/11 context of appropriating Sufis into state-funded wars on terror (and thereby helping turn Sufi shrines into targets of antigovernment groups), there is hardly the possibility of an apolitical scholar.

Historically, as scholars, our conceptual, ethical, and political flaws have not been in attempting to understand various populations and their traditions, however imperfectly understanding can be had in the exchange and imbalance of languages and mores, wealth and power, that makes up scholarly investigations. Our flaws are the hubris of believing that anything close to perfect understanding can be attained, and the consistent failure to question how our work might be instrumentalized for various political ends. As the work of contributors to this volume reminds us, yet again, the fact of politics is inevitable, but the shape of politics is not. The politics of producing religion—and knowledge of it—is no exception.

Notes

Introduction

1. The term *salaf* (predecessors) points to the Prophet and the first three generations of his followers, whom Salafis use as exemplars of true Islam. Modern Salafis trace their roots to reformist movements that arose in eighteenth century Arabia, but in recent years the term has been applied to, and taken up by, a range of Muslims who are concerned with strict adherence to sharia and the condemnation of *bidʿah* (innovation).
2. Itzchak Weismann, "Modernity from Within: Islamic Fundamentalism and Sufism," *Der Islam*, 86, no. 1 (October 2011): 142.
3. Other components of the Luce project included "Islam, Democracy, and Toleration in Muslim Nations" and "Choreographies of Sharing Sacred Sites."
4. Carl W. Ernst, *The Shambhala Guide to Sufism* (Boston: Shambhala, 1997), 8, 19; and Katherine Pratt Ewing, *Arguing Sainthood: Modernity, Psychoanalysis, and Islam* (Durham, NC: Duke University Press, 1997), 45–47.
5. Louis Massignon, and Bernd Radtke, "Tasawwuf," in *Encyclopedia of Islam*, 2nd ed., ed. L. Massignon et al., accessed October 21, 2017, http://dx.doi.org/10.1163/1573-3912_islam_COM_1188.
6. Ernst, *Shambhala Guide to Sufism*, 8.
7. Rosemary R. Hicks, "Comparative Religion and the Cold War Transformation of Indo-Persian 'Mysticism' into Liberal Islamic Modernity," in *Secularism and Religion-Making*, ed. Marcus Dressler and Arvind Pal S. Mandair (New York: Oxford University Press, 2011), 148.
8. R. C. Gupta, ed., *Panjab Notes and Queries: A Monthly Periodical*, vol. 1. (Allahabad: Pioneer Press, 1883–84).
9. Ewing, *Arguing Sainthood*, 47.
10. Muhammad Iqbal, *Thoughts and Reflections of Iqbal*, ed. Syed Abdul Vahid (Lahore: Sh. Muhammad Ashraf, 1964), 81; and Ewing, *Arguing Sainthood*, 69.
11. Rex S. O'Fahey and Bernd Radtke, "Neo-Sufism Reconsidered," *Der Islam* 70, no. 1 (1993): 54.

12. John Stratton Hawley, *A Storm of Songs: India and the Idea of the Bhakti Movement* (Cambridge, MA: Harvard University Press, 2015).
13. Though the Ahl-e Hadith are often called "Wahhabis," the movement did not directly originate from the Wahhabi movement based in Saudi Arabia.
14. Barbara Daly Metcalf, *Islamic Revival in British India: Deoband, 1860–1900* (Princeton, NJ: Princeton University Press, 1982); Muhammad Qasim Zaman, *The Ulama in Contemporary Islam: Custodians of Change* (Princeton, NJ: Princeton University Press, 2002); and Brannon Ingram, "The Portable Madrasa: Print, Publics, and the Authority of the Deobandi Ulama," *Modern Asian Studies*, 48, no. 4 (October 2014): 845–71.
15. Usha Sanyal, *Ahmad Riza Khan Barelwi: In the Path of the Prophet* (Oxford: Oneworld Publications, 2005); and S. Jamal Malik, "The Luminous Nurani: Charisma and Political Mobilization Among the Barelwis in Pakistan," *Social Analysis: The International Journal of Social and Cultural Practice*, 28 (July 1990): 38–50.
16. Hicks, "Comparative Religion." Hicks is Corbett's former name.
17. For a brief biography of Fazlur Rahman, see Tamara Sonn, "Rahman, Fazlur," in *The Oxford Encyclopedia of the Modern Islamic World*, ed. John L. Esposito (Oxford: Oxford University Press, 1995), 63–75.
18. O'Fahey and Radtke make this attribution in "Neo-Sufism Reconsidered."
19. Fazlur Rahman, *Islam* (Garden City, NY: Doubleday, 1966), 254.
20. O'Fahey and Radtke, "Neo-Sufism Reconsidered," 55.
21. John O. Voll, "Neo-Sufism: Reconsidered Again," *Canadian Journal of African Studies/La Revue canadienne des études africaines*, 42, no. 2/3 (2008): 320.
22. Nehemia Levtzion, "The Dynamics of Sufi Brotherhoods," in *The Public Sphere in Muslim Societies*, ed. Miriam Hoexter, Shmuel N. Eisenstadt, and Nehemia Levtzion (Albany, NY: SUNY Press, 2002), 111.
23. This reliance on such forms can be understood as an example of how public religion today may take on the forms and practices of modern bureaucracy. See Bill Maurer, *Mutual Life, Limited: Islamic Banking, Alternative Currencies, Lateral Reason* (Princeton, NJ: Princeton University Press, 2005); and Birgit Meyer and Annelies Moors, eds., *Religion, Media, and the Public Sphere* (Bloomington: Indiana University Press, 2005) for other examples of this phenomenon.
24. Charles Taylor, *A Secular Age* (Cambridge, MA: Harvard University Press, 2007); and Akeel Bilgrami, *Secularism, Identity, and Enchantment* (Cambridge, MA: Harvard University Press, 2014).
25. Mahmood Mamdani, *Good Muslim, Bad Muslim: America, the Cold War, and the Roots of Terror* (New York: Pantheon Books, 2004), 23–24.
26. Ernst, *Shambhala Guide to Sufism*, 19.
27. Nile Green, *Sufism: A Global History* (Oxford: Wiley-Blackwell, 2012), 3.
28. See, for example, George Makdisi, "Ibn Taimiya: A Sufi of the Qadiriya Order," *American Journal of Arabic Studies* 1 (1973): 118–29.

    The issue of Ibn Taymiyyah's relationship to Sufism has generated considerable debate among Muslims, as a quick Google search on "Ibn Taymiyyah Sufism" demonstrates. One site, entitled "Deoband," includes an English translation of a detailed, well-documented account of Ibn Taymiyyah's relationship to Sufis of his time as revealed in his writings and the writings of his contemporaries. Mawlana 'Abd al-Hafiz al-Makki, "Shaykh al-Islam Ibn Taymiyyah and Sufism (Part One), " trans. Ismaeel Nakhuda, September 20,

2015, https://www.deoband.org/2015/09/tasawwuf/shariah-and-tariqah-tasawwuf/shaykh-al-islam-ibn-taymiyyah-and-sufism-part-one/,accessed July 28, 2019.

29. Rosemary Corbett, "Islamic 'Fundamentalism:' The Mission Creep of an American Religious Metaphor," *Journal of the American Academy of Religion* 83, no. 4 (December 2015): 977–1004.
30. Romila Thapar, "Imagined Religious Communities: Ancient History and the Modern Search for a Hindu Identity," *Modern Asian Studies* 23, no. 2 (1989): 209–31.
31. See Ewing, *Arguing Sainthood*; and Naveeda Khan, *Muslim Becoming: Aspiration and Skepticism in Pakistan* (Durham, NC: Duke University Press, 2012).
32. For discussions of the modernity of fundamentalisms and Islamic reform movements, see Bruce B. Lawrence, *Defenders of God: The Fundamentalism Revolt Against the Modern Age* (San Francisco: Harper and Row, 1989); and Katherine Pratt Ewing, "The Misrecognition of a Modern Islamist Organization: Germany Faces 'Fundamentalism,'" in *From Orientalism to Cosmopolitanism: Changing Approaches to Islamic Studies*, ed. Carl W. Ernst and Richard C. Martin (Columbia: University of South Carolina Press, 2010), 52–71.
33. Javid Iqbal, *The Ideology of Pakistan and Its Implementation* (Lahore: Ghulam Ali, 1959).
34. For a more detailed account of the development of *awqāf* in Pakistan, see Ewing, *Arguing Sainthood*, 70.
35. See Katherine Pratt Ewing, "The Politics of Sufism: Redefining the Saints of Pakistan," *Journal of Asian Studies* 42, no. 2 (February 1983): 251–68.
36. See Thomas K. Gugler, "Barelwis: Developments and Dynamics of Conflict with Deobandis," in *Sufis and Salafis in the Contemporary Age*, ed. Lloyd Ridgeon (London: Bloomsbury Academic, 2015), 171–89.
37. Jeffrey Gettleman, Kai Schultz, Ayesha Venkataraman, and Sameer Yasir, "India Election Gives Modi a 2nd Term. Here Are 5 Takeaways," *New York Times*, May 23, 2019, https://www.nytimes.com/2019/05/23/world/asia/india-election-narendra-modi.html.
38. Arshad Alam, "The Enemy Within: Madrasa and Muslim Identity in North India," *Modern Asian Studies* 42, no. 2/3 (March–May 2008): 606.
39. Rachana Umashankar, "Defending Sufism, Defining Islam: Asserting Islamic Identity in India" (PhD diss., University of North Carolina, Chapel Hill, 2012).
40. Athar Zafar and Anas Omair, "World Sufi Forum: India's Outreach to Global Community," Issue Brief, Indian Council of World Affairs, May 6, 2016, icwa.in/pdfs/IB/2014/WorldSufiForumIB06052016.pdf
41. "PM Narendra Modi Hands Over 'Chadar' to be Offered at Ajmer," *Times of India*, March 2, 2019. http://timesofindia.indiatimes.com/articleshow/68233868.cms?utm_source=contentofinterest&utm_medium=text&utm_campaign=cppst
42. Shahid Amin, *Conquest and Community: The Afterlife of Warrior Saint Ghazi Miyan* (Chicago: University of Chicago Press, 2016).
43. For example, see Anna Bigelow, *Sharing the Sacred: Practicing Pluralism in Muslim North India* (Oxford: Oxford University Press, 2010); Carla Bellamy, *The Powerful Ephemeral: Everyday Healing in an Ambiguously Islamic Place* (Berkeley: University of California Press, 2011); and Joyce Burkhalter Flueckiger, *In Amma's Healing Room: Gender and Vernacular Islam in South India* (Bloomington: Indiana University Press, 2006).
44. Torsten Tschacher, "From 'Rational' to 'Sufi Islam'?: The Changing Place of Muslims in Tamil Nationalism," in *Islam, Sufism, and Everyday Politics of Belonging in South Asia*, ed. Deepra Dandekar and Torsten Tschacher (Milton Park, UK: Taylor and Francis, 2016), 196.
45. Tschacher, "From 'Rational' to 'Sufi Islam'?," 210.

46. Deepra Dandekar and Torsten Tschacher, "Introduction," in *Islam, Sufism, and Everyday Politics of Belonging in South Asia*, ed. Deepra Dandekar and Torsten Tschacher (Milton Park, UK: Taylor and Francis, 2016), 14.
47. Peter van der Veer, "Playing or Praying: A Sufi Saint's Day in Surat," *Journal of Asian Studies* 51, no. 3 (August 1992): 545–64.
48. See Anand Vivek Taneja, *Jinnealogy: Time, Islam, and Ecological Thought in the Medieval Ruins of Delhi* (Stanford, CA: Stanford University Press, 2017).
49. Katherine Pratt Ewing, "Creating New Sufi Publics at an Old Sufi Shrine," Rethinking Public Religion: Word, Image, Sound, *The Immanent Frame*, SSRC, June 11, 2019, https://tif.ssrc.org/2019/06/11/creating-new-sufi-publics-at-an-old-sufi-shrine/?fbclid=IwAR37GMvMZNpEpa5ePc53Gh_2OZg61Q2BBZ0Dg4flni4gmcV9Kb7rY8Gk1fc.
50. *Waqf*, or wakf, is the singular form of *awqāf*.
51. For example, see Tabasum Rasool, "*Waqf* Administration in India: Issues and Challenges of State *Waqf* Boards," *Journal of Islamic Thought and Civilization* 7, no. 1 (Spring 2017): 1–12.
52. Syed Masroor Hasan, "Waqf Land Grab Exposed: India's Biggest Land Scam," *India Today*, September 19, 2017, https://www.indiatoday.in/india/story/waqf-land-grab-scam-muslim-charitable-assets-1048007-2017-09-19.
53. Alam, "The Enemy Within," 605–6.
54. Van der Veer, "Playing or Praying," 545.
55. "Indian Islam: Deobandi-Barelwi Tension Changing Mainstream Islam in India," *WikiLeaks*, February 2, 2010. https://wikileaks.org/plusd/cables/10NEWDELHI207_a.html. Thanks to one of the anonymous readers for calling my attention to this point.
56. Kelly Pemberton, "Sufis and Social Activism: A Chishti Response to Communal Strife in India Today," in *In Search of South Asian Sufis*, ed. Clinton Bennett and Charles Ramsey (New York: Continuum Books, 2012), 269–84.
57. Pemberton, "Sufis and Social Activism," 273.
58. Pemberton, "Sufis and Social Activism," 275.
59. Ewing, *Arguing Sainthood*.
60. Ronie Parciack, "Islamic Deshbhakti: Inscribing a Sufi Shrine into the Indian Nation-Space," *Contributions to Indian Sociology* 48, no. 2 (May 2014): 249–77.
61. Umashankar, "Defending Sufism, Defining Islam."
62. For example, see Manya Gugliani, "AIUMB Urges Sunni Muslims to Reject Hardline Wahabism," *Times of India*, November 27, 2011, https://timesofindia.indiatimes.com/city/lucknow/AIUMB-urges-Sunni-Muslims-to-reject-hardline-Wahabism/articleshow/10886872.cms.
63. "All India Ulema and Mashaikh Board," Wikipedia, accessed January 8, 2018, https://en.wikipedia.org/wiki/All_India_Ulema_and_Mashaikh_Board.
64. Vidya Subrahmaniam, "When Anyone Tries to Recruit You into Terrorism, Hand Him Over to the Police," *The Hindu*, October 16, 2011, http://www.thehindu.com/news/national/sufi-maha-panchayat-denounces-wahabi-extremism/article2543620.ece.
65. Sangeeta Ojha, "PM Modi to Inaugurate World Sufi Forum Today," *India Today*, March 17, 2016, http://indiatoday.intoday.in/story/pm-modi-inaugurate-world-sufi-forum-today/1/622426.html.
66. "Syed Babar Ashraf," Wikipedia, edited December 17, 2017, https://en.wikipedia.org.wiki/Syed_Babar_Ashraf.
67. Marshall Hodgson, *The Venture of Islam, Conscience and History in a World Civilization*, vols. 1–3 (Chicago: University of Chicago Press, 1974).
68. Richard W. Bulliet, *Islam: The View from the Edge* (New York: Columbia University Press, 1994.)

69. Shahab Ahmed, *What Is Islam? The Importance of Being Islamic* (Princeton, NJ: Princeton University Press, 2015).
70. Green, *Sufism: A Global History.*
71. As Philip Jenkins wrote for the *New Republic,* "Until his death in 1979, Mawdudi was the critical link between the various theaters of transnational activism, between the Muslim Brotherhood and the Iranian Revolution, between Kashmir and Western Europe. Mawdudi's thinking was South Asian in origin and character, as was the international Islamist movement he inspired—a movement whose flowering we are still watching today." His basic argument was that the roots of radical Islam are to be found as much in South Asia as in the Arab Middle East. Philip Jenkins, "Clerical Terror," *New Republic,* December 24, 2008, https://newrepublic.com/article/61223/clerical-terror.
72. Souleymane Bachir Diagne, "Bergson et la pensée de LS Senghor," *La lettre du Collège de France* 29 (2010): 10–11.
73. Gayatri Chakravorty Spivak, *A Critique of Postcolonial Reason* (Cambridge, MA: Harvard University Press, 1999).

1. Anti-Colonial Militants or Liberal Peace Activists?

1. UNESCO, "800th Anniversary of the Birth of Mawlana Jalal ud-Din Balkhi-Rumi," 2007, http://portal.unesco.org/culture/en/ev.php-URL_ID=34694&URL_DO=DO_TOPIC&URL_SECTION=201.html.
2. Sabrina Tavernise, "Turkish Schools Offer Pakistan a Gentler Version of Islam," *New York Times,* May 8, 2008, https://www.nytimes.com/2008/05/04/world/asia/04islam.html; and Waleed Ziad, "In Pakistan, Islam Needs Democracy," *New York Times,* February 16, 2008, https://www.nytimes.com/2008/02/16/opinion/16ziad.html?mtrref=www.google.com&gwh=E9EC02525F9F25A97547D22DB6844065&gwt=pay&assetType=REGIWALL.
3. The feature article the cover referenced was Nicholas Schmidle, "Faith and Ecstasy," *Smithsonian Magazine,* December 2008. The cover photo can be found here with the editor's take on the Sufi-extremist dichotomy: "Pakistan's violent extremists may get most of the attention, but the nation's peaceful, life-affirming Sufis have numbers and history on their side." https://www.smithsonianmag.com/issue/december-2008/. The text of the article can be found at http://www.smithsonianmag.com/people-places/pakistans-sufis-preach-faith-and-ecstasy-92998056/?onsite_source=relatedarticles&onsite_campaign=SmithMag&onsite_medium=internallink&onsite_content=Pakistan%27s+Sufis+Preach+Faith+and+Ecstasy&page=1.
4. See Cheryl Benard, *Civil Democratic Islam: Partners, Resources, and Strategies* (Santa Monica, CA: RAND Corporation, 2003), 46, 63–64; and Angela Rebasa, Cheryl Benard, Lowell H. Schwartz, and Peter Sickle, *Building Moderate Muslim Networks* (Santa Monica, CA: RAND Corporation, 2007), 74.
5. Rosemary R. Hicks, "Comparative Religion and the Cold War Transformation of Indo-Persian Mysticism into Liberal Islamic Modernity," in *Secularism and Religion-Making,* ed. Markus Dressler and Arvind Mandair (New York: Oxford University Press, 2011), 141–68.
6. For an overview of some of these conflicts, see Fait Muedini, "The Promotion of Sufism in the Politics of Algeria and Morocco," *Islamic Africa* 3, no 2 (Fall 2012): 201–26; as well as Elizabeth Surriyeh, *Sufis and Anti-Sufis: The Defence, Rethinking, and Rejection of Sufism in the Modern World* (New York: Routledge, 1998), 14–16.

7. I discuss Gibb's work in Rosemary R. Corbett, "'Islamic Fundamentalism:' The Mission Creep of an American Religious Metaphor," *Journal of the American Academy of Religion* 83, no. 4 (December 2015): 977–1004; and the Rockefeller Foundation's role in supporting it in Rosemary R. Corbett, "How the Rockefeller Foundation Shaped Islamic Studies While Avoiding 'Religion,'" in *The Politics of Religion and Philanthropy*, ed. Phillip Goff and David King (Bloomington, IN: University of Indiana Press, forthcoming).
8. One of the most comprehensive studies of foundation work in this area is Patricia L. Rosenfield's *A World of Giving: Carnegie Corporation of New York, a Century of International Philanthropy* (New York: Public Affairs, 2014). Despite the title, Rosenfield devotes significant attention to the Rockefeller and Ford Foundations' roles in funding such inquiries. See also Timothy Mitchell, "The Middle East in the Past and Future of Social Science," in *The Politics of Knowledge: Area Studies and the Disciplines*, ed. David Szanton (Berkeley: University of California Press, 2004), 74–118.
9. Waldo G. Leland, letter and proposal to Rockefeller Foundation (December 7, 1942), quoted in Rosenfield, *A World of Giving*, 157.
10. For more on the Rockefeller Foundation's Near East funding, see Corbett, "How the Rockefeller Foundation Shaped Islamic Studies." On the Rockefeller-funded General Education Board's support of Oriental studies at the University of Chicago, see Mitchell, "The Middle East," 77. As Mitchell rightly notes, foundation support for studies of the contemporary Near East also began before World War II but were interrupted during the war and then reinstated in a new Cold War environment. Many scholars have mistaken these reinstituted studies for initial attempts and assumed that Cold War concerns inaugurated such work.
11. For a discussion of Marshall's primary work with the Rockefeller Foundation, see Evan Kindley, "Big Criticism," *Critical Inquiry* 38, no. 1 (Autumn 2011): 71–95; and William J. Buxton, "John Marshall and the Humanities in Europe: Shifting Patterns of Rockefeller Foundation Support," *Minerva* 41, no. 2 (2003): 133–53.
12. John Marshall, "Reminiscences of John Marshall and Charlotte T. Marshal," interview by Pauline Madow, 1974, transcript, Columbia University Rare Book and Manuscript Library, 617, 775–57.
13. In the most well-known example of CIA co-optation, the agency actively funneled money through the Luce Foundation in order to "de-radicalize" American literary magazines such as *Partisan Review*. See, for example, Frances Stonors Saunders, *The Cultural Cold War: The CIA and the World of Arts and Letters* (1999; New York: New Press, 2013), 135–37.
14. Saunders, *Cultural Cold War*, 118.
15. Saunders, *Cultural Cold War*, 120–21.

    I find it necessary to disclose here my personal acquaintance with David Rockefeller, who was my husband's grandfather until he passed in 2017 at the age of 101. Although we at times briefly spoke about foreign policy and his travels in the Middle East during World War II and after on behalf of Chase Manhattan Bank, Rockefeller was already ninety-six years old when I met him in 2011 and struggling with the onset of dementia. Our conversations were limited and, often, elliptical. For discussion of the Rockefeller family's role in some of the mid-century policy explorations discussed here, see Darren Dochuck, *Anointed with Oil: How Christianity and Crude Made Modern America* (New York: Basic Books, 2019).
16. Marshall, "Reminiscences," 621–22.
17. JM (John Marshall) Diary Excerpt, March 6, 1952, Online Collection and Catalog of Rockefeller Archive Center, http://dimes.rockarch.org/a0f4001d-0846-49a6-b547-3ee6011ff299.

These conferences were not overtly described as sessions devoted to modernization. Rather, the rubric was that elite Arab intellectuals would investigate and discuss contemporary issues facing Arab countries in a way that non-Arabs could understand. However, during the course of each session, Marshall would reframe the Arab participants' stated interests and plans to focus on what their research could reveal about the future development of Arab countries, as Marshall—holding to the Orientalist canard about Arab fatalism and attachment to past glory—believed Arabs had great difficultly preparing for the future or appreciating anything but past achievements and present needs. See, for example, JM Diary Excerpts, April 1–3, 1954, Online Collection and Catalog of Rockefeller Archive Center, http://dimes.rockarch.org/d1c5c7c9-8ed7-47bf-9b15-30867494aefc.

18. CG (Chadbourne Gilpatric) Diary Excerpts, April 20, 1955, and September 26, 1955, Folder 413, Box 53, Series 100, RG 1.2, Projects, FA 387, Rockefeller Foundation Records, Rockefeller Archive Center.
19. As Mitchell notes, Gibb was instrumental in the formation of Near East studies in Britain prior to World War II and had traveled to Chicago in 1942 to participate in a conference (attended by academics, business leaders, and government officials) on contemporary issues in the region. "The Middle East," 80.
20. H. A. R. Gibb, *Modern Trends in Islam* (Chicago: University of Chicago Press, 1947). On the substance of that work and its legacy in promoting the idea that Sufis are the counter to fundamentalists, see Corbett, "'Islamic Fundamentalism.'"

    On RF funding for the Chicago trip, see Marshall, "Memoirs," 433, and "A Special Grant in Aid to Professor and Mrs. H.A.R. Gibb" (February 20, 1952), Folder 407, Box 53, Series 100, RG 1.2, Projects, FA387, Rockefeller Foundation Records, Rockefeller Archive Center. Mention of the earlier grants is included under the "Previous Interest" heading.
21. Marshall, "Reminiscences," 632.
22. See, for example, Marshall's recounting of a conversation in Tehran in 1950 with a General Arfa, for whom he promised to purchase a copy of Gibb's work. JM Diary Excerpt, April 28, 1950, Online Collection and Catalog of Rockefeller Archive Center, http://dimes.rockarch.org/6d180dd6-9fde-4d0a-a139-afb6d7529d98.
23. Marshall's belief, and that of other foundation officers, that Muslims must assist in such modernization also reflected changes in social science philosophies at the time. As the social sciences professionalized between the 1930s and 1960s and segmented into discrete units, it became more common to study not a society's civilization, but its component parts: politics, economy, culture, and so on. The question was how to approach non-Western (often deemed "pre-modern" societies) in which such diversification had ostensibly not yet taken place. Mitchell, "The Middle East," 83–86. The answer for Marshall and other RF officers appears to have been employing two strategies at once: encouraging studies of discreet components of Near Eastern and Islamic societies, while also enlisting Muslims in modernizing them because Islam was ostensibly so inextricable from these societies' operations.
24. Gibb, *Modern Trends in Islam*, viii–ix.
25. Gibb, *Modern Trends in Islam*, ix–x. On Smith's changing opinions of Iqbal, see Hicks, "Comparative Religion."
26. Gibb, *Modern Trends in Islam*, viii.
27. JM Diary Excerpt, March 1, 1951, Online Collection and Catalog of Rockefeller Archive Center, http://dimes.rockarch.org/94ed470f-9bc2-49e4-8f6e-084643ded699.

Although Laoust's works remain primarily in French, a brief introduction to some of it can be found in Albert Hourani, "Rashid Rida and the Sufi Orders: A Footnote to Laoust," *Bulletin d'études orientales* 29 (1977): 231–41. Elsewhere, Henri Lauzi discusses Laoust's perpetuation of Massignon's erroneous claims that Muhammad 'Abduh founded the Salafi movement (a claim that Gibb reiterated when relying on Laoust for his 1947 book). See Henri Lauzi, *The Making of Salafism: Islamic Reform in the Twentieth Century* (New York: Columbia University Press, 2016), 43.

28. John Marshall, "Grant in Aid," October 8, 1951, Folder 405, Box 53, Series 100R, RG 1.2, Projects, FA 387, Rockefeller Foundation Records, Rockefeller Archive Center.
29. Arberry to Marshall, July 15, 1953, Folder 405, Box 53, Series 100R, RG 1.2, Projects, FA 387, Rockefeller Foundation Records, Rockefeller Archive Center.
30. "Special Grant-in-Aid Fund—Visits to Islam," May 31, 1951, Folder 404, Box 53, Series 100, RG 1.2, Projects, FA 387, Rockefeller Foundation Records, Rockefeller Archive Center.
31. JM (John Marshall) Diary Excerpt, April 3, 1954, Online Collection and Catalog of Rockefeller Archive Center, http://dimes.rockarch.org/d1c5c7c9-8ed7-47bf-9b15-30867494aefc.
32. John Marshall, "A Special Grant in Aid," July 27, 1951, Folder 410, Box 53, Series 100, RG 1.2, Projects, FA 387, Rockefeller Foundation Records, Rockefeller Archive Center. Quote from JM Diary Excerpts, April 4, 6, 1951, Online Collection and Catalog of Rockefeller Archive Center, http://dimes.rockarch.org/d9a49fa5-3413-4b19-a210-444695ba4992. For more on this aim of synthesizing cultures into a global modern whole, see Corbett, "How the Rockefeller Foundation Shaped Islamic Studies."
33. Marshall, "Reminiscences," 772, 777.
34. Marshall, "Reminiscences," 736–37. Marshall claimed to have first heard this sentiment from an Iraqi friend.
35. Smith mentions his study (lent to Marshall) in Smith to Marshall, April 25, 1951, Folder 93, Box 10, Series 427, RG 1.2, Projects, FA 387, Rockefeller Foundation Records, Rockefeller Archive Center. In reply, Marshall wrote, "I can't help wondering what some of your more orthodox Arab friends would think of it. On the other hand, it is an expression of views which they should take into account." Marshall to Smith, April 27, 1951, Folder 93, Box 10, Series 427, RG 1.2, Projects, FA 387, Rockefeller Foundation Records, Rockefeller Archive Center.
36. JM Diary Excerpt, May 24, 1951, Folder 93, Box 10, Series 427, RG 1.2, Projects, FA 387, Rockefeller Foundation Records, Rockefeller Archive Center. The insistence on making reform concerns incidental came from RF director of humanities Charles Fahs. Marshall, by contrast, seemed to agree with Smith on the need for it.
37. JM Diary Excerpt, May 24, 1951.
38. Smith to Gilpatric, December 14 and 16, 1952, Folder 94, Box 10, Series 427, RG 1.2, Projects, FA 387, Rockefeller Foundation Records, Rockefeller Archive Center. Smith's earlier conversation with Gilpatric and Fahs had occurred during the early planning stages of the Institute. "Interview: Wilfred Cantwell Smith," April 6, 1951, Folder 93, Box 10, Series 427, RG 1.2, Projects, FA 387, Rockefeller Foundation Records, Rockefeller Archive Center.
39. CG Diary excerpt, January 11, 1955.
40. CG Diary Excerpt, January 12, 1955.
41. Smith to Fahs, March 12, 1955, Folder 413, Box 53, Series 100, RG 1.2, Projects, FA 387, Rockefeller Foundation Records, Rockefeller Archive Center.
42. Smith to Fahs, March 12, 1955; and CG Diary Excerpt, July 14, 1955.

43. See Maureen Patterson, "Context for Development of Pakistan Studies in North America: Pre-Partition Interest in Proposed Pakistan Area of South Asia," *Pakistan Studies News: Newsletter of the American Institute of Pakistan Studies* 6, no. 1 (Spring 2002): 1–3; and Maureen Patterson, "Pakistan Studies in North America: 1947–1989," *Pakistan Studies News: Newsletter of the American Institute of Pakistan Studies* 6, no. 11 (Fall 2003): 8–10.
44. Maron to Gilpatric, September 30, 1955, Folder 413, Box 53, Series 100, RG 1.2, Projects, FA 387, Rockefeller Foundation Records, Rockefeller Archive Center.
45. Stanley Maron, "A Report of the Third Meeting of the Group on Pakistan Studies," October 30, 1956; and Keith Callard to Gilpatric, December 7, 1956, both in Folder 414, Box 53, Series 100, RG 1.2, Projects, FA 387, Rockefeller Foundation Records, Rockefeller Archive Center.
46. CG Diary Excerpt, March 31, 1955.
47. I discuss Rahman's understanding of Iqbal in Hicks, "Comparative Religion." For a more detailed account, see the account of Rahman's student at McGill, Sheila McDonough, *The Flame of Sinai: Hope and Vision in Iqbal* (Lahore: Iqbal Academy Pakistan, 2002).
48. Smith to Gilpatric, October 26, 1955, (Keith Callard's institute proposal appended), Folder 413, Box 53, Series 100, RG 1.2, Projects, FA387, Rockefeller Foundation Records, Rockefeller Archive Center.
49. See Fazlur Rahman, "Revival and Reform in Islam," in *The Cambridge History of Islam*, vol. 2, *The Further Islamic Lands, Islamic Society, and Civilization*, ed. P. M. Holt, Ann K. S. Lambton, and Bernard Lewis (Cambridge: Cambridge University Press, 1970), 632–56; as well as his posthumously published manuscript on the subject, Fazlur Rahman and Ebrahim Moosa, *Revival and Reform in Islam: A Study of Islamic Fundamentalism* (New York: Oneworld, 1999).
50. Corbett, "'Islamic Fundamentalism.'"
51. For Rahman's work in Karachi and return to the United States, see Earle H. Waugh, "Beyond Scylla and Kharybdis: Fazlur Rahman and Islamic Identity," and Donald L. Berry, "Fazlur Rahman: A Life in Review," both in *The Shaping of an American Islamic Discourse: A Memorial to Fazlur Rahman*, ed. Earle H. Waugh and Frederick M. Denny (Atlanta, GA: Scholars Press, 1998), 15–36, 37–48.
52. RWJ (Robert W. July) Diary Excerpt, March 2, 1959, Folder 41, Box 4, Series 495R, RG 1.2, Projects, FA387, Rockefeller Foundation Records, Rockefeller Archive Center.
53. John Parry, "Progress and Development Report Submitted to the Rockefeller Foundation, May, 1961," Folder 42, Box 4, Series 495R, RG 1.2, Projects, FA387, Rockefeller Foundation Records, Rockefeller Archive Center.
54. "University of Ibadan Department of Arabic and Islamic Studies Report for the Year 1963/1964," Folder 43, Box 4, Series 495R, RG 1.2, Projects, FA387, Rockefeller Foundation Records, Rockefeller Archive Center.
55. Clifford Geertz, *Islam Observed: Religious Development in Morocco* (1968; Chicago: University of Chicago Press, 1971), 8–9.
56. Clifford Geertz, "Suq: the Bazaar Economy in Sefrou," in *Meaning and Order in Moroccan Society: Three Essays in Cultural Analysis*, ed. Clifford Geertz, Hildred Geertz, and Laurence Rosen (Cambridge: Cambridge University Press, 1979), 123–276.
57. Geertz, *Islam Observed*, 51, 52.
58. Muedini, "Promotion of Sufism," 209–10.
59. For this history of Kabbani and the U.S. government's more recent interest in Sufism, see Paul Barrett, *American Islam: The Struggle for the Soul of a Religion* (New York: Picador, 2007),

197; and Rosemary R. Corbett, *Making Moderate Islam: Sufism, Service, and the "Ground Zero Mosque" Controversy* (Stanford, CA: Stanford University Press, 2016).

60. See Ron Geaves, "Who Defines Moderate Islam 'Post'-September 11?," in *Islam and the West, Post 9/11*, ed. Ron Geaves, Yvonne Haddad, and Jane Idelman Smith (Burlington, VT: Ashgate, 2004), 67.

2. From *Taṣawwuf* Modern to Neo-Sufism

I am grateful to this volume's editors as well as Megan Brankley Abbas and Michael Laffan for their helpful comments on earlier drafts of this chapter. I also thank the two anonymous reviewers. Any remaining mistakes or shortcomings are my own.

1. Fazlur Rahman, *Islam and Modernity* (Chicago: University of Chicago Press, 1982), 124.
2. Nurcholish Madjid, *The True Face of Islam: Essays on Islam and Modernity in Indonesia* (Ciputat: Voice Center Indonesia, 2003), 60.
3. Greg Barton, "Neo-Modernism: A Vital Synthesis of Traditionalist and Modernist Islamic Thought in Indonesia," *Studia Islamika—Indonesian Journal for Islamic Studies* 2, no. 3 (1995): 1–76, esp. 5.
4. See Carool Kersten, *Cosmopolitans and Heretics: New Muslim Intellectuals and the Study of Islam* (New York: Columbia University Press, 2011), 96–99, for a critique of Neo-Modernism as used by Barton and a summary of the different views on the extent on Rahman's influence on Madjid. Kersten largely agrees with Barton that Madjid's position did not change radically but rather resulted in a shift in focus.
5. Megan Brankley Abbas, "Knowing Islam: The Entangled History of Western Academia and Modern Islamic Thought," PhD diss., Princeton University, 2015; and Kersten, *Cosmopolitans and Heretics*.
6. Abbas, "Knowing Islam," 196.
7. For Madjid's biography, see Kersten, *Cosmopolitans and Heretics*, 45–100; and Ann Kull, *Piety and Politics: Nurcholish Madjid and his Interpretation of Islam in Modern Indonesia* (Lund: Department of History and Anthropology of Religion, Lund University, 2005).
8. On Snouck Hurgronje, see Michael Laffan, *Islamic Nationhood and Colonial Indonesia: The Umma Below the Winds* (New York: Routledge, 2002), 92–95.
9. See Harry Benda, *The Crescent and the Rising Sun: Indonesian Islam under the Japanese Occupation, 1942–1945* (The Hague and Bandung: W. van Hoeve, 1958); and Chiara Formichi, *Islam and the Making of the Nation: Kartosuwiryo and Political Islam in 20th Century Indonesia* (Leiden: KITLV Press, 2012) for an extended discussion of Indonesian Islam and its entanglements with political history before independence.
10. Benda, *Crescent and Rising Sun*, 185–86.
11. See R. E. Elson, "Another Look at the Jakarta Charter Controversy of 1945," *Indonesia* 88 (2009): 105–30, for more on the context of the Jakarta Charter's emergence and the controversies it engendered.
12. For detailed presentations of political Islam in Indonesia after independence, see Robert Hefner, *Civil Islam: Muslims and Democratization in Indonesia* (Princeton, NJ: Princeton University Press, 2000); and M. C. Ricklefs, *Islamization and Its Opponents in Java: A Political, Social, Cultural, and Religious History, c. 1930 to the Present* (Honolulu: University of Hawai'i Press, 2012).
13. Abbas, "Knowing Islam," 134–93; Hefner, *Civil Islam*, 96.

14. Kull, *Piety and Politics*, 53.
15. Greg Barton, "Indonesia's Nurcholish Madjid and Abdurrahman Wahid as Intellectual Ulama: The Meeting of Islamic Traditionalism and Modernism in Neo-Modernist Thought," *Islam and Christian-Muslim Relations* 8, no. 3 (1997): 323–50, esp. 331–32.
16. An English translation of the talk is published in Madjid, *The True Face*, 315–22.
17. Madjid, *The True Face*, 318. See also Hefner, *Civil Islam*, 118–19; and Kersten, *Cosmopolitans and Heretics*, 57–67, for more in-depth discussions of Madjid's understanding of Islam and progress.
18. Madjid himself emphasized that his rise to prominence was unintentional, as he did not expect the paper to be leaked to the public; see Kull, *Piety and Politics*, 59–60. For a detailed discussion of the paper and its aftermath, see Barton, "Neo-Modernism," 15–24.
19. At $360,000, this was the largest grant the Ford Foundation had ever made in support of a project on religion at the time, in hopes of better understanding the effects of religious dynamics on development efforts in Muslim-majority countries. For an overview of Binder and Rahman's program, see Abbas, "Knowing Islam," 211–17.
20. Kull, *Piety and Politics*, 64.
21. Barton, "Indonesia's Nurcholish Madjid," 333.
22. Fazlur Rahman, *Islam*, 2nd ed. (Chicago: University of Chicago Press, 1979), 114–15. For a discussion of Madjid's use of Ibn Taymiyyah, see Kersten, *Cosmopolitans and Heretics*, 93–94.
23. Nurcholish Madjid, "Sufisme Baru dan Sufisme Lama: Masalah Kontinuitas dan Perkembangan dalam Esoterisme Islam," in *Sufisme dan Masa Depan Agama*, ed. Djohan Effendi (Jakarta: Pustaka Firdaus, 1993), 104–5; and Madjid, *The True Face*, 153; 257–58. For Rahman's view, see Rahman, *Islam*, 166.
24. In 1973 NU had been forced by Soeharto to merge with three other Islamic parties. This forced consolidation resulted in internal conflicts that weakened political Islam and disabled effective opposition. Under the chairmanship of Abdurrahman Wahid, NU left the party in 1984 to revert to its status as a socio-political organization. For more information on Abdurrahman's program and his similarities with Madjid, see Barton, "Indonesia's Nurcholish Madjid," 337–42.
25. Julia Day Howell, "Sufism and Neo-Sufism in Indonesia Today," *Review of Indonesian and Malaysian Affairs* 46, no. 2 (2012): 1–24, esp. 6; see also Kull, *Piety and Politics*, 74.
26. On Madjid's involvement in ICMI, see Hefner, *Civil Islam*, 143–44; 154–55.
27. Kull, *Piety and Politics*, 78.
28. The term *masyarakat madani* was first coined in 1995 by the Malay politician Anwar Ibrahim. Madjid and other Indonesian intellectuals conceptualized *masyarakat madani* as the example set by the Prophet Muḥammad in the city of Medina, thus claiming its normativity, even as the specific content of a *masyarakat madani* remained contested. See Azyumardi Azra, *Menuju Masyarakat Madani: Gagasan, Fakta, dan Tantangan* (Bandung, Indonesia: Penerbit PT Remaja Rosdakarya, 1999); Hefner, *Civil Islam*, 186–89; Kull, *Piety and Politics*, 146–47.
29. Abbas, "Knowing Islam," 265.
30. For an overview of opposition to certain strands of Sufi thought and practice and the relation between Sufism and reform in the Malay-Indonesian archipelago since the seventeenth century, see Azyumardi Azra, *The Origins of Islamic Reformism in Southeast Asia* (Honolulu: University of Hawaiʻi Press, 2004).
31. See Laffan, *Islamic Nationhood*, 142–80, for an analysis of Southeast Asian receptions of and responses to Arabic media in colonial times.

32. Martin van Bruinessen, "Controversies and Polemics Involving the Sufi Orders in Twentieth-Century Indonesia," in *Islamic Mysticism Contested: Thirteen Centuries of Controversies and Polemics*, ed. Frederick de Jong and Bernd Radtke (Leiden: Brill, 1999), 705–72.
33. Nurcholish Madjid, "Tasauf dan Pesantren," in *Pesantren dan Pembaharuan*, ed. M. Dawam Rahardjo (1974; Jakarta: LP3ES, 1988), 95–120.
34. Madjid, "Tasauf dan Pesantren," 116.
35. Madjid, "Tasauf dan Pesantren," 109–10.
36. Nurcholish Madjid, "Pondok Pesantren 'Darul ʿUlum' di Rejoso, Peterongan, Jombang, Jawa Timur," in *Bulletin Proyek Penelitian Agama dan Perubahan Sosial*, ed. Lembaga Ekonomi dan Kemasyarakatan Nasional (Jakarta: Lembaga Ekonomi dan Kemasyarakatan Nasional, 1977), 53–66.
37. As cited in James Rush, *Hamka's Great Story: A Master Writer's Vision of Islam for Modern Indonesia* (Madison: University of Wisconsin Press, 2016), 127.
38. Rush, *Hamka's Great Story*, 195. This clash happened in the aftermath of Madjid's aforementioned controversial talk from 1970 and his subsequent series of speeches and publications.
39. As cited in Rush, *Hamka's Great Story*, 172.
40. For Madjid's acknowledgment of Hamka's influence on him, see Madjid, *The True Face*, 95.
41. Julia Day Howell, "Indonesia's Salafist Sufis," *Modern Asian Studies* 44, no. 5 (2010): 1029–51, esp. 1031–32.
42. Hamka, *Tasauf Modern* (1939; Jakarta: Republika Penerbit, 2015), 2, 126–29.
43. Hamka, *Tasauf Modern*, 263.
44. Hamka, *Tasauf Modern*, 5.
45. Hamka, *Tasauf Modern*, 131.
46. Hamka, *Tasauf Modern*, 309.
47. Hamka, *Tasauf Modern*, 272.
48. Budhy Munawar-Rahman, *Ensiklopedi Nurcholish Madjid: Pemikiran Islam di Kanvas Peradaban* (Jakarta: Paramadina dan Mizan, 2006), 2188.
49. See Abbas, "Knowing Islam," 114–21, for Rahman's methodological fusionism, which he shared with Smith, and the reception of his work in the wider academy. Abbas shows that the McGill institute provided an intellectual space for many Muslims who would later occupy important posts in their home country.
50. Rahman, *Islam and Modernity*, 5.
51. Rahman, *Islam and Modernity*, 147.
52. Madjid, *The True Face*, 60. Of course, the understanding of *ijtihād* as an epistemological rather than a legal concept that is incumbent upon every Muslim rather than just trained specialists is very common in Islamic reform movements, especially those inspired by Egyptian modernism, including liberal reform movements. For more on changes in the conceptualization of *ijtihād*, see Indira Gesink, "'Chaos on the Earth': Subjective Truths Versus Communal Unity in Islamic Law and the Rise of Militant Islam," *American Historical Review* 108, no. 3 (2003): 710–33.
53. Madjid, *The True Face*, 188.
54. For information on other influential Indonesian graduates, see Abbas, "Knowing Islam." Further prominent graduates of McGill's Institute of Islamic Studies who later occupied influential positions in academia and politics include the Pakistani scholar Muhammad

Khalid Masud, who, like Madjid, wrote his dissertation on a medieval Muslim scholar (in Masud's case, the Mālikī jurist al-Shāṭibī, d. 1388) as an example of adapting Islamic thought to accommodate changing social conditions through *ijtihād* and *maṣlaḥah*. See Muhammad Khalid Masud, *Islamic Legal Philosophy: A Study of Abū Isḥāq al-Shāṭibī's Life and Thought* (Islamabad: Publications of the Islamic Research Institute, 1977).

55. Fazlur Rahman, "Iqbāl's Idea of the Muslim," *Islamic Studies* 2 (1963): 439–45, esp. 441.
56. Fazlur Rahman, "Revival and Reform in Islam," in *The Cambridge History of Islam*, vol. 2, *The Further Islamic Lands, Islamic Society and Civilization*, ed. P. M. Holt, Ann Lambton, and Bernard Lewis (Cambridge: Cambridge University Press, 1970), 633-34.
57. Rahman, *Islam*, 195.
58. Rahman, *Islam*, 205–6.
59. Rahman, *Islam*, 194–95.
60. Rahman, "Revival and Reform," 637.
61. Madjid, "Sufisme Baru," 95.
62. Madjid, "Sufisme Baru," 104–5. See also Rahman, *Islam*, 206; and Howell, "Indonesia's Salafist Sufis," 1032–40, for a summary of Hamka's understanding of Sufism as following the example of the Prophet, which is also echoed in Madjid, "Tasauf dan Pesantren," 99.
63. This article was originally published in Indonesian. See Nurcholish Madjid, "Tasawuf sebagai Inti Keberagamaan," *Pesantren* 2, no. 3 (1985): 3–9; see also Madjid, "Tasauf dan Pesantren," 100.
64. Madjid, "Tasawuf sebagai Inti Keberagamaan," 6; see also Madjid, "Tasauf dan Pesantren," 101–3.
65. Madjid, "Tasawuf sebagai Inti Keberagamaan," 7–8; see also Madjid, "Tasauf dan Pesantren," 102.
66. Tellingly, Madjid employs a pun, calling *fiqh* an "Islamic science" (*ilmu keislaman*) and *taṣawwuf* a "science of Islam" (*keilmuan Islam*). As in English, the two Indonesian expressions are almost interchangeable in meaning, indicating perhaps that they are two different forms of the same truth.
67. This book was originally published in Indonesian. See Nurcholish Madjid, *Islam: Doktrin dan Peradaban* (Jakarta: Paramadina, 1992), 254–57.
68. Madjid, *Doktrin dan Peradaban*, 259–62.
69. Madjid, *Doktrin dan Peradaban*, 266.
70. Madjid, "Sufisme Baru," 93.
71. Madjid, "Sufisme Baru," 96.
72. Madjid, "Sufisme Baru," 98.
73. See Rex S. O'Fahey and Bernd Radtke, "Neo-Sufism Reconsidered," *Der Islam* 70, no. 1 (1993): 55, for their claim that Rahman was the first one to use the term. O'Fahey and Radtke challenge the use of the term, questioning its meaning and utility in designating a rich and complex range of movements and traditions. See also Voll's response to their criticism in John Voll, "Neo-Sufism: Reconsidered Again," *Canadian Journal of African Studies* 42, no. 2/3 (2008): 317–18. Voll defends the use of the term, arguing that Rahman's innovation in terminology and the use of Rahman's term in his own and Levtzion's work builds on scholarship by Gibb and Trimingham, among others. See Nehemia Levtzion and John O. Voll, eds., *Eighteenth-Century Renewal and Reform in Islam* (Syracuse, NY: Syracuse University Press, 1987).

74. For an English translation of the talk, see Madjid, *The True Face*, 79–112.
75. Madjid, *The True Face*, 87–89.
76. Madjid, *The True Face*, 93.
77. Nurcholish Madjid, "Islamic Roots of Modern Pluralism: Indonesian Experiences," *Studia Islamika—Indonesian Journal for Islamic Studies* 1, no. 1 (1994): 64.
78. Madjid, "Islamic Roots," 65.
79. Madjid, "Islamic Roots," 72.

3. Beyond Barelwiism

1. For example, a 2002 publication in Urdu collects newspaper and other sources reporting on Qadri under the title "The Most Contradictory Personality: A Critical Evaluation of Professor Tahir al-Qadri." See Muḥammad Nawāz Kharal, ed., *Mutanāzi'ah tarīn shakhṣiyyat: Professor Tahir ul-Qadri kī shakhṣiyyat kā tanqīdī jā'iza* (Lahore: Fateh Publishers, 2002).
2. *Minhaj-ul-Quran International Webpage*, http://www.minhaj.org/english/index.html in English, Arabic, and Urdu, Accessed March 17, 2019.
3. See Tahir-ul Qadri, *Fatwa on Terrorism and Suicide Bombings* (London: Minhaj-ul-Qur'an International, 2010). The 2019 ten-year cumulative ranking of influential Muslims known as the *Muslim 500* places Qadri at #81, just above the current Pakistani prime minister, Imran Khan. See https://www.themuslim500.com/ten-year-list-7/. Accessed March 17, 2019.

   For an example of Qadri's status as a counterterrorism expert, see "Islamic Curriculum on Peace and Counter-Terrorism (Clerics, Imams)," http://www.minhajpublications.com/product/islamic-curriculum-peace-counter-terrorism-clerics-imams/, accessed December 20, 2015.
4. This Arabic phrase, meaning "the people of the Sunna and the community," emerged in about the fourth Islamic century to refer to Muslims who were neither Shiʿa nor Kharijite—thus the proto-Sunnis. It has a connotation among Sunnis of "mainstream," "majority," or "core" identity. As we will see, it has therefore been appropriated by many subsequent Muslim groups, including South Asian Barelwis.
5. See Ira Lapidus, "Islamic Revival and Modernity: The Contemporary Movements and the Historical Paradigms" in *Journal of the Economic and Social History of the Orient* 40, no. 4 (1997): 448. Traditional Islam in the sense of the current global movement is discussed more extensively in Ronald Geaves, "Transformations and Trends Among British Sufis," in *Sufism in Britain*, ed. Ronald Geaves and Theodore Gabriel (London: Bloomsbury Academic, 2014), 47–51.
6. Marcia Hermansen, "American Sufis and American Islam: From Private Spirituality to the Public Sphere," in *Islamic Movements and Islam in the Multicultural World: Islamic Movements and Formation of Islamic Ideologies in the Information Age*, ed. Denis Brilyov (Kazan: Russian Federation, Kazan Federal University Publishing House, 2014), 189–208.
7. Mumtaz Ahmad, "Media-Based Preachers and the Creation of New Muslim Publics in Pakistan," in *Who Speaks for Islam? Muslim Grassroots Leaders and Popular Preachers in South Asia*, NBR Special Report 22, February 2010, http://www.nbr.org/publications/specialreport/pdf/Free/SR22.pdf, 9–10.
8. "Profile: Dr. Muhammad Tahirul Qadri," *Dawn*, January 12, 2013, http://www.dawn.com/news/778260/profile-dr-muhammad-tahirul-qadri.
9. Ahmad, "Media-Based Preachers," 11.

10. See the Minhaj "Directorate of Foreign Affairs" website, which also features a Google map and contact information of centers abroad: http://minhajoverseas.com, accessed March 21, 2019.
11. Alix Philippon, "When Sufi Tradition Reinvents Islamic Modernity: The Minhaj-ul Qur'an, a Neo-Sufi Order in Pakistan," in *South Asian Sufis: Devotion, Deviation, and Destiny*, ed. Clinton Bennett and Charles M. Ramsey (London: Bloomsbury, 2012), 113.
12. Israr Ahmed (d. 2010) was well known in his own right as an Islamist preacher and activist. He was originally part of Mawdudi's Islamist movement Jamaat-e Islami, and then founded his own organization, Tanzeem-e Islami.
13. Ahmad, "Media-Based Preachers," 11.
14. Ahmad, "Media-Based Preachers," 11.
15. "Islamic Library-Minhaj Books," https://www.minhajbooks.com/english/index.html, accessed March 17, 2019.
16. "Dr Muhammad Tahir-ul-Qadri," https://www.facebook.com/Tahirulqadri/, accessed March 21, 2019.
17. "Profile: Dr. Muhammad Tahirul Qadri."
18. Philippon, "When Sufi Tradition Reinvents Islamic Modernity," 114.
19. Zofshan Taj, "The Political Thought of Tahir-ul-Qadri in Its Islamic Context: Understanding the Concept of Khilafa and Its Relevance to Modern Society in Light of Medieval Islamic Teachings," *Intermountain West Journal of Religious Studies* 3, no. 1 (2011): 12–32.
20. Philippon, "When Sufi Tradition Reinvents Islamic Modernity," 116.
21. Documented and discussed by Philippon, who was allowed to accompany the group, in "When Sufi Tradition Reinvents Islamic Modernity," 119 and beyond; also discussed by M. Amer Morgahi, in "Reliving the 'Classical Islam:' Emergence and Working of the Minhajul Quran Movement in the UK," in *Sufism in Britain*, ed. Ron Geaves and Theodore Gabriel (London: Bloomsbury Academic, 2014), 227.
22. Shaykh al-Islam was an honorific title used in classical Islam for any highly accomplished scholar, but in the Ottoman period it came to refer to the state-appointed head of all Islamic scholars.
23. An Azharī-style turban is a red fez with a long white scarf tightly wrapped around it, as worn by theology graduates of al-Azhar University in Egypt. Qadri's headgear has attracted various forms of attention. See Zarrar Khuhro, "Topi Drama: The Hat Matters as Much as the Head," *Express Tribune*, February 3, 2013, https://tribune.com.pk/story/500563/topi-drama-revolution-begins-with-a-hat/.
24. See "Habib Ali Al Jifri Visits Mawlana Shaykh Nazim al-Haqqani in Cyprus," https://www.youtube.com/watch?v=6UMLucWM9Q4, August 2009. Incidentally, the video has over 900,000 views as of January 23, 2020.
25. See "USA: Shaykh Hisham Kabbani Addresses Milad Ceremony," Minhaj-ul Quran International, January 18, 2015, http://www.minhaj.org/english/tid/31787/USA-Shaykh-Hisham-Kabbani-addresses-Milad-ceremony.html. Kabbani and Qadri made statements of approval, and Kabbani appeared at Minhaj Milads in the United States.
26. A collection of related press clippings may be accessed at "Media Coverage Islamic Curriculum on Peace and Counter Terrorism," http://www.minhaj.net/downloads/Media-Coverage-Curriculum-on-Peace-and-Counter-Terrorism.pdf, accessed March 21, 2019.
27. This was the slogan for a rally held at Minar-e Pakistan, Karachi, in December 2012. See Rana Tanveer, "'Save the State, Not Politics': Qadri Returns in Style," *Express Tribune*,

December 24, 2012, http://tribune.com.pk/story/483635/save-the-state-not-politics-qadri-returns-in-style/.

28. This movement used to be called the "Muhajir Qaumi Movement," and it was founded in the late 1970s/early 1980s, drawing on the desire to mobilize Urdu-speaking Pakistanis of Indian migrant (*muhajir*) background, especially those based in Karachi, where its influence has been strongest.
29. "Profile: Dr. Muhammad Tahirul Qadri."
30. "Nawaz Vows to Defy Qadris 'Imported Agenda,'" *Dawn*, January 3, 2013, http://www.dawn.com/news/776006/nawaz-vows-to-defy-qadris-imported-agenda.
31. PILDAT (Pakistan Institute of Legislative Development and Transparency), "Assessment of the Quality of Democracy in Pakistan," June 2013–December 2014, published February 1, 2015, https://pildat.org/assessment-of-democracy1/assessment-of-the-quality-of-democracyin-pakistan, 11, accessed October 11, 2016.
32. Freedom House, "Freedom of the Press 2015: Pakistan," https://freedomhouse.org/report/freedom-press/2015/pakistan, accessed February 14, 2016; International Federation of Journalists, "IFJ Calls on Pakistan Government, Political Parties to Respect Media Rights," September 5, 2014, http://www.ifj.org/nc/news-single-view/backpid/51/article/ifj-calls-on-pakistan-government-political-parties-to-respect-media-rights/, accessed October 9, 2016.
33. See note 4 above for a definition of this term. It is noteworthy that, in one of his talks, Qadri explicitly declares that he is not "Barelwi," but rather "Ahl-e Sunnat wa-l Jamāʿat." "Why Barelvi Ulama Think Dr Tahir-ul-Qadri a non-Sunni?" https://www.youtube.com/watch?v=r-VZh3Fcvs4, accessed October 11, 2016.
34. These are the other two major Sunni orientations among South Asian Muslims.
35. Commemoration ceremonies of the birth of the Prophet.
36. The politicization of Barelwis is discussed by Ethan Epping in "Politics and Pirs: The Nature of Sufi Political Engagement in 20th and 21st Century Pakistan," *Pakistaniyaat: A Journal of Pakistan Studies* 5, no. 3 (2013): 1–25.
37. Barbara Daly Metcalf, *Islamic Revival in British India: Deoband, 1860–1900* (Princeton, NJ: Princeton University Press, 1982), 296–97.
38. The Barelwi movement has been studied in detail by historian Usha Sanyal, in *Devotional Islam and Politics in British India: Ahmad Riza Khan Barelwi and His Movement, 1870–1920*, 2nd ed. (New York: Oxford University Press, 1999).
39. Usha Sanyal, "Aḥmad Rizā Khān Barelwī," *Encyclopaedia of Islam*, 3rd ed, ed. Gudrun Krämer, Denis Matringe, John Nawas, and Everett Rowson (Leiden: Brill, 2007), 71–75.
40. Philippon, "When Sufi Tradition Reinvents Islamic Modernity," 113.
41. Anatol Lieven, *Pakistan: A Hard Country* (New York: Public Affairs, 2011), 142.
42. Epping, "Politics and Pirs," 13.
43. Philippon, "When Sufi Tradition Reinvents Islamic Modernity," 112.
44. Philippon, "When Sufi Tradition Reinvents Islamic Modernity," 112.
45. Philippon, "When Sufi Tradition Reinvents Islamic Modernity," 112, citing Olivier Roy, L'islam mondialisē (Paris: Seuil, 2002), 51.
46. Fazlur Rahman, *Islam* (Chicago: University of Chicago, 1979), 206.
47. One reason for avoiding the term "Neo-Sufi" is that it was used with a specific meaning when first coined by Fazlur Rahman in the book *Islam* (1966) to refer to Sufi moral reformers who argued for the strong intellectual moorings of Sufism in Islamic law and hadith

sources. Subsequently Rex S. O'Fahey and Bernd Radtke, in "Neo-Sufism Reconsidered," *Der Islam* 70, no. 1 (1993): 52–87, argued against the Neo-Sufi hypothesis. For a review of this debate, see John O. Voll, "Neo-Sufism: Reconsidered Again," *Canadian Journal of African Studies* 42, no. 2/3 (2008): 314–30. Verena Meyer, in chapter 2 of this volume, refers to how Rahman's concept of Neo-Sufism was applied in a normative reformist way by the Indonesian modernist Nurcholish Madjid.

48. Morgahi, "Reliving the 'Classical Islam,'" 226–27.
49. Morgahi, "Reliving the 'Classical Islam,'" 226.
50. Morgahi, "Reliving the 'Classical Islam,'"226.
51. Morgahi, "Reliving the 'Classical Islam,'" 229.
52. Usha Sanyal, "Are Wahhabis Kafirs? Ahmad Riza Khan Barelwi and His Sword of the Haramayn," in *Islamic Legal Interpretation: Muftis and Their Fatwas*, ed. Muhammad Khalid Masud, Brinkley Morris Messick, and David Stephan Powers (Cambridge, MA: Harvard University Press, 1996), 204–13. Some of these debates and issues are treated chapter 4 by Brannon Ingram in this volume.
53. Ahmad, "Media-Based Preachers," 10.
54. See, for example, "Who Are Against Dr Tahir ul Qadri?," posted October 28, 2012, https://www.facebook.com/notes/basharath-siddiqui/who-are-against-dr-tahir-ul-qadri/481282188578670/, accessed October 11, 2016.
55. Philippon describes some such musical sessions during the tour of 2005 in "When Sufi Tradition Reinvents Islamic Modernity," 120–21.
56. This video of Qadri at a session with a *nashīd* has more than one million views: "Tahir Ul Qadri Dancers Reply—Tahir ul Qadri Lovers," https://www.youtube.com/watch?v=hMiM6OEoniO, posted October 26, 2008; Qadri's response to criticism (in Urdu): "Reply to Tahir Ul Qadri Dancers Video," https://www.youtube.com/watch?v=CwOfuTyLsRQ, no post date; Qadri giving hadith evidence for such dancing being permitted (in English): "Shaykh Tahir ul Qadri's Islam & Sufi Dancers," https://www.youtube.com/watch?v=V_mAo1dv-lg, posted December 28, 2008. All accessed October 10, 2016.
57. "Tahir ul Qadri Talking to Grave—Astaghfirullah," https://www.youtube.com/watch?v=yvKpOSY9kWo&fbclid=IwAR3PMRvrz9SI4QUcFpLxV_GKKbGCibO9uRTXuNZg0hrz1FIfV-odPfbQdOc, posted January 15, 2013, accessed March 17, 2019.
58. The original footage of Qadri recounting the dream, "Dream of Dr Tahir ul Qadri about Prophet MUHAMMAD (PBUH)_TRUE OR FAKE Decide," is posted at https://www.dailymotion.com/video/x3dvsj8, accessed January 23, 2020. In a response video, Qadri states that excessive attention has been given to this one incident that occurred during a private session. The dream was never promoted as a publicity stunt. See "The Reality behind the (Dream Video) of Dr Tahir ul Qadri 1of2," https://www.youtube.com/watch?v=dshXcyA0CG4, no post date, but ca. 2012, accessed October 1, 2016.
59. The content of this video is discussed in Tahir ul-Qadri, *Khwāboñ aur bashārāt par aʿtrāżāt kā ʿilimi maḥākmah* (Delhi: Adabī Dunyā, ca. 2009), 18. The rebuttal video with the same name is found at https://www.youtube.com/watch?v=6HZP0_NCk4A, accessed January 18, 2020.
60. For example, Syed Sami-uz-Zafar Naushahi, "Objections on Dr. Qadri's Dreams Clarified," https://minhajian.wordpress.com/2007/05/06/objections-on-dr-qadris-dreams-clarified-full/, accessed March 21, 2019.
61. Qadri, *Khwāboñ aur bashārāt.*

62. Thus the category of the "good" Muslim is by definition contaminated because it implies uncritical support for Western governmental policies. See Mahmood Mamdani, *Good Muslim, Bad Muslim: America, the Cold War, and the Roots of Terror* (New York: Pantheon, 2004).
63. Cheryl Benard, *Civil Democratic Islam Partners, Resources, and Strategies* (Santa Monica, CA: Rand Corporation, 2003), https://www.rand.org/content/dam/rand/pubs/monograph_reports/2005/MR1716.pdf; http://www.rand.org/pubs/monograph_reports/MR1716.html, accessed October 8, 2016.
64. Ahmad, "Media-Based Preachers," 12.
65. In a YouTube video (in English) in response to questions at the Danish conference, Qadri categorically distances himself from the formulation of the law under Zia-ul-Haq and criticizes contemporary procedures that he denounces as being unfair to minorities. See "Clarification on You Tube Propaganda Against Dr Tahir ul Qadri on the Issue of Blasphemy Law," https://www.youtube.com/watch?v=LQR_CRQynjE&feature=youtu.be, accessed October 9, 2016.
66. Qadri, *Fatwa on Terrorism.*
67. Qadri, *Fatwa on Terrorism,* 22–26.
68. See Katherine Pratt Ewing, "The Politics of Sufism: Redefining the Saints of Pakistan," *Journal of Asian Studies* 42, no. 2 (February 1983): 251–68. For a survey of Pakistan government attempts to use Sufism and court Barelwi elements since 9/11, see Muhammad Suleman, "Insitutionalisation of Sufi Islam after 9/11 and the Rise of Barelwi Extremism in Pakistan," *Counter Terrorist Trends and Analyses* 10, no. 2 (February 2018): 6–10.
69. A PhD dissertation has been written on the Pakistan Sufi Council and its role. See Teresa Ann Drage, "The National Sufi Council: Redefining the Islamic Republic of Pakistan through a Discourse on Sufism after 9/11" (PhD diss., Western Sydney University, 2015).
70. See Alix Philippon, "A Sublime, yet Disputed, Object of Political Ideology? Sufism in Pakistan at the Crossroads," *Commonwealth and Comparative Politics* 52, no. 2 (2014): 283–86; and Ali Eteraz, "State Sponsored Sufism: Why Are US Think Tanks Pushing for State-Sponsored Sufism in Pakistan?," *Foreign Policy*, June 10, 2009, https://foreignpolicy.com/2009/06/10/state-sponsored-sufism/.
71. Qadri's speech (in Urdu) is on YouTube: "Dr. Tahir-ul-Qadri's Speech at RamlilaGround, New Delhi, India—International Sufi Conference," https://www.youtube.com/watch?v=WTy7xSNW7LA, accessed March 21, 2019.

Commentary on Part I: Ambiguities and Ironic Reversals in the Categorization of Sufism

1. Carl W. Ernst, "Early Orientalist Concepts of Sufism," in *It's Not Just Academic! Essays on Sufism and Islamic Studies* (New Delhi: SAGE Publications India/Yoda Press, 2017), 463–82.
2. Carl W. Ernst, "The *Dabistān* and Orientalist Views of Sufism," in *Sufism East and West: Reorientation and Dynamism of Mystical Islam in the Modern World*, ed. Jamal Malik and Saeed Zarrabi-Zadeh (Leiden: Brill, 2018), 33–52.
3. Jonathan Z. Smith, "Religion, Religions, Religious," in *Critical Terms for Religious Studies*, ed. Mark Taylor (Chicago: University Chicago Press, 1998), 269.

4. George R. Trumbull, "French Colonial Knowledge of Maraboutism," in *Islam and the European Empires*, ed. David Motadel (Oxford: Oxford University Press, 2016).
5. Arthur John Arberry, *Sufism, An Account of the Mystics of Islam* (London: Allen & Unwin, 1950), 119–33.
6. Nile Green, *Islam and the Army in Colonial India: Sepoy Religion in the Service of Empire* (Cambridge: Cambridge University Press, 2009).
7. Fazlur Rahman, *Islam* (Garden City, NY: Doubleday, 1966), 239–40.
8. Rahman, *Islam*, 253.
9. Charles Tripp, *Islam and the Moral Economy* (Cambridge: Cambridge University Press, 2006).
10. See Maciej Sulmicki, "A Plenitude of Prefixes: Delineating the Boundaries of Neo-, Retro-, Faux- and Post-Victorian Literature," *Zagadnienia Rodzajów Literackich* 58, no. 1 (2015): 9–26; and Nancy S. Love, "Anti-, Neo-, Post-, and Proto—: Conservative Hybrids, Ironic Reversals, and Global Terror(ism)," *New Political Science* 31, no. 4 (December 2009): 443–59.
11. Aḥmad Sirhindī, *Intikhāb-i maktūbāt-i Shaykh Aḥmad Sirhindī*, ed. Fazlur Rahman (Karāchī: Iqbāl Academy Pākistān, 1968).
12. For a comprehensive critique, see Ahmad S. Dallal, *Islam Without Europe: Traditions of Reform in Eighteenth-Century Islamic Thought* (Chapel Hill: University of North Carolina Press, 2018), 94–139.
13. Mark J. Sedgwick, "Neo-Sufism," in *The Cambridge Companion to New Religious Movements*, ed. Olav Hammer and Mikael Rothstein (Cambridge: Cambridge University Press, 2012), 198–214.
14. Bruce Lawrence, "Sufism and Neo-Sufism," in *The New Cambridge History of Islam*, ed. Robert W. Hefner (Cambridge: Cambridge University Press, 2010), 355–84, doi: 10.1017/CHOL9780521844437.016
15. Mahkama Auqaf, *Fihrist-ei aʿras-i māzārāt zir tahawwul Mahkama Auqaf Panjāb* (Lahore, n.d.), 9.
16. Thomas A. Tweed, "Nightstand Buddhists and Other Creatures: Sympathizers, Adherents and the Study of Religion," in *American Buddhism: Methods and Findings in Recent Scholarship*, ed. Christopher Queen and Duncan Ryuken Williams (Richmond, Surrey, UK: Curzon, 1999), 71–90.

4. Is the Taliban Anti-Sufi?

1. On the rise of the Pakistani Taliban, see Hassan Abbas, *The Taliban Revival: Violence and Extremism on the Pakistan-Afghanistan Border* (New Haven, CT: Yale University Press, 2014), 141–67.
2. Sher Alam Shinwari, "Footprints: Rahman Baba's Devotees in Grip of Fear," *Dawn*, April 5, 2015.
3. Alix Philippon, *Soufisme et politique au Pakistan: Le mouvement barelwi à l'heure de "la guerre contre le terrorisme"* (Paris: Éditions Karthala/Sciences Po Aix, 2011), 284.
4. Declan Walsh, "Suicide Bombers Kill Dozens at Pakistan Shrine," *The Guardian*, July 2, 2010.
5. The TTP explicitly denied involvement in this attack. "TTP Condemns Lahore Strike, Denies Involvement," *Dawn*, July 3, 2010.
6. Huma Imtiaz, "Sufi Shrine in Pakistan Is Hit by a Lethal Double Bombing," *New York Times*, October 7, 2010.

7. Ashraf Buzdar, "Suicide Hits at Sakhi Sarwar Shrine Kill 41," *The Nation* (Pakistan), April 4, 2011. I return below to the links between these attacks and Taliban attitudes toward the government.
8. Iftikhar Firdous, "Extremists Pull Down Two Shrines in Khyber," *Express Tribune*, December 11, 2011.
9. On this topic, see, among many others: Rosemary R. Corbett, *Making Moderate Islam: Sufism, Service, and the "Ground Zero Mosque" Controversy* (Stanford, CA: Stanford University Press, 2017); Carl W. Ernst, *Sufism: An Introduction to the Mystical Tradition of Islam* (Boston: Shambhala, 2011); Fait Muedini, *Sponsoring Sufism: How Governments Promote "Mystical Islam" in Their Domestic and Foreign Policies* (New York: Palgrave MacMillan, 2015); and Mark Sedgwick, "Sufis as 'Good Muslims': Sufism in the Battle Against Jihadi Salafism," in *Sufis and Salafis in the Contemporary Age*, ed. Lloyd Ridgeon (London: Bloomsbury, 2015), 105–17.
10. Rania Abouzeid, "Taliban Targets, Pakistan's Sufi Muslims Fight Back," *Time*, November 10, 2010. The author interviewed Sayyid Safdar Shah Gilani, head of a Barelwi organization, the Sunni Ittehad Council, who proposed among other things a ban on "incendiary Deobandi literature," according to Abouzeid.
11. Thomas Barfield, *Afghanistan: A Cultural and Political History* (Princeton, NJ: Princeton University Press, 2010), 261.
12. On the early history of the Deoband movement, see Barbara Daly Metcalf, *Islamic Revival in British India: Deoband, 1860–1900* (Princeton, NJ: Princeton University Press, 1982).
13. On the Deoband movement and Sufism, see Brannon D. Ingram, *Revival from Below: The Deoband Movement and Global Islam* (Oakland: University of California Press, 2018).
14. Samiul Haq, *Afghan Taliban: War of Ideology, Struggle for Peace* (Islamabad: Emel Publications, 2015), xvii.
15. Ḥaqqānī is an epithet that a scholar earns by virtue of graduating from Dār al-ʿUlūm Ḥaqqāniyya. On the Ḥaqqānī network, see Vahid Brown and Don Rassler, *Fountainhead of Jihad: The Haqqani Nexus, 1973–2012* (New York: Oxford University Press, 2013).
16. In fact, one of the Dār al-ʿUlūm Ḥaqqāniyya's muftis responded to an inquiry about whether it was permissible to kill the custodian of a shrine where "un-Islamic" practices took place; the mufti made it clear that it was not acceptable. The same mufti argued elsewhere that destroying tombs was a "Najdi" (i.e., Wahhabi) practice. Muhammad Qasim Zaman, *Islam in Pakistan: A History* (Princeton, NJ: Princeton University Press, 2018), 343n174.
17. The Deobandis conceptualized *bidʿah* not so much as beliefs and practices that arose after the era of the Prophet Muḥammad and his Companions as beliefs and practices that simulate, or compete with, revealed religion (*dīn*). See Ingram, *Revival from Below*, 56–64, 77–80.
18. Quoted in Ali Riaz, *Faithful Education: Madrassahs in South Asia* (New Brunswick, NJ: Rutgers University Press, 2008), 31.
19. Christina Lamb, "The Pakistan Connection: Focus Special," *Sunday Times*, July 17, 2005. Similarly, Jessica Stern, writing for *Foreign Affairs*, presaged in 2000 that Dār al-ʿUlūm Ḥaqqāniyya, "the madrasah that created the Taliban," was among those Pakistani institutions bent on "exporting holy war" across the globe. Jessica Stern, "Pakistan's Jihad Culture," *Foreign Affairs* 79, no. 6 (2000): 115–26.
20. To my knowledge, the only other scholar who has studied these fatwas is Muhammad Qasim Zaman, who refers to the collection in a discussion of how contemporary ulama approach honor crimes. Muhammad Qasim Zaman, *Modern Islamic Thought in a Radical Age: Religious Authority and Internal Criticism* (Cambridge: Cambridge University Press, 2012), 179n15.

21. Muḥammad Akbar Shāh Bukhārī, *Akābir-e 'Ulamā-yi Deoband* (Karachi: Idāra-yi Islāmiyya, 1999), 417.
22. Not to be confused with Aḥmad Rażā Khān (1856–1921), founder of the Barelwi movement, discussed by other authors in this volume. Aḥmad Rażā Khān was born in the north Indian town of Bareilly, hence the eponym "Barelwi." Sayyid Aḥmad Barelwī (1786–1831), born in Rae Bareli, was a reformist who called for Islamic revival, amassed large numbers of followers, and was killed in 1831 fighting Sikh armies at Balakot, now part of the Khyber Pakhtunkhwa Province. The writings of his associate Shāh Muḥammad Ismāʿīl (1779–1831) heavily influenced early Deobandis. See especially Ingram, *Revival from Below*, chap. 2.
23. Ḥaqq, *Afghan Taliban*, 4.
24. Bukharī, *Akābir-e 'Ulamā-yi Deoband*, 419.
25. ʿAbd al-Ḥaqq et al. in *Fatāwa-e Ḥaqqāniyya*, ed. Mukhtār Allāh Ḥaqqānī et al. (Akora Khattak: Jāmiʿa Dār al-ʿUlūm Ḥaqqāniyya, 2002), 1:82–8. From the beginning, the Dār al-Iftāʾ has explicitly aimed to accommodate the needs of the general public, mostly lay Muslims (non-ulama) from the surrounding region, though only very rarely do the fatwas provide any information on the background of those requesting them. When the demand for fatwas exceeded his ability to meet it, a second Dār al-Iftāʾ was established under direction of Muftī Ghulām al-Raḥmān to assist with the queries and research. ʿAbd al-Ḥaqq reviewed and signed off on fatwas written by other muftis at Dār al-ʿUlūm Ḥaqqāniyya.
26. Hājji Ṣāḥib Turangzai (d. 1937), a student of Maḥmūd al-Ḥasan's at Dār al-ʿUlūm Deoband and a Sufi pupil of Hājjī Imdādullah al-Makkī, organized Pakhtun resistance against the British in the late nineteenth century. See Sana Haroon, *Frontier of Faith: Islam in the Indo-Afghan Borderland* (New York: Columbia University Press, 2007), 98–99, as well as James Caron, "Sufism and Liberation Across the Indo-Afghan Border: 1880–1928," *South Asian History and Culture* 7, no. 2 (2016): 135–54.
27. ʿAbd al-Ḥaqq et al., *Fatāwa-e Ḥaqqāniyya*, 1:87. All translations from this source are my own.
28. ʿAbd al-Ḥaqq et al., *Fatāwa-e Ḥaqqāniyya*, 1:87. On the Deobandi critique of "customs" (*rusūm*), see Brannon D. Ingram, "Crises of the Public in Muslim India: Critiquing 'Custom' at Aligarh and Deoband," *South Asia: Journal of South Asian Studies* 38, no. 3 (2015): 403–18.
29. ʿAbd al-Ḥaqq et al., *Fatāwa-e Ḥaqqāniyya*, 110.
30. ʿAbd al-Ḥaqq et al., *Fatāwa-e Ḥaqqāniyya*, 112. Many of his fatwas appeared in *Al-Ḥaqq*, as well as the Lahore weekly *Khuddām al-Dīn*.
31. Samiul Haq and Iṣlāḥ al-Dīn Ḥaqqānī, eds. *Zain al-Mahāfil: Sharḥ al-Shamāʾil li Imām al-Tirmidhī* (Lahore: Al-Matbaʿ al-ʿArabiyya, 2007).
32. Samiul Haq and ʿAbd al-Qayyūm Ḥaqqānī, eds., *Ṣalībī Dehshatgardī aur ʿAlām al-Islām* (Akora Khattak: Dār al-ʿUlūm Ḥaqqāniyya, 2004).
33. ʿAbd al-Ḥaqq et al., *Fatāwa-e Ḥaqqāniyya*, 1:111. Indeed, for most of the latter half of the twentieth century, Samiul Haq and the Dār al-ʿUlūm Ḥaqqāniyya have been known far more for anti-Ahmadi agitation than jihadi activism, let alone anti-Sufi sentiment. See Samiul Haq and Muḥammad Taqī ʿUsmānī, *Qādiyānī Fitna aur Millat-e Islāmiyya ka Mawqif* (London: Khatm-e Nubuwwat Academy, 2005), based in part on anti-Ahmadi speeches delivered in Pakistan's National Assembly in 1974; and Samiul Haq, *Qādiyān se Israil tak* (Akora Khattak: n.p., 1978).
34. ʿAbd al-Ḥaqq et al., *Fatāwa-e Ḥaqqāniyya*, 1:114.
35. Including, especially, the *Badāʿi al-Sanāʿi* of ʿAlāʾ al-Dīn al-Kāsānī, the *Hidāya* of Burhān al-Dīn al-Marghinānī, and the *Radd al-Muḥtār ʿala al-Dur al-Muhktār* of Ibn ʿĀbidin.

36. ʿAbd al-Ḥaqq et al., *Fatāwa-e Ḥaqqāniyya*, 1:ii.
37. ʿAbd al-Ḥaqq et al., *Fatāwa-e Ḥaqqāniyya*, 2:243.
38. ʿAbd al-Ḥaqq et al., *Fatāwa-e Ḥaqqāniyya*, 2:261.
39. ʿAbd al-Ḥaqq, ed., *Ṣuḥbat-e ba Ahl-e Ḥaqq*, by ʿAbd al-Qayyūm Ḥaqqānī (Nowshera: Idāra al-ʿIlm wa-l Taḥqīq, 1998), 170.
40. ʿAbd al-Ḥaqq et al., *Fatāwa-e Ḥaqqāniyya*, 2:247.
41. ʿAbd al-Ḥaqq et al., *Fatāwa-e Ḥaqqāniyya*, 2:245.
42. ʿAbd al-Ḥaqq et al., *Fatāwa-e Ḥaqqāniyya*, 2:247.
43. Samiul Haq, *Islāmī Muʿāshira ke Lāzimī Khad o Khāl* (Nowshera: Al-Qāsim Academy, n.d.), 1:155.
44. ʿAbd al-Ḥaqq et al., *Fatāwa-e Ḥaqqāniyya*, 2:243–44.
45. ʿAbd al-Ḥaqq et al., *Fatāwa-e Ḥaqqāniyya*, 2:249. On *Niẓām al-Qulūb* and its centrality for the Chishtī-Ṣābirī lineage, for which Ḥājjī Imdādullah al-Makkī (d. 1899) was especially central in propagating among early Deobandis, see Scott Kugle, *Sufis and Saints' Bodies: Mysticism, Corporeality, and Sacred Power in Islam* (Chapel Hill: University of North Carolina Press, 2007), 232. Ḥājjī Imdādullah outlines the *zikr ḥaddādī* in his manual on *zikr*, "Ẓiyā al-Qulūb," in *Kulliyāt-e Imdādiyya* (Karachi: Dār al-Ishaʿāt, 1977), 21–22.
46. ʿAbd al-Ḥaqq et al., *Fatāwa-e Ḥaqqāniyya*, 2:254.
47. ʿAbd al-Ḥaqq et al., *Fatāwa-e Ḥaqqāniyya*, 1:166–67. See also 1:242.
48. ʿAbd al-Ḥaqq et al., *Fatāwa-e Ḥaqqāniyya*, 2:255.
49. ʿAbd al-Ḥaqq et al., *Fatāwa-e Ḥaqqāniyya*, 2:264–65. These categories are an essential part of Sufi cosmology at least as early as Tirmidhī (d. 869). The *quṭb* and *ghaus* (Arabic, *ghawth*) are generally understood to be the highest saints in the hierarchy and the axis around which the world turns. For a general overview of this typology, see Annemarie Schimmel, *Mystical Dimensions of Islam* (Chapel Hill: University of North Carolina Press, 1975), 200–203.
50. ʿAbd al-Ḥaqq et al., *Fatāwa-e Ḥaqqāniyya*, 2:267.
51. ʿAbd al-Ḥaqq et al., *Fatāwa-e Ḥaqqāniyya*, 2:256–57.
52. ʿAbd al-Ḥaqq et al., *Fatāwa-e Ḥaqqāniyya*, 1:189.
53. ʿAbd al-Ḥaqq et al., *Fatāwa-e Ḥaqqāniyya*, 1:190.
54. ʿAbd al-Ḥaqq et al., *Fatāwa-e Ḥaqqāniyya*, 1:217.
55. ʿAbd al-Ḥaqq et al., *Fatāwa-e Ḥaqqāniyya*, 1:182–3.
56. ʿAbd al-Ḥaqq et al., *Fatāwa-e Ḥaqqāniyya*, 1:186.
57. ʿAbd al-Ḥaqq et al., *Fatāwa-e Ḥaqqāniyya*, 1:187.
58. ʿAbd al-Ḥaqq et al., *Fatāwa-e Ḥaqqāniyya*, 1:186.
59. See William C. Chittick, *The Sufi Path of Knowledge: Ibn al-ʿArabi's Metaphysics of Imagination* (Albany: State University of New York Press, 1989), 15.
60. Rashīd Aḥmad Gangohī (d. 1905) was a prominent early Deobandi Sufi-scholar, Qāżī SanāʾAllāh Pānīpatī (d. 1810) was a Naqshbandī Sufi and legal scholar whose work the Deobandis cite and study, and Shāh Walī Allāh (d. 1762) was the foremost Muslim reformist thinker of eighteenth-century India, whose work had a profound impact on the Deobandis as well as rival scholarly movements.
61. ʿAbd al-Ḥaqq et al., *Fatāwa-e Ḥaqqāniyya*, 2:254.
62. ʿAbd al-Ḥaqq et al., *Fatāwa-e Ḥaqqāniyya*, 2:268.
63. ʿAbd al-Ḥaqq et al., *Fatāwa-e Ḥaqqāniyya*, 2:274.
64. ʿAbd al-Ḥaqq et al., *Fatāwa-e Ḥaqqāniyya*, 1:402.

65. Ingram, *Revival from Below*, 7–8. And as Brian Bond discusses in chapter 6 of this volume, it was a Barelwi mufti, not a Deobandi one, who issued a fatwa deeming music "impermissible" in Islam. Bond's chapter is one among a number of recent works complicating the dominant image of Barelwis.
66. One of Samiul Ḥaq's works, a detailed treatise on Quranic ethics, draws on much of the standard language of Deobandi works on Sufism, including ethical reform (*iṣlāḥ-e ahklāq*) of the self (*nafs*) and targeting love of wealth (*ḥubb-e māl*) and lust (*shawat*) as particularly harmful among the "negative ethical traits" (*raẓā'il-e akhlāq*). These are the negative attributes that nearly all Deobandi Sufi texts also single out. But there is no mention of Sufism in the entire text; indeed, for Samiul Ḥaq, the Quran alone, along with the core ritual commandments of Islam, are singlehandedly equipped to effect this ethical reform of the self. Samiul Ḥaq, *Quran aur Taʿmīr-e Akhlāq* (Akora Khattak: Maktaba al-Ḥaqq, 1984), 46 and passim.
67. On Thānawī's approach to Sufism, see Muhammad Qasim Zaman, *Ashraf Ali Thanawi: Islam in Modern South Asia* (London: Oneworld, 2008), chap. 4, as well as Ingram, *Revival from Below*, chap. 4.
68. ʿAbd al-Ḥaqq praised Thānawī for his prolific writings and service to Islam, calling him a "wellspring of divine grace" (*chashma-yi faiẓ*), but it is by far the example of Madanī that inspires ʿAbd al-Ḥaqq, and he takes Madanī's activist politics as a model for the ulama. ʿAbd al-Ḥaqq, *Ṣuḥbat-e ba Ahl-e Ḥaqq*, 49 and passim.
69. Zaman, *Modern Islamic Thought*, 292.
70. Barbara Daly Metcalf, *Husain Ahmad Madani: The Jihad for Islam and India's Freedom* (Oxford: Oneworld, 2009), 7.
71. See Barbara D. Metcalf, "Maulana Husain Ahmad Madani and the Jamiʿat ʿUlama-i-Hind: Against Pakistan, Against the Muslim League," in *Muslims Against the Muslim League: Critiques of the Idea of Pakistan*, ed. Ali Usman Qasmi and Megan Eaton Robb (New York: Oxford University Press, 2017), 35–64.
72. ʿAbd al-Wāhid Bukharī, *Shaykh Ḥusain Aḥmad Madanī, ek shakhsiyat, ek muṭālaʿa* (Gujrat: Maktaba-yi Ẓafar, 1972), 218.
73. On the political legacies of Thānawī and Madanī, respectively, see Zaman, *Ashraf Ali Thanawi*, and Metcalf, *Husain Ahmad Madani*. On Madanī's relationship with his Sufi master, Rashīd Aḥmad Gangohī, see Metcalf, *Husain Ahmad Madani*, 62–64.
74. This is less the case for Deobandis affiliated with the Dār al-ʿUlūm Karachi, perhaps the only Deobandi Dār al-ʿUlūm in Pakistan that surpasses Dār al-ʿUlūm Ḥaqqāniyya in terms of prestige and notoriety. It was founded by Muḥammad Shafīʿ, a disciple of Ashraf ʿAlī Thānawī whose works evince a wide interest in Sufism, as do the works of his sons, Muḥammad Rafīʿ ʿUsmānī and Muḥammad Taqī ʿUsmānī. This might suggest a "Thanawite" line running through Karachi and a "Madanite" line running through Akora Khattak.
75. Ron Geaves, "The Contested Milieu of Deoband: 'Salafis' or 'Sufis?,'" in Lloyd Ridgeon, ed. *Sufis and Salafis in the Contemporary Age* (London: Bloomsbury Academic, 2015), 191–216.
76. Mufti Muḥammad Rafīʿ ʿUsmānī, *Fiqh aur Taṣawwuf: Ek Taʿarruf* (Karachi: Idāra al-Maʿārif, 2004), 37.
77. Ernst, *Sufism*, 79. See also Alix Philippon, "Sunnis Against Sunnis: The Politicization of Doctrinal Fractures in Pakistan," *Muslim World* 101, no. 2 (2011): 348.
78. Zaman, *Islam in Pakistan*, 223.

79. Zaman, *Islam in Pakistan*, 223.
80. See Finbarr Barry Flood, "Between Cult and Culture: Bamiyan, Islamic Iconoclasm, and the Museum," *Art Bulletin* 84, no. 4 (2002): 641–59; and Jamal Elias, "Un/Making Idolatry: From Mecca to Bamiyan," *Future Anterior: Journal of Historic Preservation* 4, no. 2 (2007): 2–29.
81. A. Afzar Moin, *The Millennial Sovereign: Sacred Kingship and Sainthood in Islam* (New York: Columbia University Press, 2012), 271n121.

5. Sufism Through the Prism of Sharia

I am grateful to David Gilmartin, Sandria Freitag, Roma Chatterji, and Sumbul Farah for their comments on earlier drafts of this chapter, which they generously gave me at very short notice. The chapter has benefited enormously from their feedback by helping me think through the issues raised by the ethnography in new ways. My thanks also to Katherine Pratt Ewing and Rosemary Corbett for their suggested revisions, which have strengthened the arguments I have tried to make here.

1. Jawad Anwar Qureshi, "Ibn al-ʿArabi's Fuṣūṣ al-ḥikam in the Deobandi Maslak," paper presented at the conference "Sufism in India and Pakistan: Rethinking Islam, Democracy, and Identity," New York, NY, September 24–25, 2015.
2. Mawlānā Aḥmad Rażā Khān Barelwi was a Sunni Muslim scholar of the Ḥanafī school, centered in the western U.P. town of Bareilly. His intellectual stance was similar to that of the Farangi Mahalli ulama of Lucknow, in that both embraced the "rationalist" (*maʿqulat*) rather than the "copied" (*manqulat*) sciences. However, this distinction, while significant in the seventeenth century when the *dars-e niẓāmī* syllabus was created by Farangi Mahalli scholar Mulla Nizam al-Din, is less important in contemporary South Asian madrasas, as the study of philosophy and logic has greatly diminished, while that of hadith has grown. Aḥmad Rażā's specialty was jurisprudence (*fiqh*), and he wrote in excess of a thousand fatwas during his lifetime, according to his biographer. See Usha Sanyal, "Aḥmad Rizā Khān Barelwī," in *Encyclopaedia of Islam, THREE*, ed. Gudrun Krämer et al. (Leiden: Brill, 2007), 71–75; and Usha Sanyal, *Devotional Islam and Politics in British India: Mawlana Ahmad Riza Khan Barelwi and His Movement, 1880–1920*, 2nd ed. (New York: Oxford University Press, 1999).
3. See Sanyal, *Devotional Islam and Politics in British India*, chap. 2.
4. Barbara D. Metcalf, *Islamic Revival in British India: Deoband, 1860–1900* (Princeton, NJ: Princeton University Press, 1982).
5. The Deobandis and Barelwis share many characteristics. Both are followers of the Ḥanafī school of law (*madhhab*), both believe that Sufism is a necessary complement to the sharia but must be subservient to it, and both believe in the concept of transfer of merit, *isal-i sawab*. The differences center on the Deobandis' embrace of the early nineteenth-century reformist tract *Taqwiyyat al-Iman* by Muhammad Ismaʿil Dihlawi (d. 1831), which Barelwis reject on theological grounds as belittling the powers of God and being disrespectful of the Prophet. On Barelwi-Deobandi differences, see Usha Sanyal, "Barelwis," in *Encyclopaedia of Islam, THREE*, ed. Gudrun Krämer et al. (Leiden: Brill, 2011), 94–99; and Sanyal, *Devotional Islam and British India*, esp. chap. 8. However, in this essay, I am more concerned with positioning the Barelwis and Deobandis within the shared universe of Islamic reform than in pointing out the ways in which they are different, because I believe academic studies

have gone too far in highlighting their differences, to the point where we fail to recognize that they come from the same milieu of nineteenth-century Sunni Muslim reform (*tajdid*) movements in South Asia. Nile Green, for instance, refers to the Barelwis as "counter reformist," a term that seems to have been coined by Green himself, not a self-description, and that suggests that the Barelwis occupy a diametrically opposed position from other Sunni Muslim groups labeled "reformist." See Nile Green, *Bombay Islam: The Religious Economy of the West Indian Ocean, 1840–1915* (New York: Cambridge University Press, 2011), 19–20, among others.

6. This is a pseudonym adopted to protect the identity of the madrasa.
7. Mareike Winkelmann, *"From Behind the Curtain": A Study of a Girls' Madrasa in India* (Amsterdam, Netherlands: Amsterdam University Press, 2005), 56–58, describes what she calls the "Thursday programme" in the Madrasatul Niswan, which is broadly similar, though the program in the Jamiʿa Nur al-Shariʿat is for madrasa students and teachers alone and has no outsiders. Nor are there any men listening to the program through a public address system, as in the Madrasatul Niswan.
8. The teachers said she had probably found it on a cell phone app, which seems likely to be the case, as Naʾim Tahsini, the poet who composed it, himself told me that his poems are easily accessible through the popular WhatsApp. Although madrasa students are not allowed to have their own cell phones, the teachers help them out by searching for suitable sources on their own phones and also in written books, though the latter seem less popular. Personal communication with Naʾim Tahsini in Bareilly, August 22, 2015.
9. Winkelmann, *"From Behind the Curtain,"* 84.
10. Sanyal, *Devotional Islam in British India*, 255–64.
11. Arshad Alam, *Inside a Madrasa: Knowledge, Power and Islamic Identity in India* (New Delhi: Routledge, 2011), 184.
12. See Alam, *Inside a Madrasa*, chap. 7, for an illuminating discussion of the ideological space of Madrasa Ashrafiyya. On the 1906 fatwa by Aḥmad Rażā Khān, see Usha Sanyal, "Are Wahhabis Kafirs? Ahmad Riza Khan Barelwi and His Sword of the Haramayn," in *Islamic Legal Interpretation: Muftis and Their Fatwas*, ed. Muhammad Khalid Masud, Brinkley Morris Messick, and David Stephan Powers (Cambridge, MA: Harvard University Press, 1996), 204–13.
13. I am grateful to Dr. Mawlana Waris Mazhari of Hamdard University, New Delhi, for helping me with the translation and meaning of this poem. Personal conversation in Delhi, August 30, 2015. I also thank Sumbul Farah, of Jamia Millia Islamia, New Delhi, who helped me further by correcting my mistakes in transcription and translation.
14. CBSE stands for Central Board of Secondary Education. It is a national accreditation organization operated by the Government of India.
15. David Gilmartin, *Empire and Islam: Punjab and the Making of Pakistan* (Berkeley: University of California Press, 1988), 117; also see Metcalf, *Islamic Revival*.
16. Sumbul Farah, "Piety and Politics in Local Level Islam: A Case Study of Barelwi Khanqahs" (PhD diss., University of Delhi, 2013).
17. Mawlānā Taḥsīn Rażā Khān was present at the founding in 1999 of the boys' madrasa in Shahjahanpur. See the introduction by Mufti Muhammad Yad Ali, in Muhammad Ehsan Miyan, *Dars-i Ibrat* (Shahjahanpur: Jamaʿat-e Mustafa Tablighi Taʿlimi Society, 1999), 7.
18. Farah, "Piety and Politics," 133.
19. Farah, "Piety and Politics,", 100–103, and see appendix for genealogical charts and trees.

20. To cite an example, a man from Bareilly who was trying to get to Shahjahanpur to meet Sayyid Sahib and myself in December 2014 boarded a train heading in the wrong direction, one that would have taken him straight to Lucknow instead. However, he was able to persuade the conductor to stop the train some ten miles outside Shahjahanpur to allow him to get off, an act of kindness that he ascribed to the blessings of his *pīr* Mustafa Rażā Khān.
21. However, a couple of Government of India grants in 2011 had been the initial source of funding for the purchase of land.
22. Personal conversation with Sayyid Sahib, December 2014.
23. Ehsan Miyan, *Dars-i Ibrat*, 11.
24. Ehsan Miyan, *Dars-i Ibrat*, 21.
25. See Ebrahim Moosa, *What Is a Madrasa?* (Chapel Hill: University of North Carolina Press, 2015); Alam, *Inside a Madrasa*; and Winkelmann, "*From Behind the Curtain*."
26. Talal Asad, *Formations of the Secular: Christianity, Islam, Modernity* (Stanford: Stanford University Press, 2003); and Saba Mahmood, *Politics of Piety: The Islamic Revival and the Feminist Subject* (Princeton, NJ: Princeton University Press, 2005).
27. Gail Minault, *Secluded Scholars: Women's Education and Muslim Social Reform in Colonial India* (Delhi: Oxford University Press, 1999), 45.
28. All responses are derived from a questionnaire I circulated to the students in 2013.
29. Aḥmad Rażā Khān, *Mālfūẓāt-e A'la Ḥażrat* (Gujarat, Pakistan: Fazl-i Nūr Academy, n.d.), 2:41.
30. On the Ahl-e Hadith, see Martin Riexinger, "How Favourable Is Puritan Islam to Modernity? A Study of the Ahl-i Hadis in Late Nineteenth/Early Twentieth Century South Asia," in *Colonialism, Modernity and Religious Movements in South Asia*, ed. Gwilym Beckerlegge (New York: Oxford University Press, 2008), 147–65.

6. Lives of a Fatwa

Acknowledgments: I thank my friends and interlocutors in Kachchh for their hospitality and generosity, and the following people for their helpful comments on drafts of this chapter: Katherine Pratt Ewing, Rosemary Corbett, Peter Manuel, Stephen Blum, Bradford Garvey, Adrienne Mills Bond, Christopher Romero Bond, and the two anonymous reviewers. All shortcomings are mine. Research for this chapter was conducted between 2014 and 2018 with funding from the Social Science Research Council, the American Institute of Pakistan Studies, the CUNY Graduate Center's Doctoral Student Research Grant, and the Franziska Dorner Fund for Musical Research.

1. The *kāfī* poetic form is performed in a range of musical styles in the Indus Valley region. Sindhi *kāfī* in Kachchh is a lively style performed with harmonium and *dholak* (barrel drum) accompaniment. Until about the 1980s, *kāfī* singers accompanied themselves on the *tanbūro* (*ektāro*) drone lute. Much of the early output of the Pakistani singer Abida Parveen consisted of *kāfīs*.
2. The Persian term *nājā'iz* is equivalent here to Arabic *ḥarām* (forbidden).
3. For a discussion of listening and modernity, see Charles Hirschkind, *The Ethical Soundscape: Cassette Sermons and Islamic Counterpublics* (New York: Columbia University Press, 2006), 13–28.
4. See, for example, Leonard Lewisohn, "The Sacred Music of Islam: Samāʿ in the Persian Sufi Tradition," *British Journal of Ethnomusicology* 6, no. 1 (1997): 1–33; Arthur Gribetz, "The *Samāʿ*

Controversy: Sufi vs. Legalist," *Studia Islamica* 74 (1991): 43–62; Jean During, "Hearing and Understanding in the Islamic Gnosis," *World of Music* 39, no. 2 (1997): 127–37; Kristina Nelson, *The Art of Reciting the Quran* (Austin: University of Texas Press, 1985).

5. While some would describe the effects of these kinds of reformist efforts as a process of "Islamization," this would imply that traditional, local practices are less Islamic.
6. John Baily, *"Can You Stop the Birds Singing?": The Censorship of Music in Afghanistan* (Copenhagen: Freemuse, 2001); John Baily, *War, Exile, and the Music of Afghanistan: The Ethnographer's Tale* (Burlington, VT: Ashgate, 2015); Magnus Marsden, *Living Islam: Muslim Religious Experience in Pakistan's North-West Frontier* (Cambridge: Cambridge University Press, 2005).
7. *Jamāʿat* in Kachchh, as elsewhere in Muslim South Asia, refers to a community-based association. Typically this association consists of members of a single endogamous community, but in some villages a *jamāʿat* may be composed of families from multiple communities, such as service communities like barbers and musicians, without sufficient representation to form their own *jamāʿat*.
8. Objections to including music at community functions do not appear to be motivated by an attempt at "ashrafization," that is, the emulation of higher-status Muslim communities, such as Sayyids.
9. Jonas Otterbeck, "Battling Over the Public Sphere: Islamic Reactions to the Music of Today," *Contemporary Islam* 2, no. 3 (2008): 211–28.
10. Saba Mahmood has pointed out that new Islamic pedagogical materials aimed at popular readership, such as fatwa collections and *fiqh* (jurisprudence) manuals "do not simply replace traditional concerns and modes of arguments; rather they point to a new set of conditions within which older commitments and themes have been given a new direction, shape, and form." Saba Mahmood, *Politics of Piety: The Islamic Revival and the Feminist Subject* (Princeton, NJ: Princeton University Press, 2005), 82.
11. Edward Simpson, *Muslim Society and the Western Indian Ocean: The Seafarers of Kachchh* (New York: Routledge, 2007).
12. Hussein Ali Agrama, "Ethics, Tradition, Authority: Toward an Anthropology of the Fatwa," *American Ethnologist* 37, no. 1 (2010): 2–18.
13. Historically, collections of legal doctrine in the Indian context have been considered "fatwa" collections despite their not taking the form of answers to questions. See Muhammad Khalid Masud, Brinkley Messick, and David S. Powers, eds., "Introduction," in *Islamic Legal Interpretation: Muftis and Their Fatwas* (Cambridge, MA: Harvard University Press, 1996), 15. For the pedagogical books I discuss below, the reader can be viewed as a kind of questioner (Ar. *mustaftī*), who chooses whether or not to accept as valid, and follow, the fatwa's ethical guidelines.
14. Michel Foucault's consideration of ethics in his study of sexuality led him to consider the "modes of subjectivation," or the "[ways] in which the individual establishes his relation to the rule and recognizes himself as obliged to put it into practice." Michel Foucault, *The Use of Pleasure*, vol. 2, *The History of Sexuality* (New York: Random House, 1985), 27.
15. See Foucault's discussion of a "thematic complex" composed of multiple "forms of [moral] problematization," by which, for example, specific practices of sexual pleasure (*aphrodisia*), such as conjugal fidelity and sexual relations between members of the same sex, came to be seen as areas of moral concern. Foucault, *The Use of Pleasure*, 14–32.
16. Edward Simpson, *The Political Biography of an Earthquake: Aftermath and Amnesia in Gujarat, India* (New York: Oxford University Press, 2014). On the anti-Muslim violence in eastern

Gujarat during the "riots" of 2002, which has been called a state-sponsored pogrom, see Ornit Shani, *Communalism, Caste and Hindu Nationalism: The Violence in Gujarat* (Cambridge: Cambridge University Press, 2007); and Parvis Ghassem-Fachandi, *Pogrom in Gujarat: Hindu Nationalism and Anti-Muslim Violence in India* (Princeton, NJ: Princeton University Press, 2012). Kachchh remained peaceful at the time, but many Muslims there now see themselves as unprotected by the police and the state.

17. See Francis Robinson, "Islamic Reform and Modernities in South Asia," *Modern Asian Studies* 42, nos. 2–3 (2008): 259–81; Gail Minault, "Women, Legal Reform, and Muslim Identity," *Comparative Studies of South Asia, Africa and the Middle East* 17, no. 2 (1997): 1–10.
18. Muslims in Kachchh who identify with the Ahl-e Sunnat movement do not refer to themselves as "Barelwi," and usually simply say that they are "Sunni." As Edward Simpson has discussed, there are also self-identified Sunnis in Kachchh who do not consider themselves as "belonging" to the Ahl-e Sunnat. See Edward Simpson, "The Changing Perspectives of Three Muslim Men on the Question of Saint Worship Over a 10-year Period in Gujarat, Western India," *Modern Asian Studies* 42, nos. 2–3 (2008): 377–403.
19. Rita Kothari, *Memories and Movements: Borders and Communities in Banni, Kutch, Gujarat* (New Delhi: Orient Blackswan, 2013).
20. Ahl-e Sunnat Muslims in Kachchh usually refer to followers of the Tablīghī Jamāʿat as "*tablīghī*" rather than "Sunni," and claim the latter term for themselves.
21. Farhana Ibrahim, *Settlers, Saints, and Sovereigns: An Ethnography of State Formation in Western India* (New Delhi: Routledge, 2008); Kothari, *Memories and Movements.*
22. Annemarie Schimmel, *Pain and Grace: A Study of Two Mystical Writers of Eighteenth-Century Muslim India* (Leiden: Brill, 1976).
23. On thinking through engagements with the Islamic discursive tradition, see Talal Asad, "The Idea of an Anthropology of Islam," *Qui Parle* 17, no. 2 (2009 [1986]): 1–30; Talal Asad, "Thinking About Tradition, Religion, and Politics in Egypt Today," *Critical Inquiry* 42, no. 1 (2015): 166–214.
24. Richard M. Eaton, "Sufi Folk Literature and the Expansion of Indian Islam," *History of Religions* 14, no. 2 (1974): 117–27; Shahab Ahmed, *What Is Islam?: The Importance of Being Islamic* (Princeton, NJ: Princeton University Press, 2015).
25. Hirschkind, *The Ethical Soundscape.*
26. Marc Gaborieau, "Criticizing the Sufis: The Debate in Early-Nineteenth Century India," in *Islamic Mysticism Contested: Thirteen Centuries of Controversies and Polemics*, ed. Frederick de Jong and Bernd Radtke (Leiden: Brill, 1999), 452–67; Barbara D. Metcalf, *Islamic Revival in British India: Deoband, 1860–1900* (Princeton, NJ: Princeton University Press, 1982).
27. Usha Sanyal, *Devotional Islam and Politics in British India: Ahmad Riza Khan Barelwi and His Movement, 1870–1920* (Delhi: Oxford University Press, 1999); Usha Sanyal, *Ahmad Riza Khan Barelwi: In the Path of the Prophet* (Oxford: Oneworld Publications, 2005).
28. Sanyal, *Ahmad Riza Khan Barelwi*, xii, 28.
29. Sanyal, *Ahmad Riza Khan Barelwi*, 129.
30. Richard Foltz, "The Central Asian Naqshbandī Connections of the Mughal Emperors," *Journal of Islamic Studies* 7, no. 2 (1996): 229–39.
31. Martin van Bruinessen, "The Origins and Development of the Naqshbandi Order in Indonesia," *Der Islam; Zeitschrift für Geschichte und Kultur des Islamischen Orients* 67, no. 1 (1990): 150–79.
32. Lewisohn, "Sacred Music of Islam," 1–33.

33. Al-Hujwīrī sometimes presents seemingly contrasting views. At one point he writes, "The results of [the inventions of physicians and philosophers who claim to possess a profound knowledge of the truth] are manifest to-day in the musical instruments which have been contrived for the sake of exciting passion and procuring amusement and pleasure, in accord with Satan." He later states that "theologians are agreed that it is permissible to hear musical instruments if they are not used for diversion, and if the mind is not lead to wickedness through hearing them." ʿAlī B. Uthmān al-Jullābī al-Hujwīrī, *Kashf al-Maḥjūb of Al Hujwiri: The Oldest Persian Treatise on Sufism*, trans. Reynold A. Nicholson (London: Gibb Memorial Trust, 1976 [1911]), 399, 401.
34. Al-Hujwīrī/Nicholson, *Kashf al-Maḥjūb of Al Hujwiri*, 409. Compare with the original Persian text: ʿAlī B. Uthmān al-Jullābī al-Hujwīrī, *Kashf al-Maḥjūb*, ed. Valentine Zhukovski and Muḥammad ʿAbbāsī (Tehran: Amīr Kabīr, 1964), 533. Gohar's Urdu translation also has *samāʿ*: see ʿAlī B. Uthmān al-Jullābī al-Hujwīrī, *Kashf al-Maḥjūb*, trans. Hazrat Allāma Fazluddīn Gohar (Lahore: Zīā al-Qurān Publications, 2010), 535.
35. Al-Hujwīrī/Nicholson, *Kashf al-Maḥjūb of Al Hujwiri*, 393.
36. See Amnon Shiloah, *Music in the World of Islam: A Socio-cultural Study* (Detroit: Wayne State University Press, 2001 [1995]), 31.
37. "Disposition" is my gloss of the Persian *tabʿ*, which Nicholson translates as "temperament."
38. Al-Hujwīrī/Nicholson, *Kashf al-Maḥjūb of Al Hujwiri*, 402.
39. Al-Hujwīrī/Nicholson, *Kashf al-Maḥjūb of Al Hujwiri*, 420.
40. Al-Hujwīrī/Nicholson, *Kashf al-Maḥjūb of Al Hujwiri*, 420.
41. Allāmah ʿAbdul Muṣṭafā Aʿẓamī, *Jannatī Zewar* [Gujarati], trans. Sayyid Haji Ahmad Shah Haji Miyan Sahib Bukhari-Qadiri (1986; Mandvi, Kachchh, Gujarat: Sayyid Anwar Shah Haji Ahmad Shah, 2014.
42. See Barbara Metcalf, *Perfecting Women: A Partial Translation of Bihishti Zewar* (Delhi: Oxford University Press, 1992).
43. Allāmah ʿAbdul Mustafa Aʿẓamī, *Jannatī Zewar* (1979; Delhi: Islamic Publisher, 2012), 288.
44. I interpret "rules of music" to mean metrical rhythm, the regularity of which has greater potential to encourage dancing.
45. Aʿẓamī, *Jannatī Zewar*, 288.
46. Musā Khān Muhammad Khān Paṭhan, *Fatāwā-e Qādarīyā* (Mandvi: Navrang Printing Press, 2014), 191–92.
47. Shāh Bhiṭāʾī is said to have invented and played the *danbūro*, which is referred to as *tanbūro* in this text.
48. Paṭhan, *Fatāwā-e Qādarīyā*, 205. I thank Dr. Asif Rayma for his help in translating from the Gujarati.
49. Name changed.
50. This is an idiosyncratic opinion that diverges from pronouncements of most Muslim scholars, including Aʿẓamī and the Muftī-e Kachchh. It is possible that Rashid considers this stringed instrument an exception because of its originary association with Shāh Bhiṭāʾī.
51. Rashid used the English words "ladies," "gents," and "modern" in what was otherwise Urdu.
52. Interview with the author, August 2015.
53. Al-Hujwīrī/Nicholson, *Kashf al-Maḥjūb of Al Hujwiri*, 420. Magnus Marsden's discussion of reformist criticism of music and poetry gatherings in Chitral (Pakistan), in which older men take pleasure in dancing with beautiful boys, and which women sometimes watch from rooftops, similarly recalls the contexts about which al-Hujwīrī warned aspirants.

Magnus Marsden, "All-Male Sonic Gatherings, Islamic Reform, and Masculinity in Northern Pakistan," *American Ethnologist* 34, no. 3 (2007): 483–85.

54. The *kāfī* singer Abdullah "Attaullah" Jat gave the example of the song "Ishq Sufiyana" from the Hindi film *The Dirty Picture* (2011). Abdullah Jat, personal communication, August 2014. The refrain of this song is "*tere vāste mera ishq sūfīyānā*," which roughly translates to: "My love for you is [like] a Sufi's love [for God]." The song's lyrics employ other Sufi concepts such as *fanā* (annihilation), thus inverting the material-divine (*majāzī-haqīqī*) love dialectic that has long been a source of inspiration for Sufi poets.
55. Turk claimed that this fatwa was issued ten to fifteen years ago, a date much later than others have given.
56. Nazar Ustād is a pseudonym. Note that Laṅgā musicians in Kachchh are referred to by the respectful title *ustād* (master) whether they are particularly accomplished or not and that the Laṅgās of Kachchh are distinct from the Laṅghā hereditary musician community of western Rajasthan.
57. Laṅgā men in Kachchh do not perform as singers in public.
58. Nazar Ustād's connection of a drum rhythm with a particular *zikr* (repetition of God's name) is a powerful example of the approach to musical and sonic practices analyzed by Richard K. Wolf, in which practitioners conceive of rhythms as ontologically connected with texts, and by extension the voice. See Richard K. Wolf, *The Voice in the Drum: Music, Language, and Emotion in Islamicate South and West Asia* (Urbana: University of Illinois Press, 2014).
59. This interview was conducted in Urdu-Hindi, but Nazar Ustād's use of *rāg* here is particular to Kachchhi/Sindhi, in which *rāġ*ᵘ, in addition to meaning "melody type," can also mean "music."
60. Interview with the author, July 30, 2015.
61. With regard to musical performance at *dargāhs* elsewhere in India, Peter Manuel has written that *qawwālī* performers in Delhi, Varanasi, and Kolkata claimed that "neither Hindu nor Muslim fundamentalism had exercised any particular impact on shrine attendance and the qawwālī milieu," but that in Ahmedabad, "the socio-musical impact of Hindutva has been overt where violence has occurred." Peter Manuel, "North Indian Sufi Popular Music in the Age of Hindu and Muslim Fundamentalism," *Ethnomusicology* 52, no. 3 (2008): 381.
62. Al-Hujwīrī/Nicholson, *Kashf al-Maḥjūb of Al Hujwiri*, 409.
63. Numerous hereditary performing communities in South Asia have had to adapt to changed circumstances wrought by socioreligious reform. See Nazir A. Jairazbhoy, "Music in Western Rajasthan: Stability and Change," *Yearbook of the International Folk Music Council* 9 (1977): 50–66; Matthew Harp Allen, "Rewriting the Script for South Indian Dance," *TDR* 41, no. 3 (1997): 63–100; and Daniel M. Neuman, *The Life of Music in North India: The Organization of an Artistic Tradition* (1980; Chicago: The University of Chicago Press, 1990).
64. Al-Hujwīrī/Nicholson, *Kashf al-Maḥjūb of Al Hujwiri*, 401.

Commentary on Part II: Sufis, Sharia, and Reform

1. The most wide-ranging critique so far of scholars positing a normative text-based core and viewing various facets of Islam in terms of the distance from it is Shahab Ahmed, *What Is Islam? The Importance of Being Islamic* (Princeton, NJ: Princeton University Press, 2015).

2. For a critique of the conceptual category of reform so far as the study of the Islamic legal tradition is concerned, see Wael B. Hallaq, *Sharīʿa: Theory, Practice, Transformations* (Cambridge: Cambridge University Press, 2009), 3–5.
3. Shāh Walī Allāh , *Al-Tafhīmāt al-Ilāhiyya*, ed. Ghulām Musṭafā Qāsimī (Hyderabad: Shāh Walī Allāh Academy, 1967–70), 2:49–50.
4. Anwār al-Ḥasan Sherkotī, ed., *Anwār-e ʿUsmānī* (Karachi: Maktaba-i Islāmiyya, n.d. [1967]), 69–70; Muhammad Qasim Zaman, *Islam in Pakistan: A History* (Princeton, NJ: Princeton University Press, 2018), 211.
5. Muftī Muḥammad Farīd, *Fatāwā-e Farīdiyya*, ed. Muḥammad Wahhāb Manglorī (Zarobi: Dār al-ʿUlūm Ṣiddīqiyya, 2013), 3:325.
6. Farīd, *Fatāwā-e Farīdiyya*, 1:307.
7. ʿAbd al-Ḥaqq et al., *Fatāwā-e Ḥaqqāniyya*, ed. Mukhtār Allāh Ḥaqqānī et al. (Akora Khattak: Jāmiʿa Dār al-ʿUlūm Ḥaqqāniyya, 2002), 1:182–83. Quoted by Ingram in chapter 4.
8. ʿAbd al-Latīf Ḥasan ʿAbd al-Raḥmān, ed., *Al-Fatāwā al-Hindiyya al-maʿrūfa bil- Fatāwā a- ʿĀ lamkīriyya* (Beirut: Dar al-kutub al-ʿilmiyya, 2000), 5:449 (from the Book of Reprehensible Matters [Kitab al-karahiyya]); ʿAbd al-Haqq et al., Fatāwa-e Haqqāniyya, 1:183.
9. Muḥammad ʿAbd al-Raḥim, *Maqālāt-e ṭarīqat maʿrūf ba-faẓāʾil-e ʿAzīziyya* (Hyderabad: Maṭbaʿ-i Matin Kartan, 1875), 24.
10. See Zaman, *Islam in Pakistan*, 200–201.

7. "A Way of Life Rather Than an Ideology?"

1. Suleman Akhtar, "Can Sufism Save Sindh?," *Dawn*, February 2, 2015, http://www.dawn.com/news/1161050.
2. The frequent invocations of Iqbal by contributors to this volume with respect to the rejection of shrine-based Sufism should not detract from the fact that, very often, *pīr* families have been labeled "feudal collaborators," as recognized by Iqbal himself when he wrote the following poem that was included in his 1935 collection *Bal-i-Jibril* (Gabriel's wing):

   To the Punjab Pirs

   STOOD by the Reformer's tomb: that dust
   Whence here below an orient splendour breaks,
   Dust before whose least speck stars hang their heads,
   Dust shrouding that high knower of things unknown
   Who to Jehangir would not bend his neck,
   Whose ardent breath fans every free heart's ardour,
   Whom Allah sent in season to keep watch
   In India on the treasure-house of Islam.
   I craved the saints' gift, other-worldliness
   For my eyes saw, yet dimly. Answer came:
   "Closed is the long roll of the saints; this Land
   Of the Five Rivers stinks in good men's nostrils.
   God's people have no portion in that country
   Where lordly tassel sprouts from monkish cap

That cap bred passionate faith, this tassel breeds
Passion for playing pander to Government."

V. G. Kiernan, trans., *Poems from Iqbal* (London: John Murray, 1955), 58, cited in David Gilmartin, "Shrines, Succession, and Sources of Moral Authority," in *Moral Conduct and Authority: The Place of Adab in South Asian Islam*, ed. Barbara D. Metcalf (Berkeley: University of California Press, 1984), 231–32. As Gilmartin points out here, "Iqbal contrasted his craving of 'the saints' gift, other worldliness' with what one could actually expect to get from *sajjada nishins* in twentieth-century Punjab."

3. Nicholas Schmidle, "Pakistan's Sufis Preach Faith and Ecstasy," *Smithsonian Magazine*, December 2008, http://www.smithsonianmag.com/people-places/pakistans-sufis-preach-faith-and-ecstasy-92998056/?onsite_source=relatedarticles&onsite_campaign=SmithMag&onsite_medium=internallink&onsite_content=Pakistan%27s+Sufis+Preach+Faith+and+Ecstasy&page=1.
4. *Pildat Background Paper: Construction of Kalabagh Dam* (Islamabad: Pildat, March 2011), http://admin.umt.edu.pk/Media/Site/UMT/SubSites/SGS/FileManager/Research/ConstructionOfKalabaghDamBackgroundPaper.pdf, accessed March 25, 2019.
5. See Oskar Verkaaik, "Reforming Mysticism: Sindhi Separatist Intellectuals in Pakistan," *International Review of Social History* 49 (2004): suppl., 65–86.
6. See "Call to Construct Dam in Thar's Mountain Range, *Dawn*, January 6, 2006, http://www.dawn.com/news/173154/call-to-construct-dam-in-thar-s-mountain-range.
7. Adeel Khan, *Politics of Identity: Ethnic Nationalism and the State in Pakistan* (London: Sage, 2005), 127.
8. Verkaaik, "Reforming Mysticism," 84.
9. Khan, *Politics of Identity*, 127.
10. Ian Talbot, *Pakistan: A Modern History* (London: Hurst, 1998), 252–54.
11. See Hamza Alavi, "Ethnicity, Muslim Society and the Pakistan Ideology," in *Islamic Reassertion in Pakistan*, ed. Anita M. Weiss (Syracuse, NY: Syracuse University Press, 1986), 21–48.
12. For a careful exploration of the introduction of British rule in the Sindhi countryside and its effects, see David Cheesman, *Landlord Power and Rural Indebtedness in Colonial Sind, 1865–1901* (Richmond, Surrey, UK: Curzon, 1997).
13. See Sarah Ansari, *Sufi Saints and State Power: The Pirs of Sind, 1843–1947* (Cambridge: Cambridge University Press, 1992), chap. 5.
14. *Dawn* (Karachi), February 10, 1948, 1.
15. Sarah Ansari, *Life After Partition: Migration, Community and Strife in Sindh, 1947–1962* (Karachi: Oxford University Press, 2005), 158. For more detail about the Pīr Pagāro's role in the sensitive intraprovince politics of 1955–56, see Despatch 565, February 3, 1956, 790D.00/2-356, U.S. National Archives.
16. "The intention of One Unit was to bring the demographic majority of East Pakistan in line with the political dominance of West Pakistan. With the resulting [constitutional] parity specifically in representation to the central legislature, the numerical majority of East Pakistan was effectively sidestepped by the ruling elite." See Fahan Hanif Siddiqi, "The Failed Experiment with Federation in Pakistan (1947–1971)," in *Defunct Federalisms: Critical Perspectives on Federal Failure*, ed. Emilian Kavalski and Magdalena Zolkos (London: Routledge, 2013), 76.

17. Verkaaik, "Reforming Mysticism," 69.
18. Cited in Ashok Behuria, *State Versus Nations in Pakistan: Sindhi, Baloch and Pukhtun Responses to Nation Building*, IDSA Monograph Series No. 43 (New Delhi: Institute for Defence Studies and Analyses, January 2015), 72, https://idsa.in/system/files/monograph/monograph43.pdf.
19. Verkaaik, "Reforming Mysticism," 71.
20. *Religion and Reality*, available online at http://www.gmsyed.org/religion/Religion%20and%20reality.pdf, is the English translation of the Sindhi publication *Jeeain ditho aahey moon*, which was published in 1967 and later republished several times. Other writings by Syed include *A Nation in Chains—Sindhudesh*, first published in 1974, http://www.gmsyed.org/nation/A%20Nation%20In%20Chains.pdf, and *The Case of Sindh* (English translation of its original Sindhi version, *Sindh Galha-ay-thee*), published in 1993, http://www.gmsyed.org/hiswork/case.html.
21. Verkaaik, "Reforming Mysticism," 78, 82.
22. For more details of the longer-term context for these protests, see Suranjan Das, *Kashmir and Sindh: Nation-Building, Ethnicity and Regional Politics in South Asia* (London: Anthem Press, 2001), 103–73.
23. Verkaaik, "Reforming Mysticism," 82.
24. Syed's aims were later restated in his 1985 *A Case for Sindhu Desh*, an abridged version of his earlier *A Nation in Chains*, in which he again called for the creation of a separate independent Sindh. http://www.sanipanhwar.com/A%20Case%20for%20Sindhu%20Desh,%20G.%20M.%20Sayed.pdf.
25. Ansari, *Sufi Saints and State Power*, 150–51.
26. Katherine Pratt Ewing, "The Politics of Sufism: Redefining the Saints of Pakistan," *Journal of Asian Studies* 42, no. 2 (February 1983): 251–68.
27. Verkaaik, "Reforming Mysticism," 83.
28. An example would be Imam Muhammad's *Hazrat Lal Shahbaz Qalandar of Sehwan-Sharif* (Karachi: n.p., 1978).
29. "Sindhi Stories: The Pir's Power, the Syed's Sway," *Express Tribune*, April 5, 2013, http://tribune.com.pk/story/531336/sindhi-stories-the-pirs-power-the-syeds-sway/.
30. Abbas Rashid, "Pakistan: The Ideological Dimension," in *Islam, Politics and the State: The Pakistan Experience*, ed. Mohammad Asghar Khan (London: Zed Press, 1985), 91.
31. Seyyed Vali Reza Nasr, "Pakistan: Islamic State, Ethnic Polity," *The Fletcher Forum of World Affairs* 16, no. 2 (Summer 1992): 86–87, http://hdl.handle.net/10427/76621, accessed March 25, 2019.
32. "The Sorry State of Sindh," *Friday Times*, May 10–16, 2013, http://www.thefridaytimes.com/beta3/tft/article.php?issue=20130510&page=26#sthash.uIch0fJB.dpuf, accessed March 25, 2019.
33. Quoted in "Poverty in Rural Sindh," *Dawn*, April 22, 2013, http://www.dawn.com/news/1024852/poverty-in-rural-sindh.
34. According to PPP leader Bilawal Bhutto Zardari, the party's two-week Sindh Cultural Festival of February 2014 was "designed to reclaim ground lost to militants and extremists. . . . This is Pakistan's history, this is Pakistan's culture and we're proud of it. We going to try to mark out a line in the sand and say this is who we are and fight back against that." "Sindh Festival: Bilawal Praised," *The News International*, February 4, 2019, https://www.thenews.com.pk/print/91381-sindh-festival-bilawal-praised.

35. Umar Farooq, "Diminishing Returns: Sufi Shrines in Pakistan's Politics," *The Revealer*, January 15, 2014, https://therevealer.org/diminishing-returns-sufi-shrines-in-pakistans-politics/.

8. Sufi Politics and the War on Terror in Pakistan

1. By "folklorization," Jean Cuisenier means the deformation and instrumentalization of cultural elements by authoritarian powers, as quoted in Katia Boissevain and Cyril Isnart, "Tourisme, patrimoine et religions en Méditerranée. Usages culturels du religieux dans le catholicisme et l'islam contemporains (Europe du Sud-Maghreb)," *Mélanges de l'École française de Rome—Italie et Méditerranée modernes et contemporaines* 129, no. 1 (September 2017), http://journals.openedition.org/mefrim/3423. All translations from the French are my own unless otherwise noted.
2. Dale Eickelman and James Piscatori, *Muslim Politics* (Princeton, NJ: Princeton University Press, 1996), 2.
3. Katherine Pratt Ewing, "The Politics of Sufism: Redefining the Saints of Pakistan," *Journal of Asian Studies* 42, no. 2 (February 1983): 251–68.
4. Gilles Bocquérat and Nazir Hussain, "Enlightened Moderation: Relevance of New Paradigm in the Face of Radical Islam," n.p, n.d.
5. S. Jamal Malik and John Hinnells, eds., *Sufism in the West* (New York: Routledge, 2006), 24–25.
6. Ewing, "Politics of Sufism," 253.
7. Quoted in Eickelman and Piscatori, *Muslim Politics*, 7.
8. Béatrice Hendrich, "Introduction—Beyond State Islam: Religiosity and Spirituality in Contemporary Turkey," *European Journal of Turkish Studies* 13 (December 2011): 1–15, http://ejts.revues.org/4527.
9. Observation of the author, February 2007, Lahore.
10. Geneviève Zubrzycki, *Beheading the Saint: Nationalism, Religion and Secularism in Quebec* (Chicago: University of Chicago Press, 2016), 164.
11. Thierry Zarcone, "La Turquie républicaine (1923–1993)," in *Les Voies d'Allah, les orders mystiques dans le monde musulman des origines à aujourd'hui*, ed. Alexandre Popovic and Gilles Veinstein (Paris: Fayard, 1996), 378.
12. In the academic literature on South Asian Islam, different definitions are given for *pīr*, all evolving around Sufi tradition: a religious leader, a spiritual leader, a Sufi master who has disciples (*murīds*), a guide and a professor of Sufism, the descendant of a Sufi saint, or even the politico-religious leader of a tribe, as *pīrs* are often political leaders and Sufi orders are often structured on segments of the population (tribes, clans etc.). Broadly, *gaddī nashīns* are "successors," those who sit on the seat of a departed *shaykh*, or saint, and are often the biological descendants of a famous Sufi saint.
13. Clifford Geertz, *The Interpretation of Cultures* (New York: Basic Books, 1973), 313–15.
14. Joel Migdal, *State in Society: Studying How States and Societies Transform and Constitute One Another* (Cambridge: Cambridge University Press, 2001), 12.
15. Ewing, "Politics of Sufism"; S. Jamal Malik, "Waqf in Pakistan: Change in Traditional Institutions," *Die Welt des Islams* n.s. 30, no. 1 (1990): 63–97.
16. Malik, "Waqf in Pakistan," 76.

17. Malik, "Waqf in Pakistan," 76.
18. Ewing, "Politics of Sufism."
19. Michel Camau and Vincent Geisser, *Le syndrome autoritaire. Politique en Tunisie de Bourguiba à Ben Ali* (Paris: Presses de Sciences Po, 2003), 75.
20. Interview with Punjab Minister of Auqaf and Religious Affairs Pir Saeedul Hassan Shah, May 2006, Lahore.
21. Quoted by Ansari, chapter 7, present volume.
22. Ewing, "Politics of Sufism," 261.
23. Khwaja Naseer, "Data's Urs Still Presses Message of Tolerance," *Daily Times* (Lahore), March 21, 2006.
24. Nadeem Shah, "Musharraf Urges Nation to Reject Fanatics," *The News* (Lahore), February 27, 2005.
25. Interview with Pīr Saeedul Hassan Shah, minister of Auqaf and Religious Affairs, April 2007, Lahore.
26. Emma Aubin-Boltanski, *Pèlerinages et Nationalisme en Palestine. Prophètes, héros et ancêtres* (Paris: Editions de l'EHESS, 2007), 9.
27. The SAARC organized a Sufi conference in Delhi in March 2006. Against the backdrop of confrontational relations between India and Pakistan, fueled by the paramilitary actions of jihadi groups and the intercommunal conflicts in India, Sufism has been identified as a panacea. The official Indian line tends to praise the "religious tolerance" of Sufism in opposition to the "fanaticism of Islam." As Carl Ernst has noted, Sufis are generally not identified as Muslims in India because they are not perceived as being sectarian. See Carl W. Ernst, *The Shambhala Guide to Sufism* (Boston: Shambhala, 1997), 209–10. The SAARC conference aimed at reviving the spirit and the pluralist cultural fabric of the subcontinent by invoking the Sufi tradition and revisiting its poetic and literary patrimony. Here again, the same process of culturalization and patrimonialization of Sufism can be witnessed. In her inaugural message, the chief organizer of the conference, the poet Ajeet Cour, presented Sufism as the only possible way to promote " democratic secularism," "pluralism," "love," and "tolerance" in the region. Sufism was also presented as being opposed to terrorism, because terrorism is the enemy of the world of poetry and of the aesthetics of the arts. Among the dozens of speakers (scholars, poets, intellectuals, writers, politicians, and so on) it was interesting to note the presence of the secretary of then Pakistani prime minister Shaukat Aziz. Observations by the author, March 2006, Delhi.
28. Interview with Youssaf Salahuddin, founding member of National Sufi Council, February 2007, Islamabad.
29. Interview with Youssaf Salahuddin, February 2007, Islamabad.
30. Interview with Youssaf Salahuddin, February 2007, Islamabad.
31. Danièle Hervieu-Léger, "Religion as a Grammar of Memory: Reflections on a Comparison Between Britain and France," in *Modernities, Memories and Mutations: Grace Davie and the Study of Religion*, ed. Abbi Day and Mia Lövheim (New York: Routledge, 2015), 19.
32. Interview with Youssaf Salahuddin, February 2007, Islamabad.
33. Observation by the author, November 2006, Islamabad.
34. "2007, the Year of Rumi," *Daily Times* (Lahore), December 12, 2006.
35. "2007, the Year of Rumi."

36. "2007, the Year of Rumi."
37. Interview with Pir Saeedul Hassan Shah, minister of Auqaf and Religious Affairs, April 2007, Lahore.
38. Interview with Youssaf Salahuddin, April 2008, Islamabad.
39. *Qawwālī* is the musical and poetical mode formalized by the Chishtī Sufi and scholar Amīr Khusrau in the thirteenth to fourteenth centuries on the basis of different musical traditions in order to attract Hindus to Islam. It was popularized around the world by the great singer Nusrat Fateh Ali Khan in the 1990s. Let us recall that some Sufi orders have granted a very central role to music as a vehicle for meditation, a means of spiritual elevation, and/or a way to reach the divine through ecstasy. *Samāʿ*, the "mystical audition" of poetry, songs, and music, which can also be accompanied by different forms of dance, is the name given to a tradition that has taken on very different ritual forms through time and space. Though originally meant to take place within a ritualized spiritual assembly, it has also gradually evolved into a more popular form of entertainment and has been widely publicized through the media. This process of diffusion is notably the case today with *qawwālī*, which can now be heard in many shrines throughout Pakistan and India but also in festivals and private concerts. Many Sufi singers have thus morphed into performing artists for wider audiences in modern settings. As a matter of fact, the lines have never been clear-cut between sacred and profane, art and spirituality.
40. Robin Denselow, "Sufi's Choice," *The Guardian*, December 2, 2015.
41. Denselow,"Sufi's Choice."
42. The Muttahida Majlis-e Amal (MMA) is an alliance of six Islamist parties that became the third parliamentary force after the 2002 elections.
43. Eickelman and Piscatori, *Muslim Politics*, 5.
44. "RPTW Bringing Musical Element of Sufism to 'Life'," *Daily Times* (Lahore), April 9, 2006.
45. Sufi Order International is an offshoot of the Chishtiyyah initially designed for Westerners in a universalist and syncretistic fashion that has recently started recruiting in the Indian subcontinent.
46. Comments by Ayeda Naqvi, guide of Sufi Order International in Lahore, at "Universalism and Islam" conference, Lahore, April 2006.
47. Faouzi Skali, "L'islam politique est une hérésie," *Intellectuel Collectif International des Mouvements Sociaux*, November 7, 2012, https://intercoll.net/SKALI-Faouzi.
48. Observation of the author, April 2007, Fès.
49. Observation of the author, April 2007, Fès.
50. Bocquérat and Hussain, "Enlightened Moderation," 21.
51. Interview with civil servant, November 2006, Lahore.
52. Interview with Ali Noor, general information secretary of JUP, April 2007, Lahore.
53. "Letters to the Editor," *Nawa-e Waqt* (Lahore), December 4, 2006.
54. See Irfan Ahmad, *Islamism and Democracy in India: The Transformation of Jama'at-e Islami* (New Delhi: Permanent Black, 2010), 6.
55. See Jean-François Bayart, *L'illusion identitaire* (Paris: Fayard, 1996), 80.
56. Bayart, *L'illusion identitaire*, 90.
57. Geertz, *Interpretation of Cultures*, 219.
58. Interview with Punjab secretary for culture, December 2006, Lahore.
59. Barbara Daly Metcalf, *Islamic Revival in British India: Deoband, 1860–1900* (Princeton, NJ: Princeton University Press, 1982).

60. The Pakistani army does not allow any of its members to affiliate with a political organization, but its progressive Islamization has taken place through religious groups or orders.
61. Interview with Arif Jamal, journalist and author specializing in South Asian radical groups, April 2007, Lahore.
62. Mahmood Mamdani, "Good Muslim, Bad Muslim: A Political Perspective on Culture and Terrorism," *American Anthropologist* 3, no. 104 (2002): 766–75.
63. Mamdani, "Good Muslim, Bad Muslim," 766.
64. See Mark Woodward, Mauhammad Sani Umar, Inyah Rohmaniyah, and Mariani Yahya, "Salafi Violence and Sufi Tolerance? Rethinking Conventional Wisdom," *Perspectives on Terrorism* 7, no. 6 (2013): 58–78.
65. Olivier Roy, *L'échec de l'Islam politique* (Paris: Seuil, 1992), 7.
66. See Alix Philippon, *Soufisme et politique au Pakistan: Le movement barelwi à l'heure de la "guerre contre le terrorisme."* (Paris: Éditions Karthala/Science Po Aix, 2011).
67. This expression designates people associating partners with God, a practice qualified as *shirk*.
68. Noah Salomon, "The New Global Politics of Religion: A View from the Other Side," Social Science Research Council, April 26, 2016, https://tif.ssrc.org/2016/04/26/the-new-global-politics-of-religion-a-view-from-the-other-side/, accessed September 22, 2018.
69. Interview with Raghib Naeemi, son of *gaddī nashīn* mufti Sarfraz Naeemi, July 2009, Islamabad.
70. Interviews with Rasul Bakhsh Rais, professor of political science at LUMS University, July 2009, Islamabad; Amir Rana, director of the Institute of Peace Studies, July 2009, Islamabad; Rifat Hussain, professor at the University of Quaid-e Azzam and director of the Department of Defense and Strategic Studies, July 2009, Islamabad; Muhammad Nadeem, journalist and researcher at the Institute of Islamic Research, July 2009, Islamabad.
71. Interview with Syed Hamid Syed Kazmi, federal minister for religious affairs, July 2009, Islamabad.
72. Interview with Riaz-ul Rehman, general secretary of the Council of the Islamic Ideology, July 2009, Islamabad.
73. Interview with Riaz-ul Rehman.
74. Interview with Shezad Qaiser, associate researcher at the Institute of Islamic Research of the International Islamic University, July 2009, Islamabad.
75. "We Will Not Surrender to Forces Harming Pakistan's Interests, Says Qureishi," *The News* (Lahore), May 4, 2009.
76. The genesis of this movement goes back to 2003, when the first incursions of the Pakistani army in the tribal areas took place to hunt the Afghan Taliban and al-Qaeda militants. But in 2007 the movement really came to light as an identifiable entity, under the leadership of Beitullah Mehsud. The radical circles in Pakistan seem to be a multi-organizational field comprising dozens of more-or-less autonomous groups (Pashtouns, Punjabis, and foreign militants), but they share common strategic, financial, or even ideological interests.
77. Ida Sofie Matzen, "Extremists of Love: Cosmological Activism Among Sufi Muslims in Contemporary Lahore, Pakistan" (PhD diss., University of Copenhagen, 2016).
78. See Romain Sèze, "L'Ahmadiyya en France," *Archives de sciences sociales des religions* 171 (2015), 247–63, http://journals.openedition.org/assr/27152.

79. See Philippe Braud, *L'émotion en politique* (Paris: Presses de la Fondation Nationale des Science-Politiques, 1996).
80. See Katherine Pratt Ewing, *Arguing Sainthood: Modernity, Psychoanalysis, and Islam* (Durham, NC: Duke University Press, 1997), 67.

9. "Our Vanished Lady"

1. Ali Usman, "Bibi Pak Daman: A Place of Solace for Everyone," *Daily Times* (Lahore), January 15, 2008, https://web.archive.org/web/20160401223526/http://archives.dailytimes.com.pk/lahore/15-Jan-2008/bibi-pak-daman-a-place-of-solace-for-everyone.
2. Haroon Khalid, "A Gnarled Tree in a Lahore Shrine Bears Witness to a Tradition That Puritans Are Bent upon Uprooting," *Scroll.in*, October 6, 2017, accessed July 1, 2019, https://scroll.in/article/853064/a-gnarled-tree-in-a-lahore-shrine-bears-witness-to-a-tradition-that-puritans-are-bent-upon-uprooting.
3. Masood Hashmi, *Makhdooma Bībī Ruqayyah Bint ʿAlī: Bībī Pāk Dāmana Lahore Meiñ* (Lahore: Al-Fazi Publications, 1990), 10.
4. Maulwi Muḥammad Bakhsh Shāh Qureshi, *Tarīkh Bībīañ Pāk Dāman (SA)* (Lahore: Sang-e-Meel, 1979), 154–55. The tragedy of Karbala occurred in 680 and is considered the seminal moment of the Shiʿi faith. The event emerged as a result of a schism in the Muslim community (*ummah*) over leadership in the aftermath of the Prophet Muḥammad's death in 632. The majority of the *ummah* supported the successful claim of Abu Bakr, a senior companion of Muḥammad. A small minority, known eventually as the Shiat-ul ʿAlī, came to back ʿAlī ibn Abu Talib, the cousin and son-in-law of Muḥammad. These followers believe that divine authority had passed from ʿAlī in a line of hereditary descent, from father to son, and that political authorities had usurped this divine will. This schism came to a head in the plains of Karbala, in present-day Iraq. Ḥusayn ibn ʿAlī, the third Shiʿi leader and head of the community (imam), had been ordered to pledge allegiance to the new Umayyad caliph, Yazīd ibn Muawiyah, but had refused, viewing Yazīd's rule as illegitimate. On the tenth day of the Islamic month of Muḥarram, the large Umayyad force killed seventy-two of Ḥusayn's male family members and companions, and the women were taken into captivity.
5. Masood Raza Khaki, *Bībīañ Pāk Dāman* (Lahore: Haidri Press, 1998), 14.
6. For more about the effects of establishing a Department of Auqaf, see Katherine Pratt Ewing, "The Politics of Sufism: Redefining the Saints of Pakistan," *Journal of Asian Studies* 42, no. 2 (February 1983): 251–68; and S. Jamal Malik, "Waqf in Pakistan: Change in Traditional Institutions," *Die Welt des Islams* n.s. 30, no. 1 (1990): 63–97.
7. Order Notification from M. Masood, C.S.P, Chief Administrator of Auqaf, West Pakistan, No. 1(71)-Auqaf/63, September 9, 1967, Issued by Office of the Chief Administrator of Auqaf, West Pakistan, Lahore, Records of Darbar Hazrat Bibi Pak Daman, Lahore. All English translations of archival sources are the author's.
8. Letter from S. Muhammad Asghar, Assistant Manager Auqaf, Central Zone Sector II, Lahore to Chief Administrator Auqaf, Lahore, September 9, 1967, Records of Darbar Hazrat Bibi Pak Daman, Lahore.
9. Letter from S. Muhammad Asghar, Assistant Manager Auqaf, Central Zone Sector II, Lahore, to Chief Administrator Auqaf, Central Zone, Memo No. 204-HMLW-1/T.O/67, September 14, 1967, Records of Darbar Hazrat Bibi Pak Daman, Lahore.

10. "Affairs at the shrine of Hazrat bibianpakhdamanan Sahiba, attn.: Administrator of Auqaf, Central Zone," Memo No. ACZ-9-2(1)-104/68/3098, March 25, 1968, Records of Darbar Hazrat Bibi Pak Daman, Lahore.
11. Hassan Abbas, "Shi'ism and Sectarian Conflict in Pakistan: Identity Politics, Iranian Influence, and Tit-for-Tat Violence," Occasional Paper Series, West Point, NY, Combating Terrorism Center, September 22, 2010.
12. Memo from Assistant Manager for Waqf Properties, Sector V to Administrator Auqaf, Central Zone, Lahore, Memo No. AMLW-V-660/69, December 22, 1969, Records of Darbar Hazrat Bibi Pak Daman.
13. Order Notification from Raja Hamid Mukhtar, Chief Administrator of Auqaf, West Pakistan, No. 1(71)-Auqaf/63: Amendment Schedule, March 31, 1970, Records of Darbar Hazrat Bibi Pak Daman, Lahore.
14. "Taking Over of Masjid," Memo No. AVZ-4(1)-104/SC/3641, April 4, 1970, Records of Darbar Hazrat Bibi Pak Daman, Lahore; see also Memo No. 1(71) DWP-Auqaf/63 from Chief Administrator of Auqaf, Government of Punjab to Manager, Waqf Properties, Sector V with reference to Memo No. A.M.LHR-V/645/70, August 20, 1970, Records of Darbar Hazrat Bibi Pak Daman, Lahore.
15. This committee comprised influential community leaders, including members of the *mutawallī* families and *gaddī nashīns*. The preeminence given to the Prophet's family versus the Prophet's companions (and the first three caliphs) is a point of doctrinal tensions between Sunnis and Shiʿa.
16. Letter from Assistant Manager for Waqf Properties, Sector V, to Chief Administrator Auqaf, Central Zone, Memo No. AMLW-V-170, July 1, 1970, Records of Darbar Hazrat Bibi Pak Daman, Lahore.
17. Memo from Muhammad Hafizullah, Chief Administrator Auqaf, Central Zone, Lahore, to Assistant Manager, Waqf Properties, Sector V, Lahore, Memo No. ACZ-4(1)-I03/RC/1720, July 4, 1970, Records of Darbar Hazrat Bibi Pak Daman, Lahore.
18. Letter from Assistant Manager, Waqf Properties Sector V, to Abdul Majid, Member RPC Hazrat Bībī Pāk Dāmana, Lahore, July 11, 1970, Records of Darbar Hazrat Bibi Pak Daman, Lahore.
19. Memo from Chief Administrator Auqaf, Central Zone, Lahore, to Assistant Manager, Waqf Properties, Sector V, Lahore, Memo No. ACZ-4(1)—I03/RC/1788, July 23, 1970, Records of Darbar Hazrat Bibi Pak Daman, Lahore.
20. For further discussion on attempts to nationalize the shrine, see Noor Zaidi, "'A Blessing on Our People': Bibi Pak Daman, Sacred Geography, and the Construction of the Nationalized Sacred," *Muslim World* 104, no. 3 (2014): 306–35; Noor Zaidi, "Making Spaces Sacred: The Sayyeda Zaynab and Bibi Pak Daman Shrines and the Construction of Modern Shia Identity" (PhD diss., University of Pennsylvania, 2015).
21. Field notes, interview with Mian Muhammad Syed, head of Auqaf Department, Bībī Pāk Dāman, Lahore, January 3, 2011.
22. Field notes, interview with Sheikh Akhlaque, member RPC, Bībī Pāk Dāman, Lahore, January 12, 2011.
23. Ghāfir Shahzād, *Hazrat Bībī Pāk Dāman*, 2nd ed. (Lahore: Department of Religious Affairs and Auqaf, Punjab, January 2005), 16.
24. Letter from Office of Manager of Auqaf to Ghulam Fatima, Ladies Attendant, Darbar Bibi Pak Daman, Memo No. 301/AMLW-II/67, December 4, 1967, Records of Darbar Hazrat Bibi Pak Daman, Lahore.

25. Shahzād, *Hazrat Bībī Pāk Dāman*, 17.
26. Hussain Haqqani, *Pakistan: Between Mosque and Military* (Washington, DC: Carnegie Endowment for International Peace, 2005), 87.
27. Zulfikar Ali Bhutto, Address as President of the National Assembly of Pakistan, April 14, 1972, Islamabad, as quoted in *Pakistan Times*, April 15, 1972.
28. For more on the challenges surrounding the dissolution of East Pakistan, see Glenn Stephenson, "Pakistan: Discontiguity and the Majority Problem," *Geographical Review* 58, no. 2 (April 1968): 195–213; Elliot L. Tepper, "Pakistan and the Consequences of Bangladesh," *Pacific Affairs* 45, no. 4 (Winter 1972–73): 573–81.
29. Shahzād, *Hazrat Bībī Pāk Dāman*, 17.
30. Shahzād, *Hazrat Bībī Pāk Dāman*, 17.
31. Maulwi Muhammad Bakhsh Shah Qureshi, "Bībīan Pāk Dāmanā ke halāt," *Al-Assad*, July 26, 1972.
32. Clifford Geertz, "Religion as a Cultural System," in *Anthropological Approaches to the Study of Religion*, ed. Michael Banton (London: Routledge, 1966), 28.
33. Memo from Manager Waqf Properties, Central Zone, Lahore to Chief Administrator, Auqaf, Central Zone, Lahore, Memo No. AMLW-III-1933/73, November 11, 1973, Records of Darbar Hazrat Bibi Pak Daman, Lahore.
34. Memo from Manager Waqf Properties, Memo No. AMLW-III-1933/73,November 11, 1973.
35. Memo from Manager Waqf Properties, Memo No. AMLW-III-1933/73, November 11, 1973.
36. Memo from Manager Waqf Properties, Memo No. AMLW-III-1933/73, November 11, 1973.

Commentary on Part III: The Problems and Perils of Translating Sufism as "Moderate Islam"

1. Saba Mahmood, *Religious Difference in a Secular Age: A Minority Report* (Princeton, NJ: Princeton University Press, 2015).
2. For an excellent recent exploration of this particular modality of moderation, see Su'ad Abdul Khabeer, *Muslim Cool: Race, Religion, and Hip Hop in the United States* (New York: New York University Press, 2016).
3. Ananda Abeysekara, "The Im-possibility of Secular Critique: The Future of Religion's Memory," *Culture and Religion* 11, no. 3 (2010): 213–46.
4. Abeysekara, "The Im-possibility of Secular Critique," 218.
5. I have explored the Barelwi-Deobandi polemic and its early nineteenth and late-eighteenth-century antecedents in greater detail in my monograph, SherAli Tareen, *Defending Muḥammad in Modernity* (South Bend, IN: University of Notre Dame Press, 2019).
6. See SherAli Tareen, "The Limits of Tradition: Competing Logics of Authenticity in South Asian Islam" (PhD diss., Duke University, 2012).

10. Is All Politics Local?

1. See Carla Bellamy, *The Powerful Ephemeral: Everyday Healing in an Ambiguously Islamic Place* (Berkeley: University of California Press, 2011); and Shail Mayaram, "Beyond Ethnicity? Being Hindu and Muslim in South Asia," in *Lived Islam in South Asia: Adaptation, Accommodation,*

and Conflict, ed. Imtiaz Ahmad and Helmut Reifeld (New Delhi: Social Science Press, 2004), 18–29.

2. See Anand Taneja, *Jinnealogy: Time, Islam, and Ecological Thought in the Medieval Ruins of Delhi* (Stanford, CA: Stanford University Press, 2017).
3. Taneja, *Jinnealogy*, 19–26.
4. Bellamy, *The Powerful Ephemeral*; Taneja, *Jinnealogy*, 48–50, 64–65. For other perspectives on the culture of Sufi saints' shrines, see Anna Bigelow, *Sharing the Sacred: Practicing Pluralism in Muslim North India* (Oxford: Oxford University Press, 2010); Claudia Liebskind, *Piety on Its Knees: Three Sufi Traditions of South Asia in Modern Times* (New Delhi: Oxford University Press, 1998); and Peter Gottschalk, *Beyond Hindu and Muslim: Multiple Identity in Narratives from Village India* (Oxford: Oxford University Press, 2005).
5. Bellamy, *The Powerful Ephemeral*, 74–76; Taneja, *Jinnealogy*, 90–91.
6. The Khoja community's religious identity is complex. They are now largely recognized as Ismaili or Ithnā ʿAsharī converts because of a nineteenth-century court case in Mumbai. See Teena Purohit, *The Aga Khan Case: Religion and Identity in Colonial India* (Cambridge, MA: Harvard University Press, 2012). Muḥarram is the month in which Shiʿi Muslims mourn the death of Ḥusayn and his male family members in a battle for leadership in the early Muslim community.
7. See Carla Bellamy, "Smoking Is Good for You: Absence, Presence, and the Ecumenical Appeal of Indian Islamic Healing Centers," *International Journal of Hindu Studies* 10, no. 2 (August 2006): 207–24.
8. The pole upon which *panje* are mounted is typically draped with decorative cloth that is changed in accordance with the season. These two special *panje* were *themselves* covered—that is, cloth was covering the hand itself, and had a concealing rather than decorative function.
9. The family told me that this woman's husband was Hindu. I have no reason to doubt this is true, but I was not able to verify it.
10. See Nathaniel Roberts, *To Be Cared For: The Power of Conversion and the Foreignness of Belonging in an Indian Slum* (Berkeley: University of California Press, 2016); Siddharth Varadarajan, ed., *Gujarat, the Making of a Tragedy* (New Delhi: Penguin Books India, 2002).
11. This is not to say that therapeutic cross-tradition and cross-caste friendships cannot develop in a local shrine context. For discussion of this type of friendship and its implications, see Joyce Burkhalter Flueckiger, *In Amma's Healing Room: Gender and Vernacular Islam in South India* (Bloomington: Indiana University Press, 2009), 60–64. Nevertheless, my research suggests that forming deep friendships and relationships with members of other communities is common at larger Muslim saint shrines, and this, too, has a therapeutic effect, allowing the pilgrim to feel that he or she is something more than that which he or she must be in the context of home and family. The anonymity of larger shrines also allows pilgrims, should they choose, to temporarily embrace aspects of other religious identities. Thus, for example, a Hindu woman may begin wearing hijab. See also Bellamy, *The Powerful Ephemeral*, 80.
12. For analysis of non-Muslim participation in Shiʿi narratives and rituals, see Afsar Mohammad, *The Festival of Pirs: Popular Islam and Shared Devotion in South India* (Oxford: Oxford University Press, 2013); Karen Ruffle, *Gender, Sainthood, and Everyday Practice in South Asian Shiʿism* (Chapel Hill: University of North Carolina Press, 2012); and Bellamy, *The Powerful Ephemeral.*

13. It is also worth noting that low-caste identity may have played a role in the family's ambivalent attitude toward the women who sat in the alley in front of the home, but I was unable to ascertain their caste status.

11. Sufi Healing and Secular Psychiatry in India

Research was funded by Deutsche Forschungs-Gemeinschaft, Cluster of Excellence "Religion and Politics," in Premodern and Modern Cultures, University of Muenster (2007–17). Thanks to the editors for helpful comments and careful editing of the chapter.

1. The chapter draws on my fieldwork on the Dava & Dua Program at the shrine of Mirā Dātār in Gujarat between 2008 and 2012. See Helene Basu, "*Davā* and *Duā*: Negotiating Psychiatry and Ritual Healing of Madness," in *Asymmetrical Conversations: Contestations, Circumventions, and the Blurring of Therapeutic Boundaries*, ed. Harish H. Naraindas, Johannes Quack, and William S. Sax (New York: Berghahn, 2014), 162–99.
2. R. Raguram et al., "Traditional Community Resources for Mental Health: A Report of Temple Healing from India," *BMJ* 325, no. 1 (July 2002): 38–40.
3. Marie Caroline Saglio-Yatzimirsky and Brigitte Sébastia, "Mixing Tirttam and Tablets: A Healing Proposal for Mentally Ill Patients in Gunaseelam (South India)," *Anthropology & Medicine* 22, no. 2 (October 2014): 127–37.
4. See Jose Casanova, "Rethinking Secularization: A Global Comparative Perspective," in *Religion, Globalization, and Culture*, ed. Peter Beyer and Lori Beaman (Leiden: Brill, 2007), 101–20.
5. See Bruno Latour, *We Have Never Been Modern* (Cambridge, MA: Harvard University Press, 1991); Bruno Latour, *On the Modern Cult of Factish Gods* (Durham, NC: Duke University Press, 2010).
6. See Johannes Quack, *Disenchanting India: Organized Rationalism and Criticism of Religion in India* (New York: Oxford University Press, 2011); Johannes Quack, "Possession and the Anti-superstition Law in Maharashtra: An Actor's Perspective on Modernization and Disenchantment," in *The Law of Possession. Ritual, Healing and the Secular State*, ed. William Sax and Helene Basu (New York: Oxford University Press, 2015), 138–61.
7. This was Narendra Dabholkar. See his Wikipedia entry: https://en.wikipedia.org/wiki/Narendra_Dabholkar. For a reaction of the Indian medical community to the murder, see Anant Phadke's editorial, "The Murder of Dr Narendra Dabholkar: A Fascist Attack on Rationalism," *Indian Journal of Medical Ethics* 10, no. 4 (2013), https://doi.org/10.20529/IJME.2013.068, https://ijme.in/articles/the-murder-of-dr-narendra-dabholkar-a-fascist-attack-on-rationalism/?galley=html, accessed January 20, 2020.
8. Catriona McKinnon, *Toleration: A Critical Introduction* (London: Routledge, 2006), 18.
9. Saglio-Yatzmirisky and Sébastia, "Mixing Tirttam and Tablets," 135.
10. See also Katherine Pratt Ewing, "The Politics of Sufism: Redefining Saints of Pakistan," *Journal of Asian Studies* 42, no. 2 (February 1983): 251–68.
11. Henrike Donner, ed. *Being Middle-Class in India: A Way of Life* (London: Routledge, 2011), 13.
12. For details, see Beatrix Pfleiderer, "Mira Datar Dargah: The Psychiatry of a Muslim Shrine," in *Ritual and Religion Among Muslims in India*, ed. Imtiaz Ahmad (Delhi: Manohar, 1981), 195–234; and Helene Basu, dir., *Spirits of Envy: The Ethnographic Film* (Muenster: Cluster of Excellence "Religion and Politics," Muenster University, 2012), DVD.

13. See "Gujarat State WAKF Board," Legal Department, Government of Gujarat, http://legal.gujarat.gov.in/wakf_board.htm, accessed July 22, 2017.
14. For others, see Carla Bellamy, *The Powerful Ephemeral: Everyday Healing in an Ambiguously Islamic Place* (Berkeley: University of California Press, 2011).
15. See Michael Dols, *Majnun: The Madman in Medieval Islamic Society* (Oxford: Clarendon Press, 1992), 223; Syed Noumanul Haq, "Occult Sciences and Medicine," in *The New Cambridge History of Islam*, ed. Michael Cook (Cambridge: Cambridge University Press, 2010), 640.
16. *Balā* is used as a cover term for Islamic spirits (jinn) created by Allah from fire, for Hindu ghosts of the dead (*pret*) or the wilderness (*bhūt*), as well as for tribal (Adivasi) categories such as "witch" (*dakan*).
17. See Beatrix Pfleiderer, *The Red Thread: Healing Possession at a Muslim Shrine in North India* (Delhi: Aakar, 2006).
18. Basu, "*Davā* and *Duā*."
19. Pfleiderer, "Mira Datar Dargah."
20. McGregor, R. S., ed. The Oxford Hindi-English Dictionary (Oxford: Oxford University Press, 1993); UrduPoint, https://www.urdupoint.com/dictionary/english-to-urdu/toleration-meaning-in-urdu/89801.html.
21. As quoted in Ira Das, *Staat und Religion in Indien: Eine rechtswissenschaftliche Untersuchung* (Tübingen: Mohr Siebeck, 2004), 43. This translation and all subsequent translations from this source are mine.
22. Rajeev Bhargava, *Secularism and Its Critics*, Themes in Politics (Delhi: Oxford University Press, 1998); Angelika Malinar, "Hinduismus und Religionsfreiheit," in *Religionsfreiheit: Positionen—Konflikte—Herausforderungen*, ed. Hans-Georg Ziebertz (Würzburg: Echter, 2015), 183–209.
23. Brenda Cossman and Ratna Kapur, "Secularism's Last Sigh?: The Hindu Right, the Courts, and India's Struggle for Democracy," *Harvard International Law Journal* 38, no. 1 (October 1997): 143.
24. Das, *Staat und Religion in Indien*, 99. A large body of scholarly literature is concerned with the problems inhering in the Indian definition of secularism, which protects distinct religious identities and minorities by accepting different codes of law (especially personal law) for these minority groups, and the link between this particular version of secularism and the rise of Hindu nationalism. See T. N. Madan, "Secularism in India: Predicaments and Prospects," in *Images of the World: Essays on Religion, Secularism, and Culture*, ed. T. N. Madan (New Delhi: Oxford University Press, 2006), 74–112; Thomas Blom Hansen and Christophe Jaffrelot, eds., *The BJP and the Compulsions of Politics in India* (New Delhi: Oxford University Press, 2001); Zakia Pathak and Rajeswari Sunder Rajan, "Shahbano," *Signs* 14, no. 3 (Spring 1989): 558–82.
25. Das, *Staat und Religion in Indien*, 44.
26. Tahir Mahmood, "Interaction of Islam and Public Law in India," in *Perspectives on Islamic Law, Justice and Society*, ed. Ravindra S. Khare (Lanham, MD: Rowman & Littlefield, 1999), 93–122.
27. Mahmood, "Interaction of Islam and Public Law in India," 94.
28. Mahmood, "Interaction of Islam and Public Law in India," 111–12.
29. Mahmood, "Interaction of Islam and Public Law in India," 108–9.
30. Mahmood, "Interaction of Islam and Public Law in India," 109.

31. See Bhargavi Davar, "Justice at Erwadi," in *The Law of Possession: Ritual, Healing, and the Secular State*, ed. William Sax and Helene Basu (New York: Oxford University Press, 2015), 117–37.
32. Since then the Indian Mental Health Act has been amended several times, most recently in 2017.
33. "Orders of the Supreme Court in Civil Writ Petition, No. 334/2001 and 562/2001—Erwady-Saarthak Public Interest Litigation," in *Mental Health: An Indian Perspective, 1946–2003*, ed. S. P. Agarwal et al. (New Delhi: Ministry of Health and Family Welfare, Directorate General of Health Services, 2004), 506.
34. "Orders of the Supreme Court in Civil Writ Petition," 511–12.
35. Oral summary by a member of the delegation in an interview with the author on October 11, 2008.
36. Howard Spodek, "In the Hindutva Laboratory: Pogroms and Politics in Gujarat, 2002," *Modern Asian Studies* 44, no. 2 (August 2010): 349–99.
37. See Christophe Jaffrelot, "Communal Riots in Gujarat: The State at Risk?" *Heidelberg Papers in South Asian and Comparative Politics* 17 (January 2003): 1–20; Parvis Ghassem-Fachandi, *Pogrom in Gujarat: Hindu Nationalism and Anti-Muslim Violence in India* (Princeton, NJ: Princeton University Press, 2012).
38. T. K. Oommen, *Reconciliation in Post-Godhra Gujarat: The Role of Civil Society* (Delhi: Pearson Longman, 2008), 64.
39. Oommen, *Reconciliation in Post-Godhra Gujarat*, 64.
40. Mushirul Hasan, "In Search of Integration and Identity: Indian Muslims Since Independence," *Economic and Political Weekly* 23, nos. 45/47 (November 1988): 2467–78.
41. Author interview with leading member of the delegation, October 11, 2008.
42. Raymond B. Williams, *A New Face of Hinduism: The Swaminarayan Religion* (Cambridge: Cambridge University Press, 1984).
43. McKinnon, *Toleration*, 14.
44. Author interview with president of the Trust, October 11, 2008.
45. Author interview with psychiatrist, October 11, 2008.

12. Sufi Sound, Sufi Space

1. *Qawwālī* is a form of Sufi ritual music characterized by verses with Islamic mystical themes, sung in a semi-classical Indian style. It is often sung by a group of male performers at Sufi shrines, accompanied by the harmonium, Indian twin drums (*tabla*), double-sided drums (*dhol*), and clapping.
2. *Qawwāls* are performers of *qawwālī*. They are usually male, though there are a few very well-known contemporary female singers. Singers often belong to *qawwāl* families in which the tradition of ritual performance is passed on generationally.
3. A *niqāb* is a veil worn to cover a woman's face.
4. Manmohan Desai, dir., *Amar Akbar Anthony*, with performances by Amitabh Bachchan and Rishi Kapoor (Hirawat Jain and Company, M.K.D. Films, and Manmohan Films, 1977), film.
5. Khalid Mohamed, dir., *Fiza*, with performances by Jaya Bhaduri, Karisma Kapoor, and Hrithik Roshan (The Culture Company and UTV Motion Pictures, 2000), film.

6. *Sherwānīs* are knee-length high-collared buttoned coats, commonly worn by men in many Muslim communities in South Asia, especially on formal occasions.
7. *Samāʿ* is a form of Sufi ritual practice, often translated as "ritual audition." It involves listening to sacred music as an act of worship, and as an aid to meditation and contemplation of the divine.
8. The only exception I could find was, interestingly, in the afore mentioned 1977 film, *Amar Akbar Anthony*. One of the *qawwālīs* that the protagonist, Akbar, sings is dedicated to the nineteenth-century Muslim figure Shirdi Sai Baba (now the focus of predominantly Hindu worship). However, the Sai Baba shrine in which the song is filmed is a set, and the interior of the shrine reflects contemporary Hindu worship of Sai Baba (with a garlanded idol of the mystic), rather than a tomb-centered Sufi courtyard.
9. For a discussion of the transplantation of *qawwālī* from its religious context to commercial music recordings, see Regula Qureshi, "'Muslim Devotional': Popular Religious Music and Muslim Identity Under British, Indian and Pakistani Hegemony," *Asian Music* 24, no. 1 (Autumn 1992/Winter 1993): 111–21. In this article Qureshi also outlines the ways in which certain forms of music and language became markers for "Muslim" in the production and marketing of these recordings.
10. Manish Jha, dir., *Anwar*, with performances by Nauheed Cyrusi and Siddharth Koirala (Dayal Creations, 2007), film.
11. The sixteenth-century poet-saint Meera was a devotee of Krishna. She is renowned for her sensual love poems to the deity, which beautifully render her unrequited love and steadfast devotion.
12. Ashutosh Gowariker, dir., *Jodhaa Akbar*, with performances by Hrithik Roshan and Aishwarya Rai Bachchan (Ashutosh Gowariker Productions and UTV Motion Pictures, 2008), film.
13. Rakesh Omprakash Mehra, dir., *Delhi-6*, with performances by Waheeda Rehman, Abhishek Bachchan, and Sonam Kapoor (Dillywood, Rakeysh Omprakash Mehra Pictures, and UTV Motion Pictures, 2009), film.
14. One prominent interreligious marriage is that of Hadiya and Shafin Jehan, who were compelled to make the case that Hadiya (a Hindu before her marriage to Shafin Jehan) entered into the relationship voluntarily and was not coerced into it or into conversion. The case made its way through the courts, and from 2017 to 2018 the Supreme Court of India ruled on various aspects of the case, in favor of the couple.
15. Srirupa Roy, *Beyond Belief: India and the Politics of Postcolonial Nationalism* (Durham, NC: Duke University Press, 2007), 15.
16. Roy, *Beyond Belief*, 15.
17. Peter Sutoris, *Visions of Development: Films Division of India and the Imagination of Progress, 1948–75* (New York: Oxford University Press, 2016).
18. Television broadcasting in India prior to 1982 was very limited in its availability and scope.
19. Purnima Mankekar, *Screening Culture, Viewing Politics: An Ethnography of Television, Womanhood, and Nation in Postcolonial India* (Durham, NC: Duke University Press, 1999).
20. Some examples of these are the iconic animated music video *Ek, Anek, aur Ekta* (1974), as well as the hugely popular *Ek Sur* (1988) (better known as *Mile Sur Mera Tumhara*) and *Baje Sargam Har Taraf Se* (1997). These pictorialized songs continue to be played on Doordarshan to the present day.
21. Mankekar, *Screening Culture, Viewing Politics*.

22. Kailash Surendranath, dir., *Ek Sur* (video on national integration). (Lok Sewa Sanchar Parishad, 1988), public service announcement for TV.
23. Mahmood Mamdani has discussed the ways in which certain forms of Muslim subjectivity are deemed as congruent with secular democracy and others as not. His work tackles this issue in terms of the United States. Mahmood Mamdani, *Good Muslim, Bad Muslim: America, the Cold War, and the Roots of Terror* (New York: Pantheon Books, 2004).
24. For the impact of television programming on, and its use for the cause of, Hindu nationalism, see Arvind Rajagopal, *Politics After Television: Religious Nationalism and the Reshaping of the Indian Public* (Cambridge: Cambridge University Press, 2001). Rajagopal analyzes the massively successful mythological TV serial *Ramayan*, produced by Doordarshan (a departure from its usual noninvolvement approach to religious themes) in the late 1980s as a pivotal point for the growth of Hindutva ideology in India.
25. The rise of Hindu nationalism as a political force can also be read as a response to the disillusionment with the state and its unmet promise of a diverse, yet integrated, India.
26. See Carla Bellamy, "Smoking Is Good for You: Absence, Presence, and the Ecumenical Appeal of Indian Islamic Healing Centers," *International Journal of Hindu Studies* 10, no. 2 (August 2006): 207–24; Carla Bellamy, *The Powerful Ephemeral: Everyday Healing in an Ambiguously Islamic Place* (Berkeley: University of California Press, 2011); Anna Bigelow, *Sharing the Sacred: Practicing Pluralism in Muslim North India* (Oxford: Oxford University Press, 2010); Rachana Rao Umashankar, "Metropolitan Microcosms: The Dynamic Spaces of Contemporary Sufi Shrines in India," *South Asian Studies* 31, no. 1 (2015): 127–43.
27. See Scott Kugle, "Qawwālī Between Written Poem and Sung Lyric, Or . . . How a Ghazal Lives," *Muslim World* 97, no. 4 (2007): 571–610; Qureshi, "'Muslim Devotional.'"
28. Scott Kugle, *When Sun Meets Moon: Gender, Eros, and Ecstasy in Urdu Poetry* (Chapel Hill: University of North Carolina Press, 2016); Annemarie Schimmel, *As Through a Veil: Mystical Poetry in Islam* (Oxford: Oneworld, 2001).
29. Supplicants at Indian Sufi shrines are indeed diverse in terms of the categories listed. However, this is not to say that these supplicants have *equal* access to the shrine space. During my work at Sufi shrines in New Delhi, Gulbarga, and Ajmer I found that hierarchies among supplicants were most evidently delineated by gender and class. In most major shrines, access to the tomb of the saint, which is the sanctum of the shrine, was denied to women. Also, as with most mosques in the subcontinent, men were given preference in using the mosque and courtyard of Sufi shrines for ritual prayer. Financial contributions to the shrine also ensured increased access to certain shrine spaces. See Carla Bellamy (chapter 10 in this volume) for a discussion of tensions arising from access (or lack thereof) to the shrine space for non-Muslim supplicants at smaller shrines.

Commentary on Part IV: Sufism in Indian National Spaces

1. For more on this saint complex, located in Madhya Pradesh, and how it relates to similar Muslim saint shrines through South Asia, see Carla Bellamy, *The Powerful Ephemeral* (Berkeley: University of California Press, 2011).
2. Helene Basu, dir., *Spirits of Envy: The Ethnographic Film* (Muenster: Cluster of Excellence "Religion and Politics," Muenster University, 2012), DVD.

3. See Rahul Bhatia, "The Year of Love Jihad in India," *The New Yorker*, December 31, 2017, https://www.newyorker.com/culture/2017-in-review/the-year-of-love-jihad-in-india.

Conclusion

1. For broader historical overviews of these dynamics, see Katherine Pratt Ewing's introduction to this volume and the commentaries by Carl Ernst, Muhammad Qasim Zaman, and SherAli Tareen.
2. For a detailed analysis of the drive to identify "good Muslims" absent the focus on Sufism, see Mahmood Mamdani, *Good Muslim, Bad Muslim: America, the Cold War, and the Roots of Terror* (New York: Penguin Press, 2005), with which many contributors to this volume are in conversation.
3. See Alix Philippon in chapter 8 of this volume for a discussion of such developments in Pakistan; Helene Basu in chapter 11 of this volume on Indian governmental attempts to render some Sufi traditions as culture rather than medical science (the province of the state); and Rosemary R. Corbett, *Making Moderate Islam: Sufism, Service, and the "Ground Zero Mosque" Controversy* (Stanford, CA: Stanford University Press, 2017), for how some Sufis in the United States came to replicate Turkish trends of presenting Sufism as apolitical culture.
4. See Corbett in chapter 1 of this volume, as well as Rosemary R. Hicks, "Comparative Religion and the Cold War Transformation of Indo-Persian Sufisms into Liberal Islamic Modernity," in *Secularism and Religion-Making*, ed. Markus Dressler and Arvind-Pal Singh Mandair (New York: Oxford University Press, 2011), 141–68; and Rosemary R. Corbett, "How the Rockefeller Foundation Shaped Islamic Studies While Avoiding 'Religion,'" in *The Politics of Philanthropy and Religion*, ed. Phillip Goff and David King (Bloomington: University of Indiana Press, forthcoming).
5. For more details on this dynamic, see Tareen's commentary on part 3 in this volume.
6. See Timothy Marr, *The Cultural Roots of American Islamicism* (New York: Cambridge University Press, 2006); Melani McAlister, *Epic Encounters: Culture, Media, and U.S. Interests in the Middle East Since 1945* (Berkeley: University of California Press, 2007); Thomas Kidd, *American Christians and Islam: Evangelical Culture and Muslims from the Colonial Period to the Age of Terrorism* (Princeton, NJ: Princeton University Press, 2009); Corbett, *Making Moderate Islam*; and Rosemary R. Corbett, "Protection," in *Religion, Law, U.S.A.*, ed. Joshua Dubler and Isaac Weiner (New York: New York University Press, 2019), 129–51.
7. On moderation as an imperative during the Reformation era, see Ethan H. Shagan, *The Rule of Moderation: Violence, Religion, and the Politics of Restraint in Early Modern England* (Cambridge: Cambridge University Press, 2011). On moderation as a shifting construct employed in some colonial engagements and, especially, over the course of American history, see Rosemary R. Corbett, "Moderation in American Religion" in *The Oxford Encyclopedia of Religion in America*, ed. John Corrigan (New York: Oxford University Press, 2018), 86–105.
8. On some of the forms of state enforcement of international religious moderation, see Elizabeth Shakman Hurd, *Beyond Religious Freedom: The New Global Politics of Religion* (Princeton, NJ: Princeton University Press, 2017).

   I find it crucial here to emphasize that, while contemporary ideas of and attempts to implement Muslim moderation are outgrowths and extensions in some ways of midcentury modernization campaigns, moderation is not synonymous with modernization. Moderation has a distinct intellectual and political history as a virtue deemed necessary to liberal political life (see note 7 above)—one that is premised on the status of the subject as a participant to some degree in the body politic. This notion of religio-political moderation became triangulated with neo-imperial modernization campaigns and applied to adherents of non-Christian traditions only in the mid-twentieth century. Prior to that, the perceived need was not to moderate non-Christians so as to make them productive, equal participants in global political and economic processes, it was to categorize, bureaucratize, and control or even exterminate them. Or, in perspectives deemed more progressive at the time, to convert and civilize them. After World War II, with the simultaneous expansion of postcolonial polities and of U.S.-based global industries (particularly, but not exclusively, the oil industry), North Americans and Europeans were again forced into dealing with Muslims as independent actors, rather than as colonial subjects, who were involved in critical political and economic developments. The impetus to moderate the influence of one Muslim constituency or another, one Muslim power or another, certainly predates the twentieth century. The impetus to moderate Muslims as individuals in order to redeem them for full (ostensibly) participation in a particular kind of political order is much more recent.

9. See Ernst, Ewing, and Meyer in this volume, as well as Corbett, "Comparative Religion."
10. Muhammad Iqbal, *The Reconstruction of Religious Thought in Islam*, new edition, ed. Saeed Sheikh (1930; Lahore: Lahore Institute of Islamic Culture, 1986), 188–89.
11. Notably, while some reformers—also operating in some relation to the ever-present pressure of proving their modernity and stripping Muslim societies of any signs of "backwardness"—insisted on the inauthenticity of Sufism altogether, other Muslims facing such pressures engaged not in attempts to "disenchant" Islam for the modern era, as Brian Bond so aptly puts it in chapter 6, but to ascertain just how enchanted it could remain and to what extent.
12. As I discuss in this volume, Rahman sought to pursue his Iqbal-inspired reformation project independently, but Smith undermined his application for independent funding and then recruited him to McGill (see Corbett, chapter 1).
13. For the Orientalist history of the supposed opposition between Sufis and fundamentalists, and how Rahman, Gibb, and Smith employed the term in ways quite different from what has since become common, see Rosemary R. Corbett, "Islamic 'Fundamentalism': The Mission Creep of an American Religious Metaphor," *Journal of the American Academy of Religion* 83, no. 4 (2015): 977–1004.

    Rahman presented his most expansive thoughts on the relationship between Sufis and fundamentalists in a study he had yet to finish at the time of his death, but that was later edited by Ebrahim Moosa into Fazlur Rahman, *Revival and Reform in Islam: A Study of Islamic Fundamentalism*, edited by Ebrahim Moosa (New York: Oneworld Publications, 1999). He first published his ideas on the Sufi-fundamentalist dialectic decades earlier, however, in a piece written for Bernard Lewis just after his years at McGill. See Fazlur Rahman, "Revival and Reform in Islam," in *Cambridge History of Islam*, Vol. 2B, *Islamic Society and Civilization*, ed. P. M. Holt, Ann K. S. Lambton, and Bernard Lewis (Cambridge: Cambridge University Press, 1970), 632–56.

    Regardless of whether Rahman independently decided to use the fundamentalist label perpetuated by Orientalists, there was no inevitably in this term's rise to prominence. Events transpiring in the United States just at the time Rahman adopted the American term would influence the weight and valences of this heuristic label, as would the continuing salience of Islam as a political ideology for some anti-colonial movements around the world, making it seem strategically useful to treat such out-of-context terms as "fundamentalist" not as metaphors but as matters of fact. See Corbett, "Islamic Fundamentalism"; David Harrington Watt, *Antifundamentalism in Modern America* (Ithaca, NY: Cornell University Press, 2017); and Simon Wood and David Harrington Watt's introduction to *Fundamentalisms: Perspectives on a Contested History*, ed. Simon Wood and David Harrington Watt (Columbia: University of South Carolina Press, 2014), 1–14.

14. Like the terms "Sufism" and "fundamentalist," the term "Wahhabi" is originally indebted to the logics of colonial encounter and definitionally freighted by political and economic interests. On the history of "Wahhabi," see Khalid Yahya Blankinship, "Muslim 'Fundamentalism,' Salafism, Sufism, and Other Trends," in *Fundamentalisms: Perspectives on a Contested History*, ed. Simon Wood and David Harrington Watt (Columbia: University of South Carolina Press, 2014), 144–62.

Glossary

abdāl: (pl. of *badal*) substitute; One of the levels in the Sufi hierarchical order of *awliyā*ʾ, who, unknown by the masses, participate in the preservation of the order of the universe by means of their powerful influence.

adhān: Announcement; the call to Friday prayers and the five daily prayers.

ʿaqīdah: Doctrine, dogma, or article of faith; *ʿaqāʾid* (pl.): articles of faith, creed.

ʿalam: Signpost, flag; in the early days of Islam, *ʿalams* were used as standards to represent individual tribes. Today they are often used by Shiʿi Muslims in religious processions.

ʿalim: Islamic legal scholar (pl. ulama).

anjuman: Society, association, or organization.

ʿĀshūrā: The tenth day of the first month (Muḥarram) of the Islamic calendar, when the Prophet Muḥammad's grandson Ḥusayn was martyred in Karbala. Shiʿi Muslims observe ʿĀshūrā as a day of mourning and lamentation in remembrance of Ḥusayn's sacrifice.

awqāf: Religious endowments, charitable trusts (s. *waqf*).

*awliyā*ʾ: Friends of God (s. *walī*).

āyat (pl. *āyāt*): A verse of the Quran.

bayʿah: A pledge of allegiance; formal initiation as a Sufi.

bidʿah: Innovation; in Islam, a belief or practice for which there is no precedent in the time of the Prophet, or has no roots in the traditional practice of the Muslim community. It can be classified into categories of good and bad, yet is mostly used to refer to practices deemed heretical.

chādar: Sheet; a large decorated cloth/fabric to be ceremonially laid over the grave of a religious/spiritual figure.

chehlum: The fortieth day after the death of an individual or important religious figure. Commonly used to refer to the fortieth day after ʿĀshūrā (day of martyrdom of Ḥusayn ibn ʿAlī), commemorated annually.

dargāh: A shrine that houses the tomb of a revered Muslim figure.

davā: Medicine.

duʿāʾ: Prayer.

fanāʾ: Annihilation, effacement; a stage of the development of the Sufi in the path of gnosis.

fiqh: Jurisprudence, the science of religious law in Islam.

gaddī nashīn: Hereditary caretaker of a shrine; a religious and administrative authority who tends to the *dargāh* of a *pīr* and leads Sufi rituals at the shrine.

hadith: A record of the sayings or customs of the Prophet Muḥammad and his Companions that is considered authoritative.

Ḥanafī: One of the Sunni Islamic schools of religious law, named after Abū Ḥanīfa al-Nuʿmān b. Thābit.

Ḥanbalī: The school of theology, law, and morality that grew up from the teaching of Aḥmad b. Ḥanbal.

ḥarām: That which has been forbidden by the Quran and/or sharia.

ʿibādah: The religious duties of worship incumbent on all Muslims when they come of age.

ijāzah: Authorization or permission from a respected scholar to be added to an existing chain of knowledge transmission.

ijtihād: Independent legal reasoning, one of four sources of Sunni law.

imām bārgāh: Enclosure of the imams; a term used in South Asia for the buildings where the Shiʿa assemble during Muḥarram and recite elegies on the martyrdom of Ḥusayn.

imāmbāṛā: See *imām bārgāh*.

īmān: Faith, belief in the metaphysical aspects of Islam.

ʿishāʾ: The nighttime prayer, one of the five compulsory daily prayers.

isnād: Chain of authorities through which a tradition/hadith is transmitted.

jamāʿat: A community-based association.

jinn: A being created by God from smokeless fire; mentioned in the Quran, along with angels and humans.

kāfī: A classical form of Sufi music, mostly in the Punjabi and Sindhi languages, and originating from the Punjab and Sindh regions of South Asia.

kufr: Disbelief/apostasy.

kyai: Teacher of Islamic sciences and community leader in traditionalist circles in Indonesia.

madhhab: A school of Islamic law. The Ḥanafī, Mālikī, Shāfiʿī, and Ḥanbalī schools are recognized by Sunni Muslims, and the Jaʿfarī and Zaydī schools are Shiʿi.

maghrib: One of the five daily prayers, offered soon after sunset.

maṣlaḥah: Utility; the term denotes "welfare" and is used by Islamic jurists to mean "general good" or "public interest."

maslak: A path or way; school of Islamic thought or law.

mātam: An act or gesture of mourning. In Shiʿi Islam, the term designates acts of lamentation for the martyrs of Karbala.

mawlid: Term for the time, place, or celebration of the birth of a person, especially that of the Prophet Muḥammad or of a saint.

muhājir: One who migrates; a term that has been applied to various groups in the course of Islamic history.

Muḥarram: First month of the Islamic calendar.

mushrik: One who recognizes the presence of any other divinity in addition to God.

nājāʾiz: (see *ḥarām*)

namāz: Obligatory ritual prayer offered five times a day; also known as *ṣalāt*.

nashīd: A piece of oratory, a chant, a hymn, and a form of vocal music.

nawḥah: Lamentation; the chanting of dirges, usually in remembrance of the Prophet's grandson Ḥusayn, who was martyred in Karbala on ʾĀshūrā.

naʿt: A panegyric poem in honor of the Prophet.

niyāz: Offering of food or other consumables made in the name of a religious figure, distributed among the people on a special occasion or presented to the visitors of a shrine.

pesantren: Islamic educational institution in Indonesia, comparable to the madrasa elsewhere in the Islamic world.

pīr: A Sufi leader and spiritual guide.

qawwāl: One who performs *qawwālī*.

qawwālī: A form of Sufi devotional music, notably popular in the Punjab and Sindh regions of Pakistan.

qirāʾat: Read or recite; often used to refer to the recitation of the Quran.

quṭb: Pole, axis; in Sufism, the perfect human being who heads the saintly hierarchy. (see also *walī*)

rusūmāt: (s. *rusm*) Rituals, customs.

samāʿ: Listening; a form of Sufi ritual practice that involves listening to sacred music as an aid to meditation and contemplation of the divine.

sanad: Support; a list of authorities who have transmitted hadith of a statement or action of the Prophet, one of his Companions, or a later authority. Its reliability determines the validity of a hadith.

sayyid: Title used for a direct descendant of the Prophet Muḥammad.
shahādah: To witness or to testify; the Islamic profession of faith "*Lā ilāha illa Allāh, Muḥammad Rasūl Allāh*," meaning "There is no god but Allah, Muḥammad is the Messenger of Allah."
shajarah: Tree; short for *shajarat al-nasab*, a family tree or pedigree chart.
shirk: The act of associating divinity with anyone other than God, for example, saint worship.
silsilah: Genealogical linkage; chain of spiritual succession.
taʿwīz: An amulet or locket usually containing verses from the Quran or other Islamic prayers and symbols, worn to protect a person from harm.
tablīgh: Proselytization.
tafsīr: Interpretation; Quranic exegesis.
taqrīr: A short talk or speech.
ṭarīqah: Way or path; a Sufi brotherhood or order.
taṣawwuf: The inward or spiritual dimension of Islam, usually translated as "Sufism."
tawḥīd: The act of believing and affirming that God is one and unique (*wāḥid*).
ʿurs: Commemoration of the death anniversary of an important religious/spiritual figure, which often takes the form of an annual festival at the shrine.
walī: A friend of God, or saint; a Sufi who is memorialized in hagiography and shrine visitation.
waqf: Religious endowment; Islamic institution of endowments or charitable trust (pl. *awqāf*).
zikr: A Sufi form of devotion involving the rhythmic repetition of the name of God or his attributes.
ziyārat: Pious visitation, pilgrimage to a holy place, tomb or shrine.

Bibliography

Abbas, Hassan. "Shi'ism and Sectarian Conflict in Pakistan: Identity Politics, Iranian Influence, and Tit-for-Tat Violence." Occasional Paper Series, West Point, NY, Combating Terrorism Center, September 22, 2010.

——. *The Taliban Revival: Violence and Extremism on the Pakistan-Afghanistan Border.* New Haven, CT: Yale University Press, 2014.

Abbas, Megan Brankley. "Knowing Islam: The Entangled History of Western Academia and Modern Islamic Thought." PhD diss., Princeton University, 2015.

Abeysekara, Ananda. "The Im-possibility of Secular Critique: The Future of Religion's Memory." *Culture and Religion* 11, no. 3 (2010): 213–46.

Agrama, Hussein Ali. "Ethics, Tradition, Authority: Toward an Anthropology of the Fatwa." *American Ethnologist* 37, no. 1 (2010): 2–18.

Ahmad, Irfan. *Islamism and Democracy in India: The Transformation of Jama'at-e Islami.* New Delhi: Permanent Black, 2010.

Ahmad, Mumtaz. "Media-Based Preachers and the Creation of New Muslim Publics in Pakistan," in *Who Speaks for Islam? Muslim Grassroots Leaders and Popular Preachers in South Asia.* NBR Special Report 22, February 2010, 1–28, http://www.nbr.org/publications/specialreport/pdf/Free/SR22.pdf.

Ahmed, Shahab. *What Is Islam? The Importance of Being Islamic.* Princeton, NJ: Princeton University Press, 2015.

Alam, Arshad. "The Enemy Within: Madrasa and Muslim Identity in North India." *Modern Asian Studies* 42, no. 2/3 (March–May 2008): 605–27.

——. *Inside a Madrasa: Knowledge, Power and Islamic Identity in India.* New Delhi: Routledge, 2011.

Alavi, Hamza. "Ethnicity, Muslim Society and the Pakistan Ideology." In *Islamic Reassertion in Pakistan,* edited by Anita M. Weiss, 21–48. Syracuse, NY: Syracuse University Press, 1986.

Allen, Matthew Harp. "Rewriting the Script for South Indian Dance." *TDR* 41, no. 3 (1997): 63–100.

Amin, Shahid. *Conquest and Community: The Afterlife of Warrior Saint Ghazi Miyan.* Chicago: University of Chicago Press, 2016.

Ansari, Sarah. *Life After Partition: Migration, Community and Strife in Sindh, 1947–1962.* Karachi: Oxford University Press, 2005.

——. *Sufi Saints and State Power: The Pirs of Sind, 1843–1947.* Cambridge: Cambridge University Press, 1992.

Arberry, Arthur John. *Sufism, An Account of the Mystics of Islam.* London: Allen & Unwin, 1950.

Asad, Talal. *Formations of the Secular: Christianity, Islam, Modernity.* Stanford: Stanford University Press, 2003.

——. "The Idea of an Anthropology of Islam." *Qui Parle* 17, no. 2 (2009 [1986]): 1–30. 10.5250/quiparle.17.2.1.

——. "Thinking About Tradition, Religion, and Politics in Egypt Today." *Critical Inquiry* 42, no. 1 (2015): 166–214.

Aubin-Boltanski, Emma. *Pèlerinages et Nationalisme en Palestine. Prophètes, héros et ancêtres.* Paris: Editions de l'EHESS, 2007.

Aʿẓamī, Allāmah ʿAbdul Mustafa. *Jannatī Zewar* [Urdu]. Delhi: Islamic Publisher, 2012. Originally published 1979.

——. *Jannatī Zewar* [Gujarati]. Translated by Sayyid Haji Ahmad Shah Haji Miyan Sahib Bukhari-Qadiri. Mandvi, Kachchh, Gujarat: Sayyid Anwar Shah Haji Ahmad Shah, 2014. Originally published 1986.

'Aẓamī, Muḥammad Ilyās. *Taḥaffuẓ-e k̲h̲aṭm-e nubuvat aur Shayk̲h̲ ul-islām Ḍākṭar Muḥammad Ṭāhir al-qādrī.* Lahore: Nūriyya Rizviyya Publications, 2010.

Azra, Azyumardi. *Menuju Masyarakat Madani: Gagasan, Fakta, Dan Tantangan.* Bandung, Indonesia: Penerbit PT Remaja Rosdakarya, 1999.

——. *The Origins of Islamic Reformism in Southeast Asia.* Honolulu: University of Hawai'i Press, 2004.

Baily, John. *"Can You Stop the Birds Singing?": The Censorship of Music in Afghanistan.* Copenhagen: Freemuse, 2001.

——. *War, Exile, and the Music of Afghanistan: The Ethnographer's Tale.* Burlington, VT: Ashgate, 2015.

Baje Sargam Har Taraf Se. Doordarshan, 1997. Short film for TV.

Barfield, Thomas. *Afghanistan: A Cultural and Political History.* Princeton, NJ: Princeton University Press, 2010.

Barrett, Paul. *American Islam: The Struggle for the Soul of a Religion.* New York: Picador, 2007.

Barton, Greg. "Indonesia's Nurcholish Madjid and Abdurrahman Wahid as Intellectual *Ulama*: The Meeting of Islamic Traditionalism and Modernism in Neo-Modernist Thought." *Islam and Christian-Muslim Relations* 8, no. 3 (1997): 323–50.

——. "Neo-Modernism: A Vital Synthesis of Traditionalist and Modernist Islamic Thought in Indonesia." *Studia Islamika—Indonesian Journal for Islamic Studies* 2, no. 3 (1995): 1–76.

Basu, Helene. "*Davā* and *Duā*: Negotiating Psychiatry and Ritual Healing of Madness." In *Asymmetrical Conversations: Contestations, Circumventions, and the Blurring of Therapeutic Boundaries,* edited by Harish H. Naraindas, Johannes Quack, and William S. Sax, 162–99. New York: Berghahn, 2014.

Basu, Helene, dir. *Spirits of Envy: The Ethnographic Film.* Muenster: Cluster of Excellence "Religion and Politics," Muenster University, 2012. DVD.

Bayart, Jean-François. *L'illusion identitaire.* Paris: Fayard, 1996.

Behuria, Ashok. *State Versus Nations in Pakistan: Sindhi, Baloch and Pukhtun Responses to Nation Building.* IDSA Monograph Series No. 43. New Delhi: Institute for Defence Studies and Analyses, January 2015. https://idsa.in/system/files/monograph/monograph43.pdf.

Bellamy, Carla. *The Powerful Ephemeral: Everyday Healing in an Ambiguously Islamic Place.* Berkeley: University of California Press, 2011.

——. "Smoking Is Good for You: Absence, Presence, and the Ecumenical Appeal of Indian Islamic Healing Centers." *International Journal of Hindu Studies* 10, no. 2 (August 2006): 207–24.

Benard, Cheryl. *Civil Democratic Islam: Partners, Resources, and Strategies.* Santa Monica, CA: RAND Corporation, 2003. https://www.rand.org/content/dam/rand/pubs/monograph_reports/2005/MR1716.pdf; and http://www.rand.org/pubs/monograph_reports/MR1716.html.

Benda, Harry J. *The Crescent and the Rising Sun: Indonesian Islam Under the Japanese Occupation, 1942–1945.* The Hague and Bandung: W. van Hoeve, 1958.

Berry, Donald L. "Fazlur Rahman: A Life in Review." In *The Shaping of an American Islamic Discourse: A Memorial to Fazlur Rahman*, edited by Earle H. Waugh and Frederick M. Denny, 37–48. Atlanta, GA: Scholars Press, 1998.

Bhargava, Rajeev. *Secularism and Its Critics.* Themes in Politics. Delhi: Oxford University Press, 1998.

Bhatia, Rahul. "The Year of Love Jihad in India." *The New Yorker.* December 31, 2017. https://www.newyorker.com/culture/2017-in-review/the-year-of-love-jihad-in-india.

Bigelow, Anna. *Sharing the Sacred: Practicing Pluralism in Muslim North India.* Oxford: Oxford University Press, 2010.

Bilgrami, Akeel. *Secularism, Identity, and Enchantment.* Cambridge, MA: Harvard University Press, 2014.

Blankinship, Khalid Yahya. "Muslim 'Fundamentalism,' Salafism, Sufism, and Other Trends." In *Fundamentalisms: Perspectives on a Contested History*, edited by Simon Wood and David Harrington Watt, 144–62. Columbia: University of South Carolina Press, 2014.

Bocquérat, Gilles, and Nazir Hussain. "Enlightened Moderation: Relevance of New Paradigm in the Face of Radical Islam." Unpublished and undated paper.

Boissevain, Katia, and Cyril Isnart. "Tourisme, patrimoine et religions en Méditerranée. Usages culturels du religieux dans le catholicisme et l'islam contemporains (Europe du Sud-Maghreb)." *Mélanges de l'École française de Rome—Italie et Méditerranée modernes et contemporaines* 129, no. 1 (September 2017). http://journals.openedition.org/mefrim/3423.

Braud, Philippe. *L'émotion en politique.* Paris: Presses de la Fondation Nationale des Science-Politiques, 1996.

Brown, Vahid, and Don Rassler, *Fountainhead of Jihad: The Haqqani Nexus, 1973–2012.* New York: Oxford University Press, 2013.

Bukharī, ʿAbd al-Wāhid. *Shaykh Ḥusain Aḥmad Madanī, ek shakhsiyat, ek muṭālaʿa.* Gujrat: Maktaba-yi Ẓafar, 1972.

Bukhārī, Muḥammad Akbar Shāh. *Akābir-e 'Ulamā-yi Deoband.* Karachi: Idāra-yi Islāmiyya, 1999.

Bulliet, Richard W. *Islam: The View from the Edge.* New York: Columbia University Press, 1994.

Buxton, William, J. "John Marshall and the Humanities in Europe: Shifting Patterns of Rockefeller Foundation Support." *Minerva* 41, no. 2 (June 2003): 133–53.

Camau, Michel, and Vincent Geisser. *Le syndrome autoritaire. Politique en Tunisie de Bourguiba à Ben Ali.* Paris: Presses de Sciences Po, 2003.

Caron, James. "Sufism and Liberation Across the Indo-Afghan Border: 1880–1928." *South Asian History and Culture* 7, no. 2 (2016): 135–54.

Casanova, John. "Rethinking Secularization: A Global Comparative Perspective." In *Religion, Globalization, and Culture*, edited by Peter Beyer and Lori Beaman, 101–20. Leiden: Brill, 2007.

Cheesman, David. *Landlord Power and Rural Indebtedness in Colonial Sind, 1865–1901.* Richmond, Surrey, UK: Curzon, 1997.

Chittick, William C. *The Sufi Path of Knowledge: Ibn al-'Arabi's Metaphysics of Imagination.* Albany: State University of New York Press, 1989.

Corbett, Rosemary, R. "Comparative Religion and the Cold War Transformation of Indo Persian 'Mysticism' into Liberal Islamic Modernity." In *Secularism and Religion-Making*, edited by Markus Dressler and Arvind Manadir, 141–69. New York: Oxford University Press, 2011.

——. "How the Rockefeller Foundation Shaped Islamic Studies While Avoiding 'Religion.'" In *The Politics of Religion and Philanthropy*, edited by Phillip Goff and David King. Bloomington: University of Indiana Press, forthcoming.

——. "Islamic 'Fundamentalism': The Mission Creep of an American Religious Metaphor." *Journal of the American Academy of Religion* 83, no. 4 (December 2015): 977–1004.

——. *Making Moderate Islam: Sufism, Service, and the "Ground Zero Mosque" Controversy.* Stanford, CA: Stanford University Press, 2017.

——. "Moderation in American Religion." In *The Oxford Encyclopedia of Religion in America*, ed. John Corrigan, 86–105. New York: Oxford University Press, 2018.

——. "Protection." In *Religion, Law, U.S.A.*, edited by Joshua Dubler and Isaac Weiner, 129–51. New York: New York University Press, 2019.

Cossman, Brenda, and Ratna Kapur. "Secularism's Last Sigh?: The Hindu Right, the Courts, and India's Struggle for Democracy." *Harvard International Law Journal* 38, no. 1 (October 1997): 113–70.

Dallal, Ahmad, S. *Islam Without Europe: Traditions of Reform in Eighteenth-Century Islamic Thought.* Chapel Hill: University of North Carolina Press, 2018.

Dandekar, Deepra, and Torsten Tschacher. "Introduction." In *Islam, Sufism, and Everyday Politics of Belonging in South Asia*, edited by Deepra Dandekar and Torsten Tschacher, 1–15. Milton Park, UK: Taylor and Francis, 2016.

Das, Ira. *Staat und Religion in Indien: Eine rechtswissenschaftliche Untersuchung.* Tübingen: Mohr Siebeck, 2004.

Das, Suranjan. *Kashmir and Sindh: Nation-Building, Ethnicity and Regional Politics in South Asia.* London: Anthem Press, 2001.

Davar, Bhargavi. "Justice at Erwadi." In *The Law of Possession: Ritual, Healing, and the Secular State*, edited by William Sax and Helene Basu, 117–37. New York: Oxford University Press, 2015.

Desai, Manmohan, dir. *Amar Akbar Anthony.* Performances by Amitabh Bachchan and Rishi Kapoor. Hirawat Jain and Company, M.K.D. Films, and Manmohan Films, 1977. Film.

Diagne, Souleymane Bachir. "Bergson et la pensée de LS Senghor." *La lettre du Collège de France* 29 (2010): 10–11.

Dochuck, Darren. *Anointed with Oil: How Christianity and Crude Made Modern America.* New York: Basic Books, 2019.

Dols, Michael. *Majnun: The Madman in Medieval Islamic Society.* Oxford: Clarendon Press, 1992.

Donner, Henrike, ed. *Being Middle-Class in India: A Way of Life.* London: Routledge, 2011.

Drage, Teresa Ann. "The National Sufi Council: Redefining the Islamic Republic of Pakistan Through a Discourse on Sufism after 9/11." PhD dissertation, Western Sydney University, 2015.

During, Jean. "Hearing and Understanding the Islamic Gnosis." *World of Music* 39, no. 2 (1997): 127–37.

Eaton, Richard M. "Sufi Folk Literature and the Expansion of Indian Islam." *History of Religions* 14, no. 2 (1974): 117–27.

Eck, Diana. *India: A Sacred Geography.* New York: Harmony Books, 2012.

Eickelman, Dale, and James Piscatori. *Muslim Politics.* Princeton, NJ: Princeton University Press, 1996.

Elias, Jamal. "Un/Making Idolatry: From Mecca to Bamiyan." *Future Anterior: Journal of Historic Preservation* 4, no. 2 (2007): 2–29.

Elson, R. E. "Another Look at the Jakarta Charter Controversy of 1945." *Indonesia* 88 (2009): 105–30.

Epping, Ethan. "Politics and Pirs: The Nature of Sufi Political Engagement in 20th and 21st Century Pakistan." *Pakistaniyaat: A Journal of Pakistan Studies* 5, no. 3 (2013): 1–25.

Ernst, Carl W. "The *Dabistān* and Orientalist Views of Sufism." In *Sufism East and West: Reorientation and Dynamism of Mystical Islam in the Modern World*, edited by Jamal Malik and Saeed Zarrabi-Zadeh, 33–52. Leiden: Brill, 2018.

——. "Early Orientalist Concepts of Sufism." In *It's Not Just Academic! Essays on Sufism and Islamic Studies*, 463–82. New Delhi: SAGE Publications India/Yoda Press.

——. *It's Not Just Academic! Essays on Sufism and Islamic Studies.* New Delhi: SAGE Publications India/Yoda Press, 2017.

——. *The Shambhala Guide to Sufism.* Boston: Shambhala, 1997.

——. *Sufism: An Introduction to the Mystical Tradition of Islam.* Boston: Shambhala, 2011.

Eteraz, Ali. "State Sponsored Sufism: Why Are US Think Tanks Pushing for State-Sponsored Sufism in Pakistan?" *Foreign Policy*, June 10, 2009, https://foreignpolicy.com/2009/06/10/state-sponsored-sufism/.

Ewing, Katherine Pratt. *Arguing Sainthood: Modernity, Psychoanalysis, and Islam.* Durham, NC: Duke University Press, 1997.

——. "Creating New Sufi Publics at an Old Sufi Shrine." Rethinking Public Religion: Word, Image, Sound. *The Immanent Frame*, SSRC, June 11, 2019. https://tif.ssrc.org/2019/06/11/creating-new-sufi-publics-at-an-old-sufi-shrine/?fbclid=IwAR37GMvMZNpEpa5ePc53Gh_2OZg61Q2BBZ0Dg4flni4gmcV9Kb7rY8Gk1fc

——. "The Misrecognition of a Modern Islamist Organization: Germany Faces 'Fundamentalism.'" In *From Orientalism to Cosmopolitanism: Changing Approaches to Islamic Studies*, edited by Carl W. Ernst and Richard C. Martin, 52–71. Columbia: University of South Carolina Press, 2010.

——. "The Politics of Sufism: Redefining the Saints of Pakistan." *Journal of Asian Studies* 42, no. 2 (February 1983): 251–68.

——. *Sharīʿat and Ambiguity in South Asian Islam.* Berkeley: University of California Press, 1998.

Farah, Sumbul. "Piety and Politics in Local Level Islam: A Case Study of Barelwi Khanqahs." PhD diss., University of Delhi, 2013.

Farīd, Muftī Muḥammad. *Fatāwā-e Farīdiyya.* Edited by Muḥammad Wahhāb Manglorī. 7 vols. Zarobi: Dār al-ʿUlūm Ṣiddīqiyya, 2013.

Flood, Finbarr Barry. "Between Cult and Culture: Bamiyan, Islamic Iconoclasm, and the Museum." *Art Bulletin* 84, no. 4 (2002): 641–59.

Flueckiger, Joyce Burkhalter. *In Amma's Healing Room: Gender and Vernacular Islam in South India.* Bloomington: Indiana University Press, 2006.

Foltz, Richard. "The Central Asian Naqshbandī Connections of the Mughal Emperors." *Journal of Islamic Studies* 7, no. 2 (1996): 229–39.

Formichi, Chiara. *Islam and the Making of the Nation: Kartosuwiryo and Political Islam in 20th Century Indonesia.* Leiden: KITLV Press, 2012.

Foucault, Michel. *The Use of Pleasure*. Vol. 2 of *The History of Sexuality*. New York: Random House, 1985.

Gaborieau, Marc. "Criticizing the Sufis: The Debate in Early-Nineteenth Century India." In *Islamic Mysticism Contested: Thirteen Centuries of Controversies and Polemics*, edited by Frederick de Jong and Bernd Radtke, 452–67. Leiden: Brill, 1999.

Geaves, Ronald. "The Contested Milieu of Deoband: 'Salafis' or 'Sufis?' " In *Sufis and Salafis in the Contemporary Age*, edited by Lloyd Ridgeon, 191–216. London: Bloomsbury Academic, 2015.

——. "Transformations and Trends Among British Sufis." In *Sufism in Britain*, edited by Ronald Geaves and Theodore Gabriel, 47–51. London: Bloomsbury Academic, 2014.

——. "Who Defines Moderate Islam 'Post'-September 11?" In *Islam and the West, Post 9/11*, edited by Ron Geaves, Yvonne Haddad, and Jane Idelman Smith, 62–74. Burlington, VT: Ashgate, 2004.

Geertz, Clifford. *The Interpretation of Cultures*. New York: Basic Books, 1973.

——. *Islam Observed: Religious Development in Morocco*. Chicago: University of Chicago Press, 1971. First published 1968.

——. "Religion as a Cultural System." In *Anthropological Approaches to the Study of Religion*, edited by Michael Banton, 1–46. London: Routledge, 1966.

——. "Suq: the Bazaar Economy in Sefrou." In *Meaning and Order in Moroccan Society: Three Essays in Cultural Analysis*, edited by Clifford Geertz, Hildred Geertz, and Laurence Rosen, 123–276. Cambridge: Cambridge University Press, 1979.

Gesink, Indira Falk. " 'Chaos on the Earth': Subjective Truths Versus Communal Unity in Islamic Law and the Rise of Militant Islam." *American Historical Review* 108, no. 3 (2003): 710–33.

Ghassem-Fachandi, Parvis. *Pogrom in Gujarat: Hindu Nationalism and Anti-Muslim Violence in India*. Princeton, NJ: Princeton University Press, 2012.

Gibb, H. A. R. *Modern Trends in Islam*. Chicago: University of Chicago, 1947.

Gilmartin, David. *Empire and Islam: Punjab and the Making of Pakistan*. Berkeley: University of California Press, 1988.

——. "Shrines, Succession, and Sources of Moral Authority." In *Moral Conduct and Authority: The Place of Adab in South Asian Islam*, edited by Barbara D. Metcalf, 221–40. Berkeley: University of California Press, 1984.

Gottschalk, Peter. *Beyond Hindu and Muslim: Multiple Identity in Narratives from Village India*. Oxford: Oxford University Press, 2005.

Gowariker, Ashutosh, dir. *Jodhaa Akbar*. With performances by Hrithik Roshan and Aishwarya Rai Bachchan. Ashutosh Gowariker Productions. and UTV Motion Pictures, 2008. Film.

Green, Nile. *Bombay Islam: The Religious Economy of the West Indian Ocean, 1840–1915*. Cambridge: Cambridge University Press, 2011.

——. *Islam and the Army in Colonial India: Sepoy Religion in the Service of Empire*. Cambridge: Cambridge University Press, 2009.

——. *Sufism: A Global History*. Oxford: Wiley-Blackwell, 2012.

Gribetz, Arthur. "The *Samāʿ* controversy: Sufi vs. Legalist." *Studia Islamica* 74 (1991): 43–62.

Gugler, Thomas K. "Barelwis: Developments and Dynamics of Conflict with Deobandis." In *Sufis and Salafis in the Contemporary Age*, edited by Lloyd Ridgeon, 171–89. London: Bloomsbury Academic, 2015.

Gupta, R. C., ed. *Panjab Notes and Queries: A Monthly Periodical*. Vol. 1. Allahabad: Pioneer Press, 1883–84.

Habib, Muhammad Rafiq. "A Critical Analysis of the Ideology of Dr. Muhammad Tahir-ul-Qadri with Special Reference to Islamic Revivalism." PhD diss., University of Aberdeen, 2012.

Hallaq, Wael B. *Sharīʿa: Theory, Practice, Transformations*. Cambridge: Cambridge University Press, 2009.

Hamka. *Tasauf Modern*. Jakarta: Republika Penerbit, 2015. Originally published 1939.

Hansen, Thomas Blom, and Christophe Jaffrelot, eds. *The BJP and the Compulsions of Politics in India*. New Delhi: Oxford University Press, 2001.

Haq, Samiul. *Afghan Taliban: War of Ideology, Struggle for Peace*. Islamabad: Emel Publications, 2015.

——. *Islāmī Muʿāshira ke Lāzimī Khad o Khāl*. 2 vols. Nowshera: Al-Qāsim Academy, n.d.

——. *Qādiyān se Israil tak*. Akora Khattak, n.p., 1978.

——. *Qur'an aur Taʿmīr-e Akhlāq*. Akora Khattak: Maktaba al-Ḥaqq, 1984.

Haq, Samiul, and ʿAbd al-Qayyūm Ḥaqqānī, eds. *Ṣalībī Dehshatgardī aur ʿAlām al-Islām*. Akora Khattak: Dār al-ʿUlūm Ḥaqqāniyya, 2004.

Haq, Samiul, and Iṣlāḥ al-Dīn Ḥaqqānī, eds. *Zain al-Mahāfil: Sharḥ al-Shamāʾil li Imām al-Tirmidhī*. Lahore: Al-Matbaʿ al-ʿArabiyya, 2007.

Haq, Samiul, and Muḥammad Taqī ʿUsmānī, *Qādiyānī Fitna aur Millat-e Islāmiyya ka Mawqif*. London: Khatm-e Nubuwwat Academy, 2005.

Haq, Syed Noumanul. "Occult Sciences and Medicine." In *The New Cambridge History of Islam*, edited by Michael Cook, 640. Cambridge: Cambridge University Press, 2010.

Ḥaqq, ʿAbd al-, ed. *Ṣuḥbat-e ba Ahl-e Ḥaqq*. By ʿAbd al-Qayyūm Ḥaqqānī. Nowshera: Idāra al-ʿIlm wa-l Taḥqīq, 1998.

——, et al. *Fatāwā-e Ḥaqqāniyya*. Edited by Mukhtār Allāh Ḥaqqānī et al. 6 vols. Akora Khattak: Jāmiʿa Dār al-ʿUlūm Ḥaqqāniyya, 2002.

Haqqani, Hussain. *Pakistan: Between Mosque and Military*. Washington, DC: Carnegie Endowment for International Peace, 2005.

Haroon, Sana. *Frontier of Faith: Islam in the Indo-Afghan Borderland*. New York: Columbia University Press, 2007.

Hasan, Mushirul. "In Search of Integration and Identity: Indian Muslims Since Independence." *Economic and Political Weekly* 23, nos. 45/47 (November 1988): 2467–78.

Hasan, Syed Masroor. "Waqf Land Grab Exposed: India's Biggest Land Scam." *India Today*, September 19, 2017. https://www.indiatoday.in/india/story/waqf-land-grab-scam-muslim-charitable-assets-1048007-2017-09-19.

Hashmi, Masood. *Makhdūma Bībī Ruqayyah Bint ʿAlī: Bībī Pak Dāmana Lahore Meiñ*. Lahore: Al-Fazi Publications, 1990.

Hawley, John Stratton. *A Storm of Songs: India and the Idea of the Bhakti Movement*. Cambridge, MA: Harvard University Press, 2015.

Hefner, Robert. *Civil Islam: Muslims and Democratization in Indonesia*. Princeton, NJ: Princeton University Press, 2000.

Hendrich, Béatrice. "Introduction—Beyond State Islam: Religiosity and Spirituality in Contemporary Turkey." *European Journal of Turkish Studies* 13 (December 2011): 1–15. http://ejts.revues.org/4527.

Hermansen, Marcia. "American Sufis and American Islam: From Private Spirituality to the Public Sphere." In *Islamic Movements and Islam in the Multicultural World: Islamic Movements and Formation of Islamic Ideologies in the Information Age*, edited by Denis Brilyov, 189–208. Kazan: Russian Federation, Kazan Federal University Publishing House, 2014.

Hervieu-Léger, Danièle. "Religion as a Grammar of Memory: Reflections on a Comparison Between Britain and France." In *Modernities, Memories and Mutations: Grace Davie and the Study of Religion*, edited by Abbi Day and Mia Lövheim, 13–30. New York: Routledge, 2015.

Hicks, Rosemary R. "Comparative Religion and the Cold War Transformation of Indo-Persian 'Mysticism' into Liberal Islamic Modernity." In *Secularism and Religion-Making*, edited by Markus Dressler and Arvind Manadir, 141–68. New York: Oxford University Press, 2011.

Hirschkind, Charles. *The Ethical Soundscape: Cassette Sermons and Islamic Counterpublics*. New York: Columbia University Press, 2006.

Hodgson, Marshall. *The Venture of Islam, Conscience and History in a World Civilization*. 3 vols. Chicago: University of Chicago Press, 1974.

Howell, Julia Day. "Indonesia's Salafist Sufis." *Modern Asian Studies* 44, no. 5 (2010): 1029–51.

——. "Sufism and Neo-Sufism in Indonesia Today." *Review of Indonesian and Malaysian Affairs* 46, no. 2 (2012): 1–24.

Hourani, Albert. "Rashid Rida and the Sufi Orders: A Footnote to Laoust." *Bulletin d'études orientales* 29 (1977): 231–41.

Hujwīrī, ʿAlī B. Uthmān al-Jullābī al- *Kashf al-Maḥjūb* [Persian]. Edited by Valentine Zhukovski and Muḥammad 'Abbāsī. Tehran: Amīr Kabīr, 1964.

——. *Kashf al-Maḥjūb of Al Hujwiri: The Oldest Persian Treatise on Sufism*. Translated by Reynold A. Nicholson. London: Gibb Memorial Trust, 1976 [1911].

——. *Kashf al-Maḥjūb* [Urdu]. Translated by Hazrat Allāma Fazluddīn Gohar. Lahore: Zīā al-Qurān Publications, 2010.

Hurd, Elizabeth Shakman. *Beyond Religious Freedom: The New Global Politics of Religion*. Princeton, NJ: Princeton University Press, 2017.

Hyder, Syed Akbar. *Reliving Karbala: Martyrdom in South Asian Memory*. New York: Oxford University Press, 2006.

Ibrahim, Farhana. *Settlers, Saints, and Sovereigns: An Ethnography of State Formation in Western India*. New Delhi: Routledge, 2008.

Imdādullah al-Makki, Ḥājjī. *Kulliyāt-e Imdādiyya*. Karachi: Dār al-Ishaʿāt, 1977.

Ingram, Brannon D. "Crises of the Public in Muslim India: Critiquing 'Custom' at Aligarh and Deoband." *South Asia: Journal of South Asian Studies* 38, no. 3 (2015): 403–18.

——. "The Portable Madrasa: Print, Publics, and the Authority of the Deobandi Ulama." *Modern Asian Studies* 48, no. 4 (July 2014): 845–71.

——. *Revival from Below: The Deoband Movement and Global Islam*. Oakland: University of California Press, 2018.

Iqbal, Javid. *The Ideology of Pakistan and Its Implementation*. Lahore: Ghulam Ali, 1959.

Iqbal, Mohammad. *The Reconstruction of Religious Thought in Islam*. New edition. Edited by Saeed Sheikh. Lahore: Lahore Institute of Islamic Culture, 1986. Originally published 1930.

——. *Thoughts and Reflections of Iqbal*, edited by Syed Abdul Vahid. Lahore: Sh. Muhammad Ashraf, 1964.

Jaffrelot, Christophe. "Communal Riots in Gujarat: The State at Risk?" *Heidelberg Papers in South Asian and Comparative Politics* 17 (January 2003): 1–20.

Jairazbhoy, Nazir A. "Music in Western Rajasthan: Stability and Change." *Yearbook of the International Folk Music Council* 9 (1977): 50–66.

Jenkins, Philip. "Clerical Terror." *New Republic*, December 24, 2008. https://newrepublic.com/article/61223/clerical-terror

Jha, Manish, dir. *Anwar*. With performances by Nauheed Cyrusi and Siddharth Koirala. Dayal Creations, 2007. Film.

Kersten, Carool. *Cosmopolitans and Heretics: New Muslim Intellectuals and the Study of Islam*. New York: Columbia University Press, 2011.

Khabeer, Su'ad Abdul. *Muslim Cool: Race, Religion, and Hip Hop in the United States.* New York: New York University Press, 2016.

Khaki, Masood Raza. *Bībiañ Pāk Dāman.* Lahore: Haidri Press, 1998.

Khan, Adeel. *Politics of Identity: Ethnic Nationalism and the State in Pakistan.* London: Sage, 2005.

Khān, Aḥmad Rażā. *Mālfūẓāt-e Aʿla Ḥażrat.* Vol. 2. Gujarat, Pakistan: Fazl-i Nūr Academy, n.d.

Khan, Naveeda. *Muslim Becoming: Aspiration and Skepticism in Pakistan.* Durham, NC: Duke University Press, 2012.

Kharal, Muḥammad Nawāz, ed. *Mutanāziʿah tarīn shakhṣiyyat: Professor Ṭāhir ul-Qādrī kī shakhṣiyyat kā tanqīdī jāʾiza.* Lahore: Fateh Publishers, 2002.

Kidd, Thomas. *American Christians and Islam: Evangelical Culture and Muslims from the Colonial Period to the Age of Terrorism.* Princeton, NJ: Princeton University Press, 2009.

Kiernan, V. G., trans. *Poems from Iqbal.* London: John Murray, 1955.

Kindley, Evan. "Big Criticism." *Critical Inquiry* 38, no. 1 (Autumn 2011): 71–95.

Kothari, Rita. *Memories and Movements: Borders and Communities in Banni, Kutch, Gujarat.* New Delhi: Orient Blackswan, 2013.

Kugle, Scott. "Qawwali Between Written Poem and Sung Lyric, Or . . . How a Ghazal Lives." *Muslim World* 97, no. 4 (2007): 571–610.

——. *Sufis and Saints' Bodies: Mysticism, Corporeality, and Sacred Power in Islam.* Chapel Hill: University of North Carolina Press, 2007.

——. *When Sun Meets Moon: Gender, Eros, and Ecstasy in Urdu Poetry.* Chapel Hill: University of North Carolina Press, 2016.

Kull, Ann. *Piety and Politics: Nurcholish Madjid and His Interpretation of Islam in Modern Indonesia.* Lund: Department of History and Anthropology of Religion, Lund University, 2005.

Laffan, Michael. *Islamic Nationhood and Colonial Indonesia: The Umma Below the Winds.* New York: Routledge, 2002.

Lapidus, Ira. "Islamic Revival and Modernity: The Contemporary Movements and the Historical Paradigms." *Journal of the Economic and Social History of the Orient* 40, no. 4 (1997): 444–60.

Latour, Bruno. *On the Modern Cult of Factish Gods.* Durham, NC: Duke University Press. 2010.

——. *We Have Never Been Modern.* Cambridge, MA: Harvard University Press, 1991.

Lauzi, Henri. *The Making of Salafism: Islamic Reform in the Twentieth Century.* New York: Columbia University Press, 2016.

Lawrence, Bruce B. *Defenders of God: The Fundamentalism Revolt Against the Modern Age.* San Francisco: Harper and Row, 1989.

——. "Sufism and Neo-Sufism." In *The New Cambridge History of Islam,* edited by Robert W. Hefner, 355–84. Cambridge: Cambridge University Press, 2010. doi:10.1017/CHOL9780521844437.016.

Lewisohn, Leonard. "The Sacred Music of Islam: Samāʿ in the Persian Sufi Tradition." *British Journal of Ethnomusicology* 6, no. 1 (1997): 1–33.

Levtzion, Nehemia. "The Dynamics of Sufi Brotherhoods." In *The Public Sphere in Muslim Societies,* edited by Miriam Hoexter, Shmuel N. Eisenstadt, and Nehemia Levtzion, 109–18. Albany: State University of New York Press, 2002.

Levtzion, Nehemia, and John O. Voll, eds. *Eighteenth-Century Renewal and Reform in Islam.* Syracuse, NY: Syracuse University Press, 1987.

Liebskind, Claudia. *Piety on Its Knees: Three Sufi Traditions of South Asia in Modern Times.* New Delhi: Oxford University Press, 1998.

Lieven, Anatol. *Pakistan: A Hard Country.* New York: Public Affairs, 2011.

Love, Nancy, S. "Anti-, Neo-, Post-, and Proto—: Conservative Hybrids, Ironic Reversals, and Global Terror(ism)." *New Political Science* 31, no. 4 (December 2009): 443–59.

Madan, T. N., ed. *Images of the World: Essays on Religion, Secularism, and Culture*. New Delhi: Oxford University Press, 2006.

——. "Secularism in India: Predicaments and Prospects." In *Images of the World: Essays on Religion, Secularism, and Culture*, edited by T. N. Madan, 74–112. New Delhi: Oxford University Press, 2006.

Madjid, Nurcholish. *Islam: Doktrin dan Peradaban*. Jakarta: Paramadina, 1992.

——. "Islamic Roots of Modern Pluralism: Indonesian Experiences." *Studia Islamika—Indonesian Journal for Islamic Studies* 1, no. 1 (1994): 55–77.

——. "Pondok Pesantren 'Darul 'Ulum' di Rejoso, Peterongan, Jombang, Jawa Timur." In *Bulletin Proyek Penelitian Agama dan Perubahan Sosial*, 53–66. Jakarta: Lembaga Ekonomi dan Kemasyarakatan Nasional, 1977.

——. "Sufisme Baru dan Sufisme Lama: Masalah Kontinuitas dan Perkembangan dalam Esoterisme Islam," in *Sufisme dan Masa Depan Agama*, edited by Djohan Effendi, 93–114. Jakarta: Pustaka Firdaus, 1993.

——. "Tasauf dan Pesantren," in *Pesantren dan Pembaharuan*, edited by M. Dawam Rahardjo, 95–120. Jakarta: LP3ES, 1988. Originally published 1974.

——. "Tasawuf sebagai Inti Keberagamaan." *Pesantren* 2, no. 3 (1985): 3–9.

——. *The True Face of Islam: Essays on Islam and Modernity in Indonesia*. Ciputat: Voice Center Indonesia, 2003.

Mahkama Auqaf. *Fihrist-ei aʿras-i māzārāt zir tahawwul Mahkama Auqaf Panjāb* . Lahore, n.d., 9.

Mahmood, Saba. *Politics of Piety: The Islamic Revival and the Feminist Subject*. Princeton, NJ: Princeton University Press, 2005.

——. *Religious Difference in a Secular Age: A Minority Report*. Princeton, NJ: Princeton University Press, 2015.

Mahmood, Tahir. "Interaction of Islam and Public Law in India." In *Perspectives on Islamic Law, Justice and Society*, edited by Ravindra S. Khare, 93–122. Lanham, MD: Rowman & Littlefield, 1999.

Makdisi, George. "Ibn Taimiya: A Sufi of the Qadiriya Order." *American Journal of Arabic Studies* 1 (1973): 118–29.

Makki, Mawlana ʿAbd al-Hafiz al-. "Shaykh al-Islam Ibn Taymiyyah and Sufism (Part One)." Translated by Ismaeel Nakhuda. September 20, 2015. https://www.deoband.org/2015/09/tasawwuf/shariah-and-tariqah-tasawwuf/shaykh-al-islam-ibn-taymiyyah-and-sufism-part-one/. Accessed July 28, 2019.

Malik, S. Jamal. "The Luminous Nurani: Charisma and Political Mobilization Among the Barelwis in Pakistan." *Social Analysis: The International Journal of Social and Cultural Practice* 28 (July1990): 38–50.

——. "Waqf in Pakistan: Change in Traditional Institutions." *Die Welt des Islams* n. s. 30, no. 1 (1990): 63–97.

Malik, S. Jamal, and John Hinnells, eds. *Sufism in the West*. New York: Routledge, 2006.

Malik, Mohammad Latif. *Aulia-e-Lahore*. Lahore: Sang-e-Meel Publishers, 1932.

Malinar, Angelika. "Hinduismus und Religionsfreiheit." In *Religionsfreiheit: Positionen—Konflikte—Herausforderungen*, edited by Hans-Georg Ziebertz, 183–209. Würzburg: Echter, 2015.

Mamdani, Mahmood. *Good Muslim, Bad Muslim: America, the Cold War, and the Roots of Terror*. New York: Pantheon Books, 2004.

——. "Good Muslim, Bad Muslim: A Political Perspective on Culture and Terrorism." *American Anthropologist* 104, no. 3 (2002): 766–75.

Mankekar, Purnima. *Screening Culture, Viewing Politics: An Ethnography of Television, Womanhood, and Nation in Postcolonial India*. Durham, NC: Duke University Press, 1999.

Manuel, Peter. "North Indian Sufi Popular Music in the Age of Hindu and Muslim Fundamentalism." *Ethnomusicology* 52, no. 3 (2008): 378–400.

Marr, Timothy. *The Cultural Roots of American Islamicism*. New York: Cambridge University Press, 2006.

Marsden, Magnus. *Living Islam: Muslim Religious Experience in Pakistan's North-West Frontier*. Cambridge: Cambridge University Press, 2005.

——. "All-Male Sonic Gatherings, Islamic Reform, and Masculinity in Northern Pakistan." *American Ethnologist* 34, no. 3 (2007): 473–90.

Marshall, John. Diary Excerpt, April 28, 1950. Online Collection and Catalog of Rockefeller Archive Center. http://dimes.rockarch.org/6d180dd6-9fde-4d0a-a139-afb6d7529d98.

Massignon, Louis, and Bernd Radtke. "Tasawwuf." *Encyclopedia of Islam*, 2nd ed. Edited by L. Massington, B. Radtke, W. C. Chittick,, F. de Jong, L. Lewisohn, Th. Zarcone, C. Ernst, Françoise Aubin, and J. O. Hunwick. Accessed October 21, 2017. http://dx.doi.org/10.1163/1573-3912_islam_COM_1188.

Masud, Muhammad Khalid. *Islamic Legal Philosophy: A Study of Abū Isḥāq al-Shāṭibī's Life and Thought*. Islamabad: Publications of the Islamic Research Institute, 1977.

Masud, Muhammad Khalid, Brinkley Messick, and David S. Powers, eds. "Introduction." In *Islamic Legal Interpretation: Muftis and Their Fatwas*. Cambridge, MA: Harvard University Press, 1996.

Matzen, Ida Sofie. "Extremists of Love: Cosmological Activism Among Sufi Muslims in Contemporary Lahore, Pakistan." PhD diss., University of Copenhagen, 2016.

Maurer, Bill. *Mutual Life, Limited: Islamic Banking, Alternative Currencies, Lateral Reason*. Princeton, NJ: Princeton University Press, 2005.

Mayaram, Shail. "Beyond Ethnicity? Being Hindu and Muslim in South Asia." In *Lived Islam in South Asia: Adaptation, Accommodation, and Conflict*, edited by Imtiaz Ahmad and Helmut Reifeld, 18–29. New Delhi: Social Science Press, 2004.

McAlister, Melani. *Epic Encounters: Culture, Media, and U.S. Interests in the Middle East Since 1945*. Berkeley: University of California Press, 2007.

McDonough, Sheila. *The Flame of Sinai: Hope and Vision in Iqbal*. Lahore: Iqbal Academy Pakistan, 2002.

McGregor, R. S., ed. *The Oxford Hindi-English Dictionary*. Oxford: Oxford University Press, 1993.

McKinnon, Catriona. *Toleration: A Critical Introduction*. London: Routledge, 2006.

Mehra, Rakesh Omprakash, dir. *Delhi-6*. With performances by Waheeda Rehman, Abhishek Bachchan, and Sonam Kapoor. Dillywood, Rakeysh Omprakash Mehra Pictures, and UTV Motion Pictures, 2009. Film.

Metcalf, Barbara Daly. *Husain Ahmad Madani: The Jihad for Islam and India's Freedom*. Oxford: Oneworld, 2009.

——. *Islamic Revival in British India: Deoband, 1860–1900*. Princeton, NJ: Princeton University Press, 1982.

——. "Maulana Husain Ahmad Madani and the Jamiʿat ʿUlama-i-Hind: Against Pakistan, Against the Muslim League," in *Muslims Against the Muslim League: Critiques of the Idea of Pakistan*, edited by Ali Usman Qasmi and Megan Eaton Robb, 35–64. New York: Oxford University Press, 2017.

——. *Perfecting Women: A Partial Translation of Bihishti Zewar*. Delhi: Oxford University Press, 1992.

Meyer, Birgit, and Moors, Annelies, eds. *Religion, Media, and the Public Sphere*. Bloomington: Indiana University Press, 2005.

Migdal, Joel. *State in Society: Studying How States and Societies Transform and Constitute One Another*. Cambridge: Cambridge University Press, 2001.

Minault, Gail. *Secluded Scholars: Women's Education and Muslim Social Reform in Colonial India*. Delhi: Oxford University Press, 1999.

——. "Women, Legal Reform, and Muslim Identity." *Comparative Studies of South Asia, Africa and the Middle East* 17, no. 2 (1997): 1–10.

Mitchell, Timothy. "The Middle East in the Past and Future of Social Science." In *The Politics of Knowledge: Area Studies and the* Disciplines, edited by David Szanton, 74–118. Berkeley: University of California Press, 2004.

Miyan, Muhammad Ehsan. *Dars-i Ibrat*. Shahjahanpur: Jamaʿat-i Mustafa Tablighi Ta'limi Society, 1999.

Mohammad, Afsar. *The Festival of Pirs: Popular Islam and Shared Devotion in South India*. Oxford: Oxford University Press, 2013.

——. "Telling Stories: Hindu-Muslim Worship in South India." *Journal of Hindu Studies* 3, no. 2 (July 2010): 157–88.

Mohamed, Khalid, dir. *Fiza*. Performances by Jaya Bhaduri, Karisma Kapoor, and Hrithik Roshan. The Culture Company and UTV Motion Pictures, 2000. Film.

Moin, A. Afzar. *The Millennial Sovereign: Sacred Kingship and Sainthood in Islam*. New York: Columbia University Press, 2012.

Morgahi, M. Amer, "Reliving the 'Classical Islam': Emergence and Working of the Minhajul Quran Movement in the UK." In *Sufism in Britain*, edited by Ronald Geaves and Theodore Gabriel, 213–35. London: Bloomsbury Academic, 2014.

Moosa, Ebrahim. *Revival and Reform in Islam: A Study of Muslim Fundamentalism*. New York: Oneworld Publications, 1999.

——. *What Is a Madrasa?* Chapel Hill: University of North Carolina Press, 2015.

Muedini, Fait. "The Promotion of Sufism in the Politics of Algeria and Morocco." *Islamic Africa* 3, no. 2 (Fall 2012): 201–26.

——. *Sponsoring Sufism: How Governments Promote "Mystical Islam" in Their Domestic and Foreign Policies*. New York: Palgrave MacMillan, 2015.

Muhammad, Imam. *Hazrat Lal Shahbaz Qalandar of Sehwan-Sharif*. Karachi: n.p., 1978.

Mulay, Vijay, dir. *Ek Anek Aur Ekta*. Films Division, 1974. Short film for TV.

Munawar-Rahman, Budhy. *Ensiklopedi Nurcholish Madjid: Pemikiran Islam di Kanvas Perabadan*. 3 vols. Jakarta: Paramadina dan Mizan, 2006.

Nasr, Seyyed Vali Reza. "Pakistan: Islamic State, Ethnic Polity." *The Fletcher Forum of World Affairs* 16, no. 2 (Summer 1992): 81–90. http://hdl.handle.net/10427/76621. Accessed March 25, 2019.

Nelson, Kristina. *The Art of Reciting the Quran*. Austin: University of Texas Press, 1985.

Neuman, Daniel M. *The Life of Music in North India: The Organization of an Artistic Tradition*. Chicago: University of Chicago Press, 1990. Originally published 1980.

O'Fahey, Rex S., and Bernd Radtke. "Neo-Sufism Reconsidered." *Der Islam* 70, no. 1 (1993): 52–87.

Ojha, Sangeeta. "PM Modi to Inaugurate World Sufi Forum Today." *India Today*, March 17, 2016. http://indiatoday.intoday.in/story/pm-modi-inaugurate-world-sufi-forum-today/1/622426.html.

Oommen, T. K. *Reconciliation in Post-Godhra Gujarat: The Role of Civil Society*. Delhi: Pearson Longman, 2008.

"Orders of the Supreme Court in Civil Writ Petition, No. 334/2001 and 562/2001—Erwady-Saarthak Public Interest Litigation." In *Mental Health: An Indian Perspective, 1946–2003*, ed. S. P. Agarwal et al., 503–20. New Delhi: Ministry of Health and Family Welfare, Directorate General of Health Services, 2004.

Otterbeck, Jonas. "Battling Over the Public Sphere: Islamic Reactions to the Music of Today." *Contemporary Islam* 2, no. 3 (2008): 211–28.

Parciack, Ronie. "Islamic Deshbhakti: Inscribing a Sufi Shrine into the Indian Nation-Space." *Contributions to Indian Sociology* 48, no. 2 (May 2014): 249–77.

Pathak, Zakia, and Rajeswari Sunder Rajan. "Shahbano." *Signs* 14, no. 3 (Spring 1989): 558–82.

Paṭhāṇ, Musā Khān Muhammad Khān. *Fatāwā-e Qādiriyyah*. Mandvi: Navrang Printing Press, 2014.

Patterson, Maureen. "Context for Development of Pakistan Studies in North America: Pre-Partition Interest in Proposed Pakistan Area of South Asia." *Pakistan Studies News: Newsletter of the American Institute of Pakistan Studies* 6, no. 1 (Spring 2002): 1–3.

——. "Pakistan Studies in North America: 1947–1989." *Pakistan Studies News: Newsletter of the American Institute of Pakistan Studies* 6, no. 11 (Fall 2003): 8–10.

Pemberton, Kelly. "Sufis and Social Activism: A Chishti Response to Communal Strife in India Today." In *In Search of South Asian Sufis*, edited by Clinton Bennett and Charles Ramsey, 269–84. New York: Continuum Books, 2012.

Pfleiderer, Beatrix. "Mira Datar Dargah: The Psychiatry of a Muslim Shrine." In *Ritual and Religion Among Muslims in India*, edited by Imtiaz Ahmad, 195–234. Delhi: Manohar, 1981.

——. *The Red Thread. Healing Possession at a Muslim Shrine in North India*. Delhi: Aakar, 2006.

Phadke, Anant. "The Murder of Dr Narendra Dabholkar: A Fascist Attack on Rationalism." *Indian Journal of Medical Ethics*, 10, no. 4 (2013). https://doi.org/10.20529/IJME.2013.068; https://ijme.in/articles/the-murder-of-dr-narendra-dabholkar-a-fascist-attack-on-rationalism/?galley=html. Accessed January 20, 2020.

Philippon, Alix. "Bons soufis" et "mauvais islamistes." La sociologie à l'épreuve de l'idéologie." *Social Compass* 62, no. 2 (2015): 187–98.

——. "Le charisme comme ressource émotionnelle du mouvement social? Dispositifs desensibilisation dans une néo-confrérie pakistanaise." *Critique internationale* 66, no. 1, (2015): 105–24.

——. "The Role of Sufism in the Identity Construction, Mobilization and Political Activism of the Barelwi Movement in Pakistan." *The Open Journal of Sociopolitical Studies* PACO 7, no. 1 (2014): 152–69.

——. *Soufisme et politique au Pakistan: Le movement barelwi a l'heure de la "guerre contre le terrorisme."* Paris: Éditions Karthala/Science Po Aix, 2011.

——. "A Sublime, yet Disputed, Object of Political Ideology? Sufism in Pakistan at the Crossroads." *Commonwealth and Comparative Politics* 52, no. 2 (2014): 271–92.

——. "Sunnis Against Sunnis. The Politicization of Doctrinal Fractures in Pakistan." *Muslim World* 101, no. 2 (2011): 347–68.

——. "When Sufi Tradition Reinvents Islamic Modernity: The Minhaj-ul Qur'an, a Neo-Sufi Order in Pakistan." In *South Asian Sufis: Devotion, Deviation, and Destiny* edited by Clinton Bennett and Charles M. Ramsey, 111–22. London: Bloomsbury, 2012.

PILDAT (Pakistan Institute of Legislative Development and Transparency). "Assessment of the Quality of Democracy in Pakistan." June 2013–December 2014. Published February 1, 2015.

https://pildat.org/assessment-of-democracy1/assessment-of-the-quality-of-democracyin-pakistan. Accessed October 11, 2016.

Purohit, Teena. *The Aga Khan Case: Religion and Identity in Colonial India.* Cambridge, MA: Harvard University Press, 2012.

Qadri, Tahir-ul. *Fatwa on Terrorism and Suicide Bombings.* London: Minhaj-ul-Qur'an International, 2010.

——. *Khwāboñ aur bashārāt par aʿtrāżāt kā ʿilmi maḥākmah.* Delhi: Adabī Dunyā, ca. 2009.

Quack, Johannes. *Disenchanting India: Organized Rationalism and Criticism of Religion in India.* New York: Oxford University Press, 2011.

——. "Possession and the Antisuperstition Law in Maharashtra: An Actor's Perspective on Modernization and Disenchantment." In *The Law of Possession. Ritual, Healing and the Secular State*, edited by William Sax and Helene Basu, 138–61. New York: Oxford University Press, 2015.

Qureshi, Jawad Anwar. "Ibn al-ʿArabi's Fuṣūṣ al-ḥikam in the Deobandi Maslak." Paper presented at the conference "Sufism in India and Pakistan: Rethinking Islam, Democracy, and Identity," New York, NY, September 24–25, 2015.

Qureshi, Maulwi Muḥammad Bakhsh Shāh. *Tarīkh Bībīañ Pāk Dāman (SA).* Lahore: Sang-e-Meel, 1979.

Qureshi, Regula. "'Muslim Devotional': Popular Religious Music and Muslim Identity Under British, Indian and Pakistani Hegemony." *Asian Music* 24, no. 1 (Autumn 1992/Winter 1993): 111–21.

Raguram, R., A. Venkateswaran, J. Ranakrishna, and M. G. Weiss. "Traditional Community Resources for Mental Health: A Report of Temple Healing from India." *BMJ* 325, no. 1 (July 2002): 38–40.

Raḥmān, ʿAbd al-Latīf Ḥasan ʿAbd al-, ed. *Al-Fatāwā al-Hindiyya al-maʿrūfa bil- Fatāwā al-ʿĀlamkīriyya.* 6 vols. Beirut: Dar al-kutub al-ʿilmiyya, 2000.

Rahman, Fazlur. "Iqbāl's Idea of the Muslim." *Islamic Studies* 2 (1963): 439–45.

——. *Islam.* 2nd ed. Chicago: University of Chicago Press, 1979.

——. *Islam.* Mass market ed. Garden City, NY: Doubleday, 1966.

——. *Islam and Modernity.* Chicago: University of Chicago Press, 1982.

Rahman, Fazlur. "Revival and Reform in Islam." In *The Cambridge History of Islam.* Vol. 2B, *Islamic Society and Civilization*, edited by P. M. Holt, Ann K. S. Lambton, and Bernard Lewis, 632–56. Cambridge: Cambridge University Press, 1970.

Rahman, Fazlur. *Revival and Reform in Islam: A study of Islamic Fundamentalism.* Edited by Ebrahim Moosa. New York: Oneworld, 1999.

Rajagopal, Arvind. *Politics After Television: Religious Nationalism and the Reshaping of the Indian Public.* Cambridge: Cambridge University Press, 2001.

Raḥim, Muḥammad ʿAbd al-. *Maqālāt-i ṭarīqat maʿrūf ba-faẓāʾil-i ʿAzīziyya.* Hyderabad: Maṭbaʿ-i Matin Kartan, 1875.

Rashid, Abbas. "Pakistan: The Ideological Dimension." In *Islam, Politics and the State: The Pakistan Experience*, edited by Mohammad Asghar Khan, 69–94. London: Zed Press, 1985.

Rasool, Tabasum. "*Waqf* Administration in India: Issues and Challenges of State *Waqf* Boards." *Journal of Islamic Thought and Civilization* 7, no.1 (Spring 2017): 1–12.

Rebasa, Angela, Cheryl Benard, H. Lowell Schwartz, and Peter Sickle, eds. *Building Moderate Muslim Networks.* Santa Monica, CA: RAND Corporation, 2007.

Records of Darbar Hazrat Bibi Pak Daman. Lahore, Pakistan.

Riaz, Ali. *Faithful Education: Madrassahs in South* Asia. New Brunswick, NJ: Rutgers University Press, 2008.

Ricklefs, Merle C. *Islamisation and Its Opponents in Java: A Political, Social, Cultural and Religious History, c. 1930 to the Present.* Honolulu: University of Hawai'i Press, 2012.

Riexinger, Martin. "How Favourable Is Puritan Islam to Modernity? A Study of the Ahl-i Hadis in Late Nineteenth/Early Twentieth Century South Asia." In *Colonialism, Modernity and Religious Movements in South Asia*, edited by Gwilym Beckerlegge, 147–65. New York: Oxford University Press, 2008.

Roberts, Nathaniel. *To Be Cared For: The Power of Conversion and the Foreignness of Belonging in an Indian Slum.* Berkeley: University of California Press, 2016.

Robinson, Francis. "Islamic Reform and Modernities in South Asia." *Modern Asian Studies* 42, nos. 2–3 (2008): 259–81.

Rockefeller Foundation Records. Rockefeller Archive Center, Sleepy Hollow, New York.

Rosenfield, Patricia. L. *A World of Giving: Carnegie Corporation of New York, a Century of International Philanthropy.* New York: Public Affairs, 2014.

Roy, Olivier. *L'échec de l'Islam politique.* Paris: Seuil, 1992.

——. *L'islam mondialisē.* Paris: Seuil, 2002.

Roy, Srirupa. *Beyond Belief: India and the Politics of Postcolonial Nationalism.* Durham, NC: Duke University Press, 2007.

Ruffle, Karen. *Gender, Sainthood, and Everyday Practice in South Asian Shi'ism.* Chapel Hill: University of North Carolina Press, 2012.

Rush, James R. *Hamka's Great Story: A Master Writer's Vision of Islam for Modern Indonesia.* Madison: University of Wisconsin Press, 2016.

Saglio-Yatzimirsky, Marie Caroline, and Brigitte Sébastia. "Mixing Tirttam and Tablets: A Healing Proposal for Mentally Ill Patients in Gunaseelam (South India)." *Anthropology & Medicine* 22, no. 2 (October 2015): 127–37.

Salomon, Noah. "The New Global Politics of Religion: A View from the Other Side." Social Science Research Council. https://tif.ssrc.org/2016/04/26/the-new-global-politics-of-religion-a-view-from-the-other-side/.

Sanyal, Usha. *Ahmad Riza Khan Barelwi: In the Path of the Prophet.* Oxford: Oneworld Publications, 2005.

——. "Aḥmad Rizā Khān Barelwī." In *Encyclopaedia of Islam, THREE.* Edited by Gudrun Krämer, Denis Matringe, John Nawas, and Everett Rowson, 71–75. Leiden: Brill, 2007.

——. "Are Wahhabis Kafirs? Ahmad Riza Khan Barelwi and His Sword of the Haramayn." In *Islamic Legal Interpretation: Muftis and Their Fatwas,* edited by Muhammad Khalid Masud, Brinkley Morris Messick, and David Stephan Powers, 204–13. Cambridge, MA: Harvard University Press, 1996.

——. "Barelwis." In *Encyclopaedia of Islam, THREE.* Edited by Gudrun Krämer, Denis Matringe, John Nawas, and Everett Rowson, 94–99. Leiden: Brill, 2011.

——. *Devotional Islam and Politics in British India: Ahmad Riza Khan Barelwi and His Movement, 1870–1920.* 2nd ed. New York: Oxford University Press, 1999.

Ṣāqib, Muḥammad ʿImrān. *Ḍākṭar Ṭāhirulqādrī kī ʿilmī k̲h̲iyānaten̲.* Gujranwala: Minhājulqur'ān val-Sunnah, 2008.

Saunders, Frances Stonors. *The Cultural Cold War: The CIA and the World of Arts and Letters.* New York: New Press, 2013. Originally published 1999.

Schimmel, Annemarie. *As Through a Veil: Mystical Poetry in Islam.* Oxford: Oneworld, 2001.

——. *Mystical Dimensions of Islam*. Chapel Hill: University of North Carolina Press, 1975.

——. *Pain and Grace: A Study of Two Mystical Writers of Eighteenth-Century Muslim India*. Leiden: Brill, 1976.

Schmidle, Nicholas. "Faith and Ecstasy." *Smithsonian Magazine*, December 2008. https://www.smithsonianmag.com/issue/december-2008/.

Sedgwick, Mark. "Sufis as 'Good Muslims:' Sufism in the Battle Against Jihadi Salafism." In *Sufis and Salafis in the Contemporary Age*, edited by Lloyd Ridgeon, 105–17. London: Bloomsbury, 2015.

——. "Neo-Sufism." In *The Cambridge Companion to New Religious Movements*, edited by Olav Hammer and Mikael Rothstein, 198–21. Cambridge: Cambridge University Press, 2012.

Sèze, Romain. "L'Ahmadiyya en France." *Archives de sciences sociales des religions* 171 (2015): 247–63 http://journals.openedition.org/assr/27152.

Shagan, Ethan, H. *The Rule of Moderation: Violence, Religion, and the Politics of Restraint in Early Modern England*. Cambridge: Cambridge University Press, 2011.

Shani, Ornit. *Communalism, Caste and Hindu Nationalism: The Violence in Gujarat*. Cambridge: Cambridge University Press, 2007.

Shahzād, Ghāfir. *Hazrat Bībī Pāk Dāman*. 2nd ed. Lahore: Department of Religious Affairs and Auqaf, Punjab, January 2005.

Sherkotī, Anwār al-Ḥasan, ed. *Anwār-i ʿUsmānī* Karachi: Maktaba-i Islāmiyya, n.d. [1967].

Shiloah, Amnon. *Music in the World of Islam: A Socio-cultural Study*. Detroit: Wayne State University Press, 2001. Originally published 1995.

Siddiqi, Fahan Hanif. "The Failed Experiment with Federation in Pakistan (1947–1971)." In *Defunct Federalisms: Critical Perspectives on Federal Failure*, edited by Emilian Kavalski and Magdalena Zolkos, 71–86. London: Routledge, 2013.

Simpson, Edward. "The Changing Perspectives of Three Muslim Men on the Question of Saint Worship Over a 10-year Period in Gujarat, Western India." *Modern Asian Studies* 42, nos. 2–3 (2008): 377–403.

——. *Muslim Society and the Western Indian Ocean: The Seafarers of Kachchh*. New York: Routledge, 2007.

——. *The Political Biography of an Earthquake: Aftermath and Amnesia in Gujarat, India*. New York: Oxford University Press, 2014.

Sirhindī, Aḥmad. *Intikhāb-i maktūbāt-i Shaykh Aḥmad Sirhindī*. Edited by Fazlur Rahman. Karāchī: Iqbāl Academy Pākistān, 1968.

Skali, Faouzi. "L'islam politique est une hérésie." *Intellectuel Collectif International des Mouvements Sociaux*, November 7, 2012. https://intercoll.net/SKALI-Faouzi.

Smith, Jonathan, Z. "Religion, Religions, Religious." In *Critical Terms for Religious Studies*, edited by Mark Taylor, 269–84. Chicago: University of Chicago Press, 1998.

Sonn, Tamara. "Rahman, Fazlur." In *The Oxford Encyclopedia of the Modern Islamic World*, edited by John L. Esposito, 63–75. Oxford: Oxford University Press, 1995.

Spivak, Gayatri Chakravorty. *A Critique of Postcolonial Reason*. Cambridge, MA: Harvard University Press, 1999.

Spodek, Howard. "In the Hindutva Laboratory: Pogroms and Politics in Gujarat, 2002." *Modern Asian Studies* 44, no. 2 (August 2010): 349–99. DOI: 10.1017/S0026749X08003612.

Stephenson, Glenn. "Pakistan: Discontiguity and the Majority Problem." *Geographical Review* 58, no. 2 (April 1968): 195–213.

Stern, Jessica. "Pakistan's Jihad Culture." *Foreign Affairs* 79, no. 6 (2000): 115–26.

Suleman, Muhammad. "Institutionalisation of Sufi Islam after 9/11 and the Rise of Barelwi Extremism in Pakistan." *Counter Terrorist Trends and Analyses* 10, no. 2 (February 2018): 6–10.

Sulmicki, Maciej. "A Plenitude of Prefixes: Delineating the Boundaries of Neo-, Retro-, Faux- and Post-Victorian Literature." *Zagadnienia Rodzajów Literackich* 58, no. 1 (2015): 9–26.

Surendranath, Kailash, dir. *Ek Sur* (video on national integration). Lok Sewa Sanchar Parishad, 1988. Public service announcement for TV.

Surriyeh, Elizabeth. *Sufis and Anti-Sufis: The Defense, Rethinking, and Rejection of Sufism in the Modern World.* New York: Routledge, 1998.

Sutoris, Peter. *Visions of Development: Films Division of India and the Imagination of Progress, 1948–75.* New York: Oxford University Press, 2016.

Taj, Zofshan. "The Political Thought of Tahir-ul-Qadri in Its Islamic Context: Understanding the Concept of Khilafa and Its Relevance to Modern Society in Light of Medieval Islamic Teachings." *Intermountain West Journal of Religious Studies* 3, no. 1 (2011): 12–32.

Talbot, Ian. *Pakistan: A Modern History.* London: Hurst, 1998.

Taneja, Anand Vivek. *Jinnealogy: Time, Islam, and Ecological Thought in the Medieval Ruins of Delhi.* Stanford, CA: Stanford University Press, 2017.

Tareen, SherAli. *Defending Muḥammad in Modernity.* South Bend, IN: University of Notre Dame Press, 2019.

——. "The Limits of Tradition: Competing Logics of Authenticity in South Asian Islam." PhD diss., Duke University, 2012.

Taylor, Charles. *A Secular Age.* Cambridge, MA: Harvard University Press, 2007.

Tepper, Elliot L. "Pakistan and the Consequences of Bangladesh." *Pacific Affairs* 45, no. 4 (Winter 1972–73): 573–81.

Thapar, Romila. "Imagined Religious Communities: Ancient History and the Modern Search for a Hindu Identity." *Modern Asian Studies* 23, no. 2 (1989): 209–31.

Tripp, Charles. *Islam and the Moral Economy.* Cambridge: Cambridge University Press, 2006.

Trumbull, George. R. "French Colonial Knowledge of Maraboutism." In *Islam and the European Empires*, edited by David Motadel, 269–86. Oxford: Oxford University Press, 2016.

Tschacher, Torsten. "From 'Rational' to 'Sufi Islam'?: The Changing Place of Muslims in Tamil Nationalism." In *Islam, Sufism, and Everyday Politics of Belonging in South Asia*, edited by Deepra Dandekar and Torsten Tschacher, 196–211. Milton Park, UK: Taylor and Francis, 2016.

Tweed, Thomas A. "Nightstand Buddhists and Other Creatures: Sympathizers, Adherents and the Study of Religion." In *American Buddhism: Methods and Findings in Recent Scholarship*, edited by Christopher Queen and Duncan Ryuken Williams, 71–90. Richmond, Surrey, UK: Curzon, 1999.

Umashankar, Rachana Rao. "Defending Sufism, Defining Islam: Asserting Islamic Identity in India." PhD diss., University of North Carolina, Chapel Hill, 2012.

——. "Metropolitan Microcosms: The Dynamic Spaces of Contemporary Sufi Shrines in India." *South Asian Studies* 31, no. 1 (2015): 127–43.

UNESCO. "800th Anniversary of the Birth of Mawlana Jalal ud-Din Balkhi-Rumi." 2007. Accessed September 3, 2019. http://portal.unesco.org/culture/en/ev.php-URL_ID=34694&URL_DO=DO_TOPIC&URL_SECTION=201.html.

ʿUsmānī, Mufti Muḥammad Rafīʿ. *Fiqh aur Taṣawwuf: Ek Taʿarruf.* Karachi: Idāra al-Maʿārif, 2004.

Van Bruinessen, Martin. "Controversies and Polemics Involving the Sufi Orders in Twentieth-Century Indonesia." In *Islamic Mysticism Contested: Thirteen Centuries of Controversies and Polemics*, edited by Frederick de Jong and Bernd Radtke, 705–28. Leiden: Brill, 1999.

——. "The Origins and Development of the Naqshbandi Order in Indonesia." *Der Islam: Zeitschrift für Geschichte und Kultur des Islamischen Orients* 67, no. 1 (1990): 150–79.

Van der Veer, Peter. "Playing or Praying: A Sufi Saint's Day in Surat." *Journal of Asian Studies* 51, no. 3 (August 1992): 545–64.

Varadarajan, Siddharth, ed. *Gujarat, the Making of a Tragedy*. New Delhi: Penguin Books India, 2002.

Verkaaik, Oskar. "Reforming Mysticism: Sindhi Separatist Intellectuals in Pakistan." *International Review of Social History* 49 (2004): suppl., 65–86.

Voll, John O. "Neo-Sufism: Reconsidered Again." *Canadian Journal of African Studies/La Revue canadienne des études africaines* 42, no. 2/3 (2008): 314–30.

Walī Allāh, Shāh. *Al-Tafhīmāt al-Ilāhiyya*, Edited by Ghulām Musṭafā Qāsimī. 2 vols. Hyderabad: Shāh Walī Allāh Academy, 1967–70.

Watt, David Harrington. *Antifundamentalism in Modern America*. Ithaca, NY: Cornell University Press, 2017.

Waugh, Earle H. "Beyond Scylla and Kharybdis: Fazlur Rahman and Islamic Identity." In *Shaping of an American Islamic Discourse: A Memorial to Fazlur Rahman*, edited by Earle H. Waugh and Frederick M. Denny, 15–36. Atlanta, GA: Scholars Press, 1998.

Weismann, Itzchak. "Modernity from Within: Islamic Fundamentalism and Sufism." *Der Islam*, 86, no. 1 (October 2011): 142–70.

Wikileaks. "Indian Islam: Deobandi-Barelvi Tension Changing Mainstream Islam in India." February 2, 2010. https://wikileaks.org/plusd/cables/10NEWDELHI207_a.html.

Wikipedia. "All India Ulema and Mashaikh Board." Accessed January 8, 2018. https://en.wikipedia.org/wiki/All_India_Ulema_and_Mashaikh_Board.

Wikipedia. "Syed Babar Ashraf." . https://en.wikipedia.org/wiki/Syed_Babar_Ashraf. Accessed January 24, 2020.

Williams, Raymond B. *A New Face of Hinduism: The Swaminarayan Religion*. Cambridge: Cambridge University Press, 1984.

Winkelmann, Mareike. *"From Behind the Curtain": A Study of a Girls' Madrasa in India*. Amsterdam, Netherlands: Amsterdam University Press, 2005.

Wolf, Richard K. *The Voice in the Drum: Music, Language, and Emotion in Islamicate South and West Asia*. Urbana: University of Illinois Press, 2014.

Wood, Simon, and Watt, David Harrington. "Introduction." In *Fundamentalisms: Perspectives on a Contested History*, edited by Simon Wood and David Harrington Watt, 1–14. Columbia: University of South Carolina Press, 2014.

Woodward, Mark, Muhammad Sani Umar, Inayah Rohmaniyah, and Mariani Yahya. "Salafi Violence and Sufi Tolerance? Rethinking Conventional Wisdom." *Perspectives on Terrorism* 7, no. 6 (2013): 58–78.

Zafar, Athar, and Omair Anas. "World Sufi Forum: India's Outreach to Global Community." Issue Brief, Indian Council of World Affairs. May 6, 2016. icwa.in/pdfs/IB/2014/WorldSufiForum IB06052016.pdf.

Zaidi, Noor. "'A Blessing on Our People': Bibi Pak Daman, Sacred Geography, and the Construction of the Nationalized Sacred." *Muslim World* 104, no. 3 (2014): 306–35.

——. "Making Spaces Sacred: The Sayyeda Zaynab and Bibi Pak Daman Shrines and the Construction of Modern Shia Identity." PhD diss., University of Pennsylvania, 2015.

Zaman, Muhammad Qasim. *Ashraf Ali Thanawi: Islam in Modern South Asia*. London: Oneworld, 2008.

——. *Islam in Pakistan: A History*. Princeton, NJ: Princeton University Press, 2018.

——. *Modern Islamic Thought in a Radical Age: Religious Authority and Internal Criticism*. Cambridge: Cambridge University Press, 2012.

——. *The Ulama in Contemporary Islam: Custodians of Change*. Princeton, NJ: Princeton University Press, 2002.

Zarcone, Thierry. "La Turquie républicaine (1923–1993)." In *Les Voies d'Allah, les orders mystiques dans le monde musulman des origines à aujourd'hui*, edited by Alexandre Popovic and Gilles Veinstein, 372–79. Paris: Fayard, 1996.

Zubrzycki, Geneviève. *Beheading the Saint: Nationalism, Religion and Secularism in Quebec*. Chicago: University of Chicago Press, 2016.

Contributors

Sarah Ansari is a historian of South Asia based at Royal Holloway, University of London, whose research focuses on places that are found in today's Pakistan. Much of her writing has engaged with historical developments in the province of Sindh and its mega port city of Karachi, including the role of local religious leaders (*pīrs*) in the colonial period, the longer-term impact of Partition-related migration, and the evolution of local ethnic nationalisms. Her main publications include *Sufi Saints and State Power: the Pirs of Sind, 1843–1947* (1992) and *Life After Partition: Migration, Community and Strife in Sindh, 1947–1962* (2005). Her latest book is *Boundaries of Belonging: Locality, Citizenship and Rights in India and Pakistan*, co-authored with William Gould (2019).

Helene Basu is professor of social anthropology at Westfaelische Wilhelms-Universitaet Muenster. She conducted fieldwork in India, Tanzania, and South Africa. Her research covers Hindu and Muslim socioreligious practices and belonging, migration across the Indian Ocean, and the "African diaspora" (Sidi) in Gujarat as well as ritual healing, emotion, and visual anthropology. She is the editor of *Journeys and Dwellings: Indian Ocean Themes in South Asia* (2008); with Pnina Werbner, *Embodying Charisma, Modernity, Locality and the Performance of Emotion* (1998); and, with Roland Littlewood and Arne Steinforth, *Spirit & Mind: Mental Health at the Intersection of Religion and Psychiatry* (2017). Her ethnographic films include *Drugs & Prayers* (2009), *Spirits of Envy* (2012), *Kabul Kiya* (2017), and *How We Got Here: Decision Matters* (2018).

Carla Bellamy is associate professor of anthropology and religious studies at Baruch College, City University of New York, and chair of the Columbia University Seminar on South Asia. Her ethnographically based research focuses on the lived realities behind the increasingly politicized terrain of religious identity in contemporary India and the effects of economic liberalization on everyday religious practices and lives. She has authored articles and book chapters on these topics as well as *The Powerful Ephemeral: Everyday Healing in an Ambiguously Islamic Place* (2011), and she is currently developing a New Delhi–based ethnography examining the reasons for and consequences of the surge in popularity of Shani, a Hindu planetary deity historically associated with misfortune.

Brian E. Bond received his PhD in ethnomusicology at The Graduate Center of the City University of New York. His dissertation, titled "A Heavy Rain Has Fallen Upon My People: Sindhi Sufi Poetry Performance, Emotion, and Islamic Knowledge in Kachchh, Gujarat," examines the use and contestation of poetry performance as a medium of Islamic knowledge transmission in rural Muslim communities of Kachchh, a border district in western India. Brian is a recipient of the Charlotte W. Newcombe Dissertation Year Fellowship (Woodrow Wilson Foundation), the International Dissertation Research Fellowship (Social Science Research Center), and the American Institute of Pakistan Studies' Junior Research Fellowship.

Rosemary R. Corbett's research focuses on the economic and gendered aspects and implications of racialized ideas about religion, particularly ideas about Islam. She is the author of *Making Moderate Islam: Sufism, Service, and the Ground Zero Mosque Controversy* (2017) and numerous articles on the subjects of race, religion, gender, and nationalism published in, among other places, *Journal of the American Academy of Religion, Religion and American Culture, Journal of Islamic Law and Culture, Culture and Religion, American Quarterly,* and *Journal of Feminist Studies in Religion.* Corbett teaches for the Bard Prison Initiative and has held fellowships as, among other things, a Young Scholar in American Religion; a Visiting Scholar at the Columbia University Institute for Religion, Culture, and Public Life; and Melon Postdoctoral Fellow at the Center for the Humanities at Tufts University. She is currently at work on a book project examining how American private foundations influenced understandings of Islam during the twentieth century.

Carl W. Ernst is William R. Kenan, Jr., Distinguished Professor of Religious Studies at the University of North Carolina, Chapel Hill. He is co-director of the Carolina Center for the Study of the Middle East and Muslim Civilizations and co-editor of the Islamic Civilization and Muslim Networks

Series, University of North Carolina Press. His most recent projects in Islamic studies have addressed issues of public scholarship relating to Islamophobia, the problem of reading the Quran, a critical rethinking of Islamic studies, and problems in understanding Islam. His studies of Sufism have engaged with the literary, historical, and contemporary aspects of Islamic mysticism, particularly in the Indo-Pakistan subcontinent and the Persianate cultural sphere. His recent books include *How to Read the Qur'an: A New Guide with Select Translations* (2011); *Sufism: An Introduction to Islamic Mysticism* (2010); and *Following Muhammad: Rethinking Islam in the Contemporary World* (2003).

Katherine Pratt Ewing is professor of religion at Columbia University and professor emerita of cultural anthropology at Duke University. She has done ethnographic fieldwork in South Asia, Northwest Africa, and among Muslims in Europe and the United States focused on debates among Muslims about the proper practice of Islam in the modern world. Her books include *Arguing Sainthood: Modernity, Psychoanalysis and Islam* (1997); and *Stolen Honor: Stigmatizing Muslim Men in Berlin* (2008).

Marcia Hermansen is director of the Islamic World Studies Program at Loyola University Chicago, where she is professor of Islam and religious studies in the Theology Department. Holding a PhD in Arabic and Islamic studies from the University of Chicago, her numerous authored and co-edited books include *Religion and Violence: Muslim and Christian Theological and Pedagogical Reflections* (2017); *Islam, Religions, and Pluralism in Europe* (2016); *Muslima Theology: The Voices of Muslim Women Theologians* (2013); *Shah Wali Allah's Treatises on Islamic Law* (2010); and *The Conclusive Argument from God* (Shah Wali Allah's *Hujjat Allah al-Baligha).* She writes on Islamic thought, Sufism, Islam and Muslims in South Asia, Muslims in America, and women and gender in Islam.

Brannon D. Ingram is assistant professor of religious studies at Northwestern University. His research focuses on Sufism and traditionally educated Muslim scholars (ulama) in South Asia and South Africa, and situates these within broader debates about Islamic law, ethics, and politics in modern Islam. He is the author of *Revival from Below: The Deoband Movement and Global Islam* (2018). He is now working on a second book project examining how modern Muslim intellectuals, scholars, and activists have debated, appropriated, and contested the category of "religion."

Bruce B. Lawrence is professor of Islamic studies emeritus at Duke University and adjunct professor at Alliance of Civilizations Institute, Ibn Haldun University, Istanbul. His research interests include contemporary Islam as religious ideology, South Asian Sufism, Islamicate cosmopolitanism, and the multiple roles and uses of the Quran. Among his monographs are *The Koran in English: A Biography* (2017); *Who Is Allah?* (2015); *The Qur'an: A Biography* (2006); and *Sufi Martyrs of Love* (with Carl Ernst, 2002). He is also working with Professor Rafey Habib on a multiyear project, *The Qur'an: A Verse Translation* (forthcoming in 2021).

Verena Meyer is a PhD candidate in Islamic studies at Columbia University. Before joining Columbia, she received an MSt in the study of religion at Oxford University. Specializing in Islam in Indonesia, her research focuses on the ways in which traditionalist and modernist Javanese Muslims construct and maintain their group identities through memory practices of authoritative founding figures and by appropriating canonical texts in Arabic, Indonesian, and Javanese. She studies traditionalist and modernist ideologies as sites where multiple epistemologies intersect and asks how conflicts between incommensurable epistemologies are understood, managed, and deployed.

Alix Philippon is assistant professor of sociology at Sciences Po Aix-en-Provence, France. She completed her PhD in political science in 2009 and is the author of two books: *Sufism and Politics in Pakistan: The Barelwi Movement in the Shadow of the War on Terror* (2011, in French) and *In the Shadow of Shrines: Sufi Traditions in Pakistan* (2016, in French). Her work mainly focuses on the political dimensions of Sufism in Pakistan. She has notably analyzed the recomposition and mobilization of (neo)-Sufi orders in Pakistan, the politicization of Sufi leaders, and studied the nationalization of shrines and the promotion of Sufism in the framework of the War on Terror. She has also authored a number of articles published in academic journals.

Usha Sanyal is an independent scholar and visiting assistant professor at Wingate University in North Carolina. Her prior research, on the history of the Barelwi, or Ahl-e Sunnat wa-l-Jamāʿat, movement in British India, was the subject of her book *Devotional Islam: Ahmad Riza Khan Barelwi and His Movement,* which is in its third edition (2013). Her new book, *Scholars of Faith: South Asian Muslim Women and the Embodiment of Religious Knowledge*, about South Asian Muslim women's and girls' religious education, is forthcoming (2020), as is her edited volume (with Nita Kumar), *Food, Faith and Gender in South Asia: The Cultural Politics of Women's Food Practices* (2020).

SherAli Tareen is associate professor of religious studies at Franklin and Marshall College. His work centers on Muslim intellectual traditions and debates in early modern and modern South Asia. He is the author of *Defending Muhammad in Modernity* (2020).

Rachana Rao Umashankar is assistant professor in the Religious Studies Department at Iona College, specializing in Islam in South Asia. She received her doctorate from the Department of Anthropology at the University of North Carolina at Chapel Hill in 2012 and her research interests are in the anthropology of religion, the politics of religious identity, history and memory, and Sufism.

Noor Zaidi is research assistant professor at the University of Maryland, Baltimore County. She has been a postdoctoral fellow in the History Department at the University of Pennsylvania. Her PhD dissertation focused on the development of sacredness in Syria and Pakistan, examining the dynamics of Shiʿi identity construction at the intersection of shrine worship and discourses of national identity. At present, she is working on a series of oral histories from Iraqi political prisoners for an upcoming book.

Muhammad Qasim Zaman is Robert H. Niehaus '77 Professor of Near Eastern Studies and Religion at Princeton University. He has written on the relationship between religious and political institutions in medieval and modern Islam, on social and legal thought in the modern Muslim world, on institutions and traditions of learning in Islam, and on the flow of ideas between South Asia and the Arab Middle East. He is the author of *Religion and Politics Under the Early Abbasids* (1997); *The Ulama in Contemporary Islam: Custodians of Change* (2002); *Ashraf Ali Thanawi: Islam in Modern South Asia* (2008); and *Modern Islamic Thought in a Radical Age: Religious Authority and Internal Criticism* (2012). With Robert W. Hefner, he is also the co-editor of *Schooling Islam: The Culture and Politics of Modern Muslim Education* (2007); with Roxanne L. Euben, of *Princeton Readings in Islamist Thought* (2009); and, associate editor, with Gerhard Bowering et al., of the *Princeton Encyclopedia of Islamic Political Thought* (2013). Among his current projects is a book on Islam in Pakistan as well as a study of South Asia and the wider Muslim world in the eighteenth and nineteenth centuries.

Index

RELIGION, CULTURE, AND PUBLIC LIFE

Series Editor: Katherine Pratt Ewing

After Pluralism: Reimagining Religious Engagement, edited by Courtney Bender and Pamela E. Klassen

Religion and International Relations Theory, edited by Jack Snyder

Religion in America: A Political History, Denis Lacorne

Democracy, Islam, and Secularism in Turkey, edited by Ahmet T. Kuru and Alfred Stepan

Refiguring the Spiritual: Beuys, Barney, Turrell, Goldsworthy, Mark C. Taylor

Tolerance, Democracy, and Sufis in Senegal, edited by Mamadou Diouf

Rewiring the Real: In Conversation with William Gaddis, Richard Powers, Mark Danielewski, and Don DeLillo, Mark C. Taylor

Democracy and Islam in Indonesia, edited by Mirjam Künkler and Alfred Stepan

Religion, the Secular, and the Politics of Sexual Difference, edited by Linell E. Cady and Tracy Fessenden

Boundaries of Toleration, edited by Alfred Stepan and Charles Taylor

Recovering Place: Reflections on Stone Hill, Mark C. Taylor

Blood: A Critique of Christianity, Gil Anidjar

Choreographies of Shared Sacred Sites: Religion, Politics, and Conflict Resolution, edited by Elazar Barkan and Karen Barkey

Beyond Individualism: The Challenge of Inclusive Communities, George Rupp

Love and Forgiveness for a More Just World, edited by Hent de Vries and Nils F. Schott

Relativism and Religion: Why Democratic Societies Do Not Need Moral Absolutes, Carlo Invernizzi Accetti

The Making of Salafism: Islamic Reform in the Twentieth Century, Henri Lauzière

Mormonism and American Politics, edited by Randall Balmer and Jana Riess

Religion, Secularism, and Constitutional Democracy, edited by Jean L. Cohen and Cécile Laborde

Race and Secularism in America, edited by Jonathon S. Kahn and Vincent W. Lloyd

Beyond the Secular West, edited by Akeel Bilgrami

Pakistan at the Crossroads: Domestic Dynamics and External Pressures, edited by Christophe Jaffrelot

Faithful to Secularism: The Religious Politics of Democracy in Ireland, Senegal, and the Philippines, David T. Buckley

Holy Wars and Holy Alliance: The Return of Religion to the Global Political Stage, Manlio Graziano

The Politics of Secularism: Religion, Diversity, and Institutional Change in France and Turkey, Murat Akan

Democratic Transition in the Muslim World: A Global Perspective, edited by Alfred Stepan

The Holocaust and the Nabka, edited by Bashir Bashir and Amos Goldberg

The Limits of Tolerance: Enlightenment Values and Religious Fanaticism, Denis Lacorne